Grid Middleware and Services
Challenges and Solutions

T0138056

Grid Middleware and Services
Challenges and Solutions

Edited by

Domenico Talia
University of Calabria, Rende, Italy

Ramin Yahyapour
University of Dortmund, Germany

Wolfgang Ziegler
Fraunhofer SCAI, Sankt Augustin, Germany

 Springer

Editors

Domenico Talia
Università della Calabria
Dip. Elettronica Informatica e
Sistemistica (DEIS)
via P. Bucci, 41 c
87036 Rende, Italy
talia@deis.unical.it

Ramin Yahyapour
Dortmund University of Technology, Germany
IT und Medien Centrum (ITMC)
44221 Dortmund, Germany
ramin.yahyapour@udo.edu

Wolfgang Ziegler
Fraunhofer-Gesellschaft
SCAI - Inst. Algorithmen und
Wissenschaftliches Rechnen
Schloss Birlinghoven
53754 Sankt Augustin, Germany
Wolfgang.Ziegler@scai.fraunhofer.de

ISBN: 978-1-4419-4614-0   e-ISBN: 978-0-387-78446-5
DOI: 10.1007/978-0-387-78446-5

Printed on acid-free paper

springer.com

Contents

Part II   Storage and Data Management

Part III   Grid Workflow and Fault Tolerance

Part IV   Service Level Agreement

Foreword

I am glad to write this foreword for this book, which is a result of the collaborative research carried out by CoreGRID, the only one Network of Excellence in Grid and P2P technologies funded by EU 6th Framework Programme. The mission, assigned to CoreGRID by the European Commission, was to build a research community in Europe to gather the expertise and the know-how of researchers in various research fields related to Grid and P2P into a single entity. After three years of existence, CoreGRID has successfully established a coherent research agenda avoiding duplication of efforts and providing a critical mass of researchers to address Grid research challenges. One of these challenges is how to build Next Generation Grid middleware systems and services. It was the goal of two workshops organized in 2007 by CoreGRID leaders. The first one was held in Dresden, in conjunction with the ISC'07 conference, on June 2007. This workshop had a particular focus on *Knowledge and Data Management, Resource Management and Scheduling* and *Information, Resource and Workflow Monitoring Services*. The second one was held in Austin in in conjunction with the Grid 2007 conference, on September 2007. This workshop was focused on *Service Level Agreements (SLAs)*.

I would like to take this opportunity to express my gratitude to the organizers of those workshops as well as to all contributors. I wish you a good reading.

Thierry Priol, CoreGRID Scientific Co-ordinator

Preface

The CoreGRID Network of Excellence includes a large number of scientists working to achieve high-level research objectives in Grid and P2P systems. CoreGRID brings together a critical mass of well-established researchers from more than forty European institutions active in the fields of distributed systems and middleware, models, algorithms, tools and environments.

Grid middleware and Grid services are two pillars of Grid computing systems and applications. Currently a large number of Grid researchers and developers are providing solutions in both those areas.

This book is the eighth volume of the CoreGRID series and it brings together scientific contributions by researchers and scientists working on knowledge and data management on Grids, Grid resource management and scheduling, Grid information, resource and workflow monitoring services, and service level agreements. The book includes revised contributions presented at two workshops organized in 2007 by CoreGRID leaders. The first one was held in Dresden in conjunction with the ISC'07 conference, on June 2007, and it was focused on middleware. The second one was held in Austin in conjunction with the Grid 2007 conference, on September 2007. This workshop was focused on Service Level Agreements (SLAs).

The book includes four parts addressing respectively Resource Management and Scheduling, Storage and Data Management, Workflow and Fault Tolerance, and Service Level Agreement. All those parts are concerned with key topics in the area Grid computing. They provide a general view of the main challenges and significant solutions in implementing complex applications in a Grid computing scenario.

The first part includes ten chapters. The first one presents Grid scheduling techniques with the ATOP-Grid. The second chapter discusses benchmarking of Grid applications. In the third chapter is presented a data model for describing Grid broker capabilities. The fourth chapter of this part discusses a meta broker for future generation Grids. A chapter discussing scheduling and replication in the LHC Grid follows. The sixth chapter presents Grid session monitoring techniques and chapter seven presents delegating contracts for resource discovery. A meta-brokering approach is described in chapter eight.

Chapter nine discusses preemption in parallel job scheduling and chapter ten discusses a scheduling architecture based on data mining prediction techniques.

The Storage and Data Management part includes five chapters. The first chapter presents a super peer architecture for public resource computing on Grids. Chapter two surveys security services in Grid storage systems. Chapter three of this part analyzes architectures for Grid storage elements. Chapter four addresses Grid information system issues and solutions. Finally, chapter five presents a metadata management system for knowledge discovery applications.

The third part includes six chapters discussing key topics in Grid workflow and fault tolerance. The first chapter describes taxonomies of the multi-criteria Grid workflow scheduling problem. The next chapter discusses workflow support in the ASKALON environment. Chapter three presents a practical approach for workflow management in Grids. Chapter four presents a fault tolerant framework with mobility support. Chapter five discusses checkpointing for fault tolerance and migration in Grids. Finally, the last chapter of part III describes a machine learning approach for automated diagnosis of faults.

The last part of the book includes seven contributions on Service Level Agreements (SLAs) in Grids. The first chapter presents a survey on current use of SLAs for Resource Management and scheduling. The second chapter addresses penalties in SLAs as a possibility to manage violations in SLAs. The third chapter reports on using bipartite SLAs for creating and operating dynamic Virtual Organisations. The fourth chapter introduces performance contracts for hierarchical component applications to meet the user expectations with respect to QoS while identifying the minimal set of resources required. The fifth chapter describes the experience of using SLAs within the context of a Catallaxy-enabled proof-of-concept prototype. The sixth chapter reports on the Implied Volatility framework developed in the European NextGRID project applying dynamic SLAs to improve business opportunities. The seventh chapter presents results of experiments with a first implementation of a negotiation service for SLAs in a Globus Toolkit 4 environment.

We would like to thank all the participants for their contributions to making the two workshops a success, the workshop program committees for reviewing the submissions, and all the authors that contributed chapter for publication in this volume. A special thank to the Springer staff, Vladimir Getov and Paolo Trunfio for their assistance in editing the book.

Our thanks also go to the European Commission for sponsoring under grant number 004265 this volume of the CoreGRID project series of publications.

Domenico Talia, Ramin Yahyapour, Wolfgang Ziegler

Contributing Authors

Ali Anjomshoaa EPCC, University of Edinburgh, Edinburgh, EH9 3JZ, United Kingdom (ali@epcc.ed.ac.uk)

Gabriel Antoniu IRISA/INRIA, Rennes Cedex, France (gabriel.antoniu@irisa.fr)

Oscar Ardaiz Department of Mathematics and Informatics, Public University of Navarra Campus de Arrosadia, Pamplona 31006, Spain (oscar.ardaiz@unavarra.es)

Dominic Battré Berlin University of Technology, Secr. E-N 50, Einsteinufer 17, 10587 Berlin, Germany (dominic.battre@tu-berlin.de)

Angelos Bilas Institute of Computer Science, Foundation for Research and Technology - Hellas, PO Box 1385, GR-71110, Heraklion, Greece (bilas@ics.forth.gr)

Frances Brazier Department of Computer Science, VU University Amsterdam, The Netherlands (frances@cs.vu.nl)

Maciej Brzezniak Poznan Supercomputing and Networking Center, 61-704 Poznan, Noskowskiego 12/14, Poland (maciekb@man.poznan.pl)

Javier Bustos-Jimenez Escuela de Ingenieria Informatica, Universidad Diego Portales, Santiago de Chile (javier.bustos@inf.udp.cl)

Xiaorong Cao University of Windsor, Computer Science, 401 Sunset Ave., Windsor, Ontario, N9B3P4, Canada (caoi@uwindsor.ca)

Pablo Chacin Computer Architecture Department, Technical University of Catalonia Jordi Girona 1-3, Campus Nord D6 Barcelona 08035, Spain (pchacin@ac.upc.edu)

Isaac Chao Computer Architecture Department, Technical University of Catalonia Jordi Girona 1-3, Campus Nord D6 Barcelona 08035, Spain (ichao@ac.upc.edu)

Augusto Ciuffoletti INFN-CNAF – Via B. Pichat 6/2, Bologna, Italy (augusto@di.unipi.it)

Dana Cojocarasu Norwegian Research Center for Computers and Law, University of Oslo, Norway (d.i.cojocarasu@jus.uio.no)

Antonio Congiusta DEIS, University of Calabria, Rende (CS), Italy (acongiusta@deis.unical.it)

Massimo Coppola Information Science and Technologies Institute, National Research Council, Via G. Moruzzi 1, 56100, Pisa, Italy (massimo.coppola@isti.cnr.it)

Julita Corbalan Barcelona SuperComputing Center, Jordi Girona 1-3, 08034 Barcelona, Spain (julita.corbalan@bsc.es)

Pasquale Cozza DEIS, University of Calabria, Rende (CS), Italy (pcozza@deis.unical.it)

Marco Danelutto Computer Science Department, University of Pisa, Largo B. Pontecorvo 3, 56100, Pisa, Italy (marcod@di.unipi.it)

Paul Donachy Belfast e-Science Centre, School of Computer Science, The Queen's University of Belfast, Belfast, BT7 1NN, United Kingdom (p.donachy@qub.ac.uk)

Bryan Esbaugh University of Windsor, Computer Science, 401 Sunset Ave., Windsor, Ontario, N9B3P4, Canada (esbaugh@uwindsor.ca)

Thomas Fahringer Institute of Computer Science, University of Innsbruck, Austria (tf@dps.uibk.ac.at)

Thomas Ferrandiz LIG Laboratory, University Joseph Fourier - Grenoble I, France (thomas.ferrandiz@imag.fr)

Michail D. Flouris Institute of Computer Science, Foundation for Research and Technology - Hellas, PO Box 1385, GR-71110, Heraklion, Greece. (flouris@ics.forth.gr)

L.L. Fong IBM T.J. Watson Research Center (llfong@us.ibm.com)

Alberto Forti Istituto Nazionale di Fisica Nucleare CNAF, viale Berti Pichat, 6/2, 40127 Bologna, Italy (alberto.forti@cnaf.infn.it)

Felix Freitag Computer Architecture Department, Technical University of Catalonia Jordi Girona 1-3, Campus Nord D6 Barcelona 08035, Spain (felix@ac.upc.edu)

Antonia Ghiselli Istituto Nazionale di Fisica Nucleare CNAF, viale Berti Pichat, 6/2, 40127 Bologna, Italy (antonia.ghiselli@cnaf.infn.it)

Francesco Giacomini Istituto Nazionale di Fisica Nucleare CNAF, viale Berti Pichat, 6/2, 40127 Bologna, Italy (francesco.giacomini@cnaf.infn.it)

A. Goyeneche University of Westminster, 115 New Cavendish Street, London, W1W 6UW (goyenea@wmin.ac.uk)

Francesc Guim Barcelona SuperComputing Center, Jordi Girona 29, 08034 Barcelona, Spain (francesc.guim@bsc.es)

René Heek High Performance Computing Center Stuttgart (HLRS), Allmandring 30, 70569 Stuttgart, Germany (heek@hlrs.de)

Lukáš Hejtmánek Institute of Computer Science, Masaryk University, Botanická 68a, 602 00 Brno, Czech Republic (xhejtman@mail.muni.cz)

Hubert Hérenger High Performance Computing Center Stuttgart (HLRS), All-mandring 30, 70569 Stuttgart, Germany (herenger@hlrs.de)

Juergen Hofer Institute of Computer Science, University of Innsbruck, Austria (juergen@dps.uibk.ac.at)

Andreas Hoheisel Fraunhofer FIRST, Kekuléstraße 7, D-12489 Berlin, Germany (andreas.hoheisel@first.fraunhofer.de)

Alexandru Iosup Faculty of Electrical Engineering, Mathematics, and Computer Science, Delft University of Technology, The Netherlands. (A.Iosup@tudelft.nl)

Gracjan Jankowski Poznan Supercomputing and Networking Center, 61-704 Poznan, Noskowskiego 12/14, Poland (gracjan@man.poznan.pl)

Radoslaw Januszewski Poznan Supercomputing and Networking Center, 61-704 Poznan, Noskowskiego 12/14, Poland (radekj@man.poznan.pl)

Liviu Joita School of Computer Science/Welsh eScience Centre, Cardiff University, UK (L.Joita@cs.cardiff.ac.uk)

Péter Kacsuk MTA SZTAKI Computer and Automation Research Institute, H-1518 Budapest, P. O. Box 63, Hungary (kacsuk@sztaki.hu)

Odej Kao Berlin University of Technology, Secr. E-N 50, Einsteinufer 17, 10587 Berlin, Germany (odej.kao@tu-berlin.de)

Ian Kelley School of Computer Science, Cardiff University, UK (I.R.Kelley@cs.cardiff.ac.uk)

Attila Kertész Institute of Informatics, University of Szeged, H-6701 Szeged, P.O. Box 652, Hungary (keratt@inf.u-szeged.hu)

Bastian Koller Höchstleistungsrechenzentrum Stuttgart, 70550 Stuttgart, Germany (koller@hlrs.de)

Jozsef Kovacs Computer and Automation Research Institute of the Hungarian Academy of Sciences, 1111 Budapest Kende u. 13-17, Hungary (smith@sztaki.hu)

Roland Kübert High Performance Computing Center Stuttgart (HLRS), Allmandring 30, 70569 Stuttgart, Germany (kuebert@hlrs.de)

Renaud Lachaiz Institute of Computer Science, Foundation for Research and Technology - Hellas, PO Box 1385, GR-71110, Heraklion, Greece. (rlachaiz@ics.forth.gr)

Domenico Laforenza Information Science and Technologies Institute, National Research Council, Via G. Moruzzi 1, 56100, Pisa, Italy (domenico.laforenza@isti.cnr.it)

Y.G. Liu IBM T.J. Watson Research Center (ygliu@us.ibm.com)

Jesus Luna Institute of Computer Science, Foundation for Research and Technology - Hellas, PO Box 1385, GR-71110, Heraklion, Greece. (jluna@ics.forth.gr)

Luca Magnoni Istituto Nazionale di Fisica Nucleare CNAF, viale Berti Pichat, 6/2, 40127 Bologna, Italy (luca.mangoni@cnaf.infn.it)

Vania Marangozova LIG Laboratory, University Joseph Fourier - Grenoble I, France (vania.marangozova@imag.fr)

Manolis Marazakis Institute of Computer Science, Foundation for Research and Technology - Hellas, PO Box 1385, GR-71110, Heraklion, Greece. (maraz@ics.forth.gr)

Carlo Mastroianni ICAR-CNR, Rende (CS), Italy (mastroianni@icar.cnr.it)

Henning Mersch Central Institute for Applied Mathematics, Research Centre Jülich, 52425 Jülich, Germany (h.mersch@fz-juelich.de)

Norbert Meyer Poznan Supercomputing and Networking Center, 61-704 Poznan, Noskowskiego 12/14, Poland (meyer@man.poznan.pl)

Rafal Mikolajczak Poznan Supercomputing and Networking Center, 61-704 Poznan, Noskowskiego 12/14, Poland (Rafal.Mikolajczak@man.poznan.pl)

Sébastien Monnet IRISA/INRIA, Rennes Cedex, France (sebastien.monnet@irisa.fr)

Gerard Murphy Belfast e-Science Centre, School of Computer Science, The Queen's University of Belfast, Belfast, BT7 1NN, United Kingdom (g.m.murphy@qub.ac.uk)

Farrukh Nadeem Institute of Computer Science, University of Innsbruck, Austria (farrukh@dps.uibk.ac.at)

Leandro Navarro Computer Architecture Department, Technical University of Catalonia Jordi Girona 1-3, Campus Nord D6 Barcelona 08035, Spain (leandro@ac.upc.edu)

Antonis Papadogiannakis FORTH – Heraklion, Crete, Greece (papadog@ics.forth.gr)

Simone Pellegrini Istituto Nazionale di Fisica Nucleare CNAF, viale Berti Pichat, 6/2, 40127 Bologna, Italy (simone.pellegrini@cnaf.infn.it)

Ron Perrot Belfast e-Science Centre, School of Computer Science, The Queen's University of Belfast, Belfast, BT7 1NN, United Kingdom (r.perrot@qub.ac.uk)

Jose Piquer Departamento de Ciencias de la Computacion, Universidad de Chile, Santiago de Chile (jpiquer@nic.cl)

Michalis Polychronakis FORTH – Heraklion, Crete, Greece (mikepo@ics.forth.gr)

Radu Prodan Institute of Computer Science, University of Innsbruck, Austria (radu@dps.uibk.ac.at)

Thomas B. Quillinan Department of Computer Science, VU University Amsterdam, The Netherlands (tb.quillinan@few.vu.nl)

Omer F. Rana School of Computer Science/Welsh eScience Centre, Cardiff University, UK (o.f.rana@cs.cardiff.ac.uk)

Ivan Rodero Barcelona SuperComputing Center, Jordi Girona 29, 08034 Barcelona, Spain (irodero@bsc.es)

S.M. Sadjadi Florida International University (sadjadi@cs.fiu.edu)

Jan Seidel Department of Bioinformatics, Fraunhofer Institute SCAI, 53754 Sankt Augustin, Germany (jan.seidel@scai.fraunhofer.de)

Jiaying Shi University of Windsor, Computer Science, 401 Sunset Ave., Windsor, Ontario, N9B3P4, Canada (shiv@uwindsor.ca)

Angela C. Sodan University of Windsor, Computer Science, 401 Sunset Ave., Windsor, Ontario, N9B3P4, Canada (acsodan@uwindsor.ca)

Federico Stagni Istituto Nazionale di Fisica Nucleare sez. di Ferrara, via Saragat 1, 44100 Ferrara, Italy. (federico.stagni@fe.infn.it)

Mike Surridge IT Innovation Centre, 2 Venture Road, Southampton, SO16 7NP, UK (ms@it-innovation.soton.ac.uk)

Domenico Talia DEIS, University of Calabria, Rende (CS), Italy (talia@deis.unical.it)

Ian Taylor School of Computer Science, Cardiff University, UK (Ian.J.Taylor@cs.cardiff.ac.uk)

Nicola Tonellotto Information Science and Technologies Institute, National Research Council, Via G. Moruzzi 1, 56100, Pisa, Italy (nicola.tonellotto@isti.cnr.it)

Paolo Trunfio DEIS, University of Calabria, Rende (CS), Italy (trunfio@deis.unical.it)

Marco Vanneschi Computer Science Department, University of Pisa, Largo B. Pontecorvo 3, 56100, Pisa, Italy (vannesch@di.unipi.it)

Cristian Varas Escuela de Ingenieria Informatica, Universidad Diego Portales, Santiago de Chile (cristian.varas2@al.udp.cl)

Kerstin Voss University of Paderborn, Fuerstenallee 11, 33102 Paderborn, Germany (kerstinv@upb.de)

Oliver Wäldrich Department of Bioinformatics, Fraunhofer Institute SCAI, 53754 Sankt Augustin, Germany (oliver.waeldrich@scai.fraunhofer.de)

Martijn Warnier Department of Computer Science, VU University Amsterdam, The Netherlands (warnier@cs.vu.nl)

Marek Wieczorek Institute of Computer Science, University of Innsbruck, Austria (marek@dps.uibk.ac.at)

Philipp Wieder Central Institute for Applied Mathematics, Research Centre Jülich, 52425 Jülich, Germany (ph.wieder@fz-juelich.de)

Ramin Yahyapour IRF, University Dortmund, 44221 Dortmund, Germany (ramin.yahyapour@udo.edu)

Riccardo Zappi Istituto Nazionale di Fisica Nucleare CNAF, viale Berti Pichat, 6/2, 40127 Bologna, Italy (riccardo.zappi@cnaf.infn.it)

Xijie Zeng University of Windsor, Computer Science, 401 Sunset Ave., Windsor, Ontario, N9B3P4, Canada (zengx@uwindsor.ca)

Wolfgang Ziegler Department of Bioinformatics, Fraunhofer Institute SCAI, 53754 Sankt Augustin, Germany (wolfgang.ziegler@scai.fraunhofer.de)

Corrado Zoccolo IAC Search & Media Italia S.r.l., Corso Italia 58, Pisa, Italy (corrado.zoccolo@ask.com)

I

RESOURCE MANAGEMENT AND SCHEDULING

GRID SCHEDULING WITH ATOP-GRID UNDER TIME SHARING

Xijie Zeng, Jiaying Shi, Xiaorong Cao, and Angela C. Sodan
University of Windsor
Computer Science, 401 Sunset Ave., Windsor, Ontario, N9B3P4
Canada
zengx@uwindsor.ca
shiv@uwindsor.ca
caoi@uwindsor.ca
acsodan@uwindsor.ca

Abstract   ATOP-Grid is an adaptive middleware which supports workload redistribution under varying resource allocation in both the space and time dimensions. In earlier work [13] [14] [15], we have already shown that time-shared execution of jobs, which splits the CPUs or cores per node between two jobs but shares the network, may provide a performance benefit vs. space sharing, which splits the nodes among the jobs. In this paper, we make a step towards providing a sounder foundation for time-sharing performance, investigating the time sharing behavior of jobs in more detail and looking into communication characteristics, memory access, and cache usage.

Keywords: Parallel job scheduling, multi-core CPUs, hyperthreaded CPUs, time sharing, cache locality

1.   Introduction

Our ATOP-Grid (Adaptive Time/Space Sharing through Over Part itioning) middleware is an approach for application-internal grid scheduling. This means that ATOP-Grid supports the application in internally adjusting its workload distribution on the grid according to the external conditions. The application may be scheduled on a single site or simultaneously across multiple sites. ATOP-Grid can run under different resource-allocation approaches. This means that ATOP-Grid is designed to execute under both time sharing and space sharing, to switch between time and space sharing, and to dynamically adapt its workload distribution to varying resource allocation in the time and space dimension. These possibilities for adaptation give the grid scheduler and local schedulers more flexibility to deal with advanced reservations.

The standard approach to allocate resources to jobs on parallel machines is dedicated resource allocation (space sharing), which assigns the individual nodes of a parallel machine exclusively to a single application. However, better resource utilization may be obtainable if letting jobs with complementary requirements run on the same nodes and share the resources per node. We apply a modified time-sharing approach which allocates the different CPUs, cores, or virtual CPUs to different jobs in a dedicated manner and time-shares the remaining resources: memory, disk, and network. We have obtained promising results from running combinations of NAS benchmarks together on different virtual CPUs of the same hyperthreaded CPU (*CPU hyper sharing*) [13] [16]. In this case, the processes also need to share the execution units and the cache per physical CPU. Nevertheless, most combinations of the NAS benchmarks ran with improved resource utilization though some pairs had too many conflicts on cache and/or network. Thus, the corresponding job scheduler selected pairs carefully and matched jobs with complementary resource needs, thereby gaining improvements in response-times of up to 50%. Similar scheduling options exist on multi-core CPUs (*multi-core sharing*) which are the current dominant trend for compute resources on cluster nodes [19]. Multi-core CPUs have separate execution units and may or may not share the cache. The results in [19] were positive but did not consider communication as the tests were carried out with a very small number of nodes (up to 4). The simplest option is to split the CPUs per SMP node among multiple jobs (*node sharing*).

We ran our own ATOP-Grid middleware successfully under CPU hyper sharing and node sharing with larger numbers of nodes involved (up to 64) [14] [15]. Though we have obtained positive results, we have only tested a Jacobi application with nearest-neighbor communication and did not look into cache effects. The performance model used was very simple. However, different communication patterns may play a role for time-sharing performance. Cache needs of a program are hard to determine as practically available compilers do not provide such information. In this paper, we make a step towards providing a sounder basis for time-sharing performance and investigate different communication patterns and communication ratios, potential memory-bandwidth problems, and cache performance. Understanding the effects is not only important to determine whether jobs can be run under time sharing but also to be able to switch between different resource allocation options in the middleware with predictable and consistent performance [14].

2.   Related work

Testing memory performance with consideration of different access patterns—consecutive, stride, and random access—was proposed in the *memperf* benchmark [18]. The performance of multi-core AMD Opteron processors was already investigated in [10] which tested integer and float SPEC2000 per node as well as the parallel Linpack benchmark. In addition, memory latency was measured. All tests were done as comparison between single-core and multi-core Opteron processors. The Linpack results showed a performance improvement of 85% by using dual-core processors. However, the results obtained from the memory tests and from the SPEC2000 benchmarks were converse to the expectations, providing better performance for the dual-core version with memory competition. Thus, the presented results are inconclusive.

Time sharing is a well known option to increase resource utilization for serial job execution. However, parallel jobs need coordinated execution across machine nodes because otherwise processes/threads may be idle while waiting for communication or too many context switches may occur (for a survey of existing research, see [15]). Using different virtual CPUs, cores, or CPUs per node to execute different applications is an easier way for coordinated execution because all threads/processes are always active. In [17], we have presented results from time sharing applications with different communication patterns on an SMP machine and shown that the effect on the jobs depends on the jobs' communication patterns and their combination.

Application-internal grid scheduling with the aim of making an application adaptive was first introduced in AppLeS [2].

3.   Time-sharing options and slowdown under time sharing

As mentioned in the introduction, we exploit 1) node sharing (splitting the CPUs per job), multi-core sharing (splitting the cores per CPU), and CPU hyper sharing (splitting the virtual CPUs per hyperthreaded CPU). In all cases, the network, memory, and disk are shared. On a hyperthreaded CPU, also the execution units and all caches are shared. The cores of a multi-core CPU have their own execution units and their own L1 cache, and, depending on the CPU type, may (e.g. IBM Power 5) or may not (e.g. Opteron [9]) share the L2 cache. The potential L3 cache is typically shared. Typically the cores share the access to the memory. Similar to multiple CPUs per node (see, e.g. [1]), this can create bottlenecks for programs with low cache locality. This problem would increase with the trend toward larger numbers of cores per CPU.

Whenever processes share resources, this may result in competition for resource access and lead to the application running slower than it would run on its own. Note that unless the slowdown is very high, still a benefit may be obtained vs. sequential execution of the jobs. We define slowdown as the relation between the runtime *T(A,B)* of Job A under shared execution with another Job B vs. the runtime *T(A)* of Job A under dedicated resource allocation, i.e. $SL(A, B) = T(A, B)/T(A)$. Note that the two jobs scheduled together may experience different slowdowns, i.e. in the general case, $SL(A, B) \neq SL(B, A)$. If in our tests one application runs longer than the other one, we calculate the slowdown for the shared execution time. The application then runs slower by $(SL(A, B) - 1) * 100\%$.

4.   ATOP-Grid

Our ATOP-Grid is designed to run with the Globus grid middleware and the MPICH-G2 communication library which are proven to work on the Tera-Grid for very large applications [5]. ATOP-Grid employs the Zoltan/ParMeTis load-balancing library [4] for the workload redistribution and supports over-partitioning (creating more data partitions via Zoltan than nodes/CPUs are used and flexibly allocating the partitions to the nodes/CPUs) to minimize workload redistribution cost. ATOP-Grid permits making reservations for a certain execution power (runtime) rather than a certain number of CPUs [14]. The job scheduler can decide the resource allocation and possibly dynamically switch between time sharing and space sharing as it is best for the overall schedule (fitting into the machine, scheduling around reservations, better utilization, etc.).

ATOP-Grid can then adjust to any possible resource allocation. This approach provides more flexibility in choosing the best resource utilization and meeting reservations, while helping to decrease the reservations' negative impact [12] on the response times of other jobs. If time sharing works well, the resource allocation ($N_{A,B}$) to obtain the same runtime is less for the time-shared execution of two jobs than would be the sum of the resource allocations N_A and N_B under space sharing, i.e. $N_{A,B} < N_A + N_B$, while $T(A, B, N_{A,B}) = T(A, N_A)$. Conversely, we can keep the overall number of resources the same ($N_{A,B} = N_A + N_B$) and may obtain a better runtime on the larger number of resources under time sharing than on part of the resources under space sharing, i.e. $T(A, B, N_{A,B}) < T(A, N_A)$. See Figure 1.

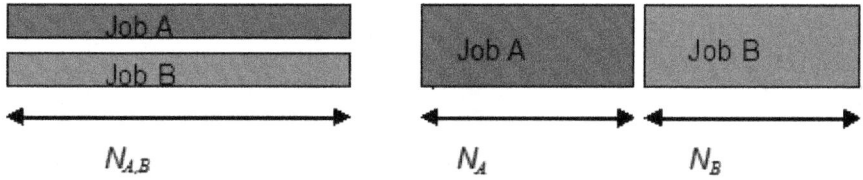

Figure 1. Resource allocation under time sharing with $N_{A,B}$ nodes for both *A* and *B* vs. resource allocation under space sharing with N_A nodes for *A* and N_B for *B*.

5. ATOP-Grid under node and CPU hyper sharing—Time vs. space adaptation

We ran tests on 64 dual-Opteronnode clusters in the Sharcnet network of clusters [1]. Since the Sharcnet job scheduler currently does not support running two jobs on the same resources, the tests with ATOP-Grid were run with manual support of the system administrator. Some additional tests were done on a 16-node cluster with 2 Ghz Intel Xeon hyperthreaded CPUs. In all cases, the interconnect was Myrinet and the communication library was MPICH-GM. To have controlled test conditions, the threads were explicitly bound to specific CPUs, specific cores, or specific virtual CPUs per node (using *setschedaffinity()*).

First we show results which we obtained for ATOP-Grid in [14] and [15] with node sharing and CPU hyper sharing, see Figure 2 and Figure 3. The application is Jacobi which uses nearest neighbor communication along the edge cuts created by an underlying graph. The application was run with different graphs, and the different instances are labeled in the figure with the names of these graphs. From Figure 2 we see that we got the same runtime under time sharing with less than double the nodes used under space sharing, i.e. obtained better resource utilization. In Figure 3 we see that conversely the runtime increased vs. time sharing if applying space sharing and giving each application half of the nodes.

For these tests, the slowdowns shown include the partitioning of the local CPUs per node. In other words, the option is to either run two threads of one application per node on two CPUs (dedicated allocation), or only one application thread on one CPU and the second application's thread on the second CPU (node sharing or CPU hyper sharing). In the latter case, the CPU computation time approximately doubles but we still get a benefit because we better utilize the network (serial execution corresponds to a factor of 2 and any slowdown below 2 means an improvement in utilization).

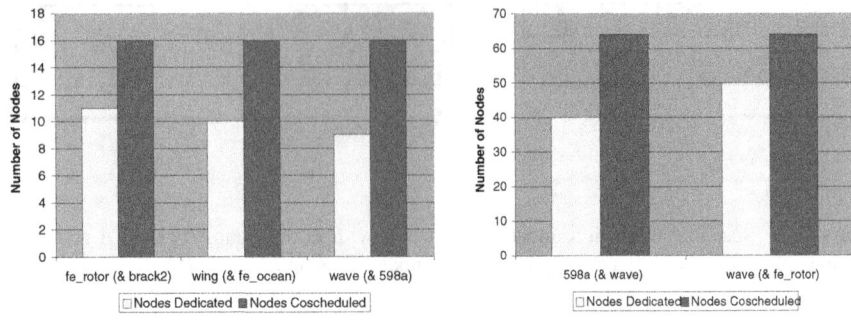

Figure 2.   Resource usage under space sharing and time sharing as required to keep the same progress/remaining runtime and meet the execution-power reservation. The coscheduled application is mentioned in parenthesis. Left graphic shows tests on 16 nodes, right graphic tests on 64 nodes.

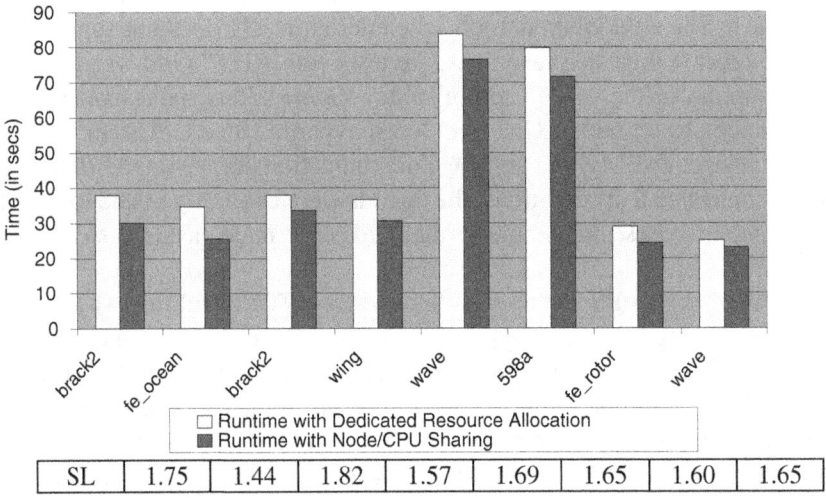

| SL | 1.75 | 1.44 | 1.82 | 1.57 | 1.69 | 1.65 | 1.60 | 1.65 |

Figure 3.   Runtimes on 16 nodes under CPU hyper sharing (brack2/fe_ocean and brack2/wing) and on 64 nodes under node sharing (598a/wave and fe_rotor/wave) vs. runtimes for the same applications under dedicated resource allocation on half of the nodes. We also show the slowdown if coscheduling the applications vs. dedicated execution on all nodes.

6.   Sharing the network—The effect of communication patterns

We now go on presenting tests targeted to investigate the effects of different communication patterns under time sharing. MPICH-GM uses buffered communication for messages of size < 32k and synchronous communication for larger messages.

In this case, we have delt with the lack of scheduler support to run 2 jobs on the same nodes by simulating resource sharing. We created two processes per node and split the overall set of processes into two communicator groups such that one process per node belongs to one of the two communicator groups and the other process to the other group. Each communicator group then represents an "application". However, this setup permitted only tests with synthetic programs but not to run benchmarks like NAS, LinPack, or Stream [7]. We used synthetic programs which employed different and common communication patterns as described below:

- *Central*: a master periodically receives messages from all its slaves (n:1), with the slaves not waiting for the master to have received all slaves' messages

- *Nearest neighbor (NN)*: processes communicates with four geometric neighbor processes periodically, while both sending and receiving messages to/from each neighbor

- *Pipeline*: the processes send messages to their right neighbors and receive messages from their left neighbors; the first process does not receive and the last process does not send

- *Broadcast*: a collective MPI communication among which sends the same data to all other processes (1:n)

- *Alltoall*: a collective MPI communication which exchanges data among all processes (n:n)

- *Random*: processes send messages to randomly selected other processes; also computation varies randomly by +/-30%. The receiver probes for incoming messages. This pattern only works for 10k message sizes with buffering because the asynchronous / random nature of computation and communication.

We configured the synthetic test programs to use message sizes of either 10k (buffered communication) or 100k (synchronous communication). The test programs are iterative, alternating (one round of) communications and (low-memory-usage) computation. We set the computation such that the communication percentage of the overall runtime is either 30% or 50% (the communication time was first measured independently, including all wait times resulting from dependencies in the patterns). We kept the communication percentage constant to investigate communication independent of the scalability of the application. All communication was blocking. In all cases, each application used

1 CPU per node, whether running under time sharing or on its own, i.e. we investigated the network sharing only. If an application would apply multi-threading per node and use both CPUs of a dual node (like ATOP-Grid, cf. Section 5), the computation time would be doubled under time sharing since it means splitting CPU resources. Thus, for the synthetic programs presented here, the projected original communication percentages under space sharing with full node-resource usage would be 46% (30% under time sharing) and 67% (50% under time sharing)—which is very high. This means that we have tested upper bounds regarding communication percentages.

Table 1 and Table 2 show the results of our measurements. All results with runtime increases over 10% are marked in bold as these are the only values that appear to be relevant at all. Results which represent more serious runtime increases over 50% have grey background.

We see that most patterns scheduled very well together (zero or very small relative increase in runtime). However, *Central* disturbed other patterns on 64 nodes with 50% communication, especially if the message size was 10k. The worst slowdown in this case is for *NN*. With message size 100k, only *Alltoall*— and to some extent *Central* if coscheduled with itself—suffered. *Alltoall* with both 10k and 100k message sizes on 32 and 64 nodes makes *Pipeline*, *NN*, and itself suffered if the communication percentage was 50%. We also observe that *NN* was most sensitive to coscheduling with any other pattern if the message size is 10k and the communication percentage was 50%.

Regarding scalability, slowdowns increased with larger number of nodes if the communication percentage was 50%, especially if the message size was 10k. This is no surprise as with larger numbers of nodes the probability for conflict on the network increases. However, in many cases, slowdown was still acceptable. For 30% communication, slowdowns were still low on 64 nodes, i.e. scalability was very good. Note that 30% (corresponding to 46% communication time if using all node resources under space sharing) is already very high and typically the maximum, i.e. many real parallel programs with lower percentages are likely to behave significantly better.

Finally, we ran some tests on a different cluster with Quadrics Elan4 interconnect. We found that communication is significantly faster (by 69% for *Central*, 26% for *Pipeline*, 48% for *NN*, 42% for *Random*, 81% for *Broadcast* and 62% for *Alltoall* if the message size was 10k; by about 27.5% for *Central*, *Pipeline*, and *NN*, 94% for *Broadcast*, and 71% for *Alltoall* if the message size was 100k). However, we have adjusted the test programs to obtain the same communication percentage. The results are shown in Table 3.

The slowdowns with the faster network were higher because the message frequency becomes higher if the same communication percentage is kept. However, the results are still acceptable except *Broadcast* which imposed extreme slowdowns. Thus, if an application relies dominantly on this communication

Table 1. Runtime increases under node sharing with different combinations of communication patterns and different communication percentages, and either 8, 32, or 64 cluster nodes. Message size is 10k. Left number in cell is increase for row application and right number in cell is increase for column application.

	Central					
	50%			30%		
	8	32	64	8	32	64
Central	0.3 / 0.3	**28.7 / 28.7**	**23.9 /23.9**	0.8 / 0.8	0.0 / 0.0	0.8 / 0.8
NN	0.2 / 0.1	**46.6 / 7.5**	**716.8** /4.6	1.6 / 0.1	**18.3 /** 1.5	**14.2** / 0.0
Pipeline	2.9 / 0.5	8.1 / 1.9	274.5/ 2.5	0.8 / 0.4	0.4 / 1.8	6.2 / 0.0
Broadcast	0.1 / 0.0	2.9 / 2.2	**62.3** /**29.8**	0.1 / 0.0	0.0 / 0.0	0.0 / 0.0
AlltoAll	6.1 / 1.0	11.6 / 0.4	**64.3** / 2.9	1.3 / 0.6	4.8 / 0.4	1.0 / 0.0
Random	0.0 / 0.0	0.3 / 3.6	1.9 /**355.3**	0.3 / 2.1	0.0 / 3.2	0.7 / 6.3
	NN					
NN	0.7 / 0.7	**18.3 / 18.3**	**27.0 /27.0**	1.0 / 1.0	**12.0 / 12.0**	7.7 / 7.7
Pipeline	1.7 / 8.0	1.5 / **25.6**	**0.0 / 32.2**	0.7 / 3.3	0.0 / 8.8	0.0 / 8.3
Broadcast	0.4 / 1.4	2.3 / **19.0**	0.0 / **13.1**	0.0 / 1.2	0.1 / 8.2	0.0 / 0.7
Alltoall	0.0 / 8.8	0.8 / **83.8**	0.0 / **96.5**	1.1 / 5.4	4.2 / **32.2**	0.0 / **38.0**
Random	0.0 / 9.7	0.4 / **32.8**	1.8 / **44.2**	0.0 / 5.3	0.0 / **11.5**	1.3 / 8.4
	Pipeline					
Pipeline	5.0 / 5.0	2.2 / 2.2	7.2/ 7.2	1.1 / 1.1	1.1 / 1.1	1.8 / 1.8
Broadcast	1.0 / 1.9	4.0 / 8.4	0.0 / 2.1	0.0 / 0.0	0.0 / 4.4	0.0 / 0.7
Alltoall	**30.0 / 14.2**	7.6 / **34.9**	0.0 / **58.9**	**10.5** / 5.0	3.6 / 17.1	0.0 / **32.5**
Random	0.1 / **29.3**	0.5 / **14.7**	1.8 / **10.1**	0.1 / 3.2	0.2 / 2.3	0.8 / 0.0
	Broadcast					
Broadcast	0.4 / 0.4	6.9 / 6.9	1.6 / 1.6	0.1 / 0.1	0.3 / 0.3	1.3 / 1.3
Alltoall	0.8 / 1.9	0.0 / 10.0	0.0 / **14.0**	0.7 / 0.8	2.2 / 4.7	0.0 / 7.1
Random	0.0 / 2.5	0.0 / 5.6	0.7 / 0.7	0.0 / 1.3	0.0 / 0.4	0.4 / 0.0
	Alltoall					
Alltoall	3.4 / 3.4	**37.4 / 7.4**	**40.1 / 40.1**	0.0 / 0.0	**18.7 / 18.7**	**15.1 /15.1**
Random	0.0 / **28.3**	0.1 / 6.4	0.6 / 8.6	0.0 / 8.8	0.0 / 8.1	0.4 / 0.0
	Random					
Random	0.3 / 0.3	1.0 / 1.0	3.3 / 3.3	0.1 / 0.1	0.0 / 0.0	0.9 / 0.9

pattern and the communication percentage is high, it should not be cosched-uled with any other application. If keeping the programs the same as in the

Table 2.   Runtime increases under node sharing with different combinations of communication patterns and different communication percentages, and either 8, 32, or 64 cluster nodes. Message size is 100k. Left number in cell is increase for row application and right number in cell is increase for column application.

	Central					
	50%			30%		
	8	32	64	8	32	64
Central	**13.4 / 13.4**	**21.2 / 21.2**	**20.0 / 20.0**	0.5 / 0.5	7.6 / 7.6	7.5 / 7.5
NN	4.6 / **13.6**	3.5 / 8.2	0.2 / 2.6	3.0 / 3.4	2.0 / 2.9	0.0 / 0.3
Pipeline	4.6 / 8.4	2.8 / 8.1	0.0 / **15.4**	3.5 / 3.7	0.5 / 3.7	0.0 / 7.3
Broadcast	3.1 / 6.4	0.0 / 0.9	1.7 / **41.1**	0.9 / 1.8	0.0 / 0.0	0.7 / **18.3**
Alltoall	3.5 / **27.6**	0.0 / **39.5**	**70.2** / 1.3	1.4 / 9.4	0.1 / 9.0	0.0 / 7.5
	NN					
NN	**19.4 / 19.4**	**13.8 / 13.8**	3.0 / 3.0	8.5 / 8.5	7.3 / 7.3	1.2 / 1.2
Pipeline	**32.3 / 25.6**	**22.8 / 19.1**	16.5 / **25.1**	10.3 / 6.4	0.5 / **11.4**	6.6 / **13.7**
Broadcast	**12.6** / 9.3	6.5 / 7.3	7.0 / 4.5	5.3 / 4.6	2.3 / 6.8	1.7 / **14.3**
Alltoall	6.4 / **31.5**	3.8 / **21.3**	0.0 / **54.5**	3.2 / **13.3**	2.0 / **17.0**	0.0 / 6.1
	Pipeline					
Pipeline	1.2 / 1.2	1.8 / 1.8	1.1 / 1.1	0.5 / 0.5	1.1 / 1.1	0.1 / 0.1
Broadcast	**23.5 /26.5**	**21.4 / 16.8**	**24.8 / 19.7**	**13.7 / 10.6**	0.5 / 7.6	9.0 / 9.1
Alltoall	9.3 / **62.8**	5.9 / **69.4**	0.0 / **61.7**	4.9 / **29.6**	2.3 / **33.2**	0.0 / **31.9**
	Broadcast					
Broadcast	0.0 / 0.0	0.0 / 0.0	1.0 / 1.0	0.0 / 0.0	0.0 / 0.0	0.0 / 0.0
Alltoall	4.8 / **53.8**	0.0 / **48.7**	0.0 / 0.0	3.6 / **17.9**	0.7 / **15.8**	0.0 / **24.7**
	Alltoall					
Alltoall	**31.3 /31.3**	**43.0 / 43.0**	**68.4 / 68.4**	**18.7 / 18.7**	**10.5 / 10.5**	**19.5 /19.5**

tests on the other cluster, the results became significantly better and acceptable, with the only exception of the combination *Broadbast/Alltoall* which still had a significant slowdown.

The overall results for our upper-bound tests demonstrate that different patterns schedule differently together and that detailed application characteristics should be recorded to decide whether running two applications under time sharing is meaningful or not. Real application with lower communication percentages may behave significantly friendlier. Communication percentages as presented here can be obtained with tools like our ScoPro monitor [16] and

Table 3. Slowdowns with faster network with 30% communication on 64 nodes. First row shows results for message size 10k (*Central* does not work because overflowing system buffers); second row shows results for message size 100k.

	Central	NN	Pipeline	Broadcast	Alltoall	Random
Central	N/A 10.0 / 10.0	N/A 1.8 / 0.6	N/A 13.7 / 0.0	N/A 20.1 / 148.0	N/A 6.7 / 0.0	N/A N/A
NN		10.8 / 0.8 2.8 / 2.8	10.4 / 11.3 19.7 / 9.5	7.4 / 74.1 10.9 / 131.0	22.8 / 0.0 6.0 / 0.0	14.7 / 9.3 N/A
Pipeline			11.6 / 11.6 24.6 / 24.6	8.4 / 61.2 18.7 / 612.2	12.9 / 7.1 34.6 / 0.0	12.9 / 9.2 N/A
Broadcast				30.8 / 30.8 228.1/228.1	60.0 / 0.0 199.6 / 0.0	51.9 / 6.4 N/A
Alltoall					20.8 / 20.8 15.0 / 12.4	0.0 / 16.3 N/A
Random						8.8 / 8.8 N/A

stored in performance directories as information for future runs of the application.

7.   Memory-access bandwidth

We tested memory-access bandwidth by creating programs which do not fit into the cache but have high memory-access rates (column-wise matrix access). We ran the program on its own and compared to the performance if running multiple copies on different cores of the same Opteron processor and on the cores of the second CPU. As Figure 4 shows, performance dropped from 138 Mbyte/sec to 119 Mbyte/sec if scheduling two programs on the same CPU, i.e., by 17% which was a moderate decrease. However, there was no further performance drop if scheduling more memory-intensive jobs on the second CPU. Thus, the performance drop appears not to be due to a memory bottleneck but to be exclusively due to the competition between the cores for the memory queue of the CPU. However, the picture may change with the trend towards larger numbers of cores and a quad-core Opteron on the horizon. Then, if sharing one memory-access interface per processor, application performance may drop unless it has very high cache locality.

Since threads of the same parallel application are likely to have the same characteristics, it then may be a significant advantage to rather run jobs with complementary memory-access characteristics together.

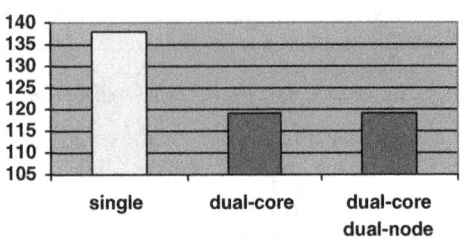

Figure 4.   Memory-access throughput for diagonal swap if running one memory-intensive job, two memory-access-intensive jobs on the same CPU, and the latter plus two memory-access-intensive jobs on the second CPU.

8.   Sharing the cache

Since caches may be shared under time sharing (cf. Section 3), we now explore cache effects. Performance can drop significantly if the applications do not fit together into the cache, and the job scheduler should therefore match jobs such that this does not occur. This requires information about the cache needs, i.e. the cache working-set sizes for the applications.

In the following, we explore the feasibility of simple black-box tests to determine the cache needs via monitoring. For one application, we pretend not to know the cache needs but want to extract them (black-box thread). We run a second application (test thread) for which we change the cache needs explicitly and incrementally. We expect the performance to drop significantly when both threads do no longer fit together into the cache, because temporal locality is fully or partially lost. Since we know the corresponding cache needs of the test thread, we can then deduce the cache needs of the black-box thread.

Since the current AMD Opteron does not share the cache (an Opteron with shared L3 cache will be on the market in the second half of 2007), we test true time sharing with CPU switching, by binding both threads to the same core. This creates a lower bound of cache impact because the threads can run undisturbed when the CPU is allocated to them, and cache locality is only lost upon switches between threads. The AMD Opteron has 1 Mbyte of L2 4-way combined cache, and cache replacement is LRU.

Even if temporal locality is lost, spatial locality per cache line still applies. Thus, programs with different memory-access patterns may suffer to a different extent if the working-sets do not fit into the cache. We therefore used synthetic programs with 1) consecutive memory access or 2) stride access (one access per cache line only) for the black-box thread. The test thread always used the stride pattern. In all cases, the programs performed dominantly read/write accesses and were kept very simple to make instruction caching negligible. We tested the cases that the black-box thread had a working-set of 256k, 512k, or 768k.

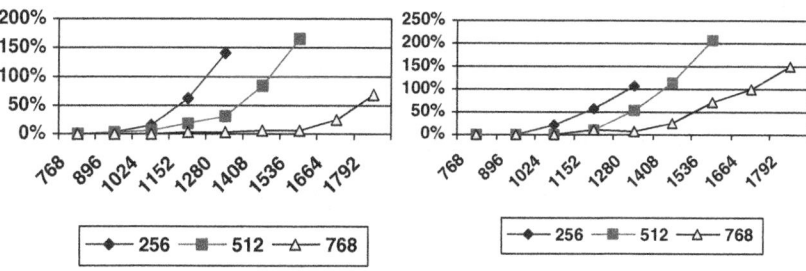

Figure 5. Percentage of runtime increase for the test thread due to cache misses under standard time sharing, shown for the sum of the two threads' cache needs (X axis) and different cache needs (256k, 512k, or 768k) for the black-box thread. Left graphic shows results for the stride-access pattern, right graphic for the consecutive-access pattern.

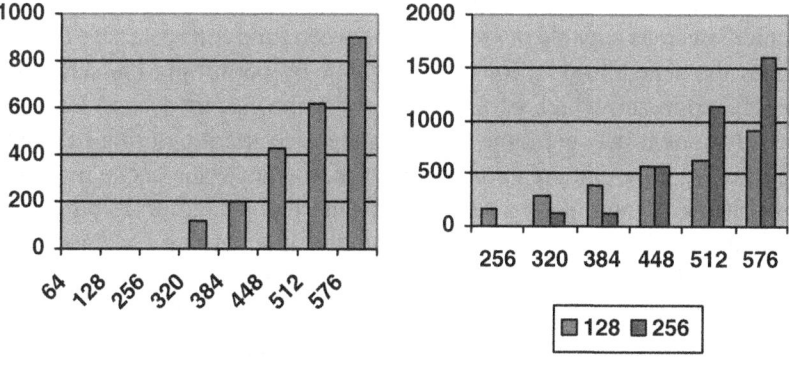

Figure 6. Left graphic shows percentage of runtime increase with increasing working set under CPU hyper sharing. Right graphic shows percentage of runtime increase for the test thread due to cache misses, shown for the sum of the two threads' cache needs (X axis), with the black-box thread needing either 128k or 256k cache.

Figure 5 shows that indeed the runtime increased significantly at the point where the two threads did not fit anymore into the cache together. The effect was clearer for the stride pattern because it does not have spatial locality per cache line. We also notice that the different cache needs for the black-box thread behaved differently. However, the difference was only gradual and the basic trend was the same.

Note that the results are also relevant for a single program if it creates a large number of threads to hide latencies [3] (switches may then occur more often than from time sharing) or to increase cache locality from smaller data chunks. In all cases, the threads need to be configured such that their data fits into the cache or such that multiple threads' data fits together into the cache. Our ATOP middleware [14] can configure and reconfigure the data partitioning (that represent chunks of work) during runtime to adjust the working-set size accordingly.

Finally, we show some tests from CPU hyper sharing where the applications share the cache simultaneously (as they would if the multiple cores of the CPU shared the L2 or L3 cache), see Figure 6. Memory access was stride-access. The synthetic programs used only memory-access or integer operations to avoid conflicts on CPU-internal resources. The cache size of the Xeon is 512k. The runtime increased significantly if the sum of the cache needs approached the cache size, and had a slightly larger jump if going beyond the cache size, i.e. from 512k to 576k. Thus, the approach is promising to extract cache-needs information.

9.   Summary and conclusion

We have shown that it be beneficial to run applications under time sharing which splits CPU resources but shares network, disk, and memory. Our ATOP-Grid middleware is capable of switching between time and space sharing which increases the scheduling options for grid jobs by permitting the scheduler to choose the approach which performs best with the current system load and to potentially switch between time sharing and space sharing during the runtime of the job. We have explored communication, memory, and cache impact. We found that the communication pattern and the percentage of communication have significant impact on the runtimes under time sharing. Memory access appears not to be a serious problem with dual core architectures like the Sharcnet clusters used (Hewlett Packard). Regarding potential cache sharing, we have proposed an approach to monitor cache of a program by running a test thread with varying cache needs and finding the point where both threads exceed the maximum cache space available. The approach is promising but needs further exploration.

Acknowledgments

We thank Sharcnet for supporting our research on the CFI-funded facilities of the Shared Hierarchical Academic Research Computing Network (www.sharcnet.ca). The 16-node cluster is funded by CFI (Grant No. 6191) with contributions from OIT and IBM. We also thank Yufei Xu, Tarik El Amsy, and Ositadimma Ejelike for their contributions.

References

[1] P. Behr, S. Pletner and A.C. Sodan. The PowerMANNA Architecture. *Proc. IEEE Conference on High Performance Computer Architecture (HPCA)*, Toulouse, France, pages 277-286, Jan. 2000.

[2] F. Berman, R. Wolski, H. Casanova, W. Cirne, et al. Adaptive Computing on the Grid Using AppLeS. *IEEE Trans. on Parallel and Distributed Systems*, 14(4):369-382, Apr. 2003.

[3] M. Bhandarkar, L.V. Kale, E. de Sturler, and J. Hoeflinger. Object-Based Adaptive Load Balancing for MPI Programs. *Proc. Internat. Conf. on Computational Science*, San Francisco/CA, USA, pages 108-117, May 2001.

[4] K. Devine, B. Hendrickson, E. Boman, M.St. John, C. Vaughan. Design of Dynamic Load-Balancing Tools for Par. Applications. *Proc. ICS*, Santa Fe, 2000.

[5] S. Dong, N.T. Karomis, and G.E. Karniadakis. Grid Solutions for Biological and Physical Cross-Site Simulations on the TeraGrid. *Proc. IPDPS*, Apr. 2006.

[6] K. Hwang and Z. Xu. *Scalable Parallel Computing*. McGraw-Hill, Boston, 1999.

[7] *Multi-core Processors—The Next Evolution in Computing*, AMD, http://multicore.amd.com/GLOBAL/WhitePapers/Multi-Core_Processors_ WhitePaper.pdf, 2005

[8] D.M. Pase and M.A. Eckl. *A Comparison of Single-Core and Dual-Core Opteron Processor Performance*. Linux Clusters—The HPC Revolution, May 2006.

[9] Sharcnet project, http://www.sharcnet.ca.

[10] W. Smith, I. Foster, and V. Taylor. Scheduling with Advanced Reservations. *Proc. IPDPS*, May 2000.

[11] A.C. Sodan and L. Lan. LOMARC-Lookahead Matchmaking for Multi-Resource Coscheduling on Hyperthreaded CPUs. *IEEE Transactions on Parallel and Distributed Computing*, Vol. 17, No. 11, Nov. 2006.

[12] A.C. Sodan, G. Gupta. Time vs. Space Adaptation with ATOP-Grid. *Proc. ACM Adaptive & Reflective Middleware Workshop*, Melbourne, Nov. 2006.

[13] A.C. Sodan and G. Gupta. ATOP-Grid for Unified Multidimensional Adaptation of Grid Applications. *Proc. PDCS*, Dallas, Nov. 2006.

[14] A.C. Sodan and L. Liu. Dynamic Multi-Resource Monitoring for Predictive Job Scheduling with ScoPro. *Proc. PDCS*, Phoenix, Nov. 2005.

[15] A.C. Sodan. Loosely Coordinated Coscheduling in the Context of Other Dynamic Approaches for Job Scheduling-A Survey. *Concurrency & Computation: Practice & Experience*, 17(15):1725-1781, Dec. 2005.

[16] A.C. Sodan and L. Lan. LOMARC—Lookahead Matchmaking for Multi-Resource Coscheduling. *Proc. JSSPP*, New York / USA, Lecture Notes in Computer Science 3277, Springer, June 2004.

[17] A.C. Sodan and M. Riyadh. Co-scheduling of MPI and adaptive thread applications under Solaris. *Proc. PDCS*, Cambridge/USA, Nov. 2002.

[18] T. Stricker and T. Gross. Global Address Space, Non-Uniform Bandwidth: A Memory System Perf. Characterization of Par. Systems. *Proc. HPCA*, Feb. 1997.

[19] J. Weinberg, A. Snavely. Symbiotic Space Sharing on SDSC's DataStar System. *Workshop on Job Scheduling Strategies for Parallel Processing (JSSPP)*, Saint-Malo, France, Lecture Notes in Computer Science 4376, Springer, June 2006.

BENCHMARKING GRID APPLICATIONS*

Farrukh Nadeem, Radu Prodan, and Thomas Fahringer
Institute of Computer Science
University of Innsbruck
{farrukh,radu,tf}@dps.uibk.ac.at

Alexandru Iosup
Faculty of Electrical Engineering, Mathematics, and Computer Science
Delft University of Technology, The Netherlands.
A.Iosup@tudelft.nl

Abstract   Application benchmarks can play a key role in analyzing and predicting the performance and scalability of Grid applications, serve as an evaluation of the fitness of a collection of Grid resources for running a specific application or class of applications [27], and help in implementing performance-aware resource allocation policies of real time job schedulers. However, application benchmarks have been largely ignored due to diversified types of applications, multi-constrained executions, dynamic Grid behavior and heavy computational costs. To remedy these, we present the GrapBench (**Gr**id **Ap**plication **Bench**marks) system. GrapBench computes the Grap Benchmarks for Grid applications which are flexible regarding variations in problem-size of the application and machine-size of the Grid-site. GrapBench dynamically controls the number of benchmarking experiments for individual applications, and manages the execution of these experiments on different Grid-sites in an easy and flexible way. We also present results from the prototype implementation of our proposed system to show the effectiveness of our approach.

Keywords: Application benchmarking, performance prediction, benchmarks measurements

*This work is partially supported by the European Union through IST-2002-004265 CoreGRID and IST-034601 edutain@grid projects. Part of this work was also carried out in the context of the Virtual Laboratory for e-Science project (www.vl-e.nl), which is supported by a BSIK grant from the Dutch Ministry of Education, Culture and Science (OC&W), and which is part of the ICT innovation program of the Dutch Ministry of Economic Affairs (EZ).

1.   Introduction

Grid infrastructure provides an opportunity to the scientific and business communities to exploit the powers of heterogeneous resources in multiple administrative domains under a single umbrella [13]. Proper characterization of Grid resources is of key importance in effective mapping and scheduling of the jobs to these resources, (to utilize maximum power of these resources). Benchmarking has been used for many years to characterize a large variety of systems ranging from CPU architectures to the file-systems, databases, parallel systems, internet infrastructures, middlewares etc. [11]. There have always been issues in optimized mapping of jobs to the Grid resources on the basis of available benchmarks [26]. Existing Grid benchmarks (or their combinations) do not suffice to measure/predict application performance and scalability, and give a quantitative comparison of different Grid-sites for individual applications while taking into effect variations in the problem-size. In addition, there are no integration mechanisms and common units available for existing benchmarks to make meaningful inferences about the performance and scalability of individual Grid applications on different Grid-sites.

Application benchmarking on the Grid can provide a basis for users and Grid middleware services (like meta scheduler, resource broker) for optimized mapping of jobs to the Grid resources by serving as evaluation of fitness to compare different computing resources in the Grid. The performance results obtained from real application benchmarking are much more useful for running applications on a highly distributed Grid infrastructure than the regular resource information provided by the standard Grid information services [26]. Application benchmarks are also helpful in predicting the performance and scalability of Grid applications, studying the effects of variations in application performance for different problem-sizes, and gaining insights into the properties of computing nodes architectures. However, the complexity, heterogeneity and the dynamic nature of Grids raise serious questions about the overall realization and applicability of application benchmarking. Moreover, diversified types of applications, multi-constrained executions, and heavy computational costs make the problem even harder. Above all, mechanizing the whole process of controlling and managing benchmarking experiments and making benchmarks available to users and Grid services in an easy and flexible fashion makes the problem more challenging.

To overcome this situation, we present GrapBench, a four layered Grid applications benchmarking system. GrapBench produces benchmarks for Grid applications taking into effect the variations in problem-size of the application and machine-size of the Grid-site, thus allowing problem-size and machine-size flexible comparison of Grid-sites for individual applications. GrapBench provides the necessary support for conducting controlled and reproducible experiments, for computing performance benchmarks accurately and for interpreting benchmarking results in the context of applications' performance and scalability predictions and application specific comparison of different Grid-sites through a graphical user interface. GrapBench takes the specifications of executables, set of problem-sizes, pre-execution requirements and set of available Grid-sites as an input in XML format. These XML specifications, along with the available resources are parsed to generate jobs to be submitted to different Grid-sites. At first, GrapBench completes pre-experiment requirements, if any, and then runs the experiments according to the experimental strategy. Benchmarks are computed from experimental results and archived in benchmarks repository for later use. Performance and scalability prediction and analysis from the benchmarks are available through a GUI and GT4 service interfaces. We do not require complex integration/analysis of measurements, or new metrics for interpretation of benchmarking results.

Among our considerations for the design of Grid application benchmarks were conciseness, portability, easy computation and adaptability for different Grid users/services. We have implemented a prototype of the proposed system under ASKALON [12], on the top of GT4 [9].

The rest of the paper follows as such: Section 2 describes performance of a Grid application and the different factors affecting it. The design of *benchmarks generation process* is described in the Section 3 . In Section 4 we describe the number of benchmarks experiments and autoGrap a semi-automatic application benchmarking tool to make benchmarking experiments. Computation of benchmarks from experimental results is explained in Section 5. In Section 6 we describe utilization of benchmarks. We present results from experiments conducted on Austrian Grid and related analysis in Section 7. Related work is presented in Section 8, and finally we conclude in Section 9.

2.   Performance of a Grid Application

Performance of an application on a Grid-site is dependent upon the performance of a couple of inter-related Grid resources at different levels of Grid infrastructure: performance of: the Grid-site, the computing node, CPU, memory hierarchy, I/O, storage node, network (LAN/WAN), network topology etc. as shown in Figure 1, adapted from [11]. Our conjecture is that, the traditional benchmarks (combination of benchmarks) and their context of use cannot be directly used for application performance prediction for multiple reasons: different performance representation of individual resources, high cost (with respect to time and money), trust worthiness of benchmarking suits and corresponding measurements, metrics interpretation, and above all the complex integration of results from different resources, to make some conclusions useful for human users and Grid middleware services. Moreover, existing sets of benchmarks do not allow *cross-platform interoperability* [9] of benchmarks results at different structural levels of the Grid, for different Grid applications. More specifically there is a need for benchmarks, which

(i) represent the performance of Grid application on different Grid sites

(ii) incorporate the individual effects of different Grid resources specific to different applications (like memory, caching etc.)

(iii) can be used for performance and scalability predictions of the application

(iv) are portable to different platforms

(v) are flexible regarding variations in problem-size and machine-size

(vi) support fast and simplified computation and management

(vii) are comprehensively understandable and usable by different users and services

On the other hand, it is also necessary to address the high cost of Grid benchmarking administration, and benchmarking computation and analysis. This requires a comprehensive system for benchmarking computation, management, with a visualization and analysis component.

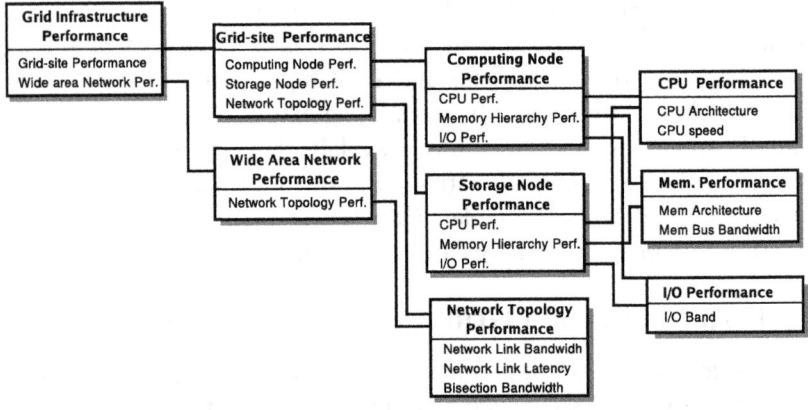

Figure 1.   Different factors affecting application performance in the Grid.

3.   GrapBench System Design

GrapBench benchmarks Grid applications on different Grid-sites. It consists of a framework containing set of tools to perform and facilitate the benchmarking process (the benchmarking experiments, computation and storage of results) in a flexible way, and later publishing the results and analysis.

The process of benchmarks generation is shown in the Figure 2. Layer 1 specifies application details for benchmarking experiments in XML based Grid

Application Description Language (GADL), and later, compiles job descriptions for individual experiments from it. GrapBench dynamically controls the total number of benchmarking experiments for individual applications w.r.t. different problem-sizes. In layer 2, these experiments are executed on available Grid-sites provided by resource manager [24]. GrapBench considers the Grid-site at both micro level (the individual Grid nodes) and macro level (the Grid-site) taking machine-size as a variable in benchmark measurements. Such application benchmarks easily incorporate the variations in application's performance associated to different problem-sizes and machine-sizes. Layer 3 computes the benchmarks and stores the results in benchmarks repository. The layer 4 is an analysis and visualization layer making the benchmarks and related analysis available to different clients through GUI and GT4 service interfaces.

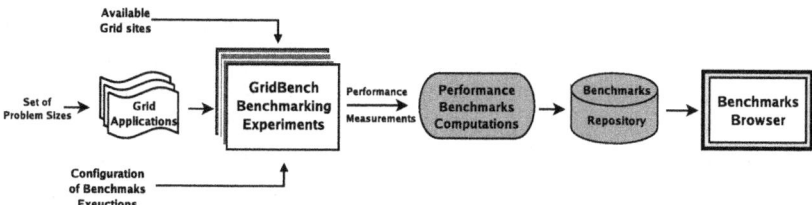

Figure 2. Process of benchmarks generation

4. Benchmarking Measurements

Controlling the number of benchmarking measurements is of key importance in the efficiency of the whole computation process. For the efficiency of computation process we focus to reduce the total number of benchmarking experiments and maximize the utility of benchmarking results.

Our methodology of reducing the number of benchmarking experiments is to enable sharing of the benchmarking information across the Grid-sites. The information sharing mechanism is explained in the Section 5. The performance comparsions (e.g. performance ratios) of different Grid-sites are different for different applications. Moreover, these also vary for different problem sizes and machine-sizes. For performance prediction and Grid-sites' comparisons while considering variations in the problem-size, we make a full factorial design of benchmarking experiments on the Grid and one benchmarking experiment for one fixed problem-size (called base problem-size) on each of other non-identical Grid-sites. We select the smallest problem-size as the base problem-size. Later, at the time of computation of benchmarks from these experimental results, the process of normalization (see Section 5) helps in completing the benchmarks computation for all the Grid-sites. The benchmarks for the base problem-size are used to share information across the Grid-sites. For scalability analysis and prediction, one benchmark experiment for each of different machine-sizes is also made.

The total number of experiments for an application A with p problem-sizes on a Grid with Grid-size of n, with m different machine-sizes is $m \times n \times p$. One of the distinctions of our work is we can greatly reduce the number of benchmarks experiments through our strategy from $m \times n \times p$ to $m + n + p - 2$ ($n + p - 1$ for execution time predictions and $m - 1$ for scalability predictions). Later, we employ prediction mechanism to serve performance values for the problem-size and machine-size combinations that were not effectively measured in the experiments.

We argue that this reduction in the number of performed benchmarks is a reasonable trade-off between duration of the benchmarking process and accuracy. In Section 5, we show experimentally that predictions based on our approach are with in 90% accuracy. A similar or better acuracy can be achieved with either more benchmarks, or by using analytical modeling techniques. However, both these alternatives are time-consuming. In addition, analytical modeling requires a separate model and expert knowledge for each new type of application. With current grid environments hosting hundreds to thousands of different applications[1], analytical modeling for individual application's performance and scalability (which requires manual efforts) is impractical, whereas, benchmarking requires only one generic setup.

4.1   Grap Benchmarking experiments with AutoGrap

To facilitate Grid administrators, application developers and end users, for comprehensive and adaptable administration and management of benchmarking experiments we have AutoGrap. The architecture of AutoGrap is presented in Figure 3. The main components of the architecture are:

- Experiments Specifications Engine (ESE) (including an RSL/JDL compiler that converts XML specifications of application to job descriptions)
- Experiment Execution Engine
- Monitoring Component
- Orchestrator
- Benchmarks Computation Component
- Archive Component
- Benchmarks Visualization and Analysis Browser
- Information Service Component (publishes results to other services)

---

[1]The Grid Workload Archive, available on line at http://gwa.ewi.tudelft.nl, hosts grid workload traces that also record the job executables.

First, a small compiler in ESE parses the application specifications written in platform-independent XML based Grid Application Description Language (GADL) and produces the job descriptions from it in a JDL. Later, these job descriptions are add resource specifications, on which these jobs are to be launched, to produce final jobs used for launching the benchmarks experiments.

In our present prototype implementations we support the RSL language of Globus [9]. The benchmark application is the actual application's executable, to be benchmarked. The Experiment Execution Engine executes benchmarks experiments designed by ESE on the Grid-sites available from our Resource Manager. The monitoring component watches the execution of the benchmarking experiments and alerts the Orchestrator component to collect the data and coordinate the start-up of the benchmarks computation component to compute the benchmarks. The Archive Component stores this information in the benchmarks repository for future use.

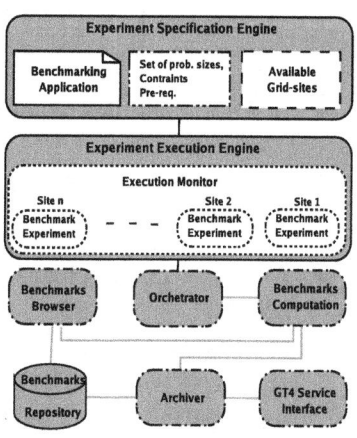

Figure 3. AutoGrap Architecture

The benchmarks Browser publishes the Grap Benchmarks on a GUI, and Information Service Component is an interface to other services for Grap Benchmarks.

4.2 Experiment specification engine

To describe application specifications we introduce Grid Application Description Language (GADL). A GADL definition specifies the application to be executed, its exact paths from resource manager, the problem-size ranges and pre-requisites of execution (some executions before the actual execution or setting of environmental variables etc.) [3, 20], if any. Every instance of GADL is described by:

- Application name with a set of problems sizes given as range (startVal:stepSize:endVal) which are described by name and value, e.g.

```
<application name="Wien2k" />
<parameter>
    <name="k-points" value=5.0:0.1:9.0>
</parameter>
```

- Resource manager [24] URI, to get the available Grid-sites and location of the executables on them.

```
<resourcemanager>
    <location path="http://karwendel.dps.uibk.ac.at:40105/wsrf/
```

```
        services/GlareService"/>
<resourcemanager/>
```

- A set of pre-requisites, comprising of the components which must be finished before the execution (of some components of) the application.

```
<prerequisites>
    <location path="http://dps.uibk.ac.at:/home/farrukh/pre-reqs"/>
</prerequisites>
```

- A set of input files required for execution of the application

```
<inputfile>
    <location path="http://dps.uibk.ac.at:/home/farrukh/input.tar"/>
<inputfile/>
```

- An executable to change the problem-size in some input files (used by ESE)

```
<probsizechange>
    <location path="http://dps.uibk.ac.at:/home/farrukh/
    changeProbSize"/>
<probsizechange/>
```

4.3   Experiment execution engine

The AutoGrap exploits *opportunistic load balancing* [22] for scheduling benchmarking experiments in the Grid. The algorithm for automatically making benchmarking experiments is shown in Algorithm 4.3. At the start, one job is submitted to each of the available Grid-sites. The next job is submitted after the completion of the previous submitted job, until all the jobs are finished from the full factorial design of experiments (Algorithm line 5 to line 13). In the next step, one experiment, for one fixed problem-size (common for all, called base problem-size), is made on each of non-identical Grid-sites (Algorithm line 14 to line 17). The benchmarks for the common problem-size are later used in the normalization 5. We categorize two Grid-sites to be identical if they have same CPU architecture, CPU speed, and memory. All benchmarking experiments are made when the Grid-site is found to be free, with the help of NWS [29]. The execution times of these experiments are archived and later used by Benchmarks Computation Component to calculate the benchmarks.

4.4   Additional benchmarking considerations

Sometimes the beckground load, that is, the applications run by other users, severely affects the performance of some (or even all) the applications in the system. This happens mostly when several applications contend for the same network or processor shares, or when resource utilization is very high and the

---

Algorithm 1 Scheduling Benchmarking Experiments

1: **makeBenchmarkExperiments()**
2: **Input:** $A : A = \{\alpha, \beta, \gamma, ...\}$ {Applications to be benchmarked}, $\lambda : \lambda = \{m_1, m_2, m_3, ..., m_n\}$ {Set of problem-sizes for each application in A}, $S : S = \{s_1, s_2, s_3, ..., s_n\}$ {Set of Grid-sites}
3: **Output:** ω - the execution time result set

4:   $Jobs = getJobDescriptions(A, \lambda, S)$;
5: **while** $Jobs \neq \phi$ **do**
6:   **if** $\exists s \in S \mid available(s)$ (when no job is running on s) **then**
7:     $j = getNextJob(Jobs)$;
8:     $\omega' := getExeTime(s, j)$;
9:     $\omega := \omega \cup \omega'$;
10:   **else**
11:     $wait()$;
12:   **end if**
13: **end while**
14: **for** $\forall s \in S$ **do**
15:   $\omega' := getExeTime(s, m_1)$;
16:   $\omega := \omega \cup \omega'$;
17: **end for**

18: **return** ω;

---

resource manager is ineffective [6]. However, our benchmarking procedure does not take into account the background load, at least for the moment. The reason is threefold. First, our goal is to quantify the best achievable performance of an application on a grid platform, that is, without the contention generated by additional users. Work in [6] helps quantifying the ratio between the maximum achievable performance and the performance achieved in practice. Second, work in hotspot or symbiotic scheduling [28], helps scheduling applications with overlapping resource requirements such that the overlap is minimized. Third, while mechanisms for ensuring the background load on the resources have been proposed, e.g., in [16], a better understanding of the structure and of the impact of the background load is needed. We plan to investigate aspects of this problem in future work.

5. Computation of Benchmarks

The Grap Benchmarks are computed by normalizing the execution times. The execution times are normalized by dividing all the execution times (for different problem-sizes) with the execution time for a base problem-size selected by default as the largest problem-size (to take in effect of inter process communication) in the set of problem-sizes specified by the user. The normalization mechanism not only makes the performance of different machines comparable but also provides a basis for translating different performance values across different Grid-sites. The normalization of values is based on the observation that for many applications, and in particular for all the applications used in our experimental work, the normalized execution times for different problem-sizes and machine-sizes are the same on all the Grid-sites, with 90% accuracy. This allows cross-platform interoperability of Grap Benchmarks. For example, the normalized execution on a Grid-site s for a certain problem-size and machine-size will be equal to that of an other Grid-site t.

$$Normalized\ Exe.\ Time(s) = Normalized\ Exe.\ Time(t)$$

On the basis of our experimental observations, we assume a simple application model under which the rate of change of execution time for a problem-size q on Grid-site s, $T_q(s)$, with respect to execution time for a problem-size r on the a Grid-site s is similar to that of on Grid-site t [17], i.e.

$$\frac{\Delta T_q(s)}{\Delta T_r(s)} = \frac{\Delta T_q(t)}{\Delta T_r(t)},\ \Delta : rate\ of\ change$$

For our set of grid applications, this assumption was over 90% accurate, and this is shown in the Figure 4(a). Similarly, we normalize the execution times when machine size is also taken as a parameter, to compute benchmarks incorporating the variations in machine size. This normalization is also based on a similar model based on our experimental observations. Under this model for CPU-intensive applications, we assume the rate of change in execution time of an application across different problem-sizes is also preserved for different machine-sizes, as shown in Figure 4(b). i.e.

$$\frac{\Delta T_{q,m}(s)}{\Delta T_{q,n}(s)} = \frac{\Delta T_{r,m}(s)}{\Delta T_{r,n}(s)}$$

Moreover, rate of change in performance behavior across different machine-sizes is also preserved for different problems-sizes. i.e.

$$\frac{\Delta T_{q,m}(s)}{\Delta T_{r,m}(s)} = \frac{\Delta T_{q,n}(s)}{\Delta T_{r,n}(s)}$$

We also found an accuracy of more than 90% on this model, and this behavior is also shown in the Figure 4(b).

6.   Grap Benchmarks Utilization

Grap Benchmarks are computed from results of benchmarks experiments and archived for future references. This is done in a manner that facilitates the comparisons between the benchmarks for different machines, problem-sizes and machine-sizes, along with the performance and scalability predictions. Benchmarks can be browsed through a GUI (see Figure 8(a)) for application performance and scalability analysis for different problem-sizes on different Grid-sites. In this section we explain how Grap Benchmarks are used for performance & scalability predictions and Grid-site comparisons.

6.1   Performance and scalability predictions

The first key use of Grap Benchmarks is application performance and scalability predictions for Grid users, as well as Grid services like meta-schedulers and performance analysis service. Grap Benchmarks can facilitate good engineering practices by allowing alternative implementations to be compared quantitatively (e.g. see Figure 7(a)). Performance of an application can be predicted, for any problem-size p on any Grid-site s from another Grid-site t (for which execution time for problem-size p exists) from Grap Benchmarks using the phenomenon of normalization as: if $T_q(s)$ represents the execution time of an application, for a problem-size q, on a Grid-site s, then;

$$T_q(s) = \frac{T_q(t)}{T_r(t)} \times T_r(s)$$

Similarly, for scalability analysis and prediction, (taking machine-size as a parameter) the performance of the parallel applications for different number of CPUs can be predicted from Grap Benchmarks as: If $T_{q,m}(s)$ represents execution time of an application for problem-size q on a Grid-site s for a machine-size m,then;

$$T_{q,m}(s) = \frac{T_{r,m}(s)}{T_{r,n}(s)} \times T_{q,n}(s)$$

For execution time and scalability predictions, normalization is done based on execution time for the closest set of parameters(problem-size and machine size). At the start, it is made based on the only common set of parameters in the benchmark repository and later, if some other performance values are available (after adding some experimental values from real runs), calculated based on the closer performance value, as it increases accuracy in the cross platform performance and scalability predictions. For our prediction results we obtained a minimum accuracy of 90% from our proposed number of experiments.

$$\frac{T_{q,m}(s)}{T_{q,n}(s)} = \frac{T_{r,m}(s)}{T_{r,n}(s)} |n \to m, q \to r$$

The benchmarks, performance and scalability predictions can be obtained through Information Service Component which is a GT4 service interface, and can also be browsed through Benchmarks Browser GUI.

6.2   Grid-site comparisons

The quantitative performance comparisons of different Grid-sites is different for individual applications. This is because of their different underlaying architectures and different performance requirements of Grid applications. This is demonstrated with quantitative comparisons of two Grid-sites *agrid1* and *altix1.uibk* for three real world applications in the Figure 7(b). In addition, the performance comparisons for the same Grid-sites are also different for different problem sizes and machine sizes. This behavior of Grid-applications is presented with performance comparisons of two Grid-sites *altix1* and *agrid1*, in terms of execution time ratios for different problems sizes in Figure 8(b).

The first key use of Grap Benchmarks is support for quantitative comparisons of different Grid-sites. Quantitative comparisons of different Grid-sites help real time schedulers for mapping jobs to different Grid-sites, and resource brokers for resource selections from the available pool of resources. Furthermore, these comparisons provide application developers with information about the systems capabilities in terms of application performance, so that they can develop and tune their applications for high-quality implementations.

Design of Grap Benchmarks helps facilitating the comparisons of applications' performance for different values of problem-sizes and machine-sizes on different Grid-sites, as the second key use. This can guide the Grid-site selection policies by the real time schedulers, resource brokers and different Grid users. The comparison of different Grid-sites for a application Wien2k is shown in the Figure 5(a).

7.   Results and Analysis

We have conducted our experiments from the prototype implementation of our system on Austrian Grid. The testbed is described in Table 1. In the test environment, the 8 sites employ 5 cluster sizes, 5 structural and communication architectures, 6 processor types, and 6 memory sizes. This ensures that the tested is heterogeneous. The experiments were conducted for three real world applications Wien2k [8], MeteoAG [21] and Invmod [25].

Wien2k application allows performing electronic structure calculations of solids using density functional theory based on the full-potential augmented plane-wave ((L)APW) and local orbital (lo) method. MeteoAG produces mete-

Table 1.   The Austrian Grid test bed sites.

Site Name	Architecture	CPUs	Processor Arch.	RAM[MB]	Location
altix1.jku	ccNUMA, SGI Altix 3000	16	Itanium 2, 1.6	1400	Linz
altix1.uibk	ccNUMA, SGI Altix 350	16	Itanium 2, 1.6	1600	Innsbruck
schafberg	ccNUMA, SGI Altix 350	16	Itanium 2, 1.6	1400	Salzburg
agrid1	NOW Fast Ethernet	20	Pentium 4, 1.8	1800	Innsbruck
hydra	COW Fast Ethernet	16	AMD Athelon 2.0	1600	Linz
hcma	NOW Fast Ethernet	206	AMD Opteron 2.2	4000	Innsbruck
zid-cc	NOW Fast Ethernet	22	Intel Xeon 2.2	2000	Innsbruck
karwendel	COW InfiniBand	80	AMD Opteron 2.6	16000	Innsbruck
Total		388			

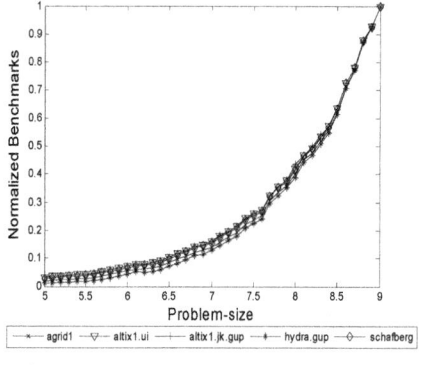

(a) Wien2k, 41 problem-sizes, 5 Grid-sites

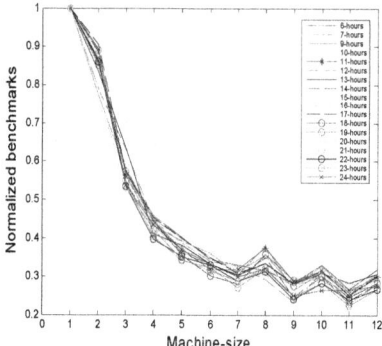

(b) MeteoAG on *zid-cc*, 19 problem-sizes, 12 machine sizes

Figure 4. Normalized benchmarks, similar curves for different Grid-sites(a), and different machine-sizes(b) exhibit the realization of normalized behavior

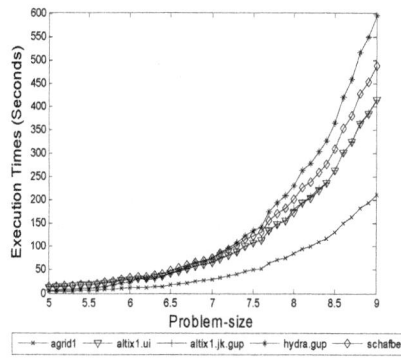

(a) Wien2k, Grid sites comparisons, performance benchmarks for 41 different problem-sizes, 5 Grid sites

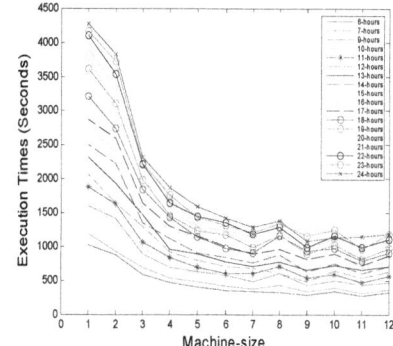

(b) MeteoAG on *zid-cc*, scalability comparisons for different machine sizes, performance benchmarks for 19 problem-sizes, 12 machine sizes

Figure 5. Grid-sites and scalability comparison for different applications

orological simulations of precipitation fields of heavy precipitation cases over the western part of Austria with RAMS, at a spatially and temporally fine granularity, in order to resolve most alpine watersheds and thunderstorms.Invmod application helps in studying the effects of climatic changes on the water balance through water flow and balance simulations, in order to obtain improved discharge estimates for extreme floods.

The Grap Benchmarks for Wien2k on different Grid-sites of the Austrian Grid are shown in Figure 4(a). Total 45 benchmark experiments were made for 41 different problem-sizes on 5 different Grid-sites. By one experiment here

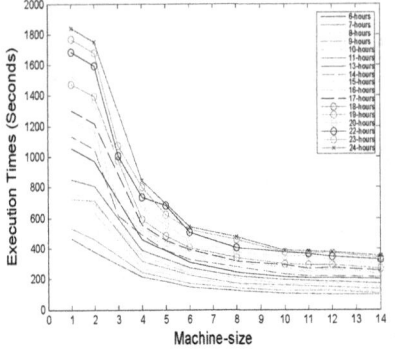

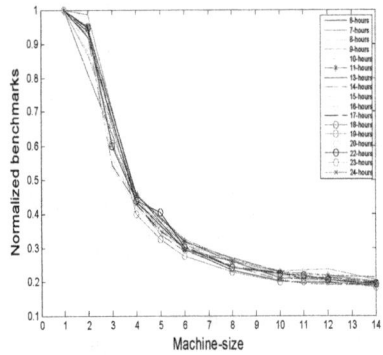

(a) MeteoAG on *hcma*, Scalability comparison for different machine-sizes for 19 different problem-sizes and 14 machine sizes

(b) MeteoAG on *hcma*, Normalized benchmarks for 19 different problem-sizes and 14 machine sizes, similar curves show the realization of normalized behavior

Figure 6.   MeteoAG Grap Benchmarks on *hcma*

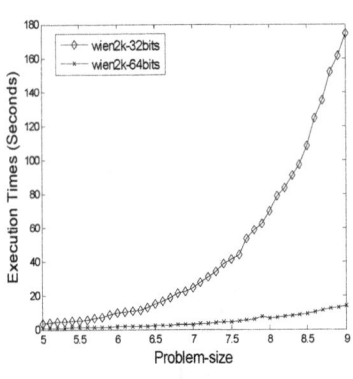

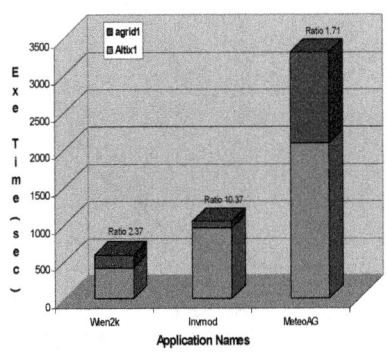

(a) Wien2k on *karwendel*, version comparisons for different problem-sizes from benchmarks, 32-bit and 64-bits

(b) Quantitative performance comparison of *altix1* and *agrid1* for 3 different applications, different ratios show different comparisons

Figure 7.   Different comparisons, based on Grap Benchmarks

we mean average of multiple repetitions to reduce the anomalies in the computations. In our presented work we repeated each computation for 5 times. For Wien2k, the execution time for problem-size 9.0 is used as base performance value for normalization. The similar benchmarks curves (for different values of problem-size) on different machines show the realization of normalized performance behavior of the Grid Benchmarks across heterogeneous platforms.

To give a glimpse of the variability in the quantitative comparisons of different Grid-sites for different applications, we present our experimental results in Figure 7(b). As shown in the figure, the comparison of two different Grid-sites *agrid1* and *altix1.uibk* yielded different ratios (*altix1.uibk* : *agrid1*) of execution times for three different applications. For Wien2k this ratio is 2.37, for Invmod 10.37 and for MeteoAG 1.71. It is noteworthy that these ratios are irrespective of the the total execution times on these Grid-sites. This is the reason that why benchmarks for individual resources (CPU, memory etc.) do not suffice for application performance and scalability predictions. Furthermore, considering one application, the comparison of execution times on Grid-sites yields different ratios for different problem sizes. This performance behavior of Grid applications urged us to make a full factorial design of experiments on the Grid, rather than modeling individual applications analytically which is complex and in-efficient. The execution time ratios of two Grid-sites *altix1.uibk* and *agrid1* for 41 different problem sizes are shown in Figure 8(b).

Performance and scalability benchmarks for different number of CPUs, for an other application MeteoAG are shown for two different Grid-sites *zid-cc* and *hcma* in Figures 5(b) and 6(a) respectively. Total 30 benchmarking experiments were made for 19 different problem-sizes and 12 different machine sizes on *zid-cc*. Total 32 benchmarking experiments were made for 19 different problem-sizes and 14 different machine sizes on *hcma*. In these experiments we have used a machine-size of 1 for normalization. The identical scalability curves demonstrate the realization of normalized performance behavior of Grid Benchmarks with respect to problem-size and machine-size on one platform.

A comparison of different Grid-sites, based on Grap Benchmarks, for Wien2k is shown in Figure 5(a). The scalability comparison for MeteoAG for different

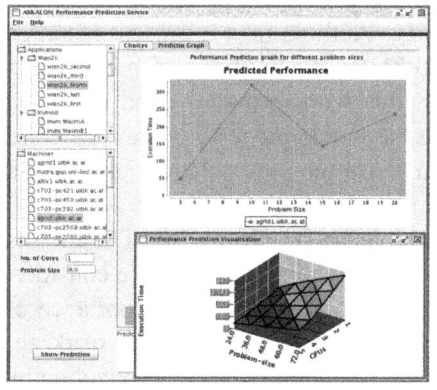

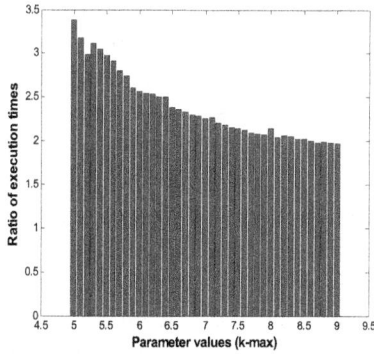

(a) Graphical user interface, for performance and scalability analysis

(b) Quantitative Grid-sites comparison for different problem sizes, execution times ratios for *altix1.uibk* and *agrid1* (*altix1.uibk* : *agrid1*) for 41 different problem sizes

Figure 8.

problem-sizes, on two different platforms (*zid-cc*(32-bits) and *hcma*(64-bits)) is shown in Figures 5(b) and 6(a) respectively. A comparison of two different version of Wien2k (32-bits version and 64-bits version) is presented in Figure 7(a) on *karwendel*. These graphs were generated from Grap Benchmarks, when only one benchmark measurement of 64-bits version was available.

We observed a maximum average variation of 10% from actual values (obtained from real runs) in our performance and scalability predictions which means a 90% accuracy in our predictions where the maximum standard deviation of 2% was observed.

8.   Related Work

There have been several good efforts at benchmarking individual Grid resources like [4, 7, 18]. The discussion presented in [10] shows that the configuration, administration and analysis of NGB requires an extensive manual effort, like other benchmarks. Moreover, these benchmarks lack some integration mechanism needed to make meaningful inferences about the performance of different Grid applications from these benchmarks.

A couple of good comprehensive tools like [27] are also available for benchmarking a wide range of Grid resources. These provide easy archiving and publishing the results. Likewise, GrenchMark [15] is a framework for analyzing, testing, and comparing grid settings. Its main focus is the generation and submission of synthetic grid workloads. By contrast, our work focuses on single application benchmarks, which are extensively supported.

Individual benchmarks have been successfully used for resource allocation [19, 5] and application scheduling [14]. Work in [19] presents good work for resource selection, by building models from resource performance benchmarks and application performance details. Authors in [5] present resource filter, resource ranker and resource MakeMatch on the basis of benchmarks and user provided information. Though this work provides good accuracy, it requires much user intervention during the whole process. Moreover, these benchmarks do not support cross-platform performance translations of different Grid applications while considering variations in problem-sizes.

A similar work has been presented by Dikaiakos et. al. in [26]. The authors present a tool for resource selection for different applications while considering variations in performance due to different machine-sizes. Importance of application specific benchmarks is also described by [23]. In this work authors present three different methodologies to benchmarks Grid application by modeling application and Grid-site, and require much manual intervention.

The distinction of our work is that we focus on controlling and specifying the total number of experiments needed for benchmarking process and our proposed benchmarks are flexible regarding variations in machine-size as well as problem-sizes (required for real time scheduling and application performance prediction). Moreover, we support a semi-automatic benchmarking process. The cross platform inter-operability of our benchmarks allows trade-off analysis and translation of performance information between different platforms.

9.   Conclusion and Future Work

Application benchmarks provide a concrete base for application's performance analysis and predictions, incorporating variations in the problem-sizes and machine-sizes on different platforms and for real quantitative comparison of different Grid-sites for individual applications. Grap Benchmarks are representative of performance of Grid applications on different Grid-sites. Computed from real execution of applications these incorporate the individual effects of different Grid resources specific to applications. Their computation, execution, performance measurements storage and management are affordable in terms of cost, such as management of the benchmarking process, execution time and storage. Performance metrics derived from the benchmarking experiments can be easily associated with the structure of the corresponding benchmarks. Grap Benchmarks are easy to compute and use in contradiction to existing benchmarking tools and techniques for different Grid resources. Experiments conducted according to our proposed strategy make the benchmarks flexible regarding problem-size and thus allow problem-size and machine-size flexible comparisons of different Grid-sites. Simple metrics of benchmarks make them directly usable and understandable to different Grid users and services.

We benchmark applications' performance only from execution times. The reason for this is general property of benchmarks that these should be repeatable and queue wait times are not normally repeatable. Grap Benchmarks can also help in designing trade-off analysis, and to exchange information between infrastructure developers and Grid applications writers. We are enhancing our present work towards application benchmarking at the level of Grid constellations comprised of multiple sites which constitute the computing platform of a Virtual Organization. We also plan to incorporate application throughput information for performance transformation across the platforms.

References

[1] http://www.netlib.org/parkbench.html/.

[2] Globus toolkit. http://www.globus.org/.

[3] Grid benchmarking group, global grid forum. http://forge.gridforum.org/projects/gb-rg (Accessed 2005).

[4] Spec benchmarks. http://www.spec.org/.

[5] E. Afgan, V. Velusamy, and P. V. Bangalore. Grid resource broker using application benchmarking. In *EGC*, pages 691–701, 2005.

[6] R. H. Arpaci-Dusseau, A. C. Arpaci-Dusseau, A. Vahdat, L. T. Liu, T. E. Anderson, and D. A. Patterson. The interaction of parallel and sequential workloads on a network of workstations. In *SIGMETRICS*, pages 267–278, 1995.

[7] D. H. Bailey, E. Barszcz, J. T. Barton, D. S. Browning, R. L. Carter, D. Dagum, R. A. Fatoohi, P. O. Frederickson, T. A. Lasinski, R. S. Schreiber, H. D. Simon, V. Venkatakrishnan, and S. K. Weeratunga. The nas parallel benchmarks. *The International Journal of Supercomputer Applications*, 5(3):63–73, 1991.

[8] P. Blaha, K. Schwarz, G. Madsen, D. Kvasnicka, and J. Luitz. *WIEN2k: An Augmented Plane Wave plus Local Orbitals Program for Calculating Crystal Properties*. Institute of Physical and Theoretical Chemistry, TU Vienna, 2001.

[9] M. De Roure, D. Surridge. Interoperability challenges in grid for industrial applications. In *In Proceedings of GGF9 Semantic Grid Workshop, Chicago IL, USA*, May 2003.

[10] R. F. V. der Wijngaart and M. A. Frumkin. Evaluating the information power grid using the nas grid benchmarks. In *IPDPS*, 2004.

[11] M. D. Dikaiakos. Grid benchmarking: vision, challenges, and current status: Research articles. *Concurr. Comput. : Pract. Exper.*, 19(1):89–105, 2007.

[12] T. Fahringer and R. P. et. al. ASKALON: A Grid Application Development and Computing Environment. In *6th International Workshop on Grid Computing (Grid 2005)*, Seattle, USA, Nov 2005.

[13] I. Foster and C. Kesselman. *The Grid: Blueprint for a New Computing Infrastructure*. San Francisco, CA, USA, 2004.

[14] E. Heymann, A. Fernández, M. A. Senar, and J. Salt. The eu-crossgrid approach for grid application scheduling. In *European Across Grids Conference*, pages 17–24, 2003.

[15] A. Iosup and D. H. J. Epema. Grenchmark: A framework for analyzing, testing, and comparing grids. In *CCGRID*, pages 313–320, 2006.

[16] H. H. Mohamed and D. H. J. Epema. Experiences with the koala co-allocating scheduler in multiclusters. In *CCGRID*, pages 784–791, 2005.

[17] F. Nadeem, M. M. Yousaf, R. Prodan, and T. Fahringer. Soft benchmarks-based application performance prediction using a minimum training set. In *E-SCIENCE '06: Proceedings of the Second IEEE International Conference on e-Science and Grid Computing*, page 71, Amsterdam, Netherlands, December 2006.

[18] Netlib. http://www.netlib.org/linpack/.

[19] G. R. Nudd and S. A. Jarvis. Performance-based middleware for grid computing: Research articles. *Concurr. Comput. : Pract. Exper.*, 17(2-4):215–234, 2005.

[20] X. D. W. Rob Allan and A. Richards. Xml schema for hpc applications and resources. Grid Technology Group. Daresbury Laboratory (2002).

[21] J. Q. Schueller Felix and F. Nadeem. Performance, Scalability and Quality of the Meteorological Grid Workflow MeteoAG. In *2nd Austrian Grid Symposium, Innsbruck, Austria*, Sep 2006.

[22] U. Schwiegelshohn and R. Yahyapour. Fairness in parallel job scheduling. *Journal of Scheduling*, 3(5):297–320, 2000.

[23] M. I. Seltzer, D. Krinsky, K. A. Smith, and X. Zhang. The case for application-specific benchmarking. In *Workshop on Hot Topics in Operating Systems*, pages 102–, 1999.

[24] M. Siddiqui, A. Villazon, J. Hofer, and T. Fahringer. Glare: A grid activity registration, deployment and provisioning framework. In *SC '05: Proceedings of the 2005 ACM/IEEE conference on Supercomputing*, page 52, Washington, DC, USA, 2005.

[25] D. Theiner and M. Wieczorek. Reduction of calibration time of distributed hydrological models by use of grid computing and nonlinear optimisation algorithms. In *Proceedings of the 7th International Conference on Hydroinformatics (HIC 2006)*, Sep. 2006.

[26] A. Tiramo-Ramos, G. Tsouloupas, M. Dikaiakos, and P. M. A. Sloot. Grid resource selection by application benchmarking: a computational haemodynamics case study. In *Computational Science - ICCS 2005, 5th International Conference Atlanta, GA, USA, May 22-25, 2005, Proceedings, Part I.*, volume 3514, pages 534–543, Atlanta, Georgia, USA, May 2005.

[27] G. Tsouloupas and M. D. Dikaiakos. Gridbench: A tool for benchmarking grids. *Grid Computing*, page 60, 2003.

[28] J. Weinberg and A. Snavely. Symbiotic space-sharing on sdsc's datastar system. In *JSSPP*, pages 192–209, 2006.

[29] R. Wolski, N. T. Spring, and J. Hayes. The network weather service: a distributed resource performance forecasting service for metacomputing. *Future Generation Computer Systems*, 15(5–6):757–768, 1999.

DATA MODEL FOR DESCRIBING
GRID RESOURCE BROKER CAPABILITIES[*]

Attila Kertész
Institute of Informatics, University of Szeged
H-6701 Szeged, P.O. Box 652, Hungary
MTA SZTAKI Computer and Automation Research Institute
H-1518 Budapest, P. O. Box 63, Hungary
CoreGRID Institute on Resource Management and Scheduling
keratt@inf.u-szeged.hu

Ivan Rodero and Francesc Guim
Barcelona SuperComputing Center
Jordi Girona 29, 08034 Barcelona, Spain
CoreGRID Institute on Resource Management and Scheduling
irodero@bsc.es
francesc.guim@bsc.es

Abstract   Since the management and the optimal utilization of the highly dynamic grid resources cannot be handled by the users themselves, various grid Resource Brokers have been developed, supporting different grids. To ease interoperability and the higher level utilization of different resource brokers, we introduce a metadata model for storing broker capabilities and show how an implementation of this model can be realized. We believe that this abstraction will help standardizing inter-broker communication to enable more efficient grid resource utilization.

Keywords: Grid, Grid resource management, Grid interoperability, broker capability language

[*] This research work is carried out under the FP6 Network of Excellence CoreGRID funded by the European Commission (Contract IST-2002-004265)

1.   Introduction

The Grid was originally proposed as a global computational infrastructure to solve grand-challenge, computational intensive problems that cannot be handled within reasonable time even with state of the art supercomputers and computer clusters [1]. Grid computing tackles these tasks by aggregating geographically and architecturally dispersed hardware and software resources into large virtual super-resources. The first decade of grid research aimed at creating relatively reliable infrastructures to serve researchers and attract users. These attempts have led to the present grid middlewares, and now development is focusing on user requirements. End-users typically access grid resources through resource management systems. Unfortunately, these tools are typically tightly coupled to one specific grid environment and do not provide multi-grid support because each center has its own resource management and scheduling system. Even if a tool is connected to multiple grids, applications that utilize services from these grids simultaneously are rarely supported.

There have been several attempts to make existing production Grids and grid services interoperable. Grid researchers seem to follow two different ways in the area of resource management.

The first one is to extend existing resource brokers with multiple grid middleware support. The Gridbus Grid Service Broker [2], Gridway [3], JSS [4], GRMS [5], GTbroker [6] and eNANOS [7], all support accessing resources of different middlewares. The GRIP [8] broker is the one that tries to support interoperability with a semantic matching of the resource descriptions enabling job submissions to Globus [9] [10] and Unicore [11] sites. This summary shows that these tools are forming separate user groups, again. They use different job descriptions and do not communicate with each other: putting an end to this separation process would need high efforts by all parties.

The second approach is to provide a higher level tool that supports different middleware services. One possible instance of this approach is a meta-scheduler, which coordinates some communication process between existing schedulers. A part of the SPA (Single Point of Access) in the HPC-Europa Project [12] was working on a similar topic. In this approach, each center implements a plug-in with its own set of supported capabilities. The user chooses manually the system to submit their jobs and the job scheduling policies are evaluated inside the context of each center. Thus, it does not take into account the broker scheduling properties: it rather operates as a job submitter.

The OGSA-RSS-WG of the OGF [13] devoted efforts to provide protocols and interface definitions for the resource selection services portion of the Execution Management Services (EMS) part of the Open Grid Services Architecture. The Resource Selection Services (RSS) consist of the Candidate Set Generator (CSG) and the Execution Planning System (EPS). The CSG can be used to generate a set of computational resources that are able to run a job in general, while the EPS uses this list to decide exactly what resources to run the job.

The GSA-RG of OGF [12] is currently working on a project enabling grid scheduler interaction. They try to define a common interface among schedulers enhancing interoperability. The greatest problem is that the existing schedulers/brokers need to support this common interface, so they need to be modified. In the following sections of this paper we introduce a meta-data model for describing various resource brokers to enable communication and interoperability among them. Furthermore, we formalize the proposed meta-data model and we specify a XML schema as a possible implementation for the model.

2. The Meta-Brokering Approach and Description Languages

Utilizing the existing, widely used and reliable resource brokers and managing interoperability among them could be new point of view in resource management. Users usually have different certificates to access different Virtual Organizations (VO). A new problem arises in this situation: which VO, which broker to choose for my specific application? Just like users needed Resource Brokers to choose proper resources within a VO, now they need a meta-brokering service to decide, which broker (or VO) is the best for them and also to hide the differences of utilizing them. Therefore, a meta-broker can be defined as the middleware component that selects the most appropriate meta-scheduler/broker to submit a job following a particular policy. In this context, a part of the interoperability mechanisms, a new area on scheduling policies is opened to the research (e.g. load-balancing across multiple VOs).

Heterogeneity appeared not only in the fabric layer of Grids, but also in the middleware. Even components and services of the same middleware may support different ways for accessing them. After a point this variety makes the users' and developers' life miserable. Languages are one of the most important factors of communication. Different resource management systems use different resource specification languages like RSL [9], JDL [13] [14], etc. The documents specifying the jobs need to be written by the users to specify all kinds of job-related requirements and data. The OGF has already started to take several steps towards interoperability among these coordinating components, and proposed a resource specification language standard called JSDL [15]. As the JSDL is general enough to describe jobs of different grids, this tool could solve the interoperability problem if it was supported by the different middleware systems regarding job descriptions.

Besides describing user jobs, we also need to describe resource brokers in order to make difference among them and help the Meta-Broker to decide, which broker to choose for submission. These brokers have various features

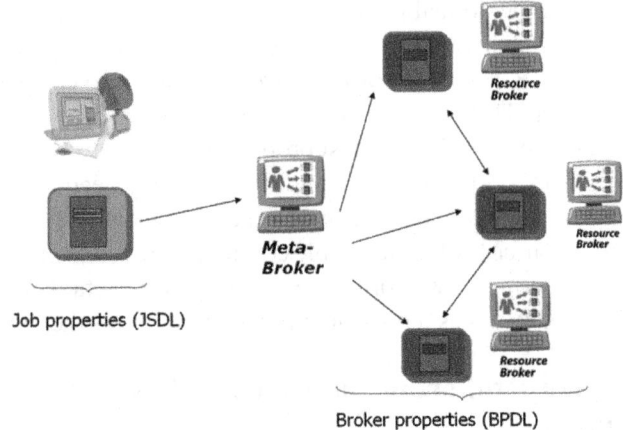

Job properties (JSDL)

Broker properties (BPDL)

Figure 1.   Languages of the Meta-Broker

for supporting different user needs and to implement scheduling policies. These needs should be able to be expressed in the users' JSDL, and identified by the Meta-Broker for each corresponding broker. Therefore we propose a Data Model for describing Resource Broker capabilities, to store metadata about brokers. We use a broker taxonomy [16] to identify the relevant properties, where various, widely used grid brokers are gathered and analyzed. These two kinds of languages are used by the Meta-Broker to communicate with the inner and outer world (Figure 1).

3.   Data Model for Broker Capabilities

3.1   Formal definition of the data model

For describing Grid Resource Broker capabilities, we introduce an extensible metadata model. Our model can be taken as an extension of the general scheduling model presented in [17]. Beside their resource and job model, there is a need for a model describing broker characteristics in order to compare, interoperate and manage different resource brokers, schedulers. We use the same notations for building up the model.

The metadata to be stored regarding resource brokers are expressed through <attribute,value> pairs – we denote with $\mathcal{P}$ the set of all possible such pairs. A broker denoted by $\mathcal{B} \subseteq \mathcal{P}$ is modeled as a pair:

$$<\text{brokerID,description}>,$$

where brokerID is a unique identifier, and description $\subseteq \mathcal{P}$ is a set of attribute/ value pairs, which contains metadata of basic and special properties. Figure 2 shows the tree of pairs in $\mathcal{P}$, which defines the whole model.

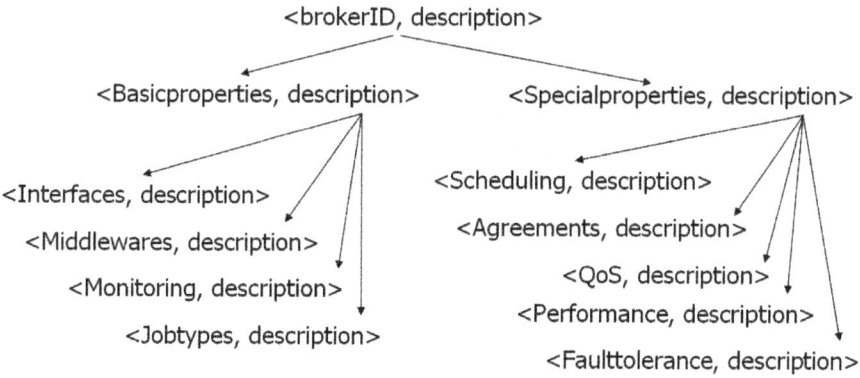

Figure 2. Structure of the Data Model for resource broker capabilities

3.2 Matchmaking function

In order to present a usage scenario we define a function over this model with the following structure:

- μ: $\mathcal{T} \times \mathcal{B}^i \to \mathcal{B}$, where $\mathcal{T}$ is a set of tasks [17] (here: jobs) and $\mathcal{B}$ is a set of brokers.

For $t \in \mathcal{T}$, $b_0, \dots, b_n \in \mathcal{B}$, n$\geq$0:

- $\mu(t, (b_1, b_2, b_3)) = b_2$ means that for a job denoted by t matched with brokers denoted by b_1, b_2 and b_3 the matchmaking function returns b_2, which is the fittest broker for the job. That means the returned broker can most efficiently execute the job. (Note that b_0 can be a special element, which is an empty description. This is the return value, when no broker fits the job requirements.)

In our scenario shown in the following section a JSDL of the job is denoted by t, and a BPDL of a broker by b_i.

4. BPDL: One possible implementation of the data model

4.1 The Broker Property Description Language

Based on the data model introduced in the previous section we have created an XML-based language called BPDL (Broker Property Description Language). The common subset of the individual broker properties are the basic properties: the supported middlewares, job types, certificates, interfaces and monitoring issues. (See the representation of this schema in Figure 3-7.) There are also special ones, such as remote file handling, fault tolerant features, agreement

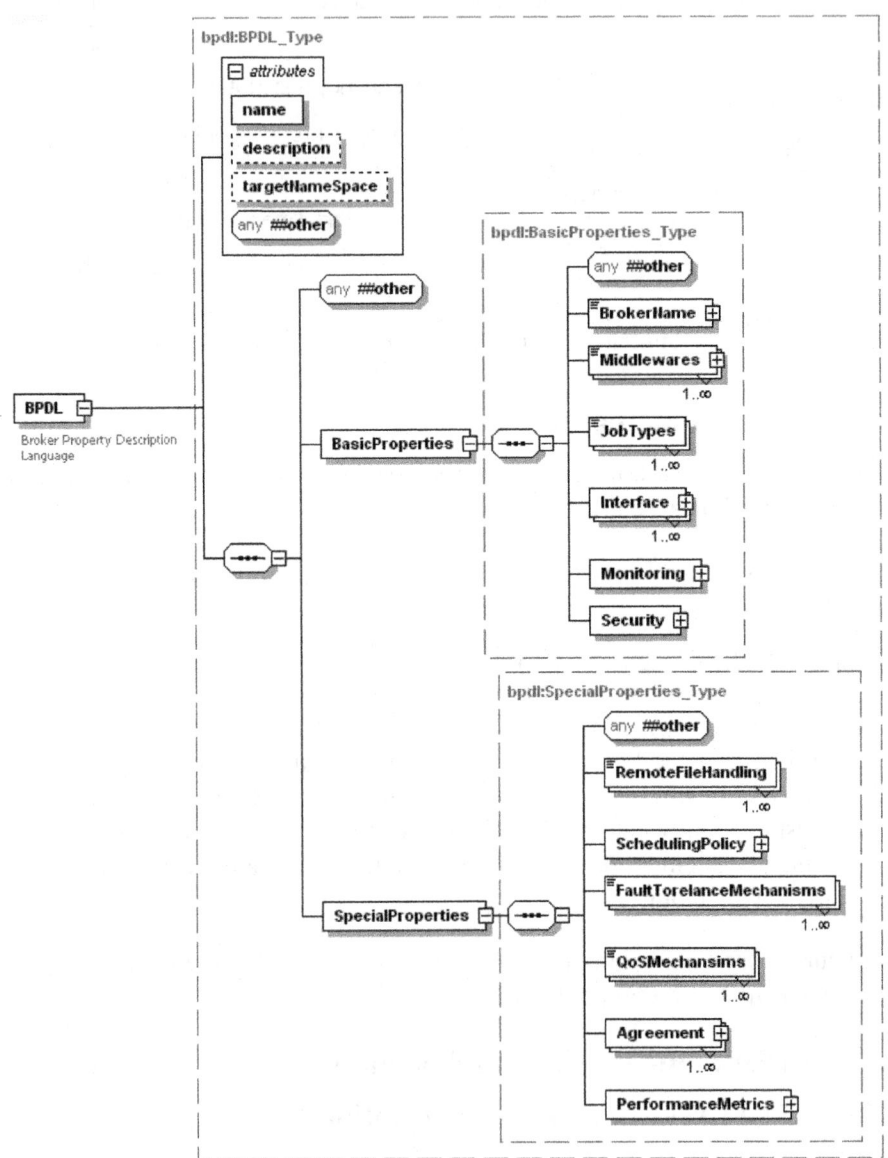

Figure 3.   General XML schema of the Broker Property Description Language

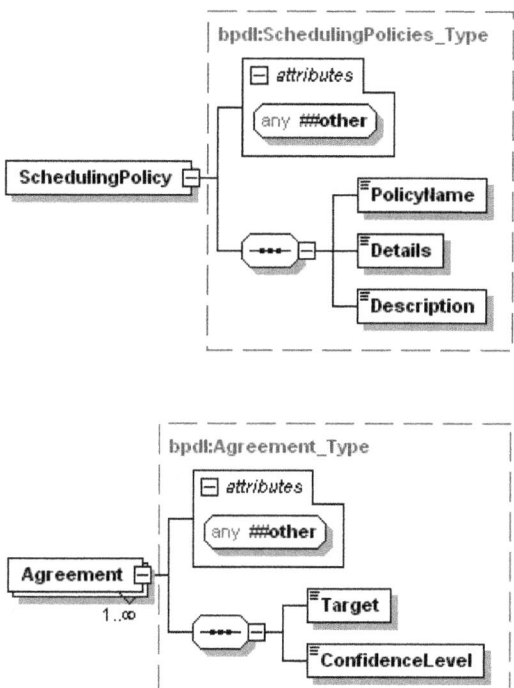

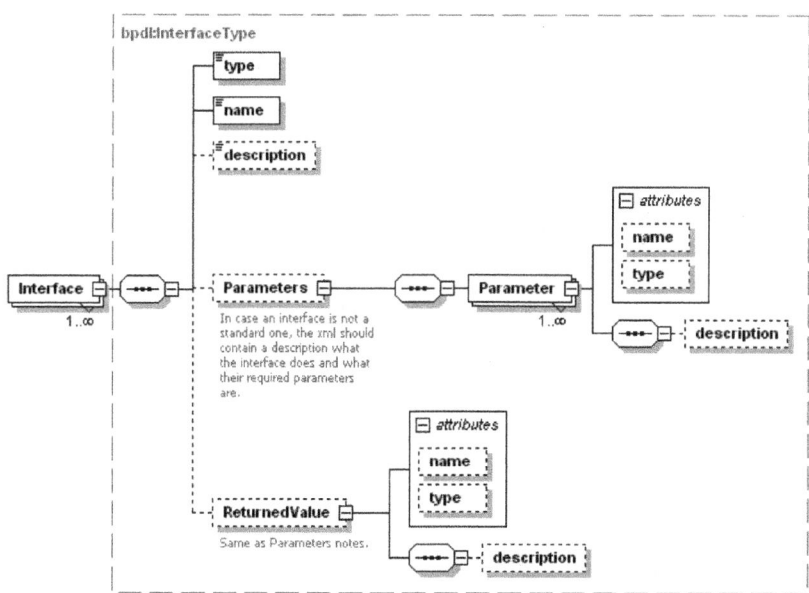

Figure 4.   Elements of the BPDL XML schema describing policies, agreements and interfaces

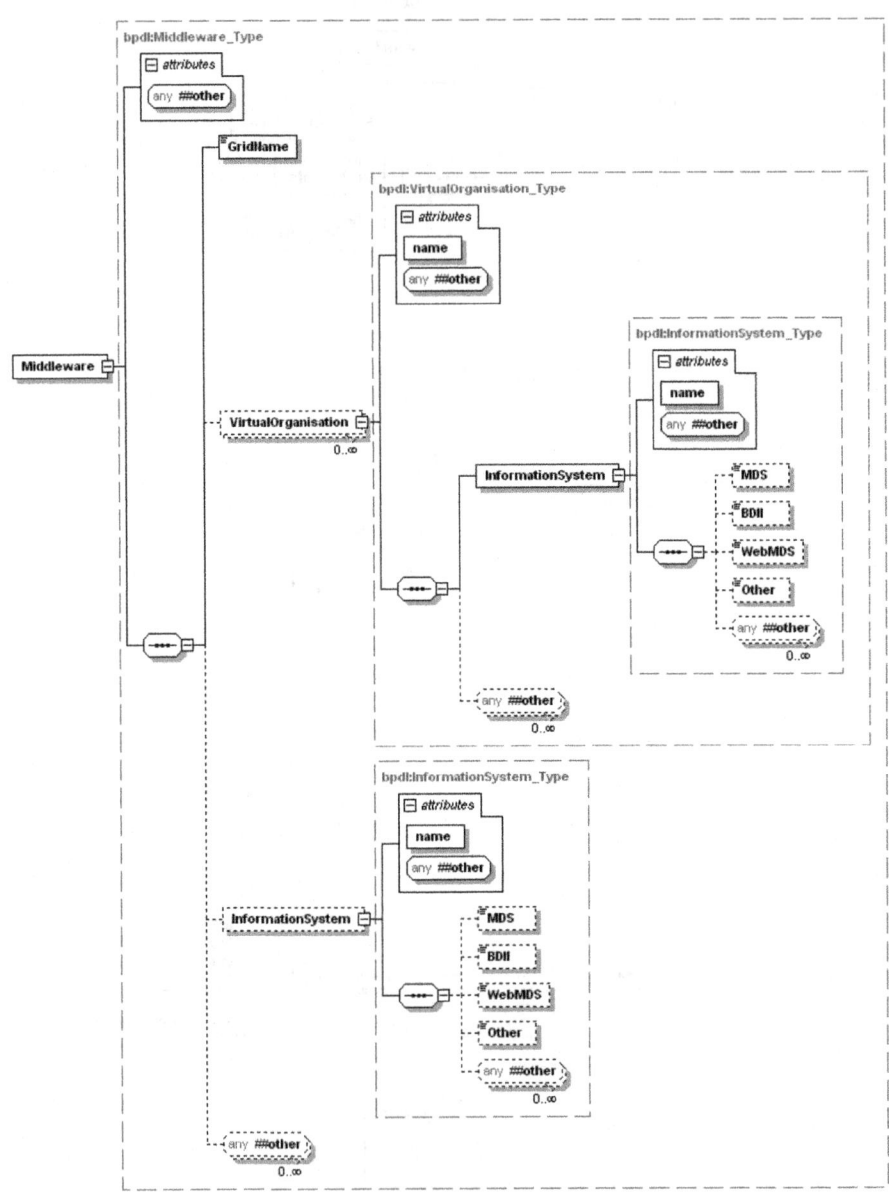

Figure 5.   Elements of the BPDL XML schema describing middlewares

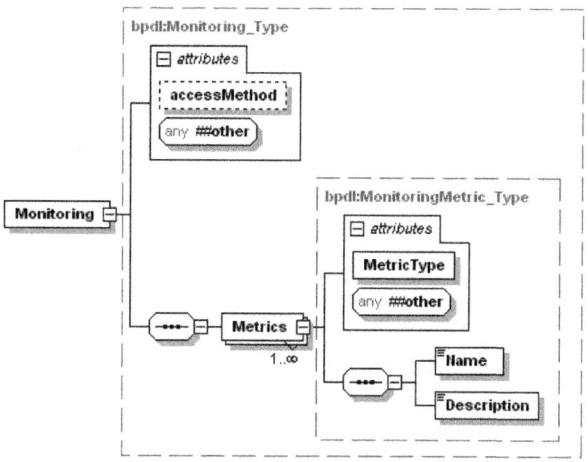

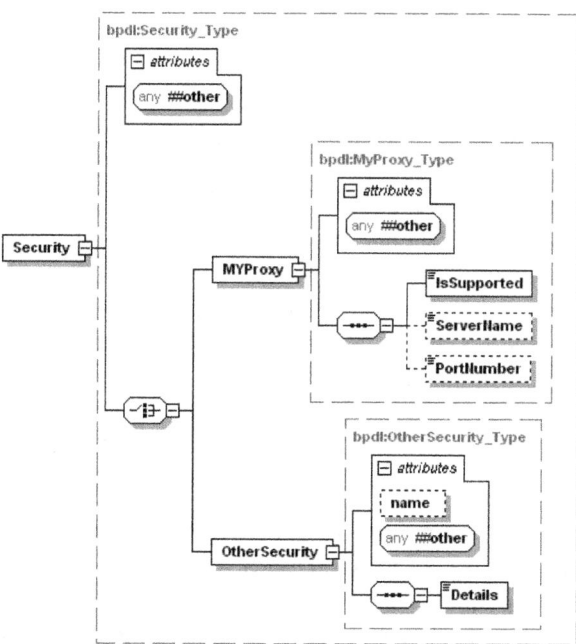

Figure 6. Elements of the BPDL XML schema describing monitoring and security types

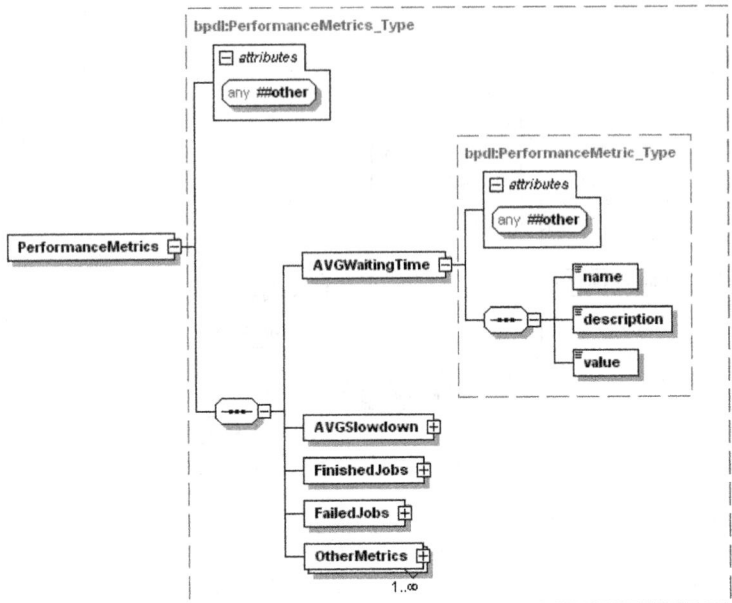

Figure 7.   Elements of the BPDL XML schema describing performance metrics

support, QoS support, performance metrics and various scheduling policies. The union of these properties forms a complete broker description document that can be filled out and regularly updated for each utilized resource broker. The special any##other type describes a mechanism that can be used to extend the schema with custom elements and attributes.

Notice that this language can also be used for peer-to-peer communication and identification in a decentralized architecture. In particular, the agreements are another mechanism typically used in this kind of architectures to broaden a domain or as a communication mechanism during the negotiation process.

4.2   Scenario for BPDL utilization in the Meta-Broker

When some years ago grid developers began to implement Grid Resource Brokers to solve the problem of resource management and scheduling, the first challenge was matchmaking: matching user jobs to grid resources. Now we are facing the same challenge at a higher level: we need to automate broker selection for job requests. The matchmaking process of the Meta-Broker uses the previously introduced language for matching the user requests to the description of the interconnected brokers. During broker utilization the successful submissions and failures should be tracked, and regarding these events a rank should be modified for each special attribute in the BPDL of the appropriate broker. The JSDL contains the user request – this supposed to be an exact specification of the user's job. During matchmaking the following steps should be taken to find the fittest broker:

1 First the Matchmaker compares the JSDL of the actual job to the BPDL of the registered resource brokers. First the basic attributes are matched against the basic properties: this selection determines a group of brokers that are able to submit the job.

2 In the second phase those brokers are kept, which are able to fulfill the special requirement attributes of the job (these capabilities are looked up from the BPDL).

3 Finally a priority list of the remaining brokers is created taking into account the ranks (stored for the requested features). The first resource broker is chosen from the list.

Since meta-brokering is in a premature state yet, during design and development we need to take into account the existing standards, data models, etc.; furthermore we need to create the missing ones. These tools should be general enough to allow the researchers to implement new grid scheduling and resource management policies based on complex criteria. Therefore we designed this data model incorporating metrics that can be used by future research (not only in matchmaking):

- Broker performance metrics (e.g. average waiting time, throughput),

- Broker historic data,

- Reputation of brokers (e.g. achieved QoS),

- Level of availability/reliability (of brokers and resources behind the brokers).

4.3   BPDL utilization in the eNANOS Broker

The eNANOS Grid Resource Broker has been recently redesigned to support new functionalities, for instance the interoperability between different brokers [19]. The BPDL presented in this paper provides a powerful schema to specify broker capabilities. Currently we are in the phase of implementing the new version of the broker extended with the BPDL schema. Some BPDL elements have already been implemented (e.g. SchedulingPolicy or Agreement elements), some are currently being included (e.g. PerformanceMetrics or Security elements) and some others will be provided in the future (e.g. Monitoring element). We use BPDL documents for managing three different kinds of information:

- Static information: this data shows the never changing characteristics of the broker that are hard-coded into the Broker Service. An example is the BrokerName element.

- Configuration information: both the user and the administrator are able to change this data in runtime. We use those attributes in the schema that define the configuration of the broker. Basically, these elements incorporate the addresses and details of the services of the broker (e.g. Information Service, Dispatching Service, etc.), its agreements and a set of other attribute-value pairs. Some examples in this category are the Agreement and the SchedulingPolicy elements.

- Runtime information: this information is obtained from the system status (e.g. execution of jobs) that can change dynamically. We use the internal services of the broker to obtain the majority of the runtime information. We are also planning to incorporate some information regarding the progress and performance of jobs through so called progress and performance indicators [18]. An example used in this category is the PerformanceMetrics element.

The BPDL language is used for different purposes in the eNANOS Grid Broker. For interoperability, we will use agreements at the center/broker/VO level. Our first approach aims at selecting resources during the resource selection phase with the help of several broker instances operating in different VOs. We submit the job to the one that utilizes the best resource. Later on we will also enable broker utilization through a common API (see [19] for more details). Moreover we can use the information stored in the BPDL directly for monitoring purposes. In the near future, we plan to investigate broker selection policies (meta-brokering), after the development of this new broker infrastructure will be finished.

5.   Conclusions

The introduced meta-brokering approach opens a new way for interoperability support. Creating such a Meta-Broker, standardized and extensible description languages are needed.

In this paper we proposed a formalization of a data model for storing grid resource broker capabilities and showed how an implementation of this model can be realized and used in a matchmaking scenario. We have presented an XML schema for the Broker Property Description Language that implements the data model. Following our approach, the current Grid Brokers should implement the BDPL (it means only using it to describe their own capabilities, not to modify the whole system) to become a member of federation of Grid Brokers managed by a global meta-brokering system.

We also have presented how to support the BPDL in the design of a real Grid Broker, how to implementing it and benefit of its usage for brokering purposes (e.g. agreements).

This work enhances establishing better interoperability among the current production grids and user groups; therefore it enables more beneficial resource utilization and collaboration by global resource management and scheduling. It also considers other mechanisms to achieve collaborative communities in a decentralized environment such as agreements mechanism. Research in this area should focus on the development of infrastructures enabling interoperability achieved by defining new standards, creating sophisticated scheduling policies in terms of global resource usage (e.g. load balancing across multiple VOs) to allow future grids to be more transparent and efficient.

References

[1] I. Foster, C. Kesselman, "Computational Grids, The Grid: Blueprint for a New Computing Infrastructure", Morgan Kaufmann, 1998. pp. 15-52.

[2] S. Venugopal, R. Buyya, L. Winton, "A Grid Service Broker for Scheduling e-Science Applications on Global Data Grids", Concurrency and Computation: Practice and Experience, Volume 18, Issue 6, 2006, pp. 685-699.

[3] E. Huedo, R. S. Montero, I. M. Llorente, "A framework for adaptive execution in grids", Software: Practice and Experience. vol. 34, 7, 2004, pp. 631-651.

[4] E. Elmroth and J. Tordsson, "An Interoperable Standards-based Grid Resource Broker and Job Submission Service", First IEEE Conference on e-Science and Grid Computing, IEEE Computer Society Press, 2005, pp. 212-220.

[5] GridLab Grid Resource Management System (GRMS), http://www.gridlab.org/Work-Packages/wp-9/res/docs/GRMS_1.9.3_UserGuide.pdf

[6] A. Kertesz, G. Sipos and P. Kacsuk, "Multi-Grid Broker Utilization with the P-GRADE Portal", Post-Proceedings of the Austrian Grid Symposium 2006, OCG Verlag, Austria, 2007.

[7] I. Rodero, J. Corbalan, R.M. Badia, J. Labarta, "eNANOS Grid Resource Broker", P.M.A. Sloot et al. (Eds.): EGC 2005, LNCS 3470, pp. 111-121, ISBN: 3-540-26918-5, Amsterdam, The Netherlands, 14-16 February, 2005.

[8] The GRIP project web site, http://www.grid-interoperability.org/grip-workpackages.htm

[9] I. Foster C. Kesselman, "The Globus project: A status report", in Proc. of the Heterogeneous Computing Workshop, IEEE Computer Society Press, 1998, pp. 4-18.

[10] Globus Team, Globus Toolkit 4.0 Release Manuals, http://www.globus.org/toolkit/docs/4.0/

[11] D. W. Erwin and D. F. Snelling., "UNICORE: A Grid Computing Environment", In Lecture Notes in Computer Science, volume 2150, Springer, 2001, pp. 825-834.

[12] The HPC-Europa Project website, http://www.hpc-europa.org

[13] OGF OGSA Resource Selection Services WG. https://forge.gridforum.org/sf/projects/ogsa-rss-wg

[14] OGF Grid Scheduling Architecture Research Group: https://forge.gridforum.org/sf/projects/gsa-rg

[15] LCG-2 User Guide, 4 August, 2005: https://edms.cern.ch/file/454439/2/LCG-2-User-Guide.html

[16] The gLite website, http://glite.web.cern.ch/glite/

[17] Job Submission Description Language: http://www.ggf.org/documents/GFD.56.pdf

[18] A. Kertesz, P. Kacsuk, "A Taxonomy of Grid Resource Brokers", 6th Austrian-Hungarian Workshop on Distributed and Parallel Systems (DAPSYS), Innsbruck, Austria, 2006.

[19] A. Pugliese, D. Talia and R. Yahyapour, "Modeling and Supporting Grid Scheduling", CoreGrid Technical Report no. 56, August 2006.

[20] I. Rodero, F. Guim, J. Corbalan, "The New Design of the eNANOS Grid Resource Broker", CoreGRID Workshop in Grid Middleware, submitted, 2007.

[21] I. Rodero, F. Guim, J. Corbalan, J. Labarta. "Design and Implementation of a General-Purpose API of Progress and Performance Indicators", Accepted in Parallel Computing (ParCo) 2007.

META-BROKER FOR FUTURE GENERATION GRIDS: A NEW APPROACH FOR A HIGH-LEVEL INTEROPERABLE RESOURCE MANAGEMENT*

Attila Kertész

Institute of Informatics, University of Szeged
H-6701 Szeged, P.O. Box 652, Hungary
MTA SZTAKI Computer and Automation Research Institute
H-1518 Budapest, P. O. Box 63, Hungary
CoreGRID Institute on Resource Management and Scheduling

keratt@inf.u-szeged.hu

Péter Kacsuk

MTA SZTAKI Computer and Automation Research Institute
H-1518 Budapest, P. O. Box 63, Hungary
CoreGRID Institute on Resource Management and Scheduling

kacsuk@sztaki.hu

Abstract   As grid technology matures the number of production grids dynamically increases. The management and the optimal utilization of these grid resources cannot be handled by the users themselves. One very important aspect of utilizing multiple Grids within one complex scientific workflow is to interact with multiple and potentially different grid brokers supported by different Grids. To ease the utilization of different resource brokers, we have introduced a meta-brokering concept to solve grid interoperability. With this new grid middleware component users and portals can utilize a growing number of Grids simultaneously for highly computation intensive applications in the future.

Keywords: Grid, Grid interoperability, Grid resource management, Grid broker, Grid scheduler

---

*This research work is carried out under the FP6 Network of Excellence CoreGRID funded by the European Commission (Contract IST-2002-004265)

1.   Introduction

The Grid was originally proposed as a global computational infrastructure to solve grand-challenge, computational intensive problems [1]. The first decade of grid research aimed at creating relatively reliable infrastructures to serve researchers and attract users. The present grid systems are mature enough to be used in production, therefore current research efforts are focusing on user requirements and interoperability. As grid technology matures the number of production grids dynamically increases, therefore end-users typically access grid resources through resource management systems or grid portals that serve as both application developer and executor environments. Unfortunately, these tools are typically tightly coupled to one specific grid environment and do not provide multi-grid support. Even if a tool is connected to multiple grids, applications that utilize services from these grids simultaneously are not supported. To enhance the manageability of grid resources and users, Virtual Organizations (VO) were founded. This kind of grouping has started an isolation process in grid development, too. Interoperability among these islands will play an important role in grid research and usage.

There have been several attempts to make existing production Grids and grid services interoperable. Grid researchers seem to follow two different ways in the area of resource management:

The first one is to extend existing resource brokers with multiple grid middleware support. The Gridbus Grid Service Broker [7] is designed for computational and data-grid applications and supports all Globus [2] [3] middleware and Unicore [4] in experimental phase. Gridway [8] has been developed in a Globus incubation project, therefore it supports all Globus versions, and it also supports EGEE [5] [6] utilization. The JSS [9] is a decentralized resource broker that is able to utilize both GT4 [3] and NorduGrid [10] resources. GTbroker [11] is a lightweight Globus-based grid broker that can simultaneously utilize Globus and LCG-2 [5] resources. The GRIP [12] broker is the one that tries to support interoperability with a semantic matching of the resource descriptions enabling job submissions to Globus and Unicore sites. This summary shows that these tools are forming separate user groups, again. They use different job descriptions and do not communicate with each other: stopping this separation process would need high efforts by all parties.

The second approach is to provide a higher level tool that supports different middleware services, including job submission, brokering or storage access. Possible instances of this approach are grid portals. The well known ones are Pegasus [13], GridFlow [14], K-Wf [15] grid portal, SPA portal of the HPC-Europa Project [16] and the P-GRADE portal [17]. Though the first 3 examples provide high-level access to grid services, they usually operate only on one middleware. The SPA (Single Point of Access) is a portal component that enables brokers to be utilized through plug-in interfaces. These interface methods need to be used by all brokers, providing the same abstract functionality. The P-GRADE Portal is a workflow-oriented multi-grid portal with the main goal to support all stages of grid workflow development and execution processes. It supports the execution of these workflows in multiple Globus-, and EGEE-based computational grids relying on user credentials. This portal is interfacing several grid brokers to reach the resources of different grids in an automated way. Another instance of this approach is a meta-scheduler, which coordinates some communication process between existing schedulers. A part of the SPA operates in a similar way, but it does not take into account the different broker properties, it rather acts as a job submitter. The GSA-RG of OGF [18] is currently working on a project enabling grid scheduler interaction. They try to define a common interface among schedulers enhancing interoperability. The greatest problem is that the existing schedulers/brokers need to support this interface, so they need to be modified.

We have already introduced the meta-brokering approach in [23], where we have stated the basic requirements that are necessary to create a higher level resource management system. In the following sections of this paper we show how the implementation of this system can be realized (which is an instance of the second, above mentioned approach).

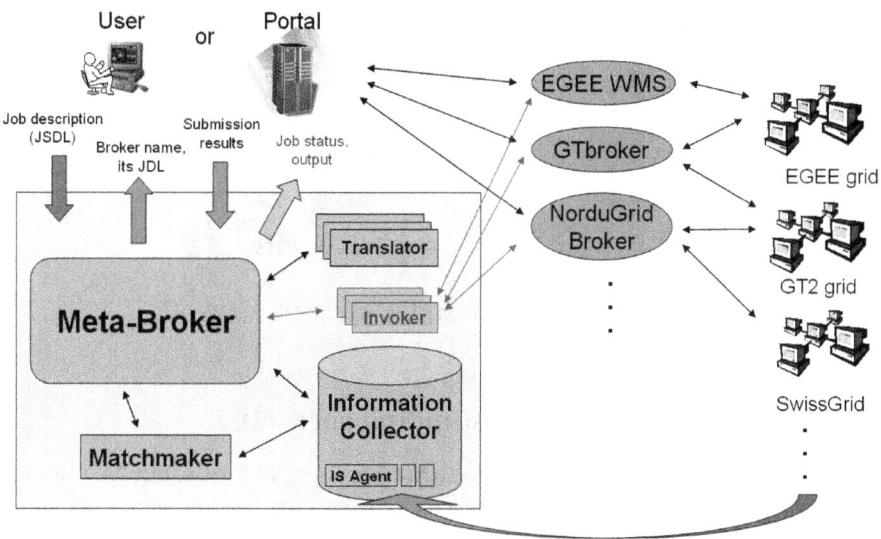

Figure 1. The Meta-Broker Architecture

2.   Meta-Brokering Approach for high-level resource management

Multiple utilization of the existing, widely used and reliable resource brokers and solving grid interoperability issues through them are still open issues in resource management. Users usually have more certificates to access different VOs. When a user wants to run an application on the grid, he/she needs to answer the following question: which VO, which broker to choose for my specific application? Just like users needed Resource Brokers to choose proper resources within a VO, now they need a meta-brokering service to decide, which broker (or VO) is the best for them and also to hide the differences of utilizing them. The solution of this problem is particularly important when a workflow is executed as a parameter sweep application. Without a meta-broker the user (portal) is not able to dynamically and evenly distribute the various workflow runs among the connected VOs [19]. Figure 1. shows the revised architecture of a Meta-Broker that enables the users to access resources of different grids through their own brokers.

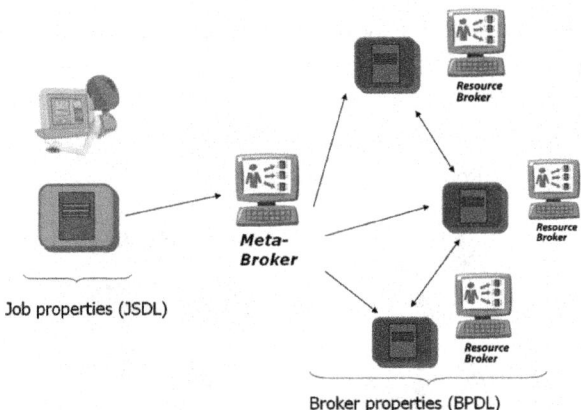

Figure 2.   Languages of the Meta-Broker: JSDL and BPDL

2.1   Languages for understanding each-other

Heterogeneity appeared not only in the fabric layer of Grids, but also in the middleware. Even components and services of the same middleware may support different ways for accessing them. After a point this variety makes the users' and developers' life miserable. Languages are one of the most important factors of communication. Different resource management systems use different resource specification languages like RSL, JDL, etc. These documents need to be written by the users to specify all kinds of job-related requirements and data. The GGF has already started to take several steps towards interoperability among these coordinating components, and developed a standard resource specification language called JSDL [20]. As the JSDL is general enough to describe jobs of different grids and brokers, we have chosen this to be the job description language of the Meta-Broker. Besides describing user jobs, we also need to describe resource brokers in order to make difference among them. These brokers have various features for supporting different user needs. These needs should be able to be expressed in the users JSDL, and identified by the Meta-Broker for each corresponding broker. Therefore we proposed a Broker Property Description Language (BPDL) [22] – similarly to the JSDL –, to store metadata about brokers. These two kinds of languages are used by the Meta-Broker to communicate with the inner and outer world (Figure 2).

Table 1. A subset of special job description language attributes.

RSL (GTbroker)	xRSL (NorduGrid)	JDL (EGEE)	JSDL
(*sched=random*) (*sched=CPU/Memory/Disk*)	(*sched=random*) (*sched=CPU/Memory/Disk*)	FuzzyRank=true; rank=other.GlueHostProcessorClockSpeed/ GlueHostMainMemoryRAMSize/ GlueSAState-AvailableSpace;	extension extension
(*minMemory=int*), (*mindisk=int*)	(memory=int), (disk=int)	Requirements: (GlueHostMainMemoryRAMSize>int); anyMatch(other.storage.CloseSEs,target.GlueSAStateAvailable-Space>int);	<resources> <jsdl:Individual-DiskSpace> <jsdl:Individual-PhysicalMemory> ... </resources>
(*skiptime=int*) rescheduling by default	(*skiptime=int*) (rerun=max.5)	/*skiptime=int*/ RetryCount=max.10;	extension extension

2.1.1 JSDL for job requirements. The Translator components of the Meta-Broker are responsible for translating the resource specification language defined by the user to the language of the appropriate resource broker that the Meta-Broker selects to use for a given job. Once a utilized broker is capable of supporting the JSDL standard, the corresponding Translator component could be removed from the Meta-Broker (since the input job description is written in JSDL). From all these job specification languages a subset of basic job attributes can be chosen, which can be denoted relatively in the same way in each document. The translation of these parts is almost trivial. The rest of these attributes describe special job handling, various scheduling features and remote storage access. Generally these cases can hardly be matched among the different systems, because only few of them support the same solution. We gathered these special attributes of the different job description languages. A sample collection of a minimal set of languages can be seen in Table 1.

If an attribute of a job description language cannot be expressed in JSDL, we specify it as an extension. These attributes are collected and specified in a proposed JSDL extension called jsdl-metabroker (the overview of the schema can be seen in Figure 3). Regarding other languages we express the missing attribute in comments in order to keep the translations consistent.

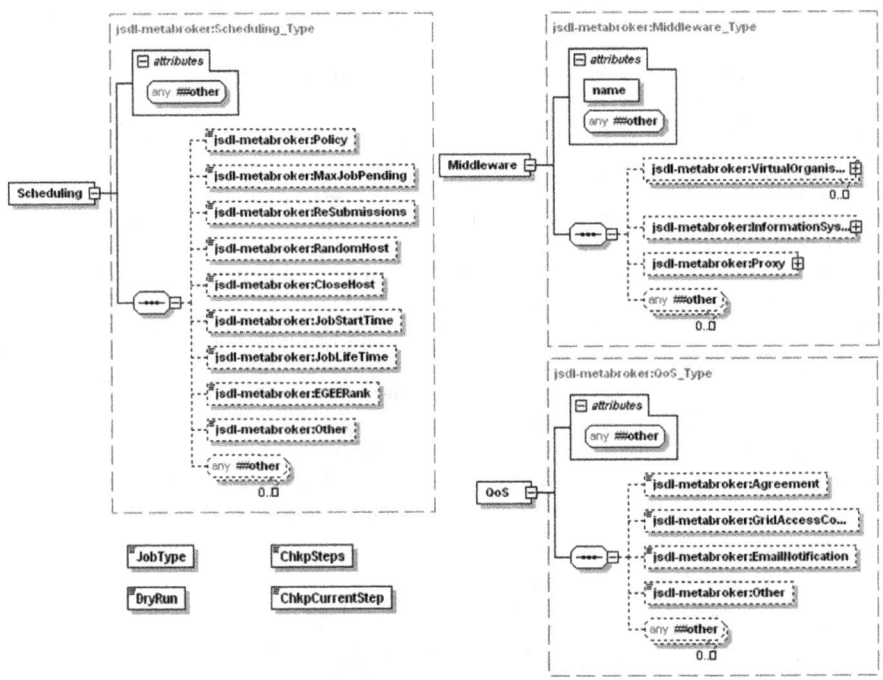

Figure 3.   General XML schema of the jsdl-metabroker JSDL extension

2.1.2   BPDL for broker properties.   For describing broker capabilities we proposed a language similar to JSDL. We have created a taxonomy of the recent Resource Brokers [21] – from this survey we could easily identify the relevant properties. This information was used to create the attributes of this XML-based language called BPDL [22]. The common subset of the individual broker properties are the basic properties: the supported middleware types, job types, certificates, job descriptions, interfaces. There are also special ones, such as remote file handling, fault tolerant features, agreement support and various scheduling policies. The overview of the schema can be seen in Figure 4. The union of these properties forms a complete broker description document that can be filled out and regularly updated for each utilized resource broker.

2.2 Information repository and matchmaking

The Information Collector stores the data of the reachable brokers and historical data of the previous submissions. This information shows whether the chosen broker is available, or how reliable its services are. The previously introduced languages are used for matching the user requests to the description of the interconnected brokers, which is the role of the Matchmaker component. During broker utilization the successful submissions and failures are tracked, and regarding these events a rank is modified for each special attribute in the BPDL of the appropriate broker. The JSDL contains the user request – this supposed to be an exact specification of the user's job, using the extended attributes. The load of the resources behind the brokers is also taken into account to help the Matchmaker to select the proper environment for the actual job. When too many similar jobs are needed to be handled by the Meta-Broker the so-called best effort matchmaking may flood a broker and its grid. That is the main reason, why load balancing is an important issue. In order to cope with this problem, there are IS Agents in the Information Collector, which regularly check the load of the underlying grids of each connected resource broker, and store this data. With this additional information the matchmaking process can adapt to the load of the utilized grids. During matchmaking the following steps are taken to find the fittest broker:

1. First the Matchmaker compares the JSDL of the actual job to the BPDL of the registered resource brokers. First the basic attributes are matched against the basic properties: this selection determines a group of brokers that are able to submit the job.

2. In the second phase those brokers are kept, which are able to fulfill the special requirement attributes of the job (these capabilities are looked up from the BPDL).

3. Finally a priority list of the remaining brokers is created taking into account the ranks (stored for the requested features) and the load of the underlying grid of each broker. The first resource broker is chosen from the list.

2.3 How to reach the Resource Brokers

Mainly two different scenarios can be done with our proposed Meta-Broker. The first one allows the users or portals to invoke and track the brokers them-

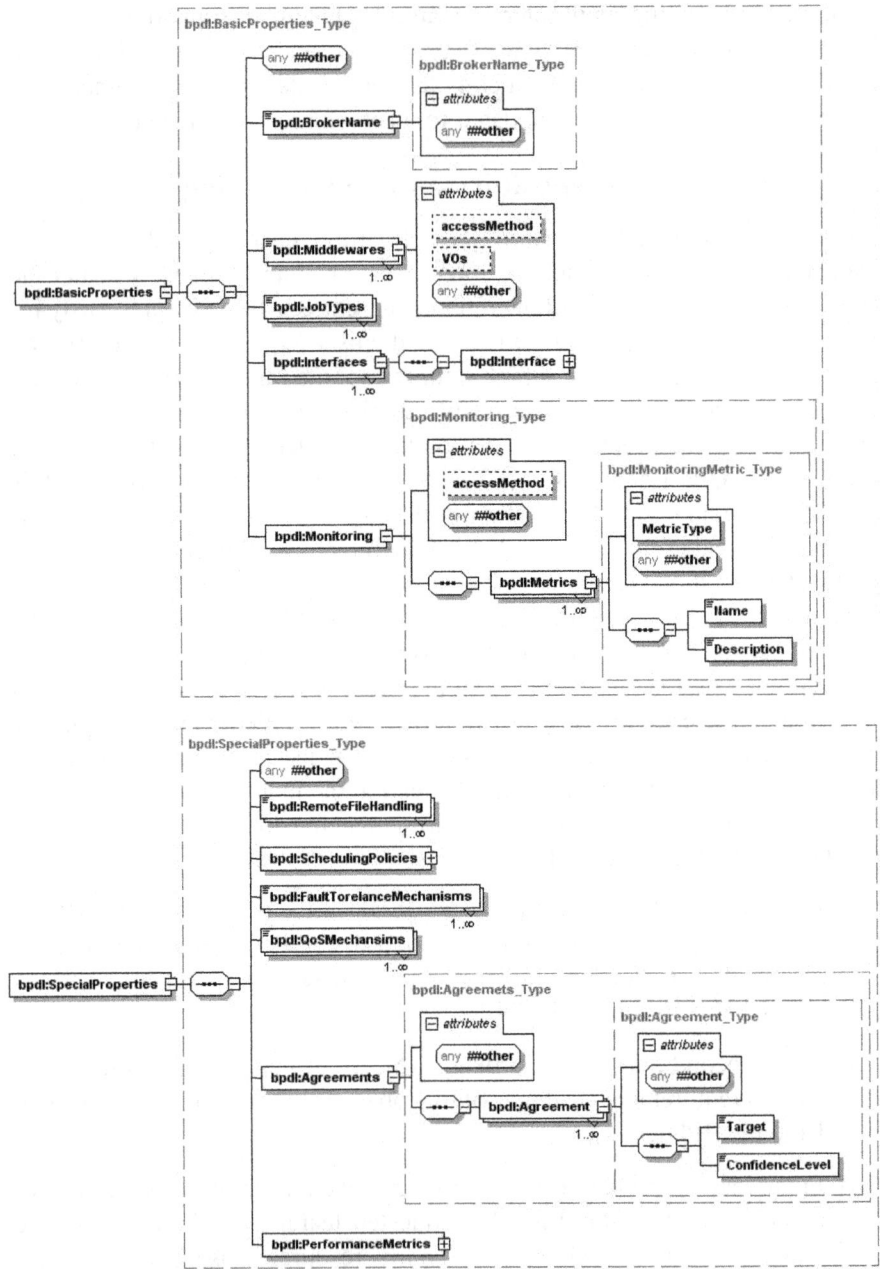

Figure 4.   General XML schema of the BPDL

selves. In this case only the JSDL document of a job needs to be provided for the Meta-Broker, and it responds with the name of the matched broker and its own job description (or with a message that none of the registered brokers is able to fulfill the specified job requirements). Finally the user/portal needs to provide the result of the submission to the Meta-Broker (to modify the broker property ranks). This limited operation is useful for systems that already have reliable connections to resource brokers and would like to use this service as broker-filtering and inter-grid load balancing. Currently these issues are not taken into account in grid portals. Even multi-grid access is rarely supported, where the users need to choose from a list of resource brokers. Furthermore this utilization can be achieved with minimal adaptation efforts and requires less data transfers. (See the direct user-broker communication in Figure 1.)

In the second scenario the utilization of the resource brokers is done by the Meta-Broker. The Invokers are broker-specific components: they communicate with the interconnected brokers, invoking them with job requests and collecting the results. Data handling is also an important task of this component. After the user uploaded the job, proxy and input files to the Meta-Broker, the Matchmaker component tries to find a proper broker for the request. If no good broker was found, the request is rejected, otherwise the JSDL is translated to the language of the selected broker. The responsible Invoker takes care of transferring the necessary files to the selected grid environment. After job submission it stages back the output files, and upgrades the historical data stored in the Information Collector with the log of the utilized broker. The core component of the Meta-Broker is responsible for managing the communication (information and data exchange) among the other components. The communication to the outer world is also done by this part through its web-service interface.

The user's job description is independent from the execution environment, and the Meta-Broker does not need to know how to access resources of different grids. It is the task of the interconnected brokers to perform the actual job submissions and to find the best resource within their scopes (the VOs they have access to). The Meta-Broker only needs to communicate with the users (via its web-service interface) and the brokers (via the Invokers). In this sense meta-brokering stands for brokering over resource brokers instead of resources.

Notice that the same way as the resource specification language was standardized, a communication protocol between the Meta-Broker and various brokers would be worth standardizing. Once it is done and brokers implement that standard the Invoker components of the Meta-Broker Architecture can be removed. In a well standardized multi-grid environment the Meta-Broker Architecture will contain only three components: Meta-Broker, Matchmaker and Information Collector.

The P-GRADE Portal already has interfaces to several grid brokers providing multi-grid usage. Our future work aims at extending the portal with the proposed meta-brokering service to ease the addition of further resource brokers and to make a better utilization of its multi-grid environment (Figure 5).

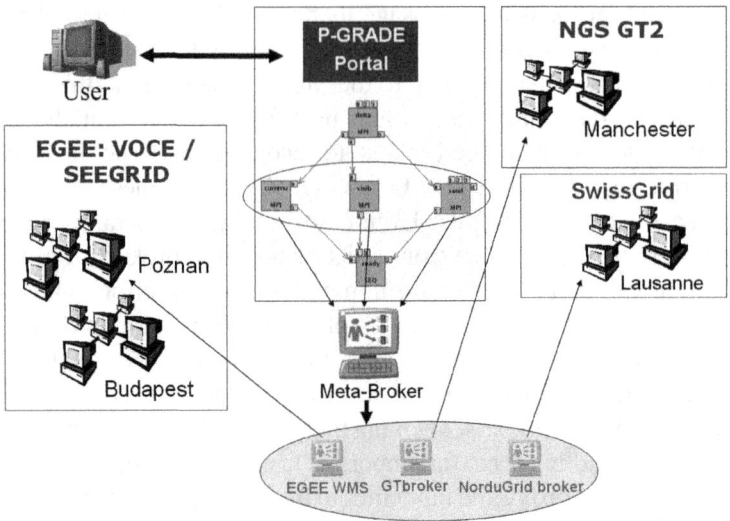

Figure 5.   Switching from Multiple Brokering to Meta-Broker Support

3.   Conclusions

The introduced meta-brokering approach opens a new way for interoperability support. The Meta-Broker itself is a standalone Web-Service that can serve both users and portals. We showed in the paper how such a service can be realized based on the latest OGF standards.

The design and the architecture of the Grid Meta-Broker enable a higher level resource management by utilizing resource brokers of different grid middleware systems. This service can act as a bridge among the separated islands of the current production Grids and user groups, therefore it enables more beneficial resource utilization and collaboration.

Recently P-GRADE portal was extended with parameter sweep execution management of workflows [19]. This new and eagerly waited feature raised the need for dynamic, well-balanced distribution of workflows and workflow components among several grids. In the future we will use the Meta-Broker to perform multi-broker utilization.

References

[1] I. Foster, C. Kesselman, "Computational Grids, The Grid: Blueprint for a New Computing Infrastructure", Morgan Kaufmann, 1998. pp. 15-52.

[2] I. Foster C. Kesselman, "The Globus project: A status report", in Proc. of the Heterogeneous Computing Workshop, IEEE Computer Society Press, 1998, pp. 4-18.

[3] Globus Team, Globus Toolkit 4.0 Release Manuals, http://www.globus.org/toolkit/docs/4.0/

[4] D. W. Erwin and D. F. Snelling., "UNICORE: A Grid Computing Environment", In Lecture Notes in Computer Science, volume 2150, Springer, 2001, pp. 825-834.

[5] LCG-2 User Guide, 4 August, 2005: https://edms.cern.ch/file/454439/2/LCG-2-User-Guide.html

[6] The gLite website, http://glite.web.cern.ch/glite/

[7] S. Venugopal, R. Buyya, L. Winton, "A Grid Service Broker for Scheduling e-Science Applications on Global Data Grids", Concurrency and Computation: Practice and Experience, Volume 18, Issue 6, 2006, pp. 685-699.

[8] E. Huedo, R. S. Montero, I. M. Llorente, "A framework for adaptive execution in grids", Software: Practice and Experience. vol. 34, 7, 2004, pp. 631-651.

[9] E. Elmroth and J. Tordsson, "An Interoperable Standards-based Grid Resource Broker and Job Submission Service", First IEEE Conference on e-Science and Grid Computing, IEEE Computer Society Press, 2005, pp. 212-220.

[10] GridLab Grid Resource Management System (GRMS), http://www.gridlab.org/Work-Packages/wp-9/res/docs/GRMS_1.9.3_UserGuide.pdf

[11] A. Kertesz, G. Sipos and P. Kacsuk, "Multi-Grid Broker Utilization with the P-GRADE Portal", Post-Proceedings of the Austrian Grid Symposium 2006, OCG Verlag, Austria, 2007.

[12] The GRIP project web site, http://www.grid-interoperability.org/grip-workpackages.htm

[13] G. Singh et al, "The Pegasus Portal: Web Based Grid Computing" In Proc. of 20th Annual ACM Symposium on Applied Computing, Santa Fe, New Mexico, 2005.

[14] J. Cao, S. A. Jarvis, S. Saini, and G. R. Nudd, "GridFlow: WorkFlow Management for Grid Computing", In Proc. of the 3rd IEEE/ACM International Symposium on Cluster Computing and the Grid (CCGRID'03), 2003, pp. 198-205.

[15] F. Neubauer, A. Hoheisel and J. Geiler, "Workflow-based Grid applications", Future Generation Computer Systems, Volume 22, Issues 1-2, January 2006, pp. 6-15.

[16] The HPC-Europa Project website, http://www.hpc-europa.org

[17] P. Kacsuk and G. Sipos, "Multi-Grid, Multi-User Workflows in the P-GRADE Grid Portal", Journal of Grid Computing, Vol. 3, No 3-4, 2005, pp. 221-238.

[18] OGF Grid Scheduling Architecture Research Group: https://forge.gridforum.org/sf/projects/gsa-rg

[19] P. Kacsuk, G. Sipos, A. Toth, Z. Farkas, G. Kecskemeti and G. Hermann, "Defining and Running Parametric Study Workflow Applications by the P-GRADE Portal", Krakow Grid Workshop, 2006

[20] Job Submission Description Language: http://www.ggf.org/documents/GFD.56.pdf

[21] A. Kertesz, P. Kacsuk, "A Taxonomy of Grid Resource Brokers", 6th Austrian-Hungarian Workshop on Distributed and Parallel Systems (DAPSYS), Innsbruck, Austria, 2006.

[22] A. Kertesz, I. Rodero and F. Guim, "BPDL: A Data Model for Grid Resource Broker Capabilities", Technical report, TR-0074, Institute on Resource Management and Scheduling, CoreGRID - Network of Excellence, March 2007

[23] A. Kertesz, P. Kacsuk, "Grid Meta-Broker Architecture: Towards an Interoperable Grid Resource Brokering Service", CoreGRID Workshop on Grid Middleware in conjunction with Euro-Par 2006, pp. 112-116, Dresden, Germany, August 28-29, 2006

MANAGING SCHEDULING AND REPLICATION IN THE LHC GRID

Thomas Ferrandiz and Vania Marangozova
LIG Laboratory, University Joseph Fourier - Grenoble I, France
thomas.ferrandiz@imag.fr
vania.marangozova@imag.fr

Abstract   In this paper, we consider the problem of data replication and its relationship with scheduling in the context of the LHC Grid. As testing replication strategies in real conditions is almost impossible because of production constraints, we propose a simulation-based approach. We study existing grid simulators and introduce a new simulator called LCGSim that should give more accurate results. We compare LCGSim to existing simulators and present some preliminary simulation results.

Keywords: Grid, simulation, scheduling, replication, LCG

1. Introduction

The goal of the LHC Grid (LCG) project is to build a grid platform for High Energy Physics experiments. Its purpose is to provide the computational and storage resources needed to manage the data that will be produced by the future Large Hadron Collider (LHC) built near Geneva in Switzerland [1]. The platform is required to provide about 15 PetaBytes of persistent storage per year and a computational capacity of about 140 million SPECint2000 which is the equivalent of 82 thousand Pentium 4 processors [2]. Deployed on the infrastructures of EGEE [3], NorduGrid [4] and OSG [5], the LCG platform counts actually about 200 sites distributed world-wide with some 32 thousand processors and 10 PetaBytes of storage.

The LCG middleware is composed of multiple grid services, each contributing to the good operation of the platform. The basic services include user authentication and security, virtual organization management, data transfer and storage, file management, monitoring and finally job scheduling. User authentication controls users' access rights to computing and storage resources. Virtual organizations isolate users, data and resources associated with different physics experiments. As there should be no losses of data, data services ensure reliable transfers among the Large Hadron Collider and the LCG storage sites. File management provides a higher level view of the data and simplifies file searches and localization. Monitoring allows for supervising the grid operation. Finally, job scheduling defines the resources and the execution order to be used for physics computations.

Scheduling is a central service, as it interacts with all the others in order to provide efficient and optimal grid operation. It uses monitoring information in order to check upon resource availability and elect suitable resources. It restrains the set of considered resources using information provided by the authentication and security services. It consults the file management services and takes into account file location in order to compare performances and choose between remote data access and replication.

In most existing grid platforms, the co-ordination between scheduling and other grid services is done in components called *resource brokers*. Their role is to match jobs' requirements to grid resources characteristics and to provide an acceptable compromise among different optimizing factors. As network usage should be optimized, brokers should minimise data transfers. They should schedule computations in a way that prevents idle CPU time and thus maximises CPU usage. When remote data access proves to be time or resource expensive, the scheduling policies should opt for replication while taking into account available storage. Finally, brokers should juggle with all this factors in order to minimise job execution time and maximise job throughput.

Experimenting with different scheduling policies in the LHC grid is a complex challenge. LCG sites have diverse hardware and software configurations and modifying the LCG global scheduling would need important software changes and reconfigurations. Now, software updates are expensive in terms of development and reconfiguration is costly in terms of administration and site production time. Knowing that LCG is a production platform meant to start full operation at the end of 2007, it is difficult to engage human and financial resources for providing scheduling policies just for the sake of testing. So, how should the LCG scheduling policies be chosen and validated?

A promising approach to this problem is given by simulation. Simulation could work with a model of the LCG platform which will represent an LCG environment freed from all low-level installation and configuration aspects. If the used LCG model is realistic, it would be possible to implement and to evaluate the performances of different LCG scheduling policies.

In this paper we discuss existing approaches to designing and evaluating grid scheduling policies. We consider both scheduling and replication as scheduling performances strongly depend on data distribution and on the possibilities for data replication. We focus on existing grid simulators and show that the proposed models have limited applicability to the LCG case. We propose a new LCG simulator, called LCGSim, whose objective is to provide a better model of the real platform. We discuss existing LCG simulators such as OptorSim [6] and Monarc II [7], present the LCGSim principles and implementation and present some preliminary results.

The article is organized as follows. Section 2 presents existing approaches to scheduling design and evaluation. Section 3 gives a short overview of the LCG platform. In section 4, we introduce the LCGSim simulator and its implementation. The scenarii used for the tests and the results of LCGSim are detailed in section 5. We discuss LCGSim limitations and future work in section 6 before concluding in section 7.

2. Scheduling in Grids

There are two major approaches to scheduling in grids. The first one, used in existing grid platforms, consists in proposing a generic scheduling architecture and implementing a small number of scheduling heuristics. As most grid platforms interconnect clusters having their own local schedulers, existing middleware propose a two-level scheduling architecture where *meta-schedulers* take global decisions before delegating to chosen local schedulers. Examples of such systems are Condor-G [8], VIOLA [9], Nimrod/G [10] and Gridbus [11]. Condor-G, used in Globus [12] and VDT [13], proposes a resource broker architecture which reconciles jobs requirements and available resources using a matching mechanism called *ClassAds* [14]. ClassAds can express jobs requirements as well as static and dynamic resource characteristics but their usage framework is left to middleware designers. VIOLA defines a generic negotiation protocol based on matching requirements to available resources and establishing QoS offers. Gridbus defines the components of a generic resource broker architecture including interpreters of application requirements, credentials and service policies, core services for scheduling and monitoring, execution feedback services, etc. Finally, Nimrod/G proposes a generic meta-scheduler architecture with an accent on economic-oriented scheduling strategies. All of these systems propose generic scheduling toolkits and neither enforce a particular scheduling policy.

The second approach to scheduling is validation through simulation. The approach is adopted in an important number of projects including ChicagoSim [15], Monarc [7], EDGSim [16], GridSim [17], SimGrid [18], BeoSim [19], etc. However, only few simulators take into account both aspects of scheduling and replication. We can namely cite GridNet [20], ChicagoSim, OptorSim [21] [22] and Monarc.

GridNet [20] is based on the ns [23] network simulator and uses a hierarchical grid model in which each grid site is represented as a node. The nodes are connected by a tree with all the children of each node connected in a ring. Each site has a *replica manager* that uses a cost function in order to decide whether a file is worth replicating. The authors show that performances are greatly increased if popular files are replicated in a cache big enough to contain all popular files. However, GridNet's tree model is not applicable to LCG.

In ChicagoSim [15] scheduling is managed with Dataset, External and Internal schedulers. Dataset schedulers use local popularity information in order to push local datasets to other sites. External schedulers decide which site jobs submitted locally will be computed on. Finally, Internal schedulers manage local site job queues. The authors investigate several replication cases but their results are not applicable to LCG because of their services model.

Monarc II [7] provides a generic framework for modeling and simulating distributed systems behaviour. It is structured in layers where the basic layer contains the simulator engine and resources modeling blocks. There is an additional layer reflecting the LCG architecture. We found two major problems with Monarc II. First, it does not focus on replication management and hence does not provide a framework for easy replication strategy configuration. The second reason is that Monarc II models in detail some real platform phenomena while ignoring other ones. In order to change these parameters, it would have been necessary to add an additional software layer and possibly to change the core Monarc engine. This would have been a problem as the simulation engine is not publicly available. Moreover there are no new Monarc II developments since 2004.

The OptorSim simulator [21] [22] is designed to explore replication and scheduling strategies in the LHC Grid. It provides several statistics like the mean job time, the resource usage ratio or the number of replications. However, OptorSim's model has several drawbacks. First, the OptorSim model ignores the internal structure of a site. There is no modeling of the network links or the data transfers in a site and network latency is considered to be null. There's no simulation of the batch scheduling, either. Another simplification point is that on a given link, the bandwidth between two communications is shared evenly no matter what the bottleneck is. For example, on a 100Mb/s link, if a file is transferred at 10Mb/s, another transfer would have a bandwidth of 50 Mb/s and not 90 Mb/s. OptorSim also considers that all communications that are not file transfers take place in no time.

3. The LHC Grid

The LHC Grid is designed as a 3-tier hierarchical grid(cf Figure 1). The Tier 0 (T0) includes only one site which is located at CERN. The role of this site is to act as a main storage for all LHC data. The Tier 1 (T1) is composed of 11 regional centres located in Europe, USA and Asia. T1 centres provide backup storage for parts of the LHC data and important computational resources. Their role is provide continuous service, guarantee data availability and run all kinds of analysis, filtering and simulation jobs. The Tier 2 (T2) is composed of sites with limited computational and storage resources provided by laboratories, research institutes and computational centres. T1 centres are connected to T0 by dedicated 10 Gb/sec connections while T1-T2 connections use local networks.

Jobs that are executed on the LHC Grid have different types depending on the physical experience they belong to. The job type defines the possible files to be used as well as the computation time needed for the treatment of a data unit.

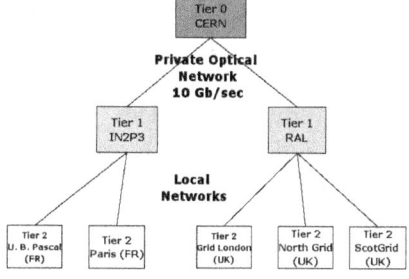

Figure 1. The LCG 3-Tier Architecture

The main services that compose LCG middleware include the Storage Element (SE), the Compute Element (CE), the Resource Broker, the

Information Service, the File Management System, the Data Access System and the Authentication Service (cf. Figure 2).

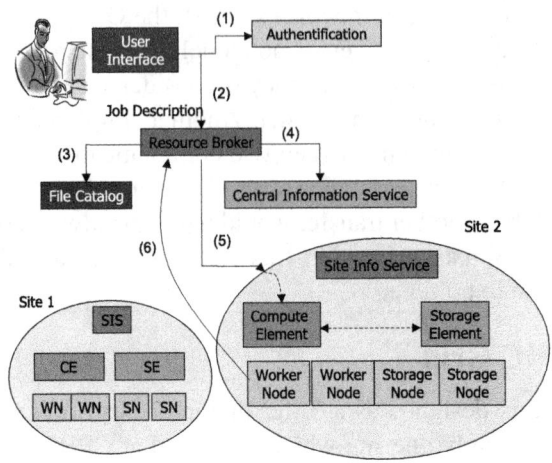

Figure 2.   Main Services in LCG

A grid site typically provides a CE which manages the site's computational resources, called Worker Nodes. The CE runs a batch scheduler, accepts the jobs submitted to the site and submits them to the nodes of the local cluster.

A grid site may provide a SE service if it has reliable mass storage resources. The SE provides an uniform interface for heterogeneous Storage Nodes and interacts with the Data Access service if a file need to be remotely accessed or copied.

Each grid site runs an Information Service which interacts with underlying monitoring services. This service reflects all the static and dynamic resource characteristics for the site and publishes the information at a global level. The Central Information Service is a collection of all the information gathered by the site information services.

The Resource Broker is a global service responsible for finding suitable execution sites for user jobs. The LCG grid runs multiple Resource Brokers referencing collections of grid sites. It is possible that different Resource Brokers send jobs to the same grid sites.

The File Management System provides a logical organization of LHC and user data. At the lowest level, files are stored at some grid site and are identified by a physical file name. However, this information is hidden from users which manipulate a File Catalog Service and work with logical file names. The conversion of logical file names to physical ones, as well as the localization of files and their replicas is done by the File Catalogue Service in a transparent way.

The workflow is the following (cf. Figure 2). When a user submits a job through a user interface, the interface identifies the user (1) and sends the job to the `Resource Broker` (2). The `Resource Broker` analyses the job's requirements, consults the `File Catalog` in order to localise the files the job needs (3) and obtains information about the sites containing these files through the global `Information Service` (4). It chooses the site containing the files and having the most available computational resources and submits the job to it (5). The job is locally scheduled and executed and its result is sent back to the `Resource Broker` (6).

4. The LCGSim Simulator

The goal of the LCGSim tool is to continue research on simulating the LHC grid and provide a more realistic model for studying scheduling and replication strategies. We decided to start from the simple OptorSim model and to add features modeling the internal site structure and network management. In order to add a network model, we decided to use the SimGrid [18] framework which has proven to provide realistic and meaningful simulation results. In the following sections we first introduce SimGrid and then describe our LCGSim implementation.

4.1 The SimGrid Framework

SimGrid [18] is a toolkit that provides core functionality for the simulation of distributed applications in heterogeneous distributed environments. It uses an advanced network model described in [24]. In this model, bandwidth is shared proportionally between communications on bottleneck links.

In SimGrid, the platform is described as a set of hosts connected by routes. Hosts have a computational power and manipulate local data. A route between two hosts is a list of links characterized by a bandwidth and a latency.

The simulated application is described as a set of *agents* running on hosts. Agents are characterized by some code and data and may communicate among themselves. If agents implement control features of the application, the calculation is modelled as set of *tasks*. A task is characterized by a computation time, a message size and some private data. The computation time gives the duration of the task, the message size characterizes the message needed for moving the task from one host to another and the private data is the data the task works on.

4.2 Model of the LCG Platform

Our model is very close to the OptorSim's one.In other terms, it represents the `Resource Broker`, the `File Management Catalog`, the CE and the SE services and ignores the internals of a grid site. We have modeled the services as a set of SimGrid agents. We have have implemented the `Resource Broker` and the `File Catalog` are implemented as centralized services. Compared to OptorSim, we have added a global `Information Service`.

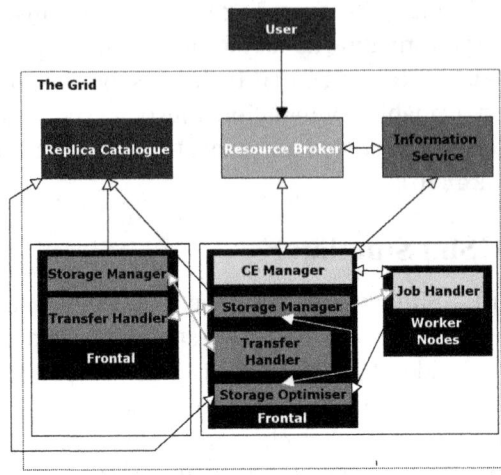

Figure 3.   The LCGSim Architecture

When a site runs a SE service, its SimGrid model includes a host running two agents. The first agent is called `Storage Manager` and manages the local storage space. It decides when a file must be inserted (possibly duplicated) or deleted. The second agent, called `Storage Optimiser`, interacts with the `File Catalog` in order to obtain information about file replicas. It probes the network and measures the round trip time in order to calculate file access cost.

When a site provides computational resources, it runs a CE service modeled as a pair of agents running on two distinct hosts: a `CE Manager` and a `Job Handler`. The `CE Manager` acts as a frontal waiting for jobs and managing the waiting queue. The `Job Handler` fetches one job at a time from the `CE Manager` and executes it. After terminating a job, it sends a notification to the `Resource Broker`.

The implemented workflow is as follows (cf 3). When a job arrives, it is submitted to the `Resource Broker` (1). The `Resource Broker` queries the `Information Service` (2) for the CE with the shortest job queue and sends the job to the corresponding site (3). The `CE Manager` listens for jobs sent by the `Resource Broker` and when one arrives, puts it in the waiting queue and sends an update to the `Information Service` (4). When all the jobs submitted previously have terminated, the job is fetched by the `Job Handler` (5). For each file associated with the job, the `Job Handler` sends a request to the `Storage Optimiser` (6) and waits for the file to become available locally. If the file is not present in the local mass storage, the `Storage Optimiser` gets a replica (7) before uploading it to the Job Handler host. If the file is present locally, it is immediately uploaded.

The `Storage Optimiser` knows whether a file is present locally by asking the local `Storage Manager`. When the file is not present, the `Storage Optimiser` will address itself to the `Replica Catalogue` for a list of the available file replicas. The list will be sorted by the `Storage Optimiser` and used by the `Storage Manager` in order to rapidly download a replica. When a new replica is created, it is registered in the local and global catalogs.

We have implemented three replication strategies for the `Storage Manager`. The first one is the simplest and involves no replication i.e files that are not locally available are accessed remotely. The second strategy is a "Least Recently Used" (LRU) one. With this strategy, remote files needed for computation are systematically duplicated and when space is needed, the least recently used files are deleted. The last strategy implements a "Least Frequently Used" (LFU) approach. Remote files are systematically duplicated and when space is needed, the least frequently used files are deleted.

The user needs to supply several input parameters to the simulator. First, he has to give a description of the grid topology and of job types. He/she will also need to provide the list of jobs with their associated files, the number of files per job and the computing time associated to jobs. There should also be a definition of the initial file distribution across grid sites. Finally, the user is to choose the replication strategy that will be used and the interval between job submissions.

As we wanted to compare LCGSim to OptorSim, we implemented the same output measures. Like OptorSim, LCGSim provides both local (i.e per site) and global statistics. Local statistics for the SE include the number of local and remote file accesses, the number of replications and a coefficient called ENU (Effective Network Usage) that measures the efficiency of a replication strategy. This coefficient is defined as $r_{enu} = \frac{N_{remote\ file\ access} + N_{replication}}{N_{remote\ file\ access} + N_{local\ file\ access}}$. The lower the ENU is, the better the strategy is. For the CE, LCGSim supplies the number of computed tasks, the proportion of time spent in computing and in waiting for file transfers along with the mean job computing time. LCGSim also calculates the total job as a sum of all computing and waiting job times. Global statistics are the same as local ones but averaged for all the sites.

5. Experimental Results

We have first experimented with OptorSim alone. We ran OptorSim for 1 000, 10 000 and 100 000 jobs and compared all the replication strategies implemented in the simulator. We confirm the results given in [22] indicating that replication decreases job execution time and that simple strategies are more efficient. However, we observe that with realistic job numbers i.e 100 000 the difference between strategies becomes insignificant.

The goal of the second experiment has been to compare the results of OptorSim and LCGSim. We used the scenario from [22] as it reflects well the LCG topology and operation. However with this realistic topology, we have been unable to obtain results with OptorSim due to simulator crashes. As a consequence, we have used a reduced grid described in the next section.

5.1   Platform configuration

Our grid configuration includes 18 sites(cf Figure 4). We find the CERN site (T0) and 4 T1 sites, each T1 site being connected to a small number (from 3 to 5) T2 sites.

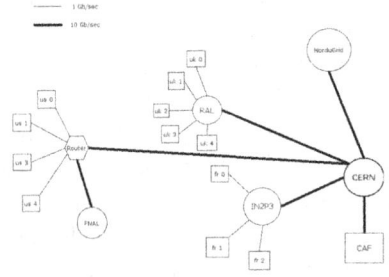

Job	Nb of files	Files per job
alice-pp	2 500	3
alice-hi	1 250	13
atlas	10 000	5
cms	3 750	3
lhcb-small	3 750	4
lhcb-big	3 750	38

Figure 4.   Simplified LCG Grid   *Figure 5.*   Jobs and Associated Files

Compared to the scenario described in [22], we scaled down the total number of files and the number of files per job. The data consists of 25,000 files of 2GB each located initially at CERN. There are six job types (cf Table 5).

We ran the scenario by modulating the number of jobs, as well as the replication strategies. We tested the no replication, LRU and LFU strategies for a workload of 1000, 10 000 and 100 000 jobs.

5.2   Results

With both simulators, we consider three metrics: the mean job completion time, the mean CE usage and the ENU.

As can be seen on Figure 6, the mean total job times results are grouped per simulator. We observe that LCGSim results are 10 000 times higher than those of OptorSim.

A possible explanation for this huge difference is that the LCGSim model takes into account network latencies and TCP acknowledgments. Indeed files are transfered via TCP connections so if the latency is important, TCP acknowledgments will slow the emitter and the rate of transmission will decrease. This is neglected in OptorSim but not in LCGSim.

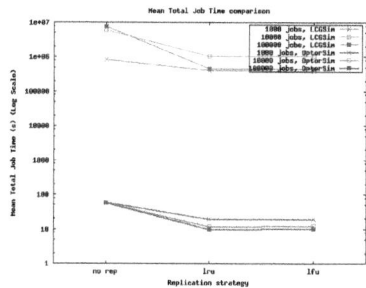

Figure 6. Mean Total Job Time Comparison for LCGSim and OptorSim

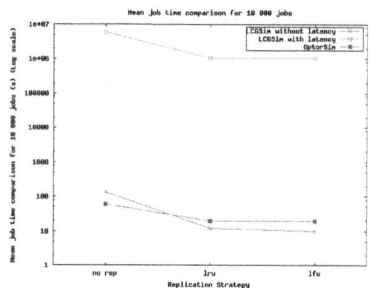

Figure 7. Mean Job Time without latency

To verify this hypothesis, we ran the same experiments on LCGSim but with latencies equal to 0. The mean job time for 10 000 jobs is shown on Figure 7. We can see that the mean job times for OptorSim and LCGSim become almost the same which confirms the hypothesis.

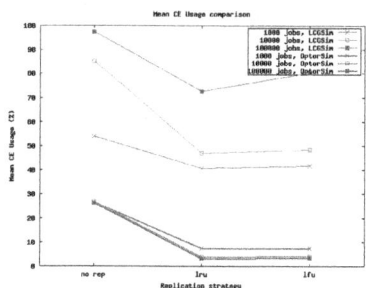

Figure 8. Mean CE Usage Comparison for LCGSim and OptorSim

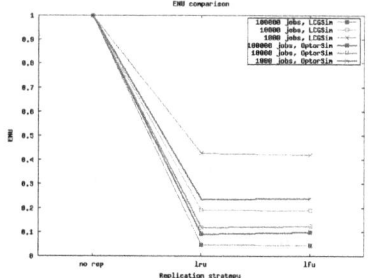

Figure 9. ENU Comparison for LCGSim and OptorSim

With or without latency, we can see that, as can be expected, using replication reduces the mean job time. We can also see on Figure 6 that replication reduces more the mean job time for a higher number of jobs which means that replication becomes more efficient when the number of jobs increases.

Results for the ENU (cf. Figure 9) show the same trend. Replication reduces the ENU, ie. the number of transfers compared to the number of file accesses, and it has a greater impact when the number of jobs increases. We can also notice that both simulators don't give the same value but that the difference becomes smaller when there are more jobs. This difference may be explained by the variations in the implementation of the two simulators. For example, the random number generators aren't the same which leads to different jobs creations and different distributions on the sites.

As for comparing replication strategies, our results show very small or even no differences between OptorSim and LCGSim predictions. We need further investigations in order to really compare replication strategies.

6.   Future Work

We have multiple ideas of continuing the work on LCGSim. At the validation level, we would like to confront the simulator with real platform results. At the model level, we are interested in zooming at the internal structure of a site and adding batch scheduling. To this purpose, we plan to use SimBatch [25], an extension of SimGrid. Finally, we are interested in investigating other measures such as measures detecting bottlenecks.

7.   Conclusion

In this paper, we tackled the problem of scheduling and replication strategy simulation in the LHC grid. We presented LCGSim, a new LCG simulator with an objective of providing a realistic LCG model. We described a first implementation inspired by the model of an existing simulator, OptorSim. Most notably, we used the SimGrid toolkit to better model inter- and intra-site communications. The improved network model influences in an important way the time related characteristics and especially the evolution of these characteristics depending on the number of jobs. However, compared to OptorSim, LCGSim has not given us more information on replication usefulness and we hope that a more detailed LCG model will provide us with a better insight on this issue.

References

[1] The LCG website. [Online]. Available: http://lcg.web.cern.ch/LCG/

[2] LHC Computing Grid: Technical Design Report. [Online]. Available: http://lcg.web. cern.ch/LCG/tdr/

[3] EGEE: Enabling Grids for E-sciencE Project. [Online]. Available: http://www.eu-egee. org/

[4] NorduGrid Project. [Online]. Available: http://www.nordugrid.org/

[5] Open Science Grid Project. [Online]. Available: http://www.opensciencegrid.org/

[6] W. H. Bell, D. G. Cameron, L. Capozza, A. P. Millar, K. Stockinger, and F. Zini, "Simulation of Dynamic Grid Replication Strategies in OptorSim," in *Proc. of the 3rd Int'l. IEEE Workshop on Grid Computing (Grid'2002)*, Baltimore, USA,, November 2002, pp. 290–294.

[7] The Monarc II Project. [Online]. Available: http://monarc.cacr.caltech.edu/

[8] J. Frey, T. Tannenbaum, I. Foster, M. Livny, and S. Tuecke, "Condor-G: A computation management agent for multi-institutional grids," *Cluster Computing*, vol. 5, pp. 237–246, 2002.

[9] K. Cristiano, P. Kuonen, R. Gruber, V. Keller, M. Spada, T.-M. Tran, S. Maffioletti, N. Nellari, M.-C. Sawley, O. Wildrich, W. Ziegler, and P. Wieder, "Integration of iss into the

viola meta-scheduling environment," CoreGRID project, CoreGRID Technical Report TR-0025, January 2006.

[10] R. Buyya, D. Abramson, J. Giddy, and H. Stockinger, "Economic models for resource management and scheduling in grid computing." *Concurrency and Computation: Practice and Experience*, vol. 14, no. 13-15, pp. 1507–1542, 2002.

[11] S. Venugopal, K. Nadiminti, H. Gibbins, and R. Buyya, "Designing a resource broker for heterogeneous grids," University of Melbourne, Australia, Grid Computing and Distributed Systems Laboratory Technical Report GRIDS-TR-2007-2, February 2007.

[12] I. Foster, "Globus Toolkit Version 4: Software for Service-Oriented Systems," in *IFIP International Conference on Network and Parallel Computing, Springer-Verlag LNCS 3779*, 2005, pp. 2–13.

[13] The Virtual Data Toolkit website. [Online]. Available: http://vdt.cs.wisc.edu/

[14] R. Raman, M. Livny, and M. Solomon, "Matchmaking: Distributed Resource Management for High Throughput Computing," in *Proceedings of the Seventh IEEE International Symposium on High Performance Distributed Computing*, Chicago, USA, July 1998, pp. 28–31.

[15] K. Ranganathan and I. Foster, "Decoupling computation and data scheduling in distributed data-intensive applications," in *Proceedings of 11th IEEE International Symposium on High Performance Distributed Computing (HPDC-11)*, Edinburgh, Scotland, July 2002.

[16] The EDGSim Project. [Online]. Available: http://www.hep.ucl.ac.uk/~pac/EDGSim/index.html

[17] R. Buyya and M. Murshed, "Gridsim: A Toolkit for the Modeling and Simulation of Distributed Resource Management and Scheduling for Grid Computing," *Journal of Concurrency and Computation: Practice and Experience*, vol. 14, Nov-Dec 2002.

[18] H. Casanova, A. Legrand, and L. Marchal, "Scheduling distributed applications: the simgrid simulation framework," in *Proceedings of the third IEEE International Symposium on Cluster Computing and the Grid*, Tokyo, 2003.

[19] The BeoSim Project. [Online]. Available: http://www.parl.clemson.edu/~wjones/research/

[20] B. S. Houda Lamehamedi, Zujun Shentu and E. Deelman, "Simulation of dynamic data replication strategies in data grids," in *Proceedingd of 12th Heterogeneous Computing Workshop*, 2003.

[21] Cameron, Millar, Nicholson, Carvajal-Schiaffino, Zini, and Stockinger, "Analysis of scheduling and replica optimisation strategies for data grids using optorsim," *Journal of Grid Computing*, vol. 2, March 2004.

[22] C. Nicholson, D. G. Cameron, A. T. Doyle, A. P. Millar, and K. Stockinger, "Dynamic data replication in lcg 2008," in *Proceedings of the UK e-Science All Hands Conference*, Nottingham, September 2006.

[23] The ns website. [Online]. Available: http://www-mash.cs.berkeley.edu/ns

[24] L. M. Henri Casanova, "A network model for simulation of grid application," INRIA, Research Report Nï¿½ 4596, October 2002.

[25] J.-S. Gay and Y. Caniou, "Simbatch: an api for simulating and predicting the performance of parallel resources and batch systems," INRIA, Research Report 6040, 11 2006, also available as LIP Research Report RR2006-32. [Online]. Available: https://hal.inria.fr/inria-00115880

NETWORK MONITORING SESSION DESCRIPTION

Augusto Ciuffoletti
INFN-CNAF – Via B. Pichat 6/2, Bologna, Italy
augusto@di.unipi.it

Antonis Papadogiannakis and Michalis Polychronakis
FORTH – Heraklion, Crete, Greece
{papadog,mikepo}@ics.forth.gr

Abstract   Network Monitoring is a complex distributed activity: we distinguish agents that issue requests and use of the results, other that operate the monitoring activity and produce observations, glued together by other agents that are in charge of routing requests and results. We illustrate a comprehensive view of a such architecture, taking into account scalability and security requirements, concentrating on the definition of the information exchanged between such agents. We address scalability by introducing monitoring sessions activated on demand, with a declared preference for passive monitoring tools, and security by enforcing authenticated communications at every step. A scalable protocol for public key diffusion is introduced in a companion paper.

Keywords: Network monitoring, workflow management, XML Schema Description, passive network monitoring, on demand network monitoring.

1.   Introduction

When we consider the information exchange related to Network Monitoring, we see that the main actors involved are the producers of monitoring data, and the consumers. We refine such view by considering consumers as parts of a complex activity that manages the tasks submitted by users: we call such distributed activity *Workflow Management* (here including also the monitoring activity successive to task allocation) and Workflow Management Agent (also WMA) the local agents that cooperate in its implementation.

While *allocating the resources* for user tasks, the interest of such agents is for snapshots of recent performances as well as for static capabilities of resources; if a reservation oriented approach is used, resource allocation is carried out by scheduling resource capabilities, without any need of a monitoring activity. In contrast, while *running a user task*, the behavior of the resource must be permanently monitored, in order to guarantee an appropriate quality of service and for accounting purposes.

Such considerations narrow our interest to a subset of what is often considered as Network Monitoring: we exclude the maintenance of pointwise historical traces, needed to respond to unanticipated requests, and instead we consider monitoring activity to be dynamically configured according with WMA requests. As a consequence we do not consider the design of a *repository* for network observations, while we are only marginally interested to the availability of generic aggregated statistics of dynamic behaviors and of static properties of network elements. Instead, we concentrate on the dynamic configuration of the monitoring activity, and to the transfer of streams of observations from producers to WMA.

On the side of the distributed functionality in charge of managing the production of Network Monitoring data, we introduce specialized agents (the Network Monitoring Agents, NMA) in charge of controlling local capabilities. Such agents are located according with a partitioning of the whole Grid: each partition, a domain in our terminology, is a set of Grid components characterized by a uniform connectivity with the rest of the system. Such abstraction is often used in the Internet architecture, so we have opted for an overloaded term to indicate it. However, it is worth stating that a Network Monitoring domain does not necessarily correspond to a DNS domain, or to a routing AS or area. Equivalence with such existing entities can be stipulated whenever non contradicting the principle of uniform connectivity.

The principle of uniform connectivity is used to justify the collection of aggregate statistics and of static capabilities for network elements between domains, thus limiting monitoring activity. As anticipated, such information is mainly directed to task allocation, which should be preferably addressed using anticipate reservation. In such case, the uniform connectivity requirement may become less stringent.

The rationale behind the introduction of NMAs is the localization of the capabilities and of the workload related to network monitoring. NMAs act as proxies for addressing monitoring requests, and manage the streaming of monitoring data for the whole domain.

Each domain may contain one or more NMAs, which may be responsible for the observation of distinct Network Elements, or related to distinct administrations living within the same domain. They are responsible of controlling Network Monitoring Elements located inside the domain. Network Monitoring Elements (NME) represent resources provided for monitoring the network using appropriate tools.

Figure 1 summarizes the above architecture in a simple system consisting of three domains (large ovals labelled with the domain ID), each with a NMA (a small circle on the border of each oval). Two NMEs are included in domains "FORTH" and "INFN-CNAF", while the other domain "INFN-NA" contains a WMA.

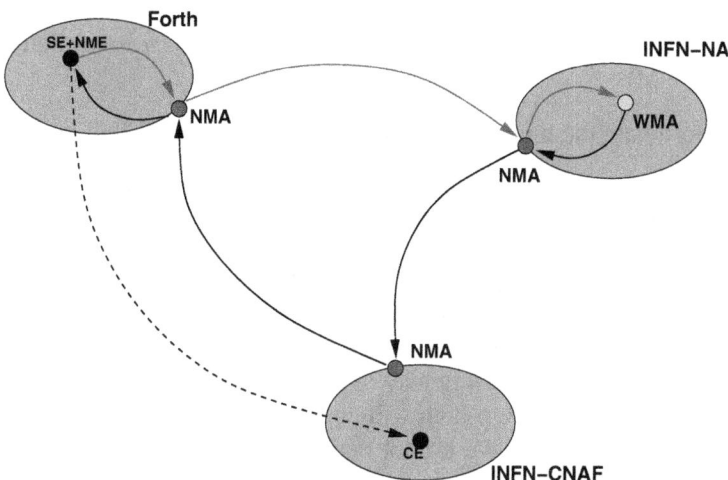

Figure 1.   Information flow related to a ping session: the green circle indicates a WMA, black arrows indicate the flow of a Network Monitoring Session description representing a request, red circles represent NMAs, black circles represent monitored sites, and red arrows represent the data stream from the NME to the WMA.

In the design of a NME we remark a relevant distinction between passive and active techniques, that impacts the scalability of the whole architecture. Since passive techniques are notably less intrusive than active ones, we prefer the former, although the latter should be provided as a fallback solution. For instance, in case of a simple request of connectivity monitoring between two sites, the option of a slow ping should be provided in case passive monitoring is not available. Other scenarios should address passive techniques.

To enforce security, NMEs should accept controls only from local NMAs. In their turn, NMAs should accept requests only from peer NMAs, as well as from local WMAs. In that sense domain partitioning improves the flexibility and expandibility of our network monitoring architecture.

The next section analyzes the activity of the NMA, and describes step by step the life-cycle of a monitoring request.

2.   The operation inside the Network Monitoring Agent

The purpose of a NMA is to coordinate the monitoring of the networking resources used by the computation coordinated by the WMA. More precisely, we distinguish four distinct activities:

- to accept (*proxying*) network monitoring requests coming from WMAs providing the description of the monitoring activity. Such requests may come either from a WMA inside the same domain, or from another NMA. In either case the request must be authenticated.

- to route the request to another NMA which is able to control an appropriate NME;

- to coordinate the monitoring activity carried out by NMEs;

- to support the streaming of Network Monitoring data to the requesting WMA, possibly through other NMAs.

In the case of *proxying*, a WMA that coordinates a given computational activity will produce a number of *Network Monitoring Session Descriptions*. Such data item is exhaustively described in next section.

Concerning the *request routing* activity, the WMA will forward session descriptions to the local NMA, which will authenticate the request, and forward it to the appropriate NMA. We do not detail how such request is routed, but consider that this operation is based on the accessibility of a database containing *Network Monitoring Agents Descriptions*. Such data items map NMAs to domains, define their monitoring capabilities, as well as their connectivity with other NMAs.

The *control of Network Elements* requires knowledge of Network Monitoring capabilities available on NMEs within the local domain.

In order to support the *streaming* of Network Monitoring results, a data channel is built between the NMA in charge of coordinating the monitoring session and the NMA proxying the WMA. In principle such path may traverse several NMAs, and should consider the possibility of optimizing the path in case the same information is requested by many different WMA tasks.

In conclusion, we have identified 3 data structures supporting our Network Monitoring architecture:

- a *local directory* that supports authentication of requests from WMAs in the local domain, as well as the description of local NMEs;

- a *global directory* that supports mutual authentication of NMAs;

- a *network monitoring session description* which contains the description of a single session.

While the design of the *local directory* does not address any challenging aspect, the other two have distinct reasons of interest from a research point of view. The implementation of a *global directory* implies the solution of a number of problems concerning distributed processing, while the *description of a monitoring session* should flexibly cope with the diversity of network monitoring requests.

Here we focus on the latter problem, addressing the reader interested in the former to a specific article [2]: in the next section we introduce the data structure describing a monitoring session as an instance of an *XML Schema Description* document.

3. The XML schema of a Network Monitoring Session

The complex type `NetworkMonitoringSessionType` (its XSD is in the appendix) is the frame for a monitoring request, whose attributes are a sort of header for the Session Description:

SessionId It is a way to identify and refer to a session. Its syntax can be constrained into a URI-like form using an appropriate pattern, which is not considered here;

StartAt It is the requested time when to start the monitoring activity;

Duration It is a timeout, in case the Session is not explicitly closed by the requesting WMA;

BandwidthLimit It is used for negotiation of the multicast facilities, and corresponds to an upper bound of the traffic generated by the monitoring activity, in bytes/second;

Priority Its usage is similar to the above.

Elements are a more composite description of the monitoring activity, which consists of a sequence of elements with complex types:

RequestFrom The agents (possibly more than one) that request the activity. This information is used to generate or extend the multicast tree, as well as to check privileges;

Route The indication of the route the stream is going to follow, represented as a tree of NMAs. The case study at page 86 exemplifies its management;

NetworkElement A session monitors a single domain-to-domain path (this is the meaning associated to a Network Element, more restrictive than in RFC2216);

MeasurementStream The description of the low level network monitoring activity. Such data should be passed to the back-end supported tool, which results in the production of a stream of data of known content and syntax.

We opt to indicate one single network element in accordance to the fact that a given session is implemented by a single Network Monitoring Agent. It is impossible to guarantee such fact if several Network Elements are monitored within the same session.

Advanced passive network monitoring tools that are able to observe distinct characteristics of traffic flowing between given endpoints may incorporate such data into a single stream.

The flexibility of the scheme is based on the definition of the type used to describe the `MeasurementStream`, which is where the monitoring tools are indicated and configured. As a general rule, a single frame in the stream will contain several numerical values produced (quasi) synchronously by the same tool activation.

A `MeasurementStream` element contains one or more elements of type `CharacteristicStream`, each containing the description of a tool activity. Such elements are passed untouched to the NME, each of them corresponding to a frame series in the stream.

Each `CharacteristicStream` element includes a choice of elements containing the controls specific for a given network monitoring tool. Note that we do not consider abstract "characteristics", for instance *roundtrip time*, but make explicit reference to the operational description of their computation. In other words, a ping is a ping, and not a roundtrip time. The WMA is free to use it as a roundtrip time, but it cannot confuse it with a roundtrip time measured during a TCP connect (which is not simply a *protocol* difference). The use of a trade mark (e.g. linux-ping) is OK, but in many cases a more abstract reference to the methodology used to measure it (e.g., ICMP ping) is preferable. The tool wrapper may accept both a tool specific name or a methodology to indicate the same operation. The WMA may indicate either a methodology or a tool specific name, and the NMA should not interfere with such indication. Descriptive statistics (historical average, stddev etc.) are indicated as tool dependent options.

Generic elements are the following:

SamplePeriod The granularity of the time axis, in seconds;

SourceIP A specific monitored IP: this details the monitoring below the *network element* level. Several *SourceIP*'s may be indicated, if the tool supports this, but all should be included in the same source domain: it is the responsibility of the WMA to ensure compliance. The role of the source in the measurement depends on the specific tool (see *SourceDomain*).

DestinationIP same as above.

Concerning the tool specific element, we outline the example of two external XSD documents describing a trivial ping, and a passive monitoring session.

The trivial ping (see the XSD in Figure 2) is characterized by the endpoints and by a ping frequency, already indicated in the `CharacteristicStream`. Such data is complemented with the length of the packet. Two distinct characteristics can be requested: the roundtrip time, and the packet loss rate.

A sophisticated passive network monitoring tool (we envision a prototype based on the MAPI monitoring library [12]) is shown in Figure 3. Based on the source and destination addresses, and optionally on the protocol name and the type of a specific application, we can filter and monitor the traffic we are interested in. The `ProtocolName` element can be any network protocol at the transport layer (such as TCP and UDP) while `ApplicationName` may correspond to any Grid-related application (such as HTTP, GridFTP, and Globus). The identification of a specific application in the Grid network traffic can be as simple as looking for a static port number, or more complex based on deep packet inspection, application-level protocol decoding, or other heuristics. The measurement frequency is defined using the `SamplePeriod` element, that is part of the `CharacteristicStreamType`.

Other options for the passive monitoring tools include requests for anonymization of sensitive fields in the results (e.g., IP addresses) and use of a third host, whenever needed, for gathering and correlating the results.

The interested reader finds in companion papers the description of the techniques used to measure round-trip time [8], packet loss rate [9], available bandwidth, and per-application bandwidth usage [1].

```
<schema
 xmlns="http://www.w3.org/2001/XMLSchema"
 xmlns:pt="http://www.di.unipi.it/~augusto/schema/PingTool.xsd"
 targetNamespace="http://www.di.unipi.it/~augusto/schema/PingTool.xsd">


 <annotation>
  <documentation xml:lang="en">
  Network Monitoring Tool Ping.
  Copyright CoreGRID. All rights reserved.
  Version 0.0
  </documentation>
 </annotation>

<complexType name="PingOptionsType">
 <sequence>
  <element name="PacketSize"
               type="integer"
               minOccurs="0"/>
 </sequence>
 <attribute name="CharacteristicId"
               type="pt:PingCharacteristicIdType"
               use="required"/>
</complexType>

<simpleType name="PingCharacteristicIdType">
 <restriction base="string">
   <enumeration value="RoundTrip"/>
   <enumeration value="PacketLoss"/>
 </restriction>
</simpleType>

</schema>
```

Figure 2.   Trivial Ping Options

3.1   A case study: monitoring Processor to Storage connectivity

A simple example illustrates the request of an active monitoring session between a Storage and a Computing Element to monitor their connectivity through an ICMP ping (see Figure 4).

The origin of the Network Monitoring Session descriptor is the WMA represented as a green circle inside the INFN-NA domain (see Figure 1). The WMA has no hints about the Network Monitoring Architecture, so it delivers a bare MeasurementStream instance to the local NMA.

At this point the Measurement Stream is encapsulated into a Network Monitoring Session description, and routes the request to the known NMA at one end of the Network Element. The identifier of the forwarding NMA is placed in the route stack.

The NMA in the INFN-CNAF domain discovers that it cannot handle the request: there is no ping wrapper on the Computing element, and therefore the monitoring activity cannot be carried out. It forwards the NetworkMonitor-

```
<schema
 xmlns="http://www.w3.org/2001/XMLSchema"
 xmlns:am="http://www.di.unipi.it/~augusto/schema/MAPIMonitoringTools-0.1.xsd"
 targetNamespace=
        "http://www.di.unipi.it/~augusto/schema/MAPIMonitoringTools-0.1.xsd">


 <annotation>
  <documentation xml:lang="en">
  Passive Network Monitoring Tools (FORTH).
  Copyright CoreGRID. All rights reserved.
  Version 0.0
  </documentation>
 </annotation>

 <complexType name="MAPIMonitoringToolsOptionsType">
  <sequence>
   <element name="ProtocolName"
               type="string"
               minOccurs="0"/>
   <element name="ApplicationName"
               type="string"
               minOccurs="0"/>
   <element name="Anonymize"
               type="string"
               minOccurs="0"/>
   <element name="ThirdParty"
               type="string"
               minOccurs="0"/>
  </sequence>
  <attribute name="CharacteristicId"
               type="am:MAPIMonitoringToolsCharacteristicIdType"
               use="required"/>
 </complexType>

 <simpleType name="MAPIMonitoringToolsCharacteristicIdType">
  <restriction base="string">
    <enumeration value="RoundTripTime"/>
    <enumeration value="PacketLossRate"/>
    <enumeration value="AvailableBandwidth"/>
    <enumeration value="UsedBandwidth"/>
  </restriction>
 </simpleType>

</schema>
```

Figure 3.   MAPI options

ingSession instance to the known NMA on the other Network Element endpoint, FORTH, pushing its own address on the stack.

The next NMA discovers that the storage element is equipped with a ping wrapper: therefore it extracts the MeasurementStream description from the Session description, and delivers it to the NME co-located with the Storage Element. It also discovers that it is adjacent to the NMA in the INFN-NA domain, and eliminates the intermediate INFN-CNAF agent from the Route stack.

```
<?xml version="1.0"?>

 <nmsd:NetworkMonitoringSession
   xmlns:nmsd="http://www.di.unipi.it/~augusto/schema/
                NetworkMonitoringSessionDescription-0.5.xsd"
   SessionId="456@this.NMagent.ip">
   <RequestFrom TaskId="WF245" WorkflowMonitoringAgentId="OurBroker@FORTH"/>
   <Schedule StartAt="2007-09-17T12:00:00.000-01:00" Duration="2H"/>
   <Route>
     <NextAgent Agent="NMAgent@FORTH" Index="1"/>
     <NextAgent Agent="Theodolite@CNAF" Index="2"/>
   </Route>
   <NetworkElement SourceDomain="FORTH" DestinationDomain="CNAF"/>
   <MeasurementStream>
     <CharacteristicStream CharacteristicStreamId="1">
       <SamplePeriod>5</SamplePeriod>
       <Path>
         <SourceIP>processor_1.ics.forth.gr</SourceIP>
         <DestinationIP>ftp.cnaf.infn.it</DestinationIP>
       </Path>
       <PingOptions CharacteristicId="RoundTrip">
         <PacketSize>2048</PacketSize>
       </PingOptions>
     </CharacteristicStream>
   </MeasurementStream>
 </nmsd:NetworkMonitoringSession>
```

Figure 4.   XML instance for the example in Figure 1

The NME activates a ping process, formatting the data coming from such process according to its specifications, and forwarding successive frames to the local NMA, which in its turn encapsulates the frames by indicating the Session they belong to and passing them to the next NMA in the stack.

In our case this is the NMA located at INFN-NA, which decapsulates the data and passes it to the WMA, which is able to unmarshall the data contained in the datagram according with tool specifications, and process the data.

The WMA finally interrupts the monitoring session notifying the local NMA, which propagates the request according to the route stack known to it. When the request reaches FORTH NMA, it stops the monitoring activity on the computing element. Alternatively, FORTH NMA will perform the same activity when the "Duration" timeout expires. Intermediate NMA's will suspend and remove the registration of the session from their soft state.

4.   Related works

The coordination of a network monitoring infrastructure is a matter of active research. The first effort in this sense is probably the Network Weather Service [13], which still offers relevant suggestions. However, such prototype indicates but solves only partially the real challenges of a coordinated network monitoring architecture: scalability and security.

Successive studies mainly focussed towards the publication of network monitoring results in view of retrospective analysis: this option limits the application of such infrastructures to those scenarios where monitoring requests are *planned* and concentrate on a restricted subset of routes. Without such limit any solution is deemed to unscalability, since the number of routes grows with the square of the number of resource elements in the network.

Such scenario is nonetheless of great practical relevance: administrative monitoring, as well as accounting or diagnosis fall into the category of a monitoring task that concentrates on few routes, known a priori. To cite some of the works on this trail, we cite the Globus MDS [11], and EGEE network performance monitoring architecture [5].

In this paper we explore another facet of the problem, which is relevant to cope with *unplanned* monitoring requests. The interest for such aspect of network monitoring is that monitoring requests from the agents responsible for the coordination of Grid jobs cannot be anticipated, they extend to a limited lifetime, they have a moderate (if any) need of historical data, mainly to improve measurement robustness. Such aspect of network monitoring is far less studied, but exhibits a number of challenges: flexibility, since new requests must be activated dynamically for scalability reasons, and security, since network monitoring is an expensive activity, and requests must be authenticated.

Our approach to this aspect of network monitoring is marginally related to the past experience with *planned* network monitoring. The problems raising in the two cases are too different to justify a common solution: one for all, *unplanned* network monitoring in principle does not need a measurements database, while *planned* network monitoring relies on the availability of a powerful repository for measurements (think for instance to the R-GMA [4] architecture). Therefore we aimed at a different approach.

The architecture we propose is an evolution of [3] and its design has been influenced by Internet streaming protocols: the basic requirements are those announced in [6], but our embrional solution for the request of a Network Monitoring Session is also inspired to the Internet SIP [7] protocol. We also take into account the RTP [10] protocol as for the components of a network monitoring request. In analogy to the *application profiles* introduced in RTP, that characterize the payload in a flexible and expandable way, we opted for a *monitoring tool* oriented description, instead of a *characteristic oriented* approach. Just like in the case of RTP, the *neutrality* of an approach that leaves to monitoring tool designers the freedom to introduce new measurements that do not exactly match existing characteristics, and to workflow managers designers the ability to use them, leaves space to research and new products in the rapidly evolving field of network monitoring tools.

5.   Conclusions

We introduce a distinction between planned and unplanned network monitoring activities: we claim that each of them exhibits challenging aspects, and requires distinct solutions, although the latter is receiving less attention than the former from the research community.

The fact that unplanned activities are requested by Workflow Management Agents introduces the need of a scalable and flexible authentication scheme. Once they are activated their output should not be stored for future use, but directly delivered to the requester with a lightweight streaming protocol. The request and reply protocol should be flexible and allow the integration of new monitoring tools.

In this paper we address a fundamental step in the design of a solution for the management of unplanned monitoring activity, which consists in the definition of the information needed to describe a single monitoring session, and the scope of such entity. In order to give an intuitive framework, we outline the architecture of the network monitoring infrastructure, identifying the actors and their inter-play.

APPENDIX – Network Monitoring Session Schema

```
<schema
 xmlns="http://www.w3.org/2001/XMLSchema"
 xmlns:pt="http://www.di.unipi.it/~augusto/schema/PingTool.xsd"
 xmlns:am="http://www.di.unipi.it/~augusto/schema/AppmonTool.xsd"
 xmlns:nmsd="http://www.di.unipi.it/~augusto/schema/
            NetworkMonitoringSessionDescription-0.4.xsd"
 targetNamespace="http://www.di.unipi.it/~augusto/schema/
                 NetworkMonitoringSessionDescription-0.4.xsd"
 elementFormDefault="unqualified"
 attributeFormDefault="unqualified">

<import namespace="http://www.di.unipi.it/~augusto/schema/PingTool.xsd"/>
<import namespace="http://www.di.unipi.it/~augusto/schema/AppmonTool.xsd"/>

<annotation>
 <documentation xml:lang="en">
 Network Monitoring Session Description.
 Copyright CoreGRID. All rights reserved.
 Version 0.1
 </documentation>
</annotation>

<element name="NetworkMonitoringSession"
            type="nmsd:NetworkMonitoringSessionType"/>

<element name="comment" type="string"/>

<complexType name="NetworkMonitoringSessionType">
 <sequence>
  <element name="RequestFrom"
            type="nmsd:WorkflowMonitoringTaskType"
            maxOccurs="unbounded"/>
  <element name="Route"
            type="nmsd:RouteStackType"
            minOccurs="0"/>
```

```
    <element name="NetworkElement"
                type="nmsd:NetworkElementType"/>
    <element name="MeasurementStream"
                type="nmsd:MeasurementStreamType"/>
  </sequence>
  <attribute name="SessionId"
                type="string"
                use="required"/>
  <attribute name="StartAt"
                type="dateTime"
                use="required"/>
  <attribute name="Duration"
                type="duration"
                use="required"/>
  <attribute name="BandwidthLimit"
                type="nonNegativeInteger"
                default="0"/>
  <attribute name="Priority"
                type="nonNegativeInteger"
                default="0"/>
</complexType>

<complexType name="WorkflowMonitoringTaskType">
  <attribute name="TaskId"
                type="string"/>
  <attribute name="WorkflowMonitoringAgentId"
                type="string"/>
</complexType>

<complexType name="RouteStackType">
  <sequence>
  <element name="NextAgent" minOccurs="0" maxOccurs="unbounded">
    <complexType>
      <attribute name="Agent"
                type="string"/>
      <attribute name="Index"
                type="nonNegativeInteger"/>
    </complexType>
  </element>
  </sequence>
</complexType>

<complexType name="NetworkElementType">
  <attribute name="SourceDomain"
                type="string"
                use="required"/>
  <attribute name="DestinationDomain"
                type="string"
                use="required"/>
</complexType>

<complexType name="MeasurementStreamType">
  <sequence>
   <element name="CharacteristicStream"
           minOccurs="1" maxOccurs="unbounded">
     <complexType>
       <sequence>
        <element name="SamplePeriod"
                type="float"
                minOccurs="0"/>
        <element name="SourceIP"
                type="string"
                minOccurs="0"
                maxOccurs="unbounded"/>
        <element name="DestinationIP"
                type="string"
                minOccurs="0"
                maxOccurs="unbounded"/>
```

```
    <choice>
     <element name="PingOptions"
                    type="pt:PingOptionsType"/>
     <element name="AppmonOptions"
                    type="am:AppmonOptionsType"/>
    </choice>
   </sequence>
   <attribute name="CharacteristicStreamId"
             type="string"/>
  </complexType>
 </element>
 </sequence>
 </complexType>

</schema>
```

References

[1] Demetres Antoniades, Michalis Polychronakis, Spiros Antonatos, Evangelos P. Markatos, Sven Ubik, and Arne Øslebø. Appmon: An application for accurate per application network traffic characterization. In *In IST Broadband Europe 2006 Conference*, 2006.

[2] A. Ciuffoletti. The wandering token: Congestion avoidance of a shared resource. In *Austrian-Hungarian Workshop on Distributed and Parallel Systems*, page 10, Innsbruck (Austria), September 2006.

[3] Augusto Ciuffoletti and Michalis Polychronakis. Architecture of a network monitoring element. In *CoreGRID workshop at EURO-Par 2006*, page 10, Dresden (Germany), August 2006.

[4] A. Cooke, A. Gray, L. Ma, W. Nutt, J. Magowan, P. Taylor, R. Byrom, L. Field, S. Hicks, and J. et Al. Leak. R-GMA: An information integration system for grid monitoring. In *Proceedings of the Eleventh International Conference on Cooperative Information Systems*, 2003.

[5] EGEE. *Network Performance Monitoring Architecture*, october 2006.

[6] Sally Floyd, Van Jacobson, Ching-Gung Liu, Steven McCanne, and Lixia Zhang. A reliable multicast framenwork for light-weight sessions and application level framing. *IEEE/ACM Transactions on Networking*, November 1996.

[7] H. Handley, H. Schultzrinne, Schooler E., and J. Rosenberg. SIP: Session initiation protocol. Request for Comment 2543, Network Working Group, March 1999.

[8] Hao Jiang and Constantinos Dovrolis. Passive estimation of TCP round-trip times. *SIGCOMM Comput. Commun. Rev.*, 32(3):75–88, 2002.

[9] Antonis Papadogiannakis, Alexandros Kapravelos, Michalis Polychronakis, Evangelos P. Markatos, and Augusto Ciuffoletti. Passive end-to-end packet loss estimation for grid traffic monitoring. In *Proceedings of the CoreGRID Integration Workshop*, 2006.

[10] H. Shultzrinne, S. Casner, R. Frederick, and V. Jacobson. RTP: A transport protocol for real-time applications. Request for Comment 1889, Audio-Video Transport Working Group, January 1996.

[11] The Globus Team. Globus Toolkit 2.2 MDS Technology Brief, Jan 2003. Draft.

[12] Panos Trimintzios, Michalis Polychronakis, Antonis Papadogiannakis, Michalis Foukarakis, Evangelos P. Markatos, and Arne Øslebø. DiMAPI: An application programming interface for distributed network monitoring. In *Proceedings of the 10th IEEE/IFIP Network Operations and Management Symposium (NOMS)*, April 2006.

[13] Rich Wolski. Dinamically forecasting network performance using the Network Weather Service. Technical Report TR-CS96-494, University of California at San Diego, January 1998.

SUB-CONTRACTS: DELEGATING CONTRACTS FOR RESOURCE DISCOVERY

Javier Bustos-Jimenez and Cristian Varas
Escuela de Ingenieria Informatica
Universidad Diego Portales
Santiago de Chile
javier.bustos@inf.udp.cl
cristian.varas2@al.udp.cl

Jose Piquer
Departamento de Ciencias de la Computacion
Universidad de Chile
Santiago de Chile
jpiquer@nic.cl

Abstract   Grid Computing promised to present a large number of resources distributed on a world-area network, ready to be used by a single user: that promise is true. Now, the problem has moved to the user side, because a normal user normally knows at most only his organization's resources, and those numbers of resources are often not enough for his purposes. Defining a Virtual Organization (VO) as a set of scientific resources, processors, clusters and Grids which are available to the user, we study the problem of resource discovery for VOs in a distributed approach. Viewing a VO-to-VO network as a Peer-to-Peer network, we present our solution based on the use of contracts to perform the query and assignment, delegating contracts if the query cannot be fully handled. We first present a blind scheme of delegation (that is, without knowing of neighbors' resource availability), evaluating it by simulations, and showing that it is not necessary to delegate the query to all neighbors to handle it. Then, a scheme knowing only direct neighbors which uses the blind scheme is presented. Finally, we will give recommendations and extensions of our scheme to improve the resource discovery process.

Keywords: Grid, resource discovery, contracts, delegation.

1.   Introduction

In large multi-cluster grids the resources suffer, most of the time, of low utilization. If, under some events, the demand exceeds the capacity of a single system, it is possible to take actions like making the system grow by adding more resources, or enqueuing the additional demand until the system can serve it, but none of them seems to be appropriate in the context of Grid Computing.

A better solution lies in making the grids inter-operate in order to drive their collective demand to achieve a stable utilization of the combined system.

For making grids to inter-operate, some design choices involving resource selection and performance must be taken. First, a meta-scheduler should be used to redirect the jobs to the appropriate grid; otherwise, the users would be forced to submit their jobs directly to the grid system arising new problems such as to know where are located the suitable resources, or availability of alien grids.

Considering that a centralized scheduler can be useful in the context of serving sets of processors, cluster or grids belonging to the same institution (also known as a *Virtual Organization* or *VO*) to perform intra-organization scheduling, to extend this approach to inter-organization scheduling (that is, scheduling into VO-to-VO networks) could turn easily into a bottleneck, and a decentralized approach is needed.

Completely decentralized solutions exist but they still have not been able to achieve enough benefits under typical grid workloads. These solutions include the Koala scheduler [1], the AliEn Resource Brokers [2] and OurGrid [3].

Our work is focused in exploiting structural properties of VO-to-VO networks (kind of natural networks), to perform inter-VO resource discovery through the use of *contracts* and delegation. A contract is used to exchange information between parties and then it can be used to transform a resource query into a resource agreement using the same infrastructure. If a VO can handle only part of the resource request, it will delegate the search for the remaining resources. Once all the resources are found and claimed by a virtual organization, the contract could be audited to generate complaints in case of error.

Our solution is partially related with the work of Baraglia et al. [4] which introduces the concept of Grid Awareness, providing to virtual organizations useful information such as network topology and QoS through query/response messages formatted by XML schemes.

This article is organized as follows: Section 2 introduces Contracts for coupling variables, which are used into Section 3 to define delegation schemes for resource discovery. Section 4 presents the behavior of the scheme in simulations for parameter tunning. Future work is presented in Section 5 followed by Conclusions in Section 6.

2. Contracts

Contracts for coupling variables were firstly defined in the work of Leyton et al. [5]. In a nutshell, a contract corresponds to the interaction between two interfaces of different parties, providing the means to define *how* information between these two parties can be shared (in Figure 1, C is the Contract between A and B). Coupling variables with contracts is a scheme similar to Condor Matchmaking [6], which allows finding suitable matches but specifying only *what* information is exchanged. Another related approach to contracts is the Web Services Agreement (WSAgreement) Specification [7], which specifies that *"an agreement defines a dynamically-established and dynamically-managed relationship between parties"*.

Contracts were studied in the context of coupling generic interfaces between two parties, and in the work of Leyton et al. contracts were studied specifically to couple distributed application with Grid deployment descriptors. In this work, we use contracts in two contexts:

1 To generate a *resource query* between parties.

2 To generate *resource delegation* between parties.

In the first case, an application with resource (or set of resources) needs sends the contract as a resource query to its parties. In the second case, if a Virtual Organization is only capable to provide a subset of the resources, it delegates the complement set of resources to its own parties.

A contract is defined as a set of *typed clauses*. A coupling between two parties is valid if and only if all clauses on the contract have the same type for both parties and all of them are valid.

Figure 1. Contracts as an interface between parties

3. Contracts for Resource Discovery

A basic contract for resource discovery has to declare four main clauses:

1 SOURCE = Reference to the VO which owns the resource query.

2 RESOURCE = Name of the resource

3 NUMBER = Number of resources wanted

4 STATUS = {QUERY, ACCEPTED, REJECTED}

The process of resource discovery begins when a user asks inside of its virtual organization (VO) for a given resource, if the VO is not able to handle the resource request, the query is delegated to other VOs. We study the behavior for two types of delegation: one-to-one and one-to-many (Figure 2).

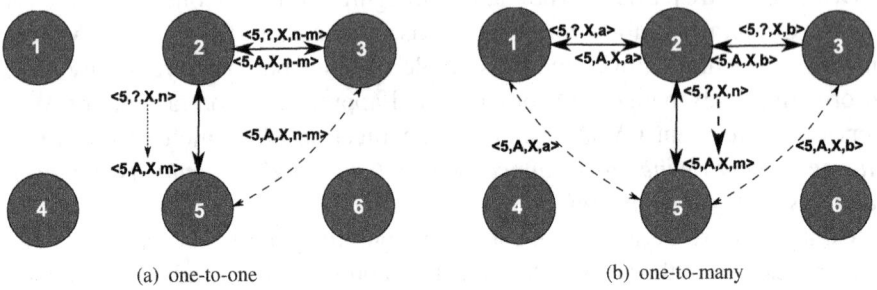

(a) one-to-one   (b) one-to-many

Figure 2.   Delegation schemes

3.1   Delegation one-to-one

A contract-query for n resources of type X is sent to another VO, if the receiver can handle the query, a contract is made between parties. Nevertheless, if the receiver can only partially handle the request (lets say, it has only m available resources of type X), it will make a reservation of its m resources for the contract and it will choose another VO to delegate the query (now requesting n-m resources). In the example of Figure 2(a) we show that the delegated query of n-m resources can be handled. Therefore, the original contract <5,QUERY,X,n> is set up as <5,ACCEPTED,X,m> and a new contract <5,ACCEPTED,X,n-m> is made between VOs 3 and 5. Note that the contract between VO 3 and VO 5 is made through VO 2 to inform that reserved resources will be used.

To avoid infinite queries inside the network (for instance, demanding more resources than the number available in the system), the delegation has a TTL parameter which is the delegation maximal depth. If after TTL delegations the last VO is not capable of handle the request, the contract status is set to REJECTED, and therefore its reserved resources are freed. For simplicity reasons, if a delegated contract is rejected, all the contracts belonging to the delegation will be set to REJECTED and therefore all the reserved resources will be free.

3.2   Delegation one-to-many

A contract-query for n resources of type X is sent to another VO, if the receiver can handle the query, a contract is made between parties. Nevertheless, if the receiver can only partially handle the request (lets say, it has only m available resources of type X, it will reserve its m resources for the contract and it will choose other VOs to delegate the query. In Figure 2(b) we show that all delegated parties are capable to handle their request, therefore the original contract <5,QUERY,X,n> is set up as <5,ACCEPTED,X,m>, and two new contracts (<5,ACCEPTED,X,a> and <5,ACCEPTED,X,b> having $a + b = n - m$) are made between the VO 5 and VOs 1 and 3 through VO 2.

As in the one-to-one scheme, a TTL parameter is set to avoid infinite queries. Moreover, using the SOURCE clause the scheme refuses multiples request of resources from the same source, noting that in this scheme is highly probable of receive two times the same contract-query. Again, if a delegated contract is rejected, all delegated contracts will be set to REJECTED and therefore all reserved resources will be freed.

3.3 The next step: sub-contracts

Placing us in the context of *VO-to-VO* networks, we can exploit structural properties of this (natural) network storing the resource information of neighbors: sending to neighbors a notification of resource utilization each time a VO make (or finish) a contract.

Therefore, if a VO (A) asks to another VO (B) for n resources of type X, B will looks into the neighboring information if all together (not including A) can handle the request. If true, a contract <X,n> is made between A and B and contracts <X,ni> (where $n = \sum ni$) are made between B and its neighbors (this process is known as *sub-contracting*). If no sub-contract can be made, B delegates the query to its neighbors as we defined above.

Due to the dynamic behavior of the VO-to-VO network in terms of resources reserved and used, a restrictive verification such as *"we can handle the query if we have **at least** n resources of type X"* could produce a fault of resources on contract claiming time, generating complaints between A and B (because finally B was not able to accomplish his contract) and complaints between B and some of its neighbors. Therefore, a ponderer $s > 1$ can be used to sub-contracting only the whole group can handle a request of $s \times n$ resources. This scheme can be used, for instance, if B manages fault-tolerance and A does not, therefore B asks for more resources than A requested to maintain always a set of n resources alive.

4. Contracts on a simulated testbed

Considering that a network made of Virtual Organizations has similar structural properties than a Peer-to-Peer network, we tested our resource discovery scheme on a VO-to-VO network simulated using PlanetSim [8]. In our simulation, we interconnected $1,000$ VOs and randomly placed $1,000$ resources on the network (values were selected considering $1,000$ a medium-size for a network). Then, we ran our scheme measuring the % of succesful requests;

that is, given a randomly chosen VO needing n items of a resource, the % of tries that the VO was capable of find the resources and a delegated contract was made.

For the one-to-one delegation scheme, we measured the % using as parameters:

- TTL = $1, 2, 3, 4, 5$.

- $n = 1,000; 500; 250; 125$ and 63.

The results of our experience are shown in Figure 3. As we expected, a use of TTL=1 produces a poor performance of the scheme, and the performance increases with TTL. The importance of this result is given by the fact that in this scheme TTL means also the number of contracts sent between parties (i.e: number of messages in the network). Therefore, if the resource wanted is popular and a VO needs only a low number of items, an one-to-one scheme could be useful.

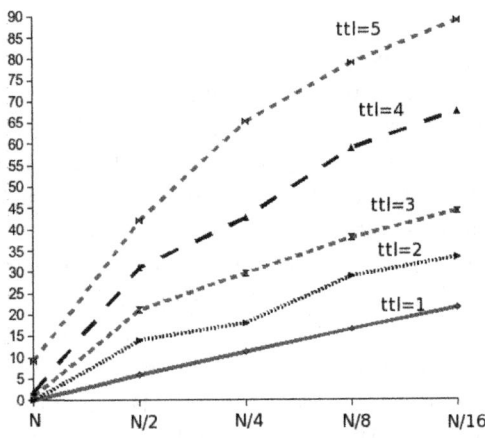

Figure 3.   % of succesful request by total number of resources (N) = $1,000$ for a one-to-one delegation scheme

For the one-to-many delegation scheme, defining v as the number of neighbors selected to perform the delegation, and m the number of resources to search in delegation. We evenly distributed the search sending to each neighbor a contract by $\lceil \frac{m}{v} \rceil$ resources. Then, we measured the % of succesful requests using the following parameters:

- Defining V as the total number of neighbors for a given VO, we used $v = V, \lceil \frac{V}{2} \rceil, \lceil \frac{V}{4} \rceil$ and $\lceil \frac{V}{8} \rceil$. The idea of dividing the query in a number less than the total number of neighbors comes from a previous work which performs efficient load-balancing on Peer-to-Peer networks [9].

- TTL = 1, 2, 3, 4, 5.

- $n = 1,000; 500; 250; 125$ and 63.

Results are presented in Figure 4, showing that a reduction in the number of delegated contracts does not produce a great reduction on the performance of the delegation scheme and, as we expected, the % of succesful queries is exponential to the search depth.

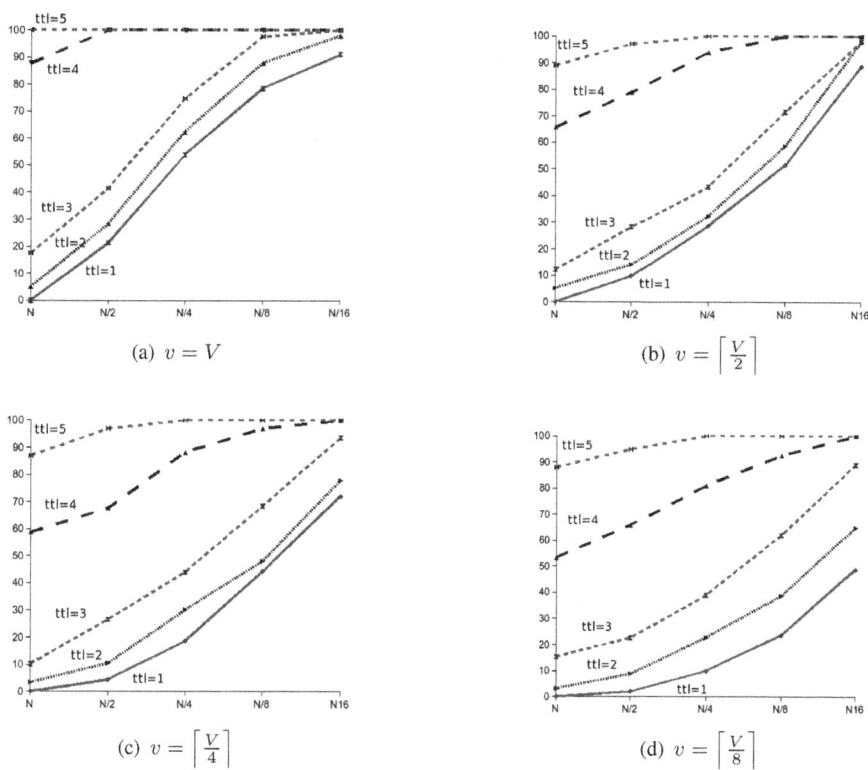

(a) $v = V$

(b) $v = \left\lceil \frac{V}{2} \right\rceil$

(c) $v = \left\lceil \frac{V}{4} \right\rceil$

(d) $v = \left\lceil \frac{V}{8} \right\rceil$

Figure 4. % of succesful request by total number of resources (N) = 1, 000 for a one-to-many delegation scheme

5. Future Work

In this work we presented how to use coupling contracts for resource discovery, validating our scheme through simulations using PlanetSim. We plan to implement our scheme in real systems such as XtreemOS [10] or ProActive [11] to provide them with a full distributed resource discovery scheme.

On the other hand, we plan to extend our scheme in the use of useful information for delegation, for instance to use the information of neighbors (as sub-contracting) to perform *smart* delegations. Also, we plan to add to contracts the number of complaints and to perform composition of resources (or services).

5.1   Complaints: Do you deserve to be part of us?

Some systems as Koala maintain an error counter [1](equivalent to a complaint counter) and, if the number of consecutive errors by an entity reaches a given threshold, the entity is marked unusable (similar to be removed from the network). We do not agree with that scheme because we are aligned with the statement: "let the user decides". A complaint counter (or complaint-per month CPM ratio) is a useful information for some testbed and it may be added to the contract. If a VO needs a reliable resource the obviously step is to add a clause limiting the CPM ratio. In the other hand, for some experimental testbeds (to test adaptive algorithms such as fault tolerance or distributed garbage collectors) will be useful to have *unstable* networks, that is, with a high CPM ratio.

Note that CPM and the ponderer s are highly related: if a VO wants to looks like very reliable, a good selection of s has to be performed. In fact, the study of s is very important to reduce the number of messages traversing the network.

5.2   The following step: Composition

Imagine now that a VO does not have a given resource, but it knows hot to compose it using other resources. For instance, in Figure 5 VO 1 asks to its neighbors VO 2 for n resources of type X, and VO 2 does not have the resource X itself but it knows that resource X can be composed by resources A,B and C. Moreover, VO 2 knows that its neighbors VO 4, VO 5 and VO 6 have availability of resources A, B and C respectively. Therefore, contracts between VO 2 and its parties can be made to acquire the needed resources and the contract status between VO 1 and VO 2 can be set up as ACCEPTED.

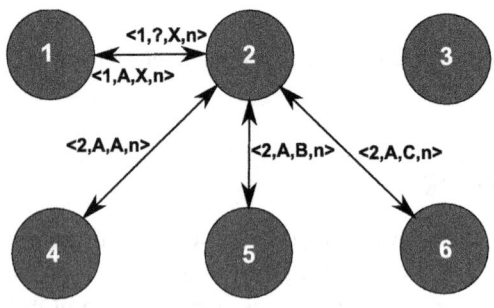

Figure 5.   Composition of resources

6. Conclusions

In this work, our solution to the distributed resource discovery problem was presented. This solution, called "sub-contracting" is based on the use of contracts to perform the resource query and assignment, delegating contracts if the query cannot be fully handled.

We first presented a blind scheme of delegation in two flavors: one-to-one and one-to-many, evaluating them by simulations, and showing that the first scheme is usefully for popular resources if the requirement is useful for low number of resources. For the second scheme, we show that it is not necessary to delegate the query to all neighbors, finding on the 85% of the experiences all the needed resources for a mid-size set of resources even using $\frac{1}{4}$ of the neighbors to delegate the query.

Following the blind schemes, a scheme knowing only direct neighbors was presented, discussing the usefulness of a strict delegation due to the dynamic nature of the network.

Finally, recommendations and extensions of our scheme to improve the resource discovery process have been discussed.

Acknowledgments

This work was partially funded by CoreGrid NoE and NIC Labs.

References

[1] H. Mohamed and D. Epema, "Experiences with the KOALA co-allocating scheduler in multiclusters," *Cluster Computing and the Grid, 2005. CCGrid 2005. IEEE International Symposium on*, vol. 2, 2005.

[2] P. Saiz, P. Buncic, and A. J. Peters, "Alien resource brokers," *CoRR*, vol. cs.DC/0306068, 2003.

[3] N. Andrade, W. Cirne, F. Brasileiro, and P. Roisenberg, "OurGrid: An Approach to Easily Assemble Grids with Equitable Resource Sharing," *Proceedings of the 9th Workshop on Job Scheduling Strategies for Parallel Processing*, pp. 61–68, 2003.

[4] R. Baraglia, D. Laforenza, R. Ferrini, N. Tonellotto, D. Adami, S. Giordano, and R. Yayhapour, "A study on network resources management," in *Proceedings of the 2nd Integrated Research in Grid Computing Workshop* (S. Gorlatch, M. Bubak, and T. Priol, eds.), (Krakow, Poland), pp. 213–224, CoreGRID, IST, Academic Computer Centre CYFRONET AGH, October 2006.

[5] J. Bustos-Jiménez, D. Caromel, M. Leyton, and J. M. Piquer, "Coupling contracts for deployment on alien grids," in *CoreGRID Workshop on Grid Middleware (in conjunction with EuroPar)*, Lecture Notes in Computer Science, Springer Berlin, September 2006.

[6] R. Raman, M. Livny, and M. Solomon, "Matchmaking: Distributed resource management for high throughput computing," in *HPDC '98: Proceedings of the The Seventh IEEE International Symposium on High Performance Distributed Computing*, (Washington, DC, USA), pp. 140–146, IEEE Computer Society, 1998.

[7] A. Andrieux, karl Czajkowski, A. Dan, K. Keahey, H. Ludwig, T. Nakata, J. Pruyne, J. Rofrano, S. Tuecke, and M. Xu, "Web Services Agreement Specification (WS-Agreement)," *Grid Resource Allocation and Agreement Protocol WG, GGF*, vol. 1, 2006.

[8] P. García, C. Pairot, R. Mondéjar, J. Pujol, H. Tejedor, and R. Rallo, "PlanetSim: A New Overlay Network Simulation Framework," *Lecture Notes in Computer Science (LNCS), Software Engineering and Middleware (SEM)*, vol. 3437, pp. 123–137, 2005.

[9] J. Bustos-Jiménez, D. Caromel, and J. M. Piquer, "Toward the infinite network, and beyond," in *Proceedings of 12th Workshop on Job Scheduling Strategies for Parallel Processing (JSSPP)*, vol. 4376 of *Lecture Notes in Computer Science*, pp. 176–191, Springer Berlin Heidelberg, June 2006.

[10] C. Morin, "Xtreemos: A grid operating system making your computer ready for participating in virtual organizations," *isorc*, vol. 00, pp. 393–402, 2007.

[11] Oasis Group at INRIA Sohpia-Antipolis, "Proactive, the java library for parallel, distributed, concurrent computing with security and mobility." http://proactive. objectweb.org, 2002.

LOOKING FOR AN EVOLUTION OF GRID SCHEDULING: META-BROKERING*

I. Rodero, F. Guim, and J. Corbalan
Barcelona Supercomputing Center (BSC) and Technical University of Catalonia (UPC)
{ivan.rodero, francesc.guim, julita.corbalan}@bsc.es

L.L. Fong and Y.G. Liu
IBM T.J. Watson Research Center
{llfong, ygliu}@us.ibm.com

S.M. Sadjadi
Florida International University
sadjadi@cs.fiu.edu

Abstract   A Grid Resource Broker for a Grid domain, or also known as meta-scheduler, is a middleware component used for matching works to available Grid resources from one or more IT organizations. A Grid meta-scheduler usually has its own interfaces for the functionalities it provides and its own job scheduling objectives. This situation causes two main problems: the user uniform access to the Grid is lost, and the scheduling decisions are taken separately while they should be done in coordination. These problems have been observed in different efforts such as the HPC-Europa project but they are still open problems. In this paper we discuss the requirements to achieve a more uniform access to the Grids through a new approach to global brokering. As the results of these discussions on brokering requirements, we propose a meta-brokering design, so called meta-meta-scheduler design, and discuss how it can be realized as a centralized model for the HPC-Europa project, and as a distributed model for the LA Grid project.

Keywords: Grid resource management, meta-brokering/scheduling, interoperability

*This research has been supported in part by the Spanish Ministry of Science and Technology under contract TIN2004-07739-C02-01, the EU project HPC-Europa under contract 506079, the CoreGRID FP6 European Network of Excellence (Contract IST-2002-004265), NSF under grant OCI-0636031, and IBM.

1.   Introduction

In a Grid environment, a resource broker, also called meta-scheduler[1], is usually used to manage user submitted jobs and the scheduling of jobs for execution to the available Grid resources from one or more IT organizations under a Grid domain. A Grid meta-scheduler has its own interfaces for the functionalities it provides and its own job scheduling objectives. However, there is not yet a standard on the interfaces of Grid meta-scheduler to support the interoperability of different meta-scheduling systems that bring us to the original idea of "The Grid", which promised an infrastructure to provide a uniform access to resources across different centers and institutions. This is an important issue because typically, a large Grid environment can be composed with different institutions or centers and each center would like to use its own scheduling system. The current Grid is managed by different meta-schedulers that manage a particular institution or virtual organization, and then the Grid becomes divided into several independent Grids without any interaction between them. In this context, the different Grid meta-schedulers are working independently, with different capabilities and using different languages for describing jobs, for submission, monitoring and so on. Different meta-scheduling projects can be found in literature, as detailed in Section 2. A meta-scheduling architecture can be based on different models, from a centralized to a distributed model as it is discussed in [26]. We also can find various approaches in scheduling policies such as economics [4], load balancing [25], or based on multi-criteria [16].

To solve the interoperability problem between different meta-scheduling systems, some initiatives have been developed. The HPC-Europa project is providing a solution to this problem through the development of a web portal to be used as a single point of access for different HPC centers in Europe [13]. In this approach, each center implements a plug-in with its own set of supported capabilities. Next, the user chooses manually the meta-scheduling system to submit their jobs. Finally, the job scheduling policies are evaluated inside the context of each center. Using the experience gained from this project, we have concluded that the portal approach is not enough to provide a transparent single point of access to Grid environments as the users are still involved with undesirable complexity and the scheduling results may less optimal. Therefore, we need to extend the model of HPC-Europa and support the mechanisms and policies on top of the meta-schedulers; basically, brokering the Grid meta-schedulers. In addition, the idea of the interoperability between different middleware and systems was studied in other projects such as in Grid Interoperability Project

---

[1]In this paper, we will use resource broker, broker, and meta-scheduler inter-changeably to refer to a grid resource broker. We will later define meta-broker as a broker on top of brokers, or a meta-meta-scheduler.

[3]. More specifically, this interoperability project tried to work on mechanisms to create Grids with a uniform access to both Globus and Unicore systems.

The idea of brokering on top of Grid meta-scheduler has been taken into account in other works such as in [15]. As a meta-broker, the scheduler on top of meta-scheduler should be called meta-meta-scheduler. Therefore, a meta-broker can be defined as the middleware component that selects the most appropriate meta-scheduler to submit a job following a particular policy. This point of view has influenced the way we are extending the approach in HPC-Europa as we propose in Section 5. Furthermore, the Open Grid Forum (OGF) is working on some recommendations regarding interoperability, but the work is still in working process. Therefore, we will consider the OGF approach only as a reference for our research activities.

In this paper, we will study the requirements for a meta-brokering system and we will define a set of requirements for common interfaces that allows accessing and managing different Grid meta-schedulers in a uniform way and provides users with single point of access. To achieve these goals we propose two approaches: (1) designing and implementing a centralized meta-brokering system on top of the different brokers; and (2) designing and implementing a distributed meta-brokering system by communicating the different brokers with a set of protocols and a certain agreement. For the first approach, we present a design in which we are working on the eNANOS [25] framework as an extension of HPC-Europa JRA2 activity, and for the second approach, we present a design based on the LA Grid meta-brokering project [17].

The rest of this paper is organized as follows. In Section 2, we present some of the current approaches in meta-brokering. In Section 3, we summarize the work done in the HPC-Europa and the lessons learned in the requirements of meta-brokering. In Section 4, we discuss the requirements and architectural elements of ideal meta-brokers for Grid environments. In Section 5, to provide the meta-brokering functions as described in Section 4, we first describe a design extension for the HPC-Europa as a centralized model; then we described the distributed design approach of LA Grid meta-brokering project; and finally we summarize the models in a table. In Section 6, we present some conclusions and some roadmap for our future works.

2. Related Work

Several projects regarding Grid meta-scheduling can be found in literature. Both specific and general-purpose initiatives have been developed during last years, and some of them are presented as follows. Condor-G [12] is based on the Condor approach for Grids that combines the inter-domain resource management protocols of the Globus Toolkit and the intra-domain resource and job management methods of Condor. AppLes [2] is a project targeted to

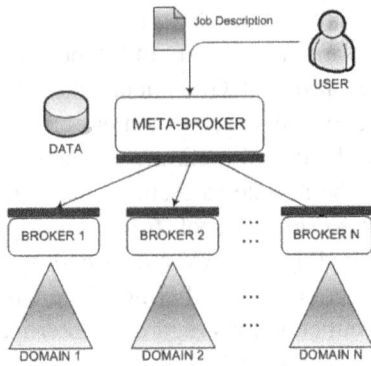

Figure 1.   General meta-broker architecture [17]

the application level scheduling. GridBus [18] is an economy-capable Data Grid service broker for scheduling distributed data oriented applications across Grid resources. GRMS [10] is an open source meta-scheduling system, which allows developers to build and deploy resource management systems to large scale distributed computing infrastructures. The GridWay framework [11] is a component for meta-scheduling in the Grid Ecosystem intended for end users and Grid applications developers. The eNANOS project [25] is based on the idea of having a good low-level support for performing a good high-level HPC scheduling.

There are some initiatives regarding the interoperability of different meta-schedulers [3]. The Grid Interoperability Project (GRIP) aim was to realize the interoperability of Globus and Unicore combining the unique strength of each system and to work towards standards for interoperability of meta-scheduling in the OGF. This goal has been achieved in a real testbed and they have extended for different meta-scheduling systems, as in the HPC-Europa project that is described in Section 3.

In terms of meta-brokering, an abstract architecture has been proposed in [15] and the objectives are similar to those discussed in HPC-Europa [13] or in the interoperability project [3]. The architecture of these proposals is similar. They are based on a meta-broker model that receives the job submission, and manages the resource brokers with some data information, as it is shown in Figure 1. In this paper, we present new designs of meta-brokering that extends the work done in the Grid community and leverages our experiences from HPC-Europa.

As the Grid standardization organization, the OGF is working on scheduling architecture in the Grid Scheduling Architecture Research Group (GSA-RG) [20]. This group has worked on a scheduling hierarchy and the communication between scheduling instances. Recently the group has started working on interoperability and on a proposal regarding the interaction between Grid schedulers. The OGSA Resource Selection Services Working Group (OGSA-RSS-WG) [19] will provide protocols and interface definitions for the resource selection services portion of the Execution Management Services (EMS) part of the Open Grid Services Architecture. The Resource Selection Services (RSS) consist of the Candidate Set Generator (CSG) and the Execution Planning System (EPS). The CSG can be used to generate a set of computational resources that are able to run a job in general, while the EPS uses this list to decide exactly what resources to run the job.

We take into account the OGF recommendations as a reference. In our approach, we promote a more practical point of view as we develop a meta-brokering system in real environments with particular solutions.

3. Lessons learned from the HPC-Europa project

One major activity of HPC-Europa project is to build a portal that provides a uniform and intuitive user interface to access and use resources from different centers. As most of the HPC centers have already deployed their own site-specific HPC and Grid infrastructure; therefore, an important requirement is to keep the autonomy of HPC centers by allowing them to use their favorite middleware, local policies, and so on. For instance, there are currently five different systems that provide a job submission and basic monitoring functionality in the HPC-Europa infrastructure: eNANOS [25], GRIA middleware [9], Grid Resource Management System (GRMS) [10], Job Scheduling Hierarchically (JOSH) [14], and UNICORE [28]. Additionally, eNANOS, GRMS and JOSH use the Globus Toolkit to access underlying resources provided for the HPC-Europa infrastructure.

The Single Point of Access (SPA) effort of HPC-Europa provides two sets of interfaces to application users. Firstly, a generic interface set that can be used by all users for most of their batch applications. To this end, this uniform interfaces are provided for the most relevant Grid functionality identified from a requirements analysis of the centers. The key set of functionalities has been determined to be required for the realization of the SPA: job submission, job monitoring, resource information, accounting, authorization, and data management. Secondly, an application-specific set of portlets are being developed to allow users to manage more complex (e.g., interactive or requiring many specific input parameters) applications in a straightforward manner.

In order to provide end-users with transparent access to resources, we developed a mechanism responsible for the management of uniform interfaces to diverse Grid middleware. Using this mechanism the Single Point of Access enables dynamic loading of components that provide access to the functionality of specific Grid middleware through a single uniform interface. These components are called plug-ins in this context (see Figure 2). These uniform interfaces

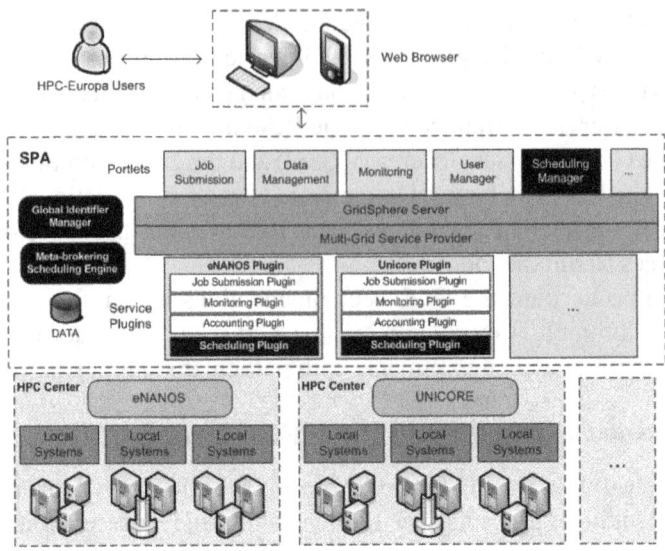

Figure 2.   HPC-Europa architecture with the proposed extensions

are based on standards where possible (e.g., JSDL for job submission [21]) and functionalities provided by Grid middleware deployed in HPC centers.

From the end-user perspective, a uniform GUI is provided that is common for all systems deployed in the HPC-Europa infrastructure. This GUI can be dynamically adapted to particular systems and still keep the same look and feel. Only slight modifications such as disabling fields and limiting lists of values are allowed. When a user wants to submit a job, the user is required to choose the center to which the job has to be submitted and to specify its requirements. There is no global scheduling and the brokering is done manually by the user.

To this end, we have implemented the ability to check the functionality of every resource broker system by retrieving the capabilities of site-specific plug-ins. These descriptions of the implemented capabilities are returned in the form of the appropriately constrained general XML schema. A plug-in returns two descriptions: a description of the methods it supports and a description of data structures (e.g., job description). In [21], this mechanism is described in more detail using the Job Submission Portlet as an example.

4.   Design of Meta-brokering

4.1   Requirements for Meta-brokering

From the experiences in HPC-Europa project we have observed some re-quirements that should be taken into account when developing a meta-brokering system:

1 Global Addressing Mechanism: We need a mechanism to address the different involved resources. In this case, the main resources of a meta-brokering system are brokers or their services, not the resources to execute the job.

2 Common Capability Description Language: Since each broker provides its own set of functionalities, it is required to have a Capability Description Language (CDL) to describe all the services capabilities (e.g., submission, monitoring, accounting, and control).

3 Common Job Description Language: To eliminate the complexity of each broker having its own job description language, it is required to have a common language for describing jobs, requirements and so on.

4 Global Job Identifiers: It is very important to have unique mapping of Grid jobs to different brokers and to the local resources. An implementation can be done using a single jobID provider for the meta-brokering system or just using each broker system to argument the job identifications. In any case jobIDs must be unique.

5 Unified Notifications Mechanism: It is required a common mechanism or protocol to notify events. The system can receive notifications from any broker and the notifications should be handled in the same way.

6 Unified Monitoring Mechanism: Since each broker has its own way to return the monitoring data, including mechanism, data type and schema, it is necessary to have a common mechanism and schema for monitoring.

7 Unified Accounting Mechanism: Usually the selection of resources is done using the accounting information especially when economic policies are applied. For meta-brokering the selection of brokers can be done in a similar way.

8 Unified Agreement Mechanism: A meta-brokering system needs a mechanism to make agreements between brokers. The agreement mechanism and an API are also required to establish protocols to communicate brokers.

9 Common Scheduling Description Language: We need a Scheduling Description Language (SDL) to describe the scheduling capabilities that a broker provides (e.g., depending on the user or the users center, a broker can offer a policy with more or less priority), and global meta-brokering policies.

In the Grid environments, this is especially important because there are interactions between several components and the different approaches can be originated from different contexts. In HPC-Europa, we adopted the standards proposed by the OGF wherever it was possible. For the requirements listed above, we propose to use at least the following set of standards: JSDL 1.0 with some extensions for job description, WS-Agreement for the agreement protocol between brokers, and WS-Addressing for addressing resources in general.

Other APIs and schemas are yet to be defined to address the remainder requirements listed above. As an example, some schema such as the one used in HPC-Europa project and presented in [13] can be used for monitoring.

4.2   The Architecture

To meet the requirements listed in section 4.1, in this paper we propose two meta-brokering models. On one hand, we consider the centralized model which is suitable for a limited number of centers and institutions. This is the model considered in the HPC-Europa extension. On the other hand, we consider the distributed model for the LA Grid meta-scheduling project, which is more suitable for more dynamic environments with a higher number of centers and institutions (i.e., centers can be added to the infrastructure dynamically). Moreover, the distributed model is more appropriate for more heterogeneous environments [19] such as the case of the LA Grid, which can be composed of different kind of resources, from a collection of desktop PCs to supercomputing centers. These two different models are discussed later sections.

4.3   The Scheduling

In addition to the architecture model and the required interfaces, there is an important functionality such as the scheduling at the meta-broker level. We can implement different kind of scheduling policies depending on the kind of information we have at the meta-brokering level. On one hand, if the meta-broker has information about the details of the resources, it can implement the typical scheduling policies studied in the literature, such as in [1] or [4], but extending them to a larger amount of resources with the lower level brokers acting as job dispatchers and execution entities. On the other hand, if the meta-broker does not have any information about the resources and only has certain information about the brokers, we can implement other kind of policies. One of the possible meta-brokering policies can be based on the capabilities of the brokers. In this case, the selection of the appropriate brokering system can be done using a multi-criteria algorithm that can take into account the brokers capabilities or even dynamic information, prediction and so on. Another kind of policies can use accounting information to select the appropriate broker for a given job in a particular situation. This kind of policies maps directly to the economic paradigm.

Furthermore, a meta-brokering scheduling algorithm can be implemented many approaches. For example, in BSC we are currently working on policies that use the historical job/resource information to take its scheduling decisions. We are designing data mining techniques that uses the historical information of Grid resources usage, Grid workloads, and a minimum set of job requirements (e.g., executable, number of processors and input files) to estimate variables about: (1) the job requirements, which estimate how much processor, disk and memory a job will use; and (2) the future state of the different resources evolved in the Grid, which estimate, for instance, how much free space will be available in a given host, or what load it will have in a given future time.

We derive this information by correlating the past executions of similar jobs using similar resources, or with similar future load using similar prediction techniques that have been proposed in other works in terms of job performance prediction [5] [8] [12] [27] and resource usage [7] but using Grid workloads. In terms of meta-brokering scheduling, we are designing techniques that use this information for matching jobs to the resources that will better satisfy their requirements.

In this paper we discuss the importance of the scheduling for a meta-broker approach. However, we do not present any particular result because we do not dispose of a testbed or simulation environment for a meta-brokering system yet.

5. Meta-broker designs

In this section, we will provide the detailed designs of the centralized and distributed models of meta-brokers.

5.1 HPC-Europa Extension Proposal

In this proposal, we extend the solution in the HPC-Europa project by adding a meta-broker on top of the individual brokers in such a way that the scheduling decisions are taken depending on the capabilities of the individual brokers. Thereby, we add a functionality to make the selection of each broker or center in the meta-broker.

This extension should include new services to perform meta-brokering. As we have identified in the list of requirements, the HPC-Europa infrastructure should incorporate a new module for the broker scheduling, a scheduling plugin for each center, a language to describe the scheduling capability of brokers and global identifiers management. Moreover, the meta-broker can include some other services such as a predictor service or a historic data catalog to improve the scheduling techniques.

The idea is to design a system following the OGF standards such as the JSDL as a language for describing jobs. In Figure 2, we show the architecture of the extended version of the HPC-Europa approach. The extension is distinguishable by the dark shading.

This meta-broker approach allows the incorporation of more scheduling functionality at the meta-broker level ("SPA" in Figure 2). For example, the meta-broker can store some useful information to improve the scheduling strategy ("DATA" in Figure 2). Some of this information can be the previous decisions regarding the selection of brokers as a historical data such as the achieved quality of service by the different brokers, the average waiting time, the reputation of brokers, or the level of availability and reliability of the resources under the broker domains.

In the new architecture, the meta-brokering scheduling engine is responsible for the broker selection and where to submit a job. At the portal level, it is evaluated one of the meta-brokering policies available in the framework and, associated to this component, a new portlet should be provided to configure policies and its main issues.

To map the scheduling performed in the meta-broker scheduling engine following the scheduling capabilities of the different brokers, we need a new plugin. This plugin implements the scheduling API and provides the functionality supported by each brokering system. Therefore, to define the scheduling capability of the different center (brokers), we need a scheduling description language. This language should include the scheduling policy capabilities, such as the quality of service, priorities, the support for co-allocations and for advanced reservations, economic issues, or the scheduling policy family. For example, in eNANOS we can offer as a scheduling capability the load-balancing of parallel applications in run-time or the support for MPI+OpenMP applications [25].

Finally, to allow the portal managing jobs coming from all the centers, we need global identifiers mechanisms. To obtain global identifiers, we need a new service (global identifier manager) that should be accessible from all the services and through the centers plugins. The global identifier service should not modify the rest of services; the different brokers should support this new functionality via the plugins. The Universally Unique Identifier (UUID) [29] seems to be a good candidate as identifier standard. It is used in software construction, standardized by the Open Software Foundation (OSF) as part of the Distributed Computing Environment (DCE). A UUID is essentially a 16-byte (128-bit) number.

5.2   Meta-brokering design in LA Grid

Latin American Grid initiative (LA Grid, pronounced "lah grid", [17]) is a multifaceted international academic and industry partnership designed to promote research, education and workforce development collaborations with major institutions in United States, Mexico, Argentina, Spain, and other locations around the world. LA Grid has developed a global living laboratory where international researchers are empowered to build new research partnerships and explore the synergies of their research strengths in areas including transparent Grid enablement, autonomic resource management, meta-brokering, and job flow Management. The meta-scheduling project in LA Grid aims to support Grid applications with resources located and managed in different domains spanned over a Grid computing cyber infrastructure. This project addresses the architecture, design, implementation and deployment issues related to meta-brokering.

The meta-broker design in LA Grid is a distributed model with multiple meta-broker instances cooperate with each other to provide Grid functions. As illustrated in Figure 4, one instance of a meta-broker consists of three functional modules: resource module, scheduling module and job module. Resource module is responsible for resource discovery, monitoring and storage. Scheduling module is responsible for locate suitable resources or brokers for a job request. Job module is responsible for management of job lifecycle: submission, dispatching and execution monitoring. A meta-broker instance interacts with existent brokers within the resource domain.

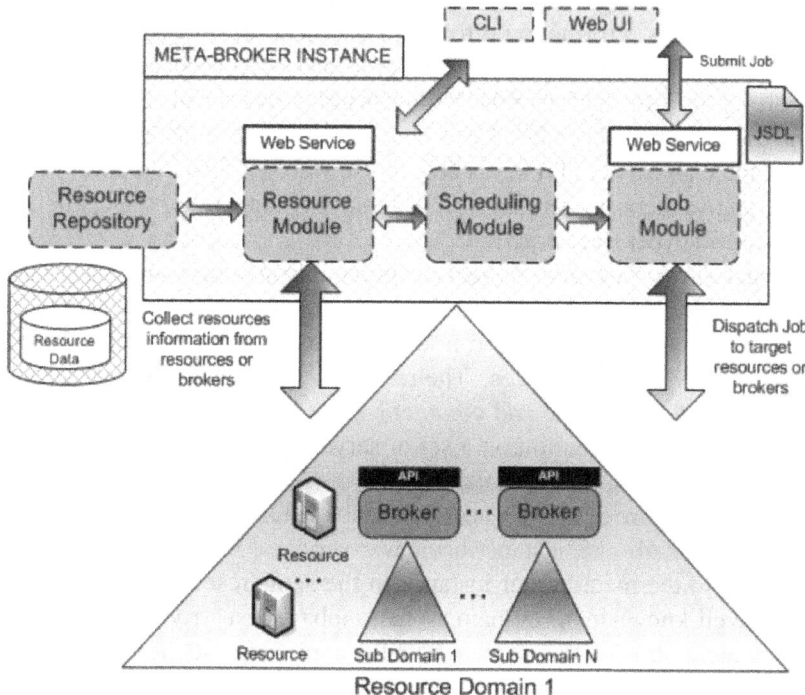

Figure 3. Meta-broker in LA Grid

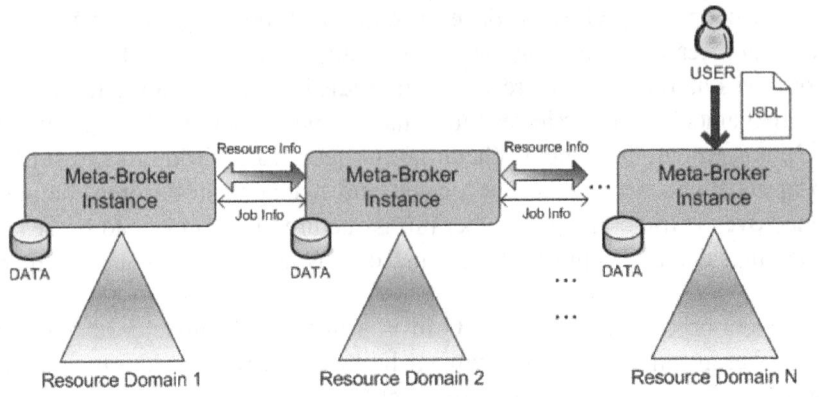

Figure 4.   Meta-broker communication model in LA Grid

In LA Grid, resources of different institutions belong to their respective resource domains and each resource domain has a meta-broker instance (see Figure 5). Inside a domain, a meta-broker instance controls resources directly and/or indirectly through other brokers in the domain. In the former case, each resource reports its information directly to the meta-broker instance using resource modules web services. In the latter case, an existent broker is responsible for reporting the information of the resources under its control. How the broker collects the resource information is within its own implementation details. In this way, once an existent broker is able to use web services to report resource information to a meta-broker instance, different existent brokers can participate in the LA Grid cyber infrastructure.

Each meta-broker instance collects resource information from its neighbors and save the information in its resource repository or in-core memory. The resource information is distributed in the Grid and each meta-broker instance will have a view of all resources. The resources information is in aggregated forms to save storage space and communication bandwidth. Example of aggregated resource information on a set of servers in a domain is: type=CPU; speed={1G,2G}; OS=Win; quantity=3.

As shown in Figure 5, a job request is described in JSDL and can be submitted to any known meta-broker instance using web services. In general, a job request is submitted to the meta-broker instance in the same resource domain whose address is well-known in the domain. When a job request arrives, a meta-broker instance matches the job to a domain with the appropriate set of resources. The matching algorithm is influenced by multiple factors. One of the factors is the location of resources such that the preference will be given to the local domain at which the job is submitted.

If the matched resources are outside of the domain, the job is dispatched to the meta-broker instance in another domain. The existent broker or meta-broker instance that the job is dispatched to has the resources required by the job and will be responsible to dispatch the job again if necessary. The resource, existent broker or meta-broker instance that the job is dispatched to will report the job status back to the original meta-broker instance.

In summary, we define a set of web services provided by meta-broker and make the incorporation of meta-brokers easy. We store a view of global resources in each meta-broker instance to provide speedy resource matching. Thus, users can experience short response time. Though storing a view of global resource locally costs storage space and communication bandwidth, we apply multiply technologies to reduce the overhead and to keep a similar performance with a incomplete view of global resources. Due to the space limitation, we shall report our efforts in these perspectives in a separate paper.

5.3 Summary of meta-brokering designs

In Figure 5, we summarize the main functionalities and some details for the discussed approaches: the original HPC-Europa approach, the HPC-Europa extension, and the LA Grid project.

	HPC-Europa	Extended HPC-Europa	LA Grid
Architecture	Centralized	Centralized	Distributed + P2P
Addressing mechanism	Plugins	Plugins	WS-addressing
Capabilities mechanism	Plugins + MultiGrid Service Provider	Plugins + MultiGrid Service Provider	Service Provider
Capability description lang.	API + XML	API + XML	API + XML
Job Submission	JSDL schema + ext.	JSDL schema + ext.	JSDL schema + ext.
Monitoring	XML schema	XML schema	XML schema
Accounting	NO	XML schema	To be defined
Scheduling	NO	XML schema (future JSDL)	XML schema (as a resource type)
Agreement	NO	WS-Agreement extension	WS-Agreement ext.
Job Description Language	JSDL 1.0 + ext.	JSDL 1.0 + ext.	JSDL 1.0 + ext.
Global identifiers	NO	YES	YES
Notification mechanism	NO	Callbacks	Callbacks
Agreement mechanism	NO	Centralized	P2P
Security	X.509 Certificates	X.509 Certificates	To be defined

Figure 5. Summary of the main functionalities of the discussed approaches

6. Conclusions and Future Work

In this paper we have discussed the convenience of the meta-brokering approach to achieve a single point of access to the Grid and to access to more resources. We also have seen how some initiatives have been carried out as the HPC-Europa project. However, they need to be extended to achieve a real global scheduling on top of different brokering systems.

One important issue to take into account is the additional overhead added to the infrastructure with another layer. We can argue that in each layer of the infrastructure the scheduling and management system is oriented to a particular target. Moreover, incorporating another layer is acceptable because of the Grid environment characteristics (e.g., timeouts are longer).

Furthermore, from the experience obtained from the HPC-Europa project, we have presented the main issues to be taken into account to develop a meta-broker. We also have proposed to use some standards to implement such an extension. We have observed a lack of a consensus in the definition of the terms used in this area (meta-scheduler, broker, meta-broker, and so on). We miss a formal definition to avoid confusions.

As for the future work we have presented two ways to achieve the meta-brokering approach. On one hand we have presented a proposal for extending the solution developed in the HPC-Europa project providing more autonomy and performance. On the other hand we have presented an overview of the distributed meta-brokering system being done in LA Grid project. Finally, we think the main line of future work regarding the meta-brokering research is toward further investigation for scheduling policies that will allow the new Grids to become transparent, autonomous and efficient.

References

[1] S. Banen, A.I.D. Bucur, and D.H.J. Epema, "A Measurement-Based Simulation Study of Processor Co-Allocation in Multicluster Systems", 9th Workshop on Job Scheduling Strategies for Parallel Processing, LNCS 2862, Seattle, 2003, pp. 105-128.

[2] F. Berman, R. Wolski, S. Figueira, J. Schopf, G. Shao, "Application-Level Scheduling on Distributed Heterogeneous Networks", Supercomputing'96, Pittsburgh, PA, November 17-22, 1996.

[3] J. Brooke, D. Fellows, K. Garwood, C. Goble, "Semantic Matching of Grid Resource Descriptions", LNCS 3165, January 2004, pp. 240-249.

[4] R. Buyya, "Economic-based Distributed Resource Management and Scheduling for Grid Computing", Ph.D. Thesis, Monash University, Melbourne, Australia, April 12, 2002.

[5] A.B. Downey, "Using queue time predictions for processor allocation", 3rd Workshop on Job Scheduling Strategies for Parallel Processing, LNCS 1291, 1997, pp.35-57.

[6] P.A. Dinda, "The statistical properties of host load", Scientific Programming, 1999.

[7] R. Gibbons, "A historical application profiler for use by parallel schedulers", Workshop on Job Scheduling Strategies for Parallel Processing, 1997.

[8] GRIA project Web Site. http://www.gria.org

[9] Grid Resource Management System (GRMS) Web Site. http://www.gridlab.org/grms

[10] GridWay Web Site. http://www.gridway.org

[11] F. Guim, J. Corbalan, J. Labarta, "Analyzing loadleveler historical information for performance prediction", Jornadas de Paralelismo, Granada, Spain, September 13-16, 2005.

[12] F. Guim, I. Rodero, J. Corbalan, J. Labarta, A. Oleksiak, J. Nabrzyski, "Uniform job monitoring using the HPC-Europa single point of access", Intl. Workshop on Grid Testbeds, in conjunction with CCGrid2006, Singapore, May 16-19, 2006.

[13] J. Frey, T. Tannenbaum, M. Livny, I. Foster, S. Tuecke, "Condor-G: A Computation Management Agent for Multi-Institutional Grids", 10th IEEE International Symposium on High Performance Distributed Computing, San Francisco, August, 2001.

[14] HPC-Europa Web Site. http://www.hpc-europa.org

[15] JOSH. http://gridengine.sunsource.net/josh.html

[16] A. Kertész, P. Kacsuk, "Grid Meta-Broker Architecture: Towards an Interoperable Grid Resource Brokering Service", CoreGRID Workshop on Grid Middleware, August, 2006.

[17] K. Kurowski, J. Nabrzyski, A. Oleksiak, J. Weglarz, "Multicriteria Aspects of Grid Resource Management", Grid Resource Management, J. Nabrzyski, J. Schopf, J. Weglarz (Eds), Kluwer Academic Publishers, Boston/Dordrecht/London, 2003.

[18] LA Grid Web Site. http://www.lagrid.fiu.edu

[19] C. Mastroianni, D. Talia, O. Verta, "A Super-Peer Model for Building Resource Discovery Services in Grids: Design and Simulation Analysis", European Grid Conference 2005, LNCS 3470, Amsterdam, The Netherlands, 14-16 February, 2005, pp. 132-143.

[20] K. Nadiminti, S. Venugopal, H. Gibbins, R. Buyya, "The Gridbus Broker Manual (v.2.0)", http://www.gridbus.org/broker

[21] OGF OGSA Resource Selection Services WG Web Site. https://forge.gridforum.org/sf/projects/ogsa-rss-wg

[22] OGF Grid Scheduling Architecture RG Web Site. https://forge.gridforum.org/sf/projects/gsa-rg

[23] A. Oleksiak, A. Tullo, P. Graham, T. Kuczynski, J. Nabrzyski, D. Szejnfeld, T. Sloan, "HPC-Europa: Towards Uniform Access to European HPC Infrastructures", 6th IEEE/ACM International Workshop on Grid Computing, Seattle, USA, 2005.

[24] I. Rodero, J. Corbalan, R. M. Badia, J. Labarta, "eNANOS Grid Resource Broker", EGC 2005, LNCS 3470, Amsterdam, The Netherlands, 14-16 February, 2005, pp. 111-121.

[25] I. Rodero, F. Guim, J. Corbalan, J. Labarta, "eNANOS: Coordinated Scheduling in Grid Environments", Parallel Computing, Malaga, Spain, 12-16 September, 2005, pp. 81-88.

[26] V. Subramani, R. Kettimuthu, S. Srinivasan, P. Sadayappan, "Distributed Job Scheduling on Computational Grids Using Multiple Simultaneous Requests", 11th Symposium on High Performance Distributed Computing, Edinburg, Scotland, 24-26 July, 2002, p. 369.

[27] D. Talby, D. Tsafrir, Z. Goldberg, D.G. Feitelson, "Session-based and estimation-less runtime prediction algorithms for parallel and grid scheduling", Technical Report, School of Computer Science and Engineering and the Hebrew University of Jerusalem, 2006.

[28] UNICORE Web Site. http://www.unicore.org

[29] Universally Unique Identifier. RFC 4122. http://www.ietf.org/rfc/rfc4122.txt

PREEMPTION AND SHARE CONTROL IN PARALLEL GRID JOB SCHEDULING

Bryan Esbaugh and Angela C. Sodan
University of Windsor
Computer Science, 401 Sunset Ave., Windsor, Ontario, N9B3P4
Canada
esbaugh@uwindsor.ca
acsodan@uwindsor.ca

Abstract   Computational grids typically involve parallel machines at the sites of the grid. We apply a grid model where the grid scheduler potentially negotiates scheduling of remote jobs for guaranteed start times with site schedulers that operate independently and autonomously. Then, response times are a main criterion to decide where to place a job for remote execution and job placement may involve advanced reservations. The latter are known to have negative impact on the response times of local jobs. In previous work, we have shown that adaptive resource allocation and gang scheduling can reduce this impact and therefore support advanced reservations. However, gang scheduling has the disadvantage of a high memory pressure. We present an approach for coarse-grain timesharing with preemption of jobs to disk. The approach is explicitly controllable regarding the resource shares allocated to different job classes with potential differentiation for different times of the day. The approach can easily be extended to support advanced reservation, group shares, and resource provisioning. The differentiation of service over the day is supported by collection and presentation of detailed statistics.

Keywords: Parallel job scheduling, preemption, time slices, fair share, advance reservation

1.   Introduction

Computational grids involve remote execution of jobs at other sites and/or simultaneous execution of jobs across multiple sites. In this paper, we focus on the former case. We apply a model where the site scheduler remains responsible for local job scheduling decisions and the grid scheduler submits jobs to the site schedulers and potentially negotiates start times with them. Thus, remote execution may or may not involve advanced reservation, i.e. the jobs may be guaranteed to start at a certain time as negotiated or simply be placed into the job scheduling queue. Reservations create road blocks in the schedule which may have negative impact on response times for local jobs as shown in [1] [3] [12] [14]. In addition, grid scheduling may lead to larger numbers of long-running jobs being executed which also may harm execution of local medium and short jobs. We aim at providing better options to deal with the execution of grid jobs and potential reservations of start times for such jobs without harming response times of local jobs.

Closely related, user satisfaction in regards to getting their jobs run on parallel machines is typically anything but good because short and medium jobs often get poor service. With our approach, we can generally provide better service to short and medium jobs.

It is necessary to modify job schedulers such that they provide more controllable response times and better service to shorter jobs and such that they can deal with reservations without harming local jobs. In [15], we have discussed various dynamic job-scheduling approaches regarding their suitability for grid scheduling and, in [14], shown that adaptive resource allocation and gang scheduling can reduce the impact of advanced reservation on the response times of local jobs. The reason is that the local jobs are given more possibilities to schedule around the reservations which create road blocks in the schedule. In this paper, we provide a practically more feasible approach to time-shared execution.

Gang scheduling creates multiple virtual machines and switches synchronously between different time slices via central control, applied to all machine nodes or hierarchically organized to subsets of them. This provides higher probabilities to get short and medium jobs scheduled quickly even in the presence of wide long-running jobs because having multiple virtual machines available to place the jobs. Time slices under gang scheduling are in the range of millisecond or a few seconds. However, gang scheduling increases the memory pressure because gang scheduling can be efficiently implemented only by keeping all active jobs in memory, meaning that the jobs from multiple slices have to share the memory [11] [15]. In addition, no explicit control regarding backfilling is provided.

Another option is to preempt jobs to disk by suspension or checkpointing and support coarse-grain time sharing (switching between jobs in long time intervals like minutes or hours) [11] or take off jobs in special cases only [5]. However, all existing preemptive approaches lack explicit control of scheduling options for individual jobs.

We present an approach which employs coarse-grain time sharing with explicit control, based on suspension of jobs to disk. Since the time slices are coarse, time slices still permit coordinated scheduling across multiple sites. In detail, our approach

- uses explicitly controlled preemption in certain long-range time slices to improve response times for short and medium jobs,

- applies safe backfilling,

- supports varying resource allocation policies over the day,

- uses a share-based control without priorities to drive the scheduling of jobs,

- supports advanced reservation for simultaneous scheduling of grid jobs.

We evaluate our approach on the basis of the simulation with large workloads, derived from the Lublin-Feitelson model, and demonstrate that our approach improves overall response times and bounded slowdown significantly, therefore being competitive to gang scheduling without the memory pressure involved in gang scheduling. We also show that especially short jobs are served very well, independent of the other jobs in the system. We obtain these results with little reduction in resource utilization.

2. Related work

Preemption has been investigated earlier and found useful in providing good utilization and response times, though only if accompanied with migration, i.e. being able to select new resources when rescheduling the job [9]. Suspension to swap disk requires continuing the job on the same resources. Migrating a job is only possible with checkpointing, but checkpointing should be done at suitable application-specific points in the execution and these may occur rather infrequently (in the order of hours based on personal communication with Sharcnet system administrators).

Gang scheduling, which switches between jobs in a coordinated manner via global time slices, is also a kind of preemption but keeps jobs in memory to reduce switching costs. Gang scheduling is known to provide better average response times and bounded slowdowns [8]. Similar benefits as from gang scheduling were found to be obtainable in [11] [16] via coarse-grain time sharing. The approach in [1] finds benefits if preempting jobs after a maximum of

1 hour runtime provided that they are over a certain size limit (this approach ignores preemption cost). This approach is also combined with migration, assuming that the application voluntarily quits and saves its state. However, these approaches do not provide any fair-share considerations. The approach in [5], however, demonstrates benefits in both average and worst-case slowdowns for all job classes with suspension only. The approach considers the relative slowdown of preemptor and preemptees and imposes limits on possible slowdown and relative sizes between preemptor and preemptees to avoid that long-running jobs suffer disadvantages.

Job schedulers normally apply backfilling which permits jobs to move ahead vs. their normal scheduling position to better utilize space. Conservative backfilling only permits this to happen if no other job in the queue is delayed. EASY backfilling only guarantees the first job in the waiting queue not to be delayed. Optimistic/speculative backfilling permits jobs to backfill even if their estimated runtimes are longer than the available backfill window by terminating and restarting them later if their actual runtimes conflict with the reservation times of other jobs [10]. In [13], different heuristics are investigated for deciding which jobs to preempt if multiple backfilled jobs run beyond the backfill window. Runtime-used and runtime-remaining were found to be the best heuristics.

Fair share scheduling was first proposed by Maui [4] though now other schedulers like LSF have included fair-share ideas, too. Maui maintains shares per user or group over time and adjusts them by considering the recent past time intervals and weighing them exponentially. Moreover, Maui pioneered the idea of combining different factors: political priorities (like group), system priorities, and user priorities. The combination of factors is then translated into priorities. The actual scheduling adds a potentially very relaxed EASY backfilling scheme (if reserving the first job of the queue only). Moab [7] is a commercial extension of Maui with more differentiated optimization and priority approaches and also supports of preemption, which can optionally be applied upon failure to meet fair share targets, upon backfilled jobs running into reservations, upon expected response times becoming too long, or upon jobs with higher priority arriving. However, the actual algorithms are not revealed.

3.   Preemption and share control

3.1   The basic approach

The basic idea of our approach is coarse-grain time sharing with time slices in the minute (or potentially hour) range. This permits suspension of jobs to disk, keeping all memory available for the next running job, and making the overhead tolerable, while accomplishing similar benefits as gang scheduling.

The time slices are primarily designated for certain job classes, i.e. each slice has a specific dominant job type. This permits for example a differentiation into short-job, medium-job, and long-job time slices. This approach provides a basis to perform controlled resource allocation for the different job classes.

In addition, we permit definition of certain resources shares (ratios of the overall resource utilization) to be defined for different job classes in different time intervals of the day. These shares are mapped to corresponding lengths of the time slices. Shares express which jobs should run at each time of the day but also indirectly determine the priority given to a job class. Thus, it makes sense to allocate higher possible shares to a job class than its average usage is (as we have done in our experiments for medium jobs). The expected benefits of our overall approach are

- To make sure that short jobs can be scheduled, independent of the currently running medium and long jobs (i.e., a wide job cannot block a short job from running) and independent of their own size (i.e. also wide short jobs, though occurring infrequently, can be served well).

- Consequently also to be able to serve medium jobs well in the presence of wide long-running jobs and being able to control how certain job classes are served over the day, e.g. to provide less share for long jobs at daytime and more at night time.

- To avoid problems like stranded jobs which may result from preemption of individual jobs by preempting the whole group of running jobs.

In addition, we have a more explicit handle to control resource allocation to jobs than using the typical priority approach which keeps the effects hard to understand and can lead to undesirable cases like a wide long-running job finally ending up being scheduled during the day.

A potential problem is that the differentiation of job classes into different time slices leads to fragmentation. However, we permit limited backfilling of other job classes and merging of slices under certain conditions as described below.

We also support reservation. If a job is reserved, it starts in a specific time interval and is always scheduled at the beginning of the interval (to make globally simultaneous scheduling possible) with a certain share.

3.2 Share definition and handling, slice calculation

We split the 24 hours of the day into a number of equidistant time intervals and permit target ratios for different job classes to be defined for every time interval. This task may be done by system administrators, based on feedback from job traces regarding the overall typical job mixes. Site policies may then determine how much resource share is allocated to different job classes at different times of the day.

To keep slice handling manageable, we define slices per each interval, i.e. we keep fixed boundaries for the slices, see Figure 1. Thus, we may have one short-job slice, one medium-job time slice, and one long-job time slice per 30 minute interval. We define the slices at the beginning of the time interval, while deciding the slice lengths for the different job classes on the basis of the target ratios. However, short jobs are handled separately and get a slice length according to the longest waiting short job. Thus, short jobs are not preempted except as a result of being backfilled into a non-short time slice. The remaining time of the time interval is split according to the ratios defined among the other job classes. If no jobs of a certain class are available, the share is attributed to another class for the corresponding interval. If using short, medium, and long job classes, the ratio defines how the time is split among medium and long jobs.

Accounting considers all used shares from the different job classes per time interval, with the sum representing the machine utilization for the time interval. The accounting considers jobs backfilled into a slice that is basically designated for a different class. In addition, it can happen that in certain time intervals no jobs of a specific class are available. Thus, we apply an adjustment of share allocation, based on target shares and past usage, with the latter being considered for a certain past time window and weights declining exponentially with time distance. Note that this corresponds to the fair-share idea as introduced by the Maui job scheduler [4]. We use m different weights, calculated as $A * B^m$ with $0 < B < 1$. B determines how quickly the weights decline and $A * \sum_{i=1,m} B^i$ determines the impact given to the past. Then, the share allocation is adapted to variations in job submission within the range of the typical job mix. See Figure 2.

For reservation, we implement a simple scheme as proof of concept (more advanced approaches like reserving a specific share are easily possible). We split the medium or long share in half to accomodate reservations and schedule the reserved-job slice as the first slice in the interval.

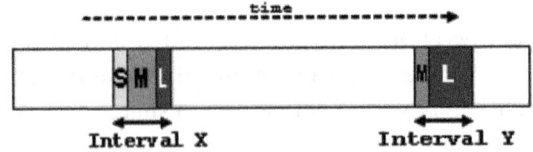

Figure 1.   Share allocation in different intervals during different times of the day. S are short, M medium, and L long-running jobs.

```
// calculate medium share, considering used vs. available shares
diffEShares[M] = 0; diffEShares[L]=0;
for (i in pastSlicesInWindow)
    diffEShares[M]+=weights[i] * (share[slot[i]]-usedShares[slot[i]][M]);
    diffEShares[L]+=weights[i] * ((1-share[slot[i]])-usedShares[slot[i][L]);
diffEshares[M] /= nPastSlicesInWindow;  diffEShares[L] /= nPastSlicesInWindow;

// M got too little, check whether L got too much or other:low load or too much S
if (diffEShares[M] > 0+delta && diffEShares[L] < 0-delta )
    targetShare=
      min(share[timeInterval]+diffEShares[M],maxShare([timeInterval][M]);
// M got too much
if (accumShareLong > = 0+delta)
    targetShare=max(share[timeInterval]-diffEshares[L],minShare[timeInterval][L]);

shortTime = maximumShortRuntime(shortJobs);
if (shortTime > 0)
    availSliceTime -= shortTime + switchOverhead;

if (mediumJobs)
  { if (longJobs)
      { mediumTime = targetShare * availSliceTime;
        longTime = availSliceTime - mediumTime - 2* switchOverhead;  }
    else {mediumTime = availSliceTime - switchOverhead;
        longTime = 0; }
else (if longJobs)
        {mediumTime = 0; longtime = availSliceTime - switchOverhead; }
    else { mediumTime = availSliceTime - switchOverhead; longTime = 0; }
```

Figure 2.   Share allocation algorithm.

3.3   Scheduling with controlled backfilling into time slices

At the beginning of each time interval, time slices of the different types for the corresponding job classes are obtained, according to the description in Section 3.2. Time slices of different types (designed to a specific job class) are currently always scheduled in the same order for each time interval, i.e. from short to long. The initial allocation for each time slice is the set of jobs that were preempted when the corresponding time slice (of same type) in the previous time interval ended. This permits jobs to be re-started on the same resources. Then, the scheduler attempts to allocate jobs of the job class which corresponds to the slice type from the head of the preemption and waiting queues. The resource-allocation approach is either first-fit or a smart-node selection heuristic as described below. Afterwards, the scheduler attempts to backfill as described below. The scheduling order per job class is FIFO. This is feasible because we no longer need priorities to give shorter-running jobs better service.

Our basic backfilling approach is EASY, adjusted to work with different job classes and our time-slice restrictions. We first try to EASY backfill from the same job class. Then we backfill from other job classes, while searching the other job classes in increasing order of their runtime ranges. The latter backfilling stage applies the following rules:

1 Any preempted jobs from other slices that can fit onto the free resources are candidates for backfilling (they are handled before any waiting jobs).

2 Any waiting jobs of other classes can be backfilled if not delaying the first waiting job of the class that corresponds to the slice type of the job to be backfilled.

3 Jobs either finish before the end of the slice or run on resources which are not yet allocated in the slice of their own corresponding type and therefore can continue running in their own slice.

4 Optionally medium jobs can be backfilled into long slices and kept in these slices for future intervals.

The abstract code is shown in Figure 3. The smart node-selection heuristic tries to allocate jobs on resources which are not yet allocated to any job in any of the slices. This makes it more likely that jobs can backfill. The heuristic counts the jobs allocated per node and then selects the nodes with the lowest count. This heuristic is less important for highly loaded systems but can play a role in cases of only sporadic arrival of certain job types.

By allocating a special slice for reserved job, these get priority over all other jobs without creating collisions on resources. We provide the options to either backfill or not with non-reserved jobs.

4.   Experimental evaluation

4.1   Experimental setup

We have used the Lublin-Feitelson model [6] for the workload generation. This model is a complex statistical workload description, considering job sizes, job runtimes, and job interarrival times. The model includes correlations between sizes and runtimes, fractions of sequential jobs, fractions of power-of-two sizes, and differing inter-arrival times according to day/night-cycles. The model can be adjusted to different machine sizes. For details of the workload parameters, see 1. We have slightly modified the interarrival times and changed the α parameter from 10.23 to 10.33. This change reduces the average work creation related to available resources from 91% to 84%. The reasons are explained below.

Statistics of the workload as obtained with these settings are included in Table 1. What is interesting to observe from the workload characteristics is that

```
// schedule preempted jobs of slice type
// collisions are possible if merging slices
for (all job in preemptionQueue[sliceType])
  if (!collision) scheduleJob(job);
  else scheduleJob(shortestFinishTimeJob());

// try to schedule waiting jobs
// avoid collisions with preempted jobs if there are any
if (scheduledPreemptedJobs)
  { excludedResources = collectResourcesUsedByScheduledPreemptedJobs();
    for (job in waitingQueue[sliceType] )
      if (jobSchedulableWithExcludedNodes(job,excludedResources))
        scheduleJob(job);
      else break;
  }
else for (job in waitingQueue[sliceType])
        if (jobScheduable(job)
          scheduleJob(job);
        else break;

tryEasyBackfill (sliceType);

// try restrictive backfilling with other job types
for (queue in preemptionQueue) // sorted by increasing runtime class
  for (job in queue)
    if (jobFits() && noCollision(job,excludedResources)
      scheduleJob(job);

for (queue in waitingQueue) // sorted by increasing runtime class
  { limit = findShortestRemainingRuntime(runningQueue);
  for (job in queue)
    if (runtime(job) <= limit && jobFits() && noCollisionInOwnSlice(job,jobType)
      scheduleJob(job);
}
```

Figure 3.   Core scheduling algorithm.

though the number of short jobs is very high, the work of the short jobs is below 1%. Furthermore, the percentages are consistent for the two workloads tested.

We currently assume that runtime estimates are equal to the actual runtimes which is no serious restriction for the evaluation, considering that our scheduling approach does not depend on correct runtime estimates.

For the tests with reservation, we randomly designate a certain percentage of medium and long jobs as reserved. The reservation time is in the range $[submitTime + 0.5h, submitTime + 1h]$.

We compare our job scheduler (TSL) to standard priority scheduling (Prio). In both cases, EASY backfilling is applied. We evaluate response times, bounded slowdowns (response times relative to runtimes with a cut-off for very short jobs), and utilization. For scheduler parameters, see Table 2.

Table 1.   Workload parameters and workload statistics.

Parameter	Value
Machine size	128
Number of jobs in workload	10,000
N_{short}	63.7%
N_{medium}	19.3%
N_{long}	17.0%
$Work_{short}$	0.5%
$Work_{medium}$	26.5%
$Work_{long}$	73.5%

Table 2.   Scheduler parameters.

Paramter	Value
Interval	30 min
Job classes supported	short, medium, long
Classification short jobs	$runtime < 10$ min
Classification medium jobs	10 min sec $\leq runtime < 3$ hours
Classification long jobs	$runtime \geq 3$ hours
Classification narrow jobs	$size \leq 10\%$ machine size
Classification medium-size jobs	10% machine size $< size \leq 50\%$ machine size
Classification wide jobs	$size > 50\%$ machine size
Switch overhead	6 sec
Medium jobs' daily shares	28% over night, 44% over day
Weights, past window	$A = 2, B = 0.81, m = 6$, window is 24 hours $\rightarrow A * \sum_{i=0,m} B^m = 1,$ $minShare$=0.05, $maxShare$=0.95

4.2   Experimental results

Results for response times and bounded slowdowns are shown in Figure 2 and Figure 3. Average response times improve by 32% vs. priority scheduling and bounded slowdowns by 87%. This is similar to the results we obtained in [14]for gang scheduling (27% improvement in response times and 84% in bounded slowdowns).

The results demonstrate that short jobs are served very well. The average response time for short jobs is 12 min and the maximum response time is 2h 36min. Response times for medium jobs also decrease significantly but long jobs currently suffer, mostly due to wide long jobs. We plan to improve the scheduling of long jobs by adding additional slices for long-wide jobs in the next scheduler version. Otherwise, longer response times for long jobs are expected because long jobs get less machine share over the day. However, these good results are due to the details of our scheduling approach. If dropping backfilling with other job types and the smart node allocation, utilization drops to 62% and the average response times increase to 54h 34 min. Response times for medium wide jobs increase by a factor of about 10. This is no surprise as we lose many of the normal fill options.

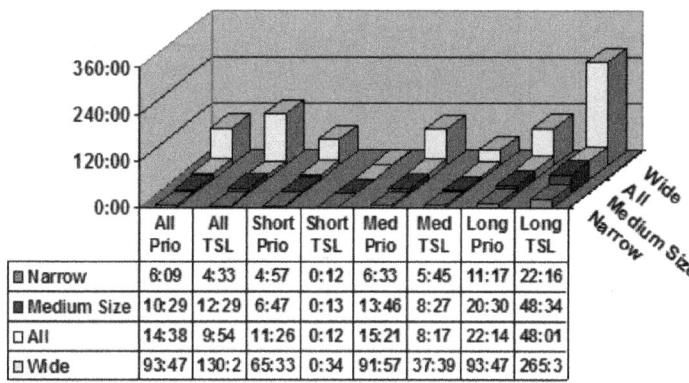

	All Prio	All TSL	Short Prio	Short TSL	Med Prio	Med TSL	Long Prio	Long TSL
Narrow	6:09	4:33	4:57	0:12	6:33	5:45	11:17	22:16
Medium Size	10:29	12:29	6:47	0:13	13:46	8:27	20:30	48:34
All	14:38	9:54	11:26	0:12	15:21	8:17	22:14	48:01
Wide	93:47	130:2	65:33	0:34	91:57	37:39	93:47	265:3

Figure 4. Average response times for the different job classes short, medium, and long and for the different sizes narrow, medium-size, and wide.

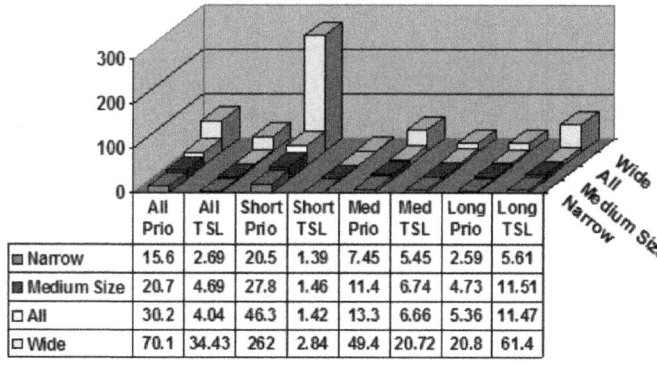

	All Prio	All TSL	Short Prio	Short TSL	Med Prio	Med TSL	Long Prio	Long TSL
Narrow	15.6	2.69	20.5	1.39	7.45	5.45	2.59	5.61
Medium Size	20.7	4.69	27.8	1.46	11.4	6.74	4.73	11.51
All	30.2	4.04	46.3	1.42	13.3	6.66	5.36	11.47
Wide	70.1	34.43	262	2.84	49.4	20.72	20.8	61.4

Figure 5. Average slowdowns for the different job classes short, medium, and long and for different sizes narrow, medium, and wide.

Our scheduling approach was capable of maintaining a high utilization: 85.92% with our scheduler vs. 88.96% with priority scheduling, i.e. the reduction in utilization is only 3%. Figure 6 and Figure 7 show that utilization is consistently high over the whole day and that the share control is effective, reducing the utilization of different job classes at different times of the day, while keeping the machine busy.

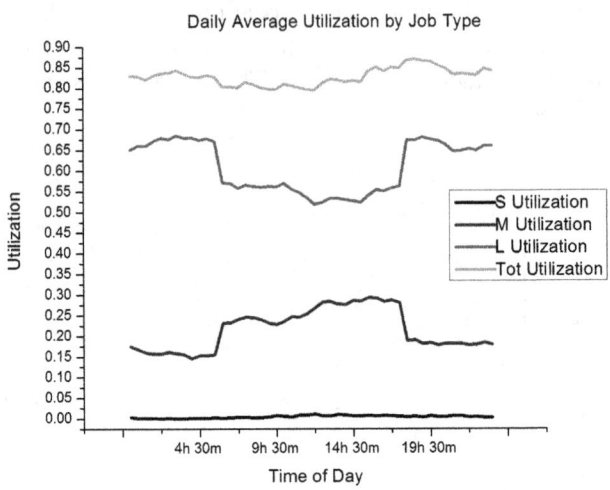

Figure 6.   Daily utilization as average over the whole workload execution.

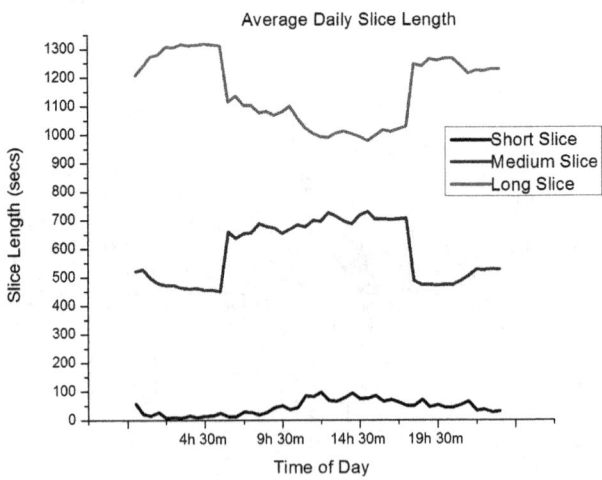

Figure 7.   Daily slice times as average over whole workload execution

Next, we show results for 5% reservation, see Figure 4. Average response times are increased by 23% for both medium jobs and long jobs. The utilization

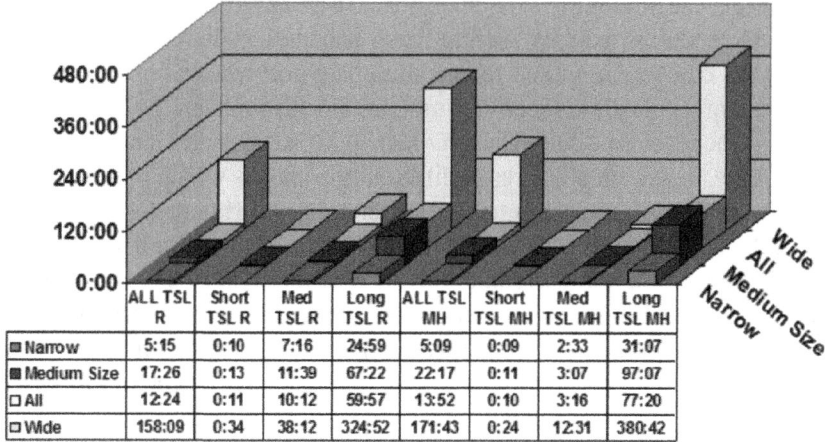

	ALL TSL R	Short TSL R	Med TSL R	Long TSL R	ALL TSL MH	Short TSL MH	Med TSL MH	Long TSL MH
▣ Narrow	5:15	0:10	7:16	24:59	5:09	0:09	2:33	31:07
▪ Medium Size	17:26	0:13	11:39	67:22	22:17	0:11	3:07	97:07
▢ All	12:24	0:11	10:12	59:57	13:52	0:10	3:16	77:20
▢ Wide	158:09	0:34	38:12	324:52	171:43	0:24	12:31	380:42

Figure 8. Average response times for TSL with 5% reservations (TSL R) and for a more sensitive priority allocation to medium jobs (TSL MH).

was 83.56% which means that the utilization drops by only by about 2%. Thus, the results are promising.

Finally, we have run the scheduler with a different fine-tuning of the share control. We now give medium jobs the maximum share if the medium work-load is high and compare the past usage to the overall averages rather than to the shares set by the scheduler. The results are shown in Figure 4. We wee that medium jobs are now served significantly better though at the expense of increasing response times for long jobs. The utilization is 82.2%, i.e. slightly decreased by 3.7%. This is not surprising. Generally speaking, our scheduler involves a trade-off between serving medium jobs well or keeping utilization high with decent response times for long jobs. The main reason is that since medium jobs are serviced quickly, fewer medium jobs queue up and therefore the options for backfilling decrease. Long jobs naturally have little potential for backfilling among each other.

5.   Summary

We have presented an approach which schedules jobs by employing coarse-grain time slicing and provides explicit control over how much time share is allocated to different job classes over the day. Time slicing is easier to handle than individual job preemption if the job allocation situation is complex (with many jobs that would need to be preempted and very different runtimes). The approach improves overall average response times and average bounded slowdowns, to a similar extent as gang scheduling. However, we accomplish this by mere suspension to disk and without any priority handling and overhead of migration and checkpointing. We therefore have a basis to deal with reservations from grid scheduling equally well as gang scheduling does [13]. Currently running jobs can be preempted to accommodate grid reservations which may be allocated in special time slices in combination with our heuristic to avoid node collisions whenever possible. The approach also provides easy and predictable control of the allocation of shares to different job classes which may be used in economic models by extension toward generation of different cost at different times of the day. The Lublin-Feitelson model used in this paper to evaluate our approach does not model correlation of job runtimes and sizes to times of the day and we expect better results with real job traces. In future work, we intend to improve our approach by special handling of wide long-running jobs and a combination of time slicing with individual job preemption (for simple cases).

References

[1] J. Cao and F. Zimmermann. Queue Scheduling and Advance Reservations with COSY. *Proc. IPDPS*, Santa Fe, April 2004.

[2] S.-H. Chiang and C. Fu. Benefit of Limited Time Sharing in the Presence of Very Large Parallel Jobs. *Proc. IPDPS*, 2005.

[3] C. Ernemann, V. Hamscher, and R. Yahyapour. Economic Scheduling in Grid Computing. *Proc. Workshop on Job Scheduling Strategies for Parallel Processing (JSSPP)*, Lecture Notes in Computer Science 2537, Springer, 2002.

[4] D. Jackson, Q. Snell, M. Clement. Core Algorithms of the Maui Scheduler. *Proc. Workshop on Job Scheduling Strategies for Parallel Processing (JSSPP)*, Lecture Notes in Computer Science 2221, Springer, 2001.

[5] R. Kettimuthu, V. Subramani, S. Srinivasan, and T. Gopalasamy. Selective Preemption Strategies for Parallel Job Scheduling. *Proc. Int. Conf. on Parallel Processing (ICPP)*, 2002.

[6] U. Lublin and D.G. Feitelson. The Workload on Parallel Supercomputers: Modeling the Characteristics of Rigid Jobs. *J. of Parallel and Distributed Computing*, 63(11):1105-1122, Nov. 2003.

[7] *Moab Workload Manager Administrator's Guide, Version 5.0.0*. Cluster Resources, available at http://www.clusterresources.com/products/ mwm/docs/index.shtml, retrieved October 2006.

[8] J.E. Moreira, W. Chan, L.L. Fong, H. Franke, and M.A. Jette. An Infrastructure for Efficient Parallel Job Execution in Terascale Computing Environments. *Proc. ACM/IEEE Supercomputing (SC)*, Nov. 1998.

[9] E.W. Parsons and K.C. Sevcik. Implementing Multiprocessor Scheduling Disciplines. *Proc. Workshop on Job Scheduling Strategies for Parallel Processing (JSSPP)*, Lecture Notes in Computer Science 1291, Springer, 1997.

[10] D. Perkovic and P.J. Keleher. Randomization, Speculation, and Adaptation in Batch Schedulers. *Proc. ACM/IEEE Supercomputing*, Dallas/TX, Nov. 2000.

[11] S. Setia, M. Squillante, and V.K. Naik. The Impact of Job Memory Requirements on Gang-scheduling Performance. *Perf. Evaluation Review*, 26(4):30-39, 1999.

[12] W. Smith, I. Foster, and V. Taylor. Scheduling with Advanced Reservations. *Proc. IPDPS*, May 2000.

[13] Q. Snell, M.J. Clement, and D.B. Jackson. Preemption Based Backfill. *Proc. Workshop on Job Scheduling Strategies for Parallel Processing (JSSPP)*, Lecture Notes in Computer Science 2537, Springer, 2002.

[14] A.C. Sodan, C. Doshi, L. Barsanti, D. Taylor. Gang Scheduling and Adaptation to Mitigate Reservation Impact. *Proc. IEEE CCGrid*, Singapore, May 2006.

[15] A.C. Sodan. Loosely Coordinated Coscheduling in the Context of Other Dynamic Approaches for Job Scheduling-A Survey. *Concurrency & Computation: Practice & Experience*, 17(15):1725-1781, Dec. 2005.

[16] A.T. Wong, L. Oliker, W.T.C. Kramer, T.L. Kaltz, and D.H. Bailey. ESP: A System Utilization Benchmark. *Proc. ACM/IEEE Supercomputing Conference (SC)*, Dallas, TX, Nov. 2000.

THE GRID BACKFILLING:
A MULTI-SITE SCHEDULING ARCHITECTURE
WITH DATA MINING
PREDICTION TECHNIQUES*

Francesc Guim, Ivan Rodero, and Julita Corbalan
Barcelona SuperComputing Center
Jordi Girona 29, 08034 Barcelona, Spain
{francesc.guim,irodero,julita.corbalan}@bsc.es

A. Goyeneche
Centre for Parallel Computing, Cavendish School of Computer Science
University of Westminster
115 New Cavendish Street, London, W1W 6UW
goyenea@wmin.ac.uk

Abstract   In large Grids, like the National Grid Service (NGS), or large distributed architecture different scheduling entities are involved. Despite a global scheduling approach would archive higher performance and could increment the utilization of global system in these scenarios usually independent schedulers carry out its own scheduling decisions. In this paper we present how a coordinated scheduling among all the different centers using data mining prediction techniques can substantially improve the performance of the global distributed infrastructure, and can provide a uniform access to the user to all the heterogeneous Grid resources. We present the Grid Backfilling meta-scheduling policy that optimizes the global utilization of the system resources and increases substantially the response time for the jobs. We also present how data mining techniques applied to historical information can provide very suitable inputs for carrying out the Grid Backfilling meta-scheduling decisions.

Keywords: Grid, meta-scheduling, backfilling, prediction

---

*This research work is carried out under the FP6 Network of Excellence CoreGRID funded by the European Commission (Contract IST-2002-004265)

1.   Introduction

The number of computational resources has increased exponentially these last decades. Scheduling policies have been adapted to these new scenarios where several independent resources have to be managed. Thus, the local policies, such as the FCFS, Gang Scheduling or Backfilling policies have also evolved to more sophisticate approaches for considering issues like multi-cluster environments, heterogeneous systems or the geographical distribution of the resources. Several global scheduling solutions have been proposed in the literature for these environments, such as centralized schedulers, centralized queues or global controllers.

The backfilling policies have been demonstrated to be the most effective policies in the local high performance computing centers. Some research works have extended the traditional backfilling policies for a distributed environments (see section 2). However one the major problem that they have is that the runtime of the scheduled applications is supposed to be known, or at least a closer estimation at submission time and should by provided by the user. However user in most of the cases will not have enough information (f.e: the user does not know in which cluster its grid application will run) or enough skills (f.e: the user just wants to submit its fluid dynamic application without knowing how many minutes it will take in a given allocation of nodes and cpus) for specify how long it will his/her job to run.

In this paper we present the Grid Backfilling scheduling policy. It extends the algorithm for the backfilling traditional policy presented in [16] for distributed architectures using a prediction service. The main goal of the presented policy is optimizing the overall performance of the system backfilling the jobs to the different available computational resources when possible requiring the minimum information from the user. In this paper we present the usage of data mining techniques for implement a prediction service that is used by the Grid Backfilling policy for estimate the job runtime. All the presented algorithms and techniques have been evaluated using a set of worklogs collected from the UK National Grid Service.

The rest of the paper is organized as follows: firstly, in the background section, we provide a discussion for the more relevant proposals concerning scheduling policies for HPC centers, including the natural evolution for the scheduling policies from local centers to more global approaches (such as: multi-site or grid architectures); secondly, we describe the Grid Backfilling meta-scheduling scheduling policy internals and the data mining techniques used for predict the run time for the jobs; and finally, we present the policy evaluation and the conclusions.

2. Background

In the area of job scheduling strategies for parallel processing the Gang Scheduling [6] and the backfilling policies have been the main goal of study these last years. Authors like Feitelson, S-H Chiang or Tsfrir have provided to the community many quality works regarding this topic. In [16] Skovira et. al presented the first paper about the EASY algorithm and its performance in the LoadLeveler system. General descriptions about the most used backfilling variants and parallel scheduling policies can be found in the report that Dror. G. Feitelson et al. provides in [7].

In the forthcoming scheduling architectures, like Grids or very heterogeneous computational resources, prediction techniques are having a crucial relevance due to user in most of the cases does not have enough information or enough skills for specify how long the job to run. Tsafrir et al. have presented several works analyzing the impact of the usage of prediction techniques rather user estimates in the backfilling policies [19]. They also formalized how the algorithm have to be extended for allow the deployment of this policies in real HPC centers.

In the current HPC infrastructures, centers may have more than one host managed by independent schedulers. In theses cases, can occurs that a job submitted to a *Host A* could start earlier in *Host B* of the same center. This global optimization has been proposed in [21] by Yue. The author proposes to apply a global backfilling within a set of independent hosts where each them is managed by an independent scheduler. The core idea of the presented algorithm is that user submits the jobs to an specific system, with an independent scheduler, and a global controller tries to find out if the job could be backfilled in another host of the center. In the case that a job can be backfilled in another host the controller will migrate the job to the chosen one. The idea is interesting due to they improve the global throughput of the center and decrease the response time of the applications. However, the algorithm requires the job runtime estimation provided by the user and not always he/she is able to provide it. This work it is only valid in very homogeneous architectures. If a job is finally executed to a different host from where the user submitted it, both configurations must be exactly the same. Otherwise, the user runtime estimation loses its validity due to it may would differ for the new host.

Similar this global backfilling approach, Sabin et al. [8] have presented the scheduling of parallel jobs in a heterogeneous multi-site environment. They propose carry out a global scheduling within a set different sites using a global meta-scheduler where users submit the jobs. Two different resource selection algorithms are proposed: the jobs are processed in order of arrival to the meta-scheduler, end each of them is assigned to the site with less instantaneous load; when the job arrives it is submitted to K different sites (each site schedules using a conservative or aggressive backfilling), once the job is started in one site the rest of submissions are canceled (technique is called multiple requests, MR). This multi-site approach still does not take into account that when the local schedulers are scheduling using the backfilling optimization the run times for the jobs may differ between two different sites.

More centralized approaches have been proposed in the literature. For instance in [5] they analyze the impact of geographical distribution of Grid resources on the machine utilization and the average response time. A centralized Grid dispatcher that controls all resource allocations is used. The local schedulers are only responsible for starting the jobs after their allocation by the Grid scheduler. Thus all the jobs are being queued in the dispatcher while the size of job wait queues of the local centers is zero. A similar approach is the once presented by Schroeder et al. in [15], where they evaluate a set of task assignment policies using the same scenario (one central dispatcher).

In [14] Pinchak et al. describe a metaqueue system to manage jobs with explicit workflow dependencies. Here the placeholder scheduling creates a user-level metaqueue that interacts with the local schedulers and queues of the overlay meta computer. In this case, instead of push model, in which jobs are submitted from the meta queue to the schedulers, placeholder is based on the pull model in which jobs are dynamically bound to the local queues on demand.

In this paper we present the Grid Backfilling scheduling policy. It extends the ideas provided by Yue, in its Global Backfilling, and uses the ideas proposed by Tsfrir about the usage of prediction in backfilling scheduling policies. The global scheduler has a reservation table with all the computational resources available on the Grid, and tries to allocate the job to the earliest available allocation. The processes of finding out the allocation is based on a prediction of the job runtime. This prediction is done using a technique built on top of C45 classifying trees, predicts the time that a given job would take to complete on a given computational node given its statical characterization.

2.1   Data mining and prediction techniques

Data mining can provide to the scheduler estimations that can guide to the meta-scheduler to carry out a more intelligent scheduling decisions. In the presented work we have derived this information correlating the past executions of similar jobs in similar resources or with similar future load using decision trees for the prediction algorithm. In the literature several prediction methodologies have been proposed. However, as will be introduced in the later paragraphs, almost all of them have been basically focused in predicting the job performance variables (such as runtime) for local environments or sites. In [10] we have proposed a set of prediction techniques that provide to the users hints about where to submit the jobs given a Grid architecture. For example, we estimate to the user how much a job will wait in a given broker before get executed with a specific job requirements (the number of processors, the input files etc.).

Works like those presented by Peter A. Dinda in [3], propose the usage of linear mathematical models for predicting the runtime for the applications submitted by the users. Dinda proposes the usage of the time series (AR, MA ARMA and ARIME) and a windowed mean for carry out host load estimations, and using such estimation for predict the job runtime. Recently, Yuanyuan presented in [22] new models, also based in time series, for predict the runtime for Grid applications. Other works [2] have proposed the usage of a state-transition model to characterize the resource usage of each program in its past executions.

In [4] Allen B. Downey characterizes the applications describing the speedup of the application on a family of curves that are parameterized by a job's average parallelism and its variance.

The other statistical approach that is also commonly used is the simulation. An example is the Dimemas simulator developed in the Barcelona Supercomputing Center [13]. The simulator reconstructs the execution trace file by estimating the time to execute each computation burst and communication burst.

Data mining techniques has became very popular during this lasts years. They are being used in a very wide range of areas, including the job performance prediction. Warren Smith et al. in [17] presented a first approximation to these techniques. Their work is mostly based on the work that previously Gibbons [9] presented before, which consisted in a static clustering of the workloads and a later usage of the mean and median inside this clusters.

3.   The Grid Backfilling policy

As has been introduced in the previous section, in multi-site or Grid architectures, the local schedulers can optimize the performance (f.e: response time) for the jobs that are currently queued to the local system or site. However, in such environments, although they are doing all the best for achieve the highest performance in the local system or site, the schedule of the whole system might be improved substantially with a global scheduling. This situation is illustrated in the figure 1a. It presents two different centers with two different schedulers. Each scheduler is carrying out a local schedule using a SJF-Backfilling allocation policy. Although the presented reservation tables are closed to the optimal in each system, there are several holes that could be filled by allocating jobs of other centers. This second situation is illustrated in the figure 1b. Jobs are scheduled using a global backfilling scheduling policy to the different centers using the meta-scheduler architecture. In this picture can be observed how the holes have been used for backfilling jobs from other centers, and how the global performance for the system (f.e: the throughput) and for the jobs (f.i: the wait time) have been improved.

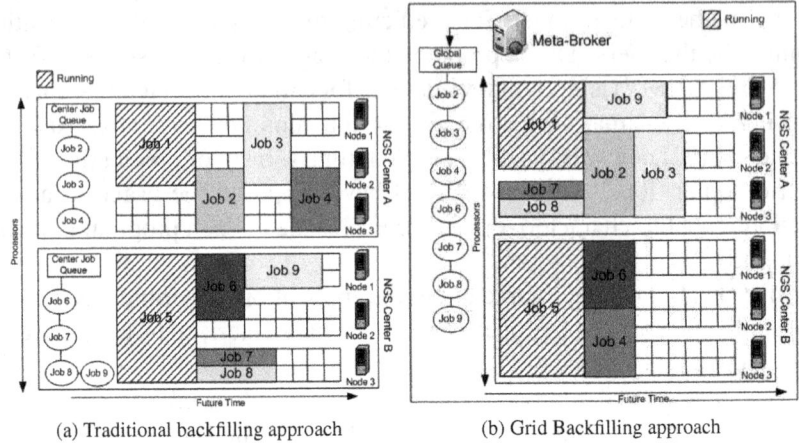

(a) Traditional backfilling approach   (b) Grid Backfilling approach

Figure 1.   Traditional VS Grid Backfilling

We define the Grid Backfilling policy based on four different events: Job arrival, Job starts, Job completion and Job deadline missed. The last event occurs when a miss-prediction in the runtime of a job occurs. The meta-scheduler is warned from the local scheduler for update its reservation table according the new estimated runtime. In the introduction section, we have already introduced the work that Tsafrir et al. have presented concerning the usage of predictors in the SJF-Backfilling policy [19]. The approach that we have followed in the design of the predictor internals, how the scheduler manages the deadline misses and how the predictor and the scheduler interacts is based on the formalizations provided in the formers work.

The different elements that are evolved in the architecture are:

- The Job α that is submitted to the system is characterized by:

    - The static description of the job $req_\alpha = \{\partial_{\{1,\alpha\}}, .., \partial_{\{n,\alpha\}}\}$ where each propierty is a pair value $\partial_{\{i,\alpha\}} = \{JobPropierty, value\}$.

- A set of computational resources $\{\sigma_1, .., \sigma_n\}$ available on the system. Like the job definition, each resource is descrived by:

    - A set of capabilities $cap_{\sigma_i} = \{\partial_{\{1,\sigma_i\}}, .., \partial_{\{n,\sigma_i\}}\}$, where each capability is composed by a pair key value
    $\partial_{\{i,\sigma_i\}} = \{ResCapability, value\}$
    (f.i: $\partial_{\{i,\sigma_i\}} = \{AvailableProcessors, 256\}$).

- The computational resource is composed by a set of nodes $\{\partial_1, .., \partial_n\}$, where each node is composed by a set of processors $\left\{\rho_{\{1,\partial\}}, .., \rho_{\{n,\partial\}}\right\}$

■ The Prediction Service γ.

■ The Meta-Scheduler β with its own global reservation table.

In the following subsections we present how the meta-scheduler behaves in each of the four enumerated events.

3.1 Job Arrival

When a job α with requirements req_α [1] is submitted to the meta-scheduler, the following scheduling algorithm is carried out:

■ It pushes the job α to the global wait queue.

■ It computes all the possible allocations to the current free nodes $outcomes_\alpha$ where the job would be able to run. Note that:

- The outcome is composed by set of nodes $\{\partial_1, .., \partial_n\}$ of the same computational resource σ_i.

- The resource σ_i satisfies the requirements of the job $\forall \partial \in cap_{\sigma_i} sat(\partial, req_\alpha)$

■ For each of the $outcomes_\alpha$ where the job would be able to run:

- It queries to the prediction service the estimation r_α of the runtime for the job α in the computational resource σ of the outcome.

- It stores the estimation and the allocation into a local hash table Ω.

■ If Ω is not empty, the meta-scheduler will choose the allocation following the backfilling algorithm $allocation_\alpha = \{\partial_1, .., \partial_n\}$ in Ω that maximizes the response time for the job. If the job can be backfilled or started (it would be the first of the wait queue), the job is deleted from the wait queue and started to run.

■ If $allocation_\alpha$ is not null. It will start the job. (see 3.2)

The priority used in the global queue is the LXWF presented by S.-H. Chiang in [1]. We have chosen this backfilling derivate due to as has been proved

---

[1] For carry out this allocation only static requirements are need from the user: the number of processors, the executable start and the input/output files. The dynamic requirements, such as the runtime, will be estimated by the prediction service

in several works [19] [1] it achieves good performance and the jobs do not suffer starvation. However, the Shortest-Job-Backfilled-First policy proposed by Tsfrir in [19] is also a valid candidate for the job selection. The evaluation results shown that both achieved similar performance.

3.2   Job starts

When a job α is chosen to start to the allocation $allocation_\alpha = \{\partial_1, .., \partial_n\}$:

- The meta-scheduler contacts to the scheduler that manages the resource specified in the allocation, provides the job credentials with it requirements and requires to start the job.

- When the job starts to run, it updates the information of the global reservation table.

- It contact to the prediction service and provide all the details the job submission, including the global id assigned to the job. This global id will be used for match the job information provided by the broker once the job is finished with its historical data base.

In this study we have considered that the local scheduler accepts the meta-scheduler resource selection about where the job has to run (nodes $\{\partial_1, .., \partial_n\}$). Thus, the local scheduler only make the resource allocation and has no say in the matter of how the scheduling is done. However, in future extensions of this policy would include interactions between all the scheduling layers of the architecture. For example, the meta-scheduler could contact to the local schedulers and start a negotiation for the acceptance of the proposed allocation

3.3   Job completion

Once the job has been executed, the scheduler contacts to the meta-scheduler providing the feedback for the job execution. This feedback includes information about variables for the job execution, for instance: run-time, disk used, memory used, final status etc. When the meta-scheduler receives a job completion notification:

- It will provide this information to the Prediction Service for allow its future usage by the prediction techniques.

- Following the algorithm presented in 3.1 it will try to allocate the head job of the global queue. If there are enough computational resources the job will start (3.2).

- Following also the same algorithm it will try to backfill (3.2) the jobs queued in the global queue. The backfilling variance used in the more aggressive once, using only one reservation. That means that jobs will be backfilling only if the start time for the first job of the queue is not delayed.

3.4 Job deadline missed

In those cases that the prediction service made a wrong prediction underestimating the runtime for the job, the local scheduler will notify to the metascheduler that a deadline missed has been reached. In normal backfilling policies, this job would be killed due to it would interfere with the execution of the following job. However, using prediction we can not take this approach. In the model proposed by Tsafrir the estimate runtime for the job is extended an t_α time. This amount of time is computed by the deadline miss managers. We have tested two times of deadline miss managers:

- Gradual Deadline miss manager: extends the job prediction runtime gradually.

- Exponential Deadline miss manager: extend the job runtime prediction in following an exponential distribution.

4. The runtime predictions

We have already emphasized that data mining techniques [13] are especially interesting because they can be applied to a very different kind of data independently of its nature. On the contrary, some statistical algorithms require the normality of the input variables for assure the correctness of the resulting conclusions. Moreover, the most interesting of their characteristics is that some of them they have an autonomic learning mechanism, and they are able to derive or discover new knowledge without the necessary interaction of a third part (user, expert or other software component).

There are several techniques can be used for the performance prediction, for example Bayessian Networks, C.45 trees, ID3 trees, K-Means or X-Means. In the presented work we have used C45 trees and discretization techniques for predicting the job runtimes. In this section we present how we have constructed and validated the model that has been used later in the grid backfilling evaluation.

4.1 The prediction model

The prediction model is built on top of the C45 decision trees algorithm. Its goal is to predict the runtime for a submitted application using the static information provided by the user. The model has been constructed and validated using the Weka [12] software and following the next steps:

- The log file used for generate the model has been preprocessed.

- The continuous variables have been converted to nominal variables.

- We have carried out an study for the selection of the response and input variables for the tree model.

- We have constructed of the decision tree validated model.

4.1.1 Log preprocessing. The log contains variables concerning the job performance (like percentage of processor used or virtual memory used), variables concerning the job identification (Grid node, job id, job owner and queue), variables concerning the data that has been used for the job execution (output, input and error paths and the working directory), and finally, variables concerning the dates of the events for the job (start time, end time, queuing time). For lack of space we do not provide a detailed analysis about the characteristics of the NGS workload used in the simulations and workload creation. However we already carried a deeper study of these traces, a characterization of them can be found in [10].

Tsafrir presented a very interesting work about detecting and deleting workload anomalies in [20]. The authors highlighted a set of phenomena, like workload flurries, that should be taken into account when analyzing workloads and proposed a set of techniques for identifying and filtering such anomalies. Before constructing the model this anomalies have been localized and deleted in the log.

4.1.2 Continuous variables discretization. We have discretized all the continuous variables into nominal values. This process has been iterated several times until find the appropriate bins according to the performance obtained in the evaluation of the resulting trees. Two different types of configurations have been tested:

- First, varying the number of been in which the continuous variables are discretized. Initially we tested several number of bins from 3 till 10. However, the final number of bins has been chose using the *findNumBins* option for the *unsupervised attribute disctretize* filter of the Weka. The interesting application of this methodology is that can be carried out in the prediction service without any external supervision.

- Secondly, varying the criteria of discretization. The options of *desired-WeightOfInstancesPerInterval*, *makeBinary* and *useEqualFrequency* for the *unsupervised attribute disctretize* filter.

The discretization for the continuous variable run time is shown in the table 1. The discretization for the rest of continous variables is not shown due to they were rejected in the construction of the C45 tree.

Table 1. Run time predictions

Interval Predicted	Numerical prediction
(-inf-12390]	12390
(12390-24780]	24780
(24780-37170]	37170
(37170-49560]	49560
(49560-inf)	49560

Table 2. Accuracy by class

TP-Rate	FP-Rate	Precision	Recall	F-Measure	Class
0.966	0.301	0.92	0.966	0.942	(-inf-12390]
0.359	0.06	0.4	0.359	0.379	(12390-24780]
0.388	0.058	0.324	0.338	0.331	(24780-37170]
0.113	0.001	0.77	0.113	0.194	(37170-49560]
0.388	0.002	0.659	0.335	0.444	(49560-inf)

4.1.3 Selection for the input variables.

The set of variables that have been chosen for built the C45 decision tree have been: executable name, number of requested processors, user id, group id and the site where the job would be submitted and the response variable runtime.

Other variables, such as the input files, working directory or output files, have been ruled out for two main reasons: the sizes of the pruned trees were big and the non availability of the variables at the submission time. Using the variables concerning the data used in the job execution resulted in a trees with a thousands of nodes with a low recall and precisions.

4.1.4 Construction and tree validation.

The resulting tree used for predicting the job runtime has 130 nodes and 120 leaves. The variables that provide more information (those that are in the upper nodes) are mainly the user credential and the number of processors used in the job execution. The resulting model has been tested using the cross validation technique with ten folds. The resulting model has classified correctly 86% of the instances. The performance of the constructed model is presented in the detailed accuracy by class presented in the table 1, and the confusion matrix 3. As can be observed in the results obtained in the cross validation analysis the model has shown good behaviour. Moreover, the main errors in the instance classification are only wrong classification between the classes *a, b and c* and we exepcted that such kind of errors should have high impact on the schedule performance.

Table 3.   Confusion matrix

a	b	c	d	e	Classified as
10354	186	160	7	15	a = (-inf-12390]
482	493	392	0	5	b = (12390-24780]
235	451	352	1	3	c = (24780-37170]
95	93	175	47	7	d = (37170-49560]
91	9	9	6	58	e = (49560-inf)

4.2   The prediction mechanism

The presented C45 tree is providing a prediction for the interval of time that a given job will need to be completed. However, the algorithm presented in the proceeding section requires a numerical value for carrying the scheduling. The prediction service, once the submitted job has been classified in one of the 5 presented classes, uses the hash 2 for return the numerical value for the estimation. The upper bound of the estimated class is used due we want to avoid overestimating the runtime for the job.

5.   The evaluation

In the experiments we have simulated four different scenarios: in the first three scenarios we have simulated independently the workload of each center using the SJF-Backfilling variant, thus we have evaluated how the different workload would behave with such policy; the last scenario has consisted on simulating the Grid Backfilling policy and the workload generated with the fusion of the four different workloads. The original log traces were collected form the NGS during five different month. In the NGS the users accessed to the different computational resources using the Globus infrastructure and they had to decide in resource their jobs had to be executed. Thereby there were no global scheduling.

The evaluation of this policy has been tested using the simulation methodology. The simulation has used a model that characterizes the computational resources for NGS architecture (see its characteristics in [10]) including the centers of Oxford, Manchester, LR and Leeds, and has simulated the Grid Backfilling policy presented in the previous sections. We have used the Alviosimulator that is a C++ event-driven simulator similar to the EASY simulator implemented by Tsafrir et al. in the paper [18], but modeling the architectures (the resources and its capabilities) for the centers.

The statistical analysis for the error in the runtime prediction using the presented prediction scheme (4) in the simulation has shown an average error of 160% and the median error is -1.7%. Our experience in the prediction errors

Table 4. Performance Variables for each workload and the Grid Backfilling

Center	Estimator	BSLD	SLD	WaitTime	Backfilled Jobs/Day
	Mean	1,1	1,9	247	0,3
Manchester	STDev	1,23	1,4	841	0,12
	95$_{th}$ Percentile	1,4	1,8	123	1
	Mean	2,4	2,5	4266,2	0,37
Leeds	STDev	3,6	3,8	3150	1,9
	95$_{th}$ Percentile	4,3	4,21	19856	2,4
	Mean	2,8	3,03	1182	2,3
LR	STDev	23	27,1	4307,3	1,2
	95$_{th}$ Percentile	2,3	2322	6223	3
	Mean	4,04	5,9	6390	1,3
Oxford	STDev	29	89,2	19420	4
	95$_{th}$ Percentile	9,1	10,1	54750	8
	Mean	1,12	1,17	153,32	3,5
GridBackfilling	STDev	0,5	0,45	1200,25	5,1
	95$_{th}$ Percentile	1,4	1,9	2200.25	14

evaluation has shown this prediction performance values can be used to understand how well the predictor behaves. However, the real benefit of the usage of a given prediction technique relies on the performance achieved on a specific scheduling policy. As has been stated in the simulation results the errors that prediction service had during the simulation were acceptable and demostrated that the presented architecture can be deployed in real systems.

Table 4 presents the average, standard deviation and $95_{th} Percentile$ for the variables Slowdown, Bounded Slowdown, Wait time and Backfilled Jobs per day for each center independently and for the global architecture with the Grid Backfilling policy. It is clear that a global scheduling carried out in top of all the centers improves qualitatively the service provided and reduces substantially the response time for the submitted jobs. The average wait time of all the centers has been reduced qualitatively. For instance the Manchester average wait is almost two times bigger than the average wait time experimented in the Grid Backfilling. Furthermore, the average wait time of the Oxford center is around forty times bigger than the Grid Backfilling once. The variable *Backfilled Jobs/Day* shows how the global backfilling approach give more chances to the jobs to start earlier rather than using independent scheduling per centers. The percentile 95_{th} shows how the ratio of backfilled jobs is at minimum two times bigger than the once achieved in the independent configurations.

6.   Conclusions and future work

In this paper we have presented the usage of backfilling scheduling techniques in distributed environments using a global reservation table and prediction techniques. We have shown how the analyzed policy provides a uniform access to the whole computational resources available in the environment and how it achieves good performance optimizing the usage of all the available resources. The policy has been evaluated using logs collected from the National Grid Service that contained the jobs that user submitted during four months to each of the four centers: Oxford, Leeds, Manchester and LR. The average wait and average wait time for all the jobs submitted to the Grid has been reduced one order of magnitude respect to the average wait time that the job of the same workloads had in the original architecture.

The usage of prediction techniques in scheduling policies has been proposed in several works for usage of such prediction rather user estimates in the scheduling decisions. In this paper we have also presented how data mining techniques are very suitable for predicting the run time for Grid environments, and how they can be used in the Grid Backfilling with high success. We have presented a prediction methodology based on classification trees C45 that having as an input static information about the job (executable name and number of requested processors) predicts the run time for this job in a given site or center. The predictions have shown only a median of error of -1.7% respect the original runtime, and a mean of 160%. The real benefit of the usage of a given prediction technique has been proved on the performance achieved scheduling policy evaluation. The usage of such techniques is specially important due to abstarct the user to the underlying complexities of the system, and allows to the scheduler to decide where to submit jobs having an estimation of how long this job would run in each of the possible allocations.

Future extensions of this policy will include interactions between all the scheduling layers of the architecture. In this extension, the meta-scheduler would reach an agreement with the local schedulers in terms of where the job can be finally allocated. On the other hand, the current allocation selection algorithm is focused on optimizing the response time for the submitted applications and does not take into account other of its requirements. We would like to take in to account economic criteria's, soft and hard requirements or resource matching criteria in the allocation selection.

References

[1] S.-H. Chiang, A. C. Arpaci-Dusseau, and M. K. Vernon. The impact of more accurate requested runtimes on production job scheduling performance. 8th International Workshop on Job Scheduling Strategies for Parallel Processing, Vol. 2537:103 – 127, 2002.

[2] M. V. Devarakonda and R. K. Iyer. Predictability of process resource usage : A measurement based study on unix. IEEE Tans. Sotfw. Eng., pp. 1579–1586, 1989

[3] P. Dinda. Online prediction of the running time of tasks. Cluster Computing SIGMETRICS/Performance, pages 225–236, 2002.

[4] A. B. Downey. Using queue time predictions for processor allocation. 3rd JSSPP, Lecture Notes In Computer Science; Vol. 1291:35 – 57, 1997.

[5] C. Ernemann, V. Hamscher, , and R. Yahyapour. Benefits of global grid computing for job scheduling. 5th IEEE/ACM International Workshop on Grid Computing, 2004.

[6] D. G. Feitelson and M. A. Jette. Improved utilization and responsiveness with gang scheduling. pages 238–261, 1997.

[7] D. G. Feitelson, L. Rudolph, and U. Schwiegelshohn. Parallel job scheduling - a status report. Job Scheduling Strategies for Parallel Processing: 10th International Workshop, JSSPP 2004, 3277 / 2005:9, June 2004.

[8] S. Gerald, K. Rajkumar, R. Arun, and S. Ponnuswamy. Scheduling of parallel jobs in a heterogeneous multi-site environment. JSSPP, 2003.

[9] R. Gibbons. A historical application profiler for use by parallel schedulers. Job Scheduling Strategies for Parallel Processing 1997, 1997.

[10] A. Goyenechea, F. Guim, I. Rodero, G. Terstyansky, and J. Corbalan. Extracting performance hints for grid users using data mining techniques: a case study in the ngs. "Mediterranean Journal: Special issue on data mining, 2006.

[11] J. Han and M. Kamber. Book: Data mining: Concepts and techniques. Book, 2001.

[12] G. Holmes, A. Donkin, and I. Witten. Weka: A machine learning workbench. In Proc 2nd Australia and New Zealand Conf. on Intelligent Information Systems, 1994

[13] T. C. Jess Labarta, Sergi Girona. Analyzing scheduling policies using dimemas. 3rd Workshop on environment and tools for parallel scientific computation, 1997.

[14] C. Pinchak, P. Lu, and M. Goldenberg. Practical heterogeneous placeholder scheduling in overlay metacomputers: Early experiences. Job Scheduling Strategies for Parallel Processing, pages 205–228, 2002. Lect. Notes Comput. Sci. vol. 2537.

[15] B. Schroeder and M. Harchol-Balter. Evaluation of task assignment policies for supercomputing servers: The case for load unbalancing and fairness. Cluster Computing 2004.

[16] J. Skovira, W. Chan, H. Zhou, and D. A. Lifka. The easy - loadleveler api project. Proceedings of the Workshop on Job Scheduling Strategies for Parallel Processing, Lecture Notes In Computer Science; Vol. 1162 archive:41 – 47, 1996.

[17] W. Smith, V. E. Taylor, and I. T. Foster. Using run-time predictions to estimate queue wait times and improve scheduler performance. Proceedings of the Job Scheduling Strategies for Parallel Processing, Lecture Notes In Computer Science; Vol. 1659:202 – 219, 1999.

[18] D. Tsafrir, Y. Etsion, , and D. G. Feitelson. Modeling user runtime estimates. In the 11th JSSPP ,Lecture Notes in Computer Science, Vol.3834:pp. 1–35, 2006.

[19] D. Tsafrir, Y. Etsion, and D. G. Feitelson. Backfilling using system-generated predictions rather than user runtime estimates. In the IEEE TPDS, 2006.

[20] D. Tsafrir and D. G. Feitelson. Instability in parallel job scheduling simulation: the role of workload flurries. In 20th Intl. Parallel and Distributed Processing Symp, 2006.

[21] J. Yue. Global backfilling scheduling in multiclusters. Asian Applied Computing Conference, AACC 2004, pages pp. 232–239, 2004.

[22] Y. Zhang, W. Sun, , and Y. Inoguchi. Cpu load predictions on the computational grid. Cluster and Grid computing, 2006.

II

STORAGE AND DATA MANAGEMENT

CACHE-ENABLED SUPER-PEER OVERLAYS FOR MULTIPLE JOB SUBMISSION ON GRIDS

Pasquale Cozza and Domenico Talia
DEIS, University of Calabria, Rende (CS), Italy
{pcozza,talia}@deis.unical.it

Carlo Mastroianni
ICAR-CNR, Rende (CS), Italy
mastroianni@icar.cnr.it

Ian Kelley and Ian Taylor
School of Computer Science, Cardiff University, UK
{I.R.Kelley,Ian.J.Taylor}@cs.cardiff.ac.uk

Abstract   Many types of distributed scientific and commercial applications require the submission of a large number of independent jobs. One highly successful and low cost mechanism for acquiring the necessary compute power is the "public-resource computing" paradigm, which exploits the computational power of private computers. Recently decentralized peer-to-peer and super-peer technologies have been proposed for adaptation in these systems. A super-peer protocol, proposed earlier by this group, is used for the execution of jobs based upon the volunteer requests of workers, and a super-peer overlay is used to perform two kinds of matching operations: the assignment of jobs to workers and providing workers the input data needed for job execution. This paper extends this super-peer protocol to account for a more dynamic and general scenario, in which: (i) workers can leave the network at any time; (ii) each job is executed multiple times, either to obtain better statistical accuracy or to perform parameter sweep analysis; and, (iii) input data is replicated and distributed to multiple data caches on-the-fly, in an effort to improve performance in terms of data availability, fault tolerance and execution time. A simulation study was performed to analyze the latest iteration of the super-peer protocol and specifically evaluate the new features.

Keywords: Grid, data caching, job execution, public resource computing, super-peer.

1.   Introduction

Distributed computing has in recent years become the next technological evolution in the high-performance and consumer computing fields. Grid computing and Peer-to-Peer (P2P) networking are two sets of such technologies that have partly addressed issues in that area and even though they have evolved from different communities, it has started to become desirable in the academic and industrial arenas to explore possible areas of convergence [12]. Super-peer systems have been proposed [10] [13] to achieve a balance between the inherent efficiency of centralized networks, and the autonomy, load balancing and fault-tolerant features offered by P2P networks. In such systems, a "super-peer" node can act as a centralized resource for a limited number of regular "peer" nodes, in a fashion similar to a current Grid system. At the same time, super peers can make interconnections with other super-peers to form a P2P overlay network at a higher level, thereby enabling distributed computing on much larger scales.

The term "public resource computing" [1] is used for applications in which jobs are executed by privately-owned and often donated computers that use their idle CPU time to support a given (normally scientific) computing project. The pioneer project in this realm is SETI@HOME [3], which has attracted millions of participants wishing to contribute to the digital processing of radio telescope data in the search for extra-terrestrial intelligence. A number of similar projects are supported today by the BOINC (Berkeley Open Infrastructure for Network Computing [2]) software infrastructure. The range of scientific objectives amongst these projects is very different, ranging from Climate@HOME's [4], which focuses on long-term climate prediction, to Einstein@HOME's [7], aiming at the detection of certain types of gravitational waves.

This paper reports on a super-peer based distributed model, firstly proposed by this group in [6], that supports applications requiring the distributed execution of a large number of jobs with similar properties to current public-resource computing systems like BOINC. Unlike BOINC, the data distribution scheme outlined here does not heavily rely on any centralized mechanisms for job and data distribution. To adapt to a P2P environment, the super-peer job submission protocol requires that job execution is preceded by two *matching* phases, the first for job assignment and the second for downloading of input data from *data centers*, which are super-peers having data storage facilities.

In the work here, we extend and enhance the data distribution scheme defined in [6] and refine its analysis to account for a more dynamic and general scenario, in which: (i) workers can leave the network at any time; (ii) each job is executed multiple times, either to obtain better statistical accuracy or to perform parameter sweep analysis; and, (iii) input data is replicated and distributed to multiple data centers on-the-fly, in an effort to improve protocol performance in terms of data availability, fault tolerance and execution time. To demonstrate these concepts, a set of simulation runs have been performed to evaluate the impact of the replication and caching mechanisms on performance indices, specifically regarding the overall time needed to execute the chosen jobs and the average utilization of data centers.

The remainder of the paper is organized as follows. Section 2 discusses related work in the field and shows how the proposed architecture here goes beyond currently supported models. Section 3 presents the super-peer model and the related protocol. Performance is analyzed in Section 4, and conclusions and future work are discussed in Section 5.

2. Related Work

Desktop Grids, in the form of volunteer computing systems, have become extremely popular as a means to garnish many resources for a low cost in terms of both hardware and manpower. The most popular volunteer computing platform currently available, the BOINC infrastructure [2] is composed of a scheduling server and a number of clients installed on users' machines. The client software periodically contacts the scheduling server to report its hardware and availability, and then receives a given set of instructions for downloading and executing a job. After a client completes the given task, it then uploads resulting output files to the scheduling server and requests more work.

The BOINC middleware is especially well suited for CPU-intensive applications but is somewhat inappropriate for data-intensive tasks due to its centralized nature that currently requires all data to be served by a set group of centrally maintained servers. BOINC allows a project to configure a fixed and static set of data servers that are maintained for a particular project and made available for data distribution. Although this scheme enables a number of servers to help load balance the network and scales well for the current applications utilizing BOINC, the topology is static and has a number of problems scaling if more data-intensive applications are introduced. For example, under the current system, an administrator must dedicate time to configure and maintain these data serving machines, which are generally independent for each BOINC project. Such machines are costly to purchase and maintain, additionally they are centrally administered; therefore cannot generally be used by other BOINC projects. The real cost, however, generally lies with the expenditure required to maintain the needed network bandwidth to support a project, especially given the extremely large scale of some public resource computing projects.

Peer-to-Peer (P2P) data sharing networks have proven to be effective in distributing both small and large files across public computing platforms in a relatively efficient manner that utilizes both participants' upload and download bandwidth. Popular super-peer based networks among these system are the Napster [11] and Kazaa projects [9]. Recently, BitTorrent [5] has become the most widely used and accepted protocol for P2P data distribution, relying on a centralized tracking mechanism to monitor and coordinate file sharing. Although this approach has proved quite scalable and efficient, it might not be appropriate to scientific volunteer computing platforms due to its "tit for tat" requirement that necessitates a ratio between upload and download bandwidth, thus requiring peers to share data if they are recipients of it on the network. Such stringent requirements are likely to prove problematic for volunteer computing platforms. For example, there are security implications of opening additional ports for traffic since every client in the network becomes a server. Further, it is difficult to establish trust for data providers in the network; that is, it is difficult to stop people acting as rogue providers and serve false data across the network or disrupt the network in some way.

The approach proposed in [6], and enhanced in this paper, attempts to combine the strengths of both a volunteer distributed computing approach like BOINC with decentralized, yet secure and customizable, P2P data sharing practices. It differs from the centralized BOINC architecture, in that it seeks to integrate P2P networking directly into the system, employing a job manager that sends data to a P2P network instead of directly to the client. Once data enters the P2P network, it is automatically propagated across the data nodes as required through simple caching schemes. Such a system helps to distribute data load dynamically in a decentralized fashion, both in topology and administratively, making it far more suitable to the Grid domain than static centralized systems. For example, inherent in BOINC-style networks is the requirement to send a needed data file to several workers multiple times to provide reliability and fault-tolerance. This replication imposes an extra and unneeded expenditure of server bandwidth, which can be avoided through a P2P caching mechanism that replicates the data across the network when it is first transferred. By replicating the data in such a way, there is an immediate decrease on the required central server bandwidth and also more advanced data distribution mechanisms can be supported, such as placing the data in locations where it is most needed on the network. Further, a number of projects require many nodes to process the same data, with different parameters, a situation that can also exploit the overlay described here. A gravitational-wave scenario presented in this paper is an example of such an algorithm.

3.   A Super-Peer Protocol for Job Submission

A data-intensive Grid application can require the distributed execution of a large number of jobs with the goal to analyze a set of data files. One representative application scenario defined for the GridOneD project [8] shows how one might conduct a massively distributed search for gravitational waveforms produced by orbiting neutron stars. In this scenario, a data file of about 7.2 MB of data is produced every 15 minutes and it must be compared with a large number of templates (between 5,000 and 10,000) by performing fast correlation. It is estimated that such computations take approximately 500 seconds. Data can be analyzed in parallel by a number of Grid nodes to speed up computation and keep the pace with data production. A single job consists of the comparison of the input data file with a number of templates, and in general it must be executed multiple times in order to assure a given statistical accuracy.

This kind of application is usually managed through a centralized framework, in which one server assigns jobs to workers, sends them input data, and then collects results; however this approach clearly limits scalability. Conversely, we propose a decentralized protocol that exploits the presence of super-peer overlays, which are more and more widely adopted to deploy interconnections among nodes of distributed systems and specifically of Grids.

The super-peer protocol relies on the definitions of different *roles* that can be assumed by Grid nodes (i.e., by super-peers or by simple nodes), as detailed in the following:

- the *data sources* are nodes that receive data from an external sensor, for example a gravitational wave detector in the GridOneD scenario, and provide this data to nodes for the execution of jobs. Each data file is associated to a *data advert*, i.e. a metadata document which describes the characteristics of this file.

- a *job manager* produces *job adverts*, i.e., files that describe the characteristics of the jobs that must be executed, and is also responsible for the collection of output results.

- the *workers* are Grid nodes that are available for job execution. A worker first issues a job query to obtain a job to be executed and then a data query to retrieve the input data file. A worker can disconnect at any time; if this occurs during the execution of a job, that one will not be completed.

- the *super-peers* constitute the backbone of the super-peer overlay. Super-peers are connected to workers through a centralized topology and to each other through a high level P2P network. In the proposed protocol, super-peers play the role of *rendezvous nodes*, since they compare job and data description documents (*job* and *data adverts*) with queries issued to discover these documents, thereby acting as a meeting place for job or data providers and consumers.

- *data cachers* are super-peers which have the additional ability to cache data (and associated data adverts) retrieved from a data source, and can directly provide such data to workers. Super peers and data cachers can be distributed on separate nodes if desired but in this experiment we hosted the data cachers on super peers for simplicity.

In the following, *data sources* and *data cachers* are collectively referred to as *data centers*, since both are able to provide data to workers, although at different phases of the process: data sources from the very beginning, data cachers after retrieving data from data sources or other data cachers. Notice that the distinction between data sources and data cachers has been introduced in this work, since here evaluation focuses on dynamic caching mechanisms. Conversely, in [6] it was assumed that all data centers possess the data files before starting the job submission process: in other words the replication and caching phase was separated from the job submission phase.

We assumed that only super-peers can assume the role of data centers, but the protocol can be easily extended to the case in which even simple peers can cache and provide data. We envisage that the same user-driven process is used to configure a peer; that is, each user can decide if a node will be a super peer and/or data center, as well as a worker. In the BOINC scenario, the existing dedicated machines would form the obvious data-center backbone and other peers (with high storage and network capacity) would also make themselves available in this mode.

3.1   Job Assignment and Data Download

Figure 1 depicts the sequence of messages exchanged among workers, super-peers and data centers for the execution of the job submission protocol in a sample topology with 5 super-peers, of which one is a data source and two others are data cachers. This example describes the behavior of the protocol when a job query is issued by the worker W_A. In this case dynamic caching is not exploited because: (i) input data is only available on the data source DS_0, i.e., no data cachers have yet downloaded data; (ii) data cannot be stored by the super-peer connected to W_A, since this is not a data cacher. The behavior of the protocol with dynamic caching is explained later.

The protocol requires that job execution is preceded by two matching phases: the *job-assignment* phase and the *data-download* phase. In the *job-assignment* phase the *job manager*(the node JM in the figure) generates a number of *job adverts*, which are XML documents describing the properties of the jobs to be executed (job parameters, characteristics of the platforms on which they must be executed, information about required input data files, etc.), and sends them to the local rendezvous super-peer, which stores the adverts. This corresponds to step 1 in the figure. Each worker, when ready to offer a fraction of its CPU time (in this case, worker W_A), sends a *job query* that travels the Grid through the super-peer interconnections (step 2), until the message time-to-live parameter is decremented to 0 or the job query finds a matching job advert. A job query is expressed by an XML document and typically contains hardware and software features of the requesting node as well as CPU time and memory amount that the node offers. A job query matches a job advert when the job query parameters are compatible with the information contained in the job advert. Whenever the job query gets to a rendezvous super-peer that maintains a matching job advert, such a rendezvous assigns the related job to the requesting worker by directly sending it a *job assignment* message (step 3).

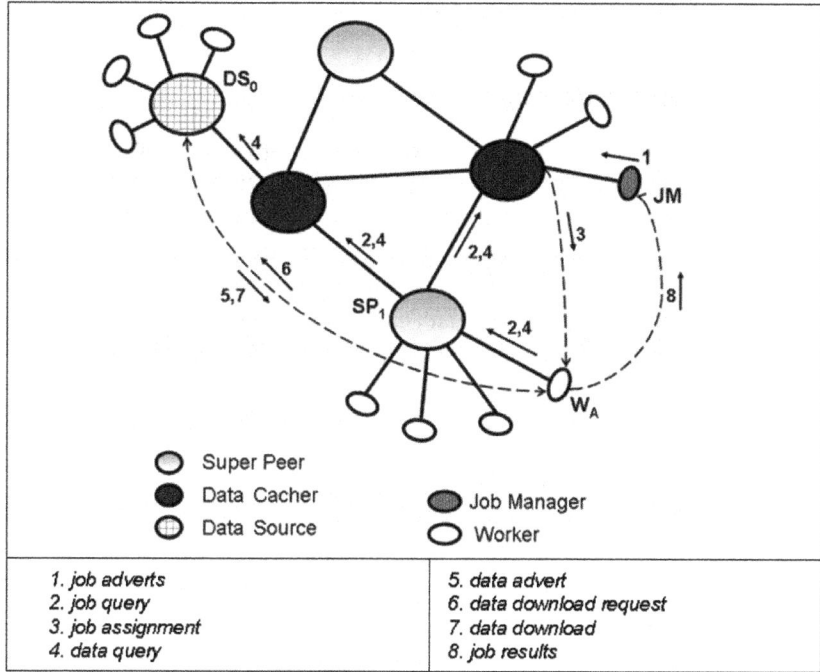

Super Peer	
Data Cacher	
Data Source	

| | Job Manager |
| | Worker |

1. *job adverts*	5. *data advert*
2. *job query*	6. *data download request*
3. *job assignment*	7. *data download*
4. *data query*	8. *job results*

Figure 1.   Super-peer job submission protocol: sample network topology and sequence of exchanged messages to execute one job at the worker W_A. Dynamic caching is not used because it is assumed that data cachers have no yet stored data.

In the *data-download* phase, the worker that has been assigned a job inspects the job advert, which contains information about the job and the required input data file, e.g., size and type of data. In a similar fashion to the job assignment phase, the worker sends a *data query* message (step 4), which travels the super-peer network searching for a matching input data file stored by a data center. Since the same file can be maintained by different data centers, a data center that successfully matches a data query does not send data directly to the worker, in order to avoid multiple transmissions of the same file. Conversely, the data center (in this example the data source DS_0) sends only a small *data advert* to the worker (step 5). The worker chooses a data center, and initiates the download operation (steps 6 and 7). After receiving the input data, the worker executes the job, reports the results to the job manager (step 8) and possibly issues another *job query*.

It can be noticed that in the job assignment phase the protocol works in a way similar to the BOINC software, except that job queries are not sent directly to the job manager, as in BOINC, but travel the super-peer network hop by hop. Conversely, the data download phase differs from BOINC in that it exploits the presence of multiple data centers in order to replicate input data files across the network.

3.2   Dynamic Caching

Dynamic caching allows for the replication of input data files on multiple data cachers. This leads to well known advantages such as increased degree of *data availability* and improved *fault tolerance*. Moreover, dynamic caching allows for a significant saving of time in the data download phase, because data queries have a greater chance to find an available data center, and most workers can download data from a neighbor data cacher instead of a remote data source. The remaining part of this section illustrates the dynamic caching mechanism, while the performance evaluation is discussed in Section 4.

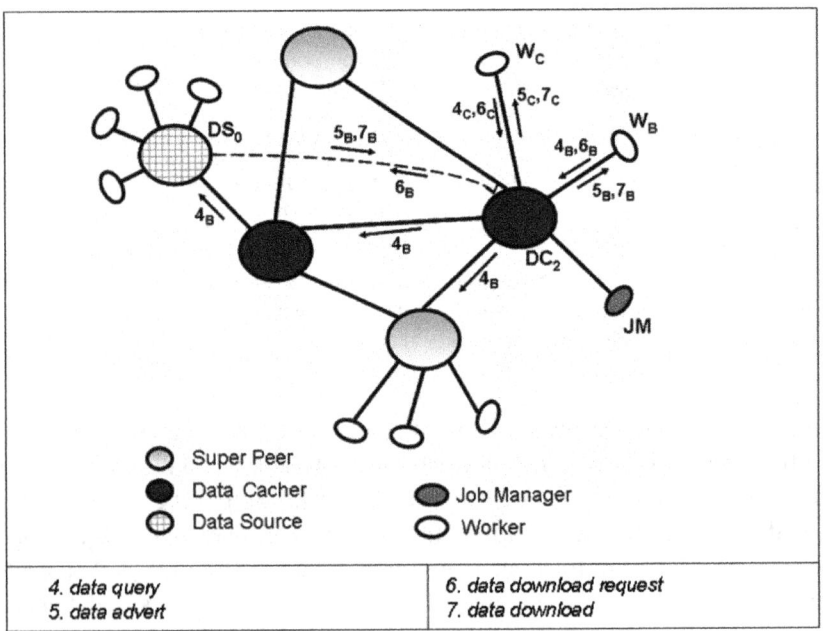

Figure 2.   Download phase of the super-peer job submission protocol, with dynamic caching. After the request of worker W_B, the data cacher DC_2 retrieves the data file from the data source DS_0, replicates and caches the file, and delivers it to W_B. Subsequently, the request of worker W_C is directly server by the data cacher DC_2.

Figure 2 shows how the protocol handles dynamic caching, both in the *replication* phase (which occurs when data is downloaded from a data source and stored by a data cacher) and in the *retrieval* phase (which occurs when data is retrieved from a data cacher by a worker). These two mechanisms are described in Figure 2 by displaying the messages exchanged when two workers W_B and W_C, connected to the same data cacher DC_2, issue two job queries at different times, first W_B then W_C. For simplicity, only messages related to the *download phase* are shown, and they are distinguished by subscripts A and B, corresponding to the two workers. The data query issued by W_B finds a matching in the data source DS_0. As opposed to the case described in Figure 1, this time the super-peer connected to W_B is a data cacher, DC_2. To let this data cacher store the data file, the data advert is not sent directly to the worker W_B, but first to DC_2 and then from DC_2 to the worker. Analogously, the data file is downloaded by DC_2, which replicates and caches it, and then passes it to the worker. Subsequently, DC_2 will act like a data source for the period of time in which it maintains the data file in its cache. In this example, the data query issued by W_C will be served directly by the cacher DC_2 instead of the data source DS_0.

To increase performance, a file splitting approach is adopted: data files are not downloaded as a whole but split in ordered fragments (of 1 Mbytes size in our case). For example, if the data cacher $DC2$ when receiving a data query does not hold the entire data file but has already received a part of it from $DS0$, it will not forward the data query, because it will soon receive the remaining fragments from $DS0$. As soon as it receives these fragments, $DC2$ will pass them to the requesting worker.

A further improvement could be obtained by enabling the parallel download of data segments from two or more data centers. The benefits and drawbacks of this enhancement are currently under investigation.

4.   Performance Evaluation

A simulation analysis was performed by means of an ad hoc event-based simulator, written in C++, to evaluate the performance of the cache-enabled super-peer protocol.

The simulation scenario is described in Table 1. The parameters of the representative astronomy scenario mentioned in Section 3 are used for the test case (file size, job execution time, etc.). It is assumed that all the jobs have similar characteristics and can be executed by any worker.

Workers can disconnect and reconnect to the network at any time. This implies that a job execution fails upon the disconnection of the corresponding worker. This is a new feature with respect to the basic protocol presented in

Table 1.   Simulation scenario.

Scenario feature	Value
Number of super-peers, N_{speer}	25 to 100
Maximum number of neighbors for a super-peer	4
Average number of workers connected to a super-peer	10
Average connection time of workers	4 h
Average disconnection time of workers	1 h
Number of data centers (data sources + data cachers)	about 50% of N_{speer}
Size of input data files	7.2 Mbytes
Latency between two adjacent super-peers *(or between two remote peers in a direct connection)*	100 ms
Latency between a super-peer and a local worker	10 ms
Bandwidth between two adjacent super-peers *(or between two remote peers in a direct connection)*	1 Mbps
Bandwidth between a super-peer and a local worker	10 Mbps
Mean job execution time	500 s
Number of jobs, N_{job}	50 to 500
Number of executions requested for each job, N_{exec}	10
Matches to live, MTL	10 to 30

[6]. Table 1 specifies the assumed average connection and disconnection times of workers.

To achieve multiple execution of every single job (which can be useful to enhance statistical accuracy or perform parameter sweep analysis) two parameters have been added: N_{exec} and MTL. Specifically, each job must be executed at least a given number of times, N_{exec}, which is set to 10. To guarantee this, a strategy based on redundant job assignment is exploited: each job advert can be matched and assigned to workers up to a number of times equal to the parameter MTL, or *Matches To Live*, which must be not lower than N_{exec}. A proper choice of MTL can compensate for possible disconnections of workers and consequent job failures.

It is assumed that local connections (i.e. between a super-peer and a local simple node) have a larger bandwidth and a shorter latency than remote connections. To compute the download time with a proper accuracy, a data file is split in 1 MB segments, and for each segment the download time is calculated assuming that the downstream bandwidth available at a data center is equally shared among all the download connections that are simultaneous active from this data center to different workers.

Simulations have been performed to analyze the overall execution time, i.e. the time needed to execute all the jobs at least N_{exec} times. The overall execution time, T_{exec}, is crucial to determine the rate at which data files can be retrieved from the data source in order to guarantee that the workers are able to keep the pace with data. We also computed the average utilization index of data centers, U, which is defined as the fraction of time that a data center is actually utilized, i.e., the fraction of time in which at least one download connection, from a worker or a data cacher, is active with this data center. The value of U is averaged on all the data centers and can be seen as an efficiency index.

4.1 Redundant Submission of Jobs

A first set of simulation was performed for a network with 25 super-peers, 1 data source and 12 data cachers. The purpose was to investigate the possible benefits of the redundant submission of jobs, in other words the impact of the Matches To Live (MTL) parameter on performance indices. Values of MTL were set to values ranging from 10 to 30, while N_{exec} was fixed to 10.

Figure 3 shows that the overall execution time increases with the number of jobs N_{job} and, more interestingly, tends to decrease as the value of MTL increases. The reason of the latter phenomenon is that a larger MTL allows to better compensate for the possible failure of jobs due to peer disconnections. However, this effect is not more evident when the MTL exceeds a threshold, in fact the execution time becomes approximately constant. Actually very large values of MTL are not even exploited since the job assignment phase is terminated as soon as the Job Manager receives, for each job, the results related to N_{exec} executions. Finally, notice that results related to MTL=10, and MTL=12 for N_{job} equal to 500, are not reported because with no or low degree of redundancy it was proved not possible to complete all the required jobs.

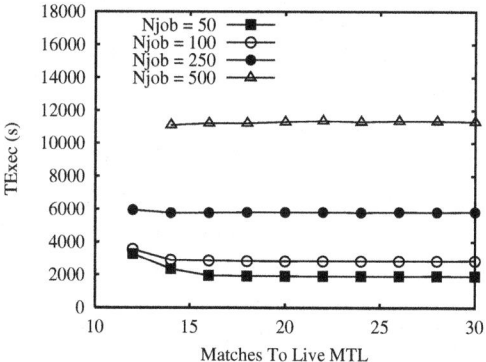

Figure 3. Overall execution time vs. the value of MTL, for different numbers of jobs.

Figure 4 shows that the average utilization of data centers, and hence the efficiency of the protocol, increases with the amount of computation assigned to workers, i.e., both with the number of jobs and with the MTL value. To understand this, it must be considered that data cachers are not very utilized in the first phase of the process, because they have not yet retrieved data from data sources, whereas they are fully exploited only after they have retrieved such data. Therefore, the utilization of data centers is high only when the number of required job executions is large enough to make the caching of data convenient. On the other hand, when the amount of computation is low, the time interval required by data cachers to retrieve data files is relevant with respect to the overall execution time, therefore data cachers are not exploited for a large fraction of time, which explains the low values of the utilization index.

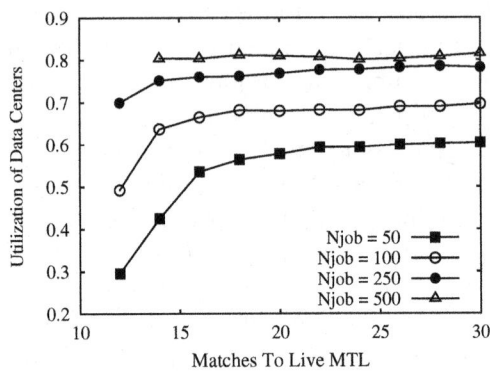

Figure 4.   Average utilization of data centers vs. the value of MTL, for different numbers of jobs.

4.2   Scalability Analysis

An additional set of simulations were performed to evaluate the behavior of the protocol in variable-sized networks. The number of super-peers was set to 25, 50, and 100, which corresponds to about 250, 500 and 1000 workers. The number of data centers was set to about half the number of super-peers, specifically to 13, 25 and 50, respectively. Two different scenarios were tested: when only one data source is available, regardless of the network size; and when the number of data sources is proportional to the network size. In this second case, we increase the number of data sources linearly with the increased network size by doubling the data sources at each stage i.e. 1, 2 and 4, respectively. This essentially compares how our approach affects a BOINC network if the BOINC administrator provides more data servers or data sources into the network. The number of jobs N_{job} was set to 250, for both scenarios.

Results are reported in Figures 5 and 6. It is interesting to note that the overall execution time may be decreased by using a larger number of workers. However, in the analyzed scenarios, this improvement is only noticed when the number of super-peers is increased from 25 to 50, while the use of larger networks is not beneficial. Furthermore, it can be noticed that the reduction of the execution time is obtained only if the MTL is larger than a threshold. Indeed, if MTL is low, it is likely that a considerable percentage of jobs are assigned to workers that are distant from the data source(s); the larger is the network, the longer are download times, and therefore the overall execution time. Conversely, with a large MTL, it is more probable that the at least N_{exec} jobs are assigned to workers directly connected to data centers, which assures lower download times; in this case, a larger number of workers actually decreases the overall execution time, because more jobs can be executed in parallel.

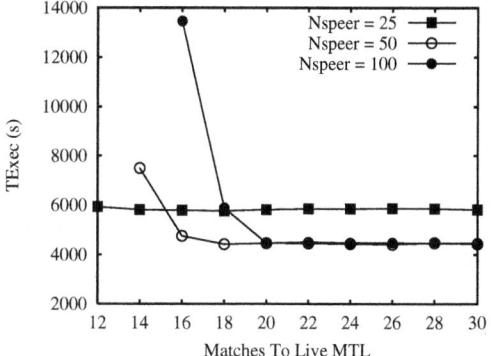

Figure 5.   Overall execution time vs. the MTL value, for different network sizes: 25, 50 and 100 super-peers. Results are obtained with 1 data source.

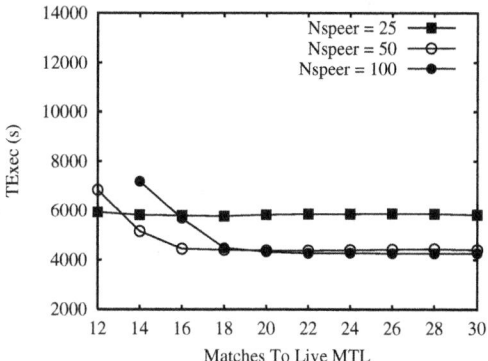

Figure 6.   Overall execution time vs. the MTL value, for different network sizes: 25, 50 and 100 super-peers. Results are obtained with a number of data sources proportional to the network size, i.e., equal to 1, 2 and 4.

Moreover, the comparison of Figures 5 and 6 shows that the execution time decreases if the number of data sources is increased from 1 to a number proportional to the network size, but again this only occurs with low values of MTL nad for large networks (num. of workers >= 500). With large values of MTL, the execution time hardly depends on the number of data sources: one data source suffices to propagate data files to data cachers and to workers.

5.   Conclusions

In this paper we have reported on the ongoing work and results of our research into a decentralized architecture for data-intensive scientific computing. This research has been undertaken according to the "public-resource computing" paradigm, where resources are distributed and generally donated by network volunteers. To take full advantage of the full spectrum of client-side capabilities in these types of networks, where participants generally have not only idle CPU cycles, but also substantial network bandwidth, we have presented a super-peer data distribution scheme that attempts to leverage the available resource capabilities for the submission of a very large number of jobs. In the scenario presented here, a small group of nodes maintains and advertises job description files and a large number of dispersed worker nodes execute the required tasks. Job assignment is performed by this group of rendezvous peers, which form a super-peer overlay network and match job descriptions with job queries when they are issued by available worker nodes.

To provide support for this scheme, a number of simulations have been performed to evaluate the impact of application (the number of jobs and the number of times that each of them is assigned to workers for statistical analysis) and network parameters (the number of workers and data centers) on performance indices such as the overall time to execute a given set of jobs and the utilization of data centers. Results for the test-case we identified show that the availability of several data centers and the use of dynamic caching bring benefits to applications. During this process, we have also observed that there is a balance between a larger number of data servers and the effective utilization of a single data center. Given the network and data parameters, the optimal number of data centers for a given problem space can be identified, thereby helping maximize the return of investment related to the deployment of new data centers. By using a system described in this paper, BOINC-like applications are able to replicate their current static data server functionality through a dynamic and decentralized data distribution system that enables projects to automatically scale their data needs without additional administrative overhead as their user-base or problem size increases.

Future work in this area will investigate a number of interesting research avenues, such as: (i) the evaluation of the pros and cons of parallel downloading of data segments from two or more data centers; and, (ii) the performance evaluation of using a super-peer schema for scenarios where input data is progressively being fed into the network from an external source as a data stream.

Acknowledgments

This research work is carried out under the FP6 CoreGRID Network of Excellence which is funded by the European Commission (Contract IST-2002-

004265). We would also like to thank Eddie Al-Shakarchi, Daniela Barbalace, Andrew Harrison, and Matthew Shields for their help in defining the distributed architecture presented here.

References

[1] David P. Anderson. Public computing: Reconnecting people to science. In *Proceedings of Conference on Shared Knowledge and the Web*, pages 17–19, November 2003.

[2] David P. Anderson. Boinc: A system for public-resource computing and storage. In *GRID '04: Proceedings of the Fifth IEEE/ACM International Workshop on Grid Computing (GRID'04)*, pages 4–10, Washington, DC, USA, 2004. IEEE Computer Society.

[3] David P. Anderson, Jeff Cobb, Eric Korpela, Matt Lebofsky, and Dan Werthimer. Seti@home: an experiment in public-resource computing. *Communications of the ACM*, 45(11), 2002.

[4] Climate@HOME Web site. http://climateprediction.net/

[5] B. Cohen. Incentives build robustness in bittorrent. In *Proceedings of the First Workshop on Economics of Peer-to-Peer Systems*, June 2003.

[6] Pasquale Cozza, Carlo Mastroianni, Domenico Talia, and Ian Taylor. A super-peer protocol for multiple job submission on a grid. In *Euro-Par 2006 Workshops*, volume 4375 of *LNCS*, pages 116–125, Dresden, Germany, 2007. Springer-Verlag.

[7] Einstein@HOME Web site. http://einstein.phys.uwm.edu/

[8] GridOneD Web site. http://www.gridoned.org/

[9] KaZaA Web site. http://www.kazaa.com/

[10] Carlo Mastroianni, Domenico Talia, and Oreste Verta. A super-peer model for resource discovery services in large-scale grids. *Future Generation Computer Systems*, 21(8):1235–1248, 2005.

[11] Napster website. http://www.napster.com/

[12] Domenico Talia and Paolo Trunfio. Toward a synergy between p2p and grids. *IEEE Internet Computing*, 7(4):96–95, 2003.

[13] Beverly Yang and Hector Garcia-Molina. Designing a super-peer network. In *19th International Conference on Data Engineering ICDE*, 2003.

AN ANALYSIS OF SECURITY SERVICES IN GRID STORAGE SYSTEMS

Jesus Luna*, Michail D. Flouris, Manolis Marazakis, and Angelos Bilas[†]
*Institute of Computer Science, Foundation for Research and Technology - Hellas (FORTH),
PO Box 1385. GR-71110. Heraklion, Greece.*
{jluna, flouris, maraz, bilas} @ics.forth.gr

Federico Stagni
*Istituto Nazionale di Fisica Nucleare sez. di Ferrara,
via Saragat 1 - 44100 Ferrara, Italy.*
federico.stagni@fe.infn.it

Alberto Forti, Antonia Ghiselli, Luca Magnoni, and Riccardo Zappi
*Istituto Nazionale di Fisica Nucleare CNAF,
viale Berti Pichat, 6/2 - 40127 Bologna, Italy*
{alberto.forti, antonia.ghiselli, luca.mangoni, riccardo.zappi} @cnaf.infn.it

Abstract   With the wide-spread deployment of Data Grids, storage services are becoming a critical aspect of the Grid infrastructure. Due to the sensitive and critical nature of the data being stored, security issues related with state of the art data storage services need to be studied thoroughly to identify potential vulnerabilities and attack vectors. In this paper, motivated by a typical use-case for Data Grid storage, we apply an extended framework for analyzing and evaluating security from the point of view of the data and metadata, considering the security capabilities provided by both the underlying Grid infrastructure and two commonly deployed Grid storage systems. This analysis leads to the identification of a set of potential security gaps, risks, and even redundant security features found in a typical Data Grid. These results are the starting point for our ongoing research on policies and mechanisms able to provide a fair balance between security and performance for Data Grid Storage Services.

Keywords: Data Grid, Grid security, OGSA security, security analysis, storage systems.

*This work was carried out for the CoreGRID IST project n°004265, funded by the European Commission
[†]Also, with the Dept. of Computer Science, University of Crete, P.O. Box 2208, Heraklion, GR 71409, Greece.

1.   Introduction

Storage systems have become an essential piece for the Data Grid, thus making it imperative to establish an integral and standardized security solution able to avoid common attacks on the data and metadata being managed. Grid security research has focused on specific high-level services (for example GSI [1] and VOMS [2]) instead of providing a systemic view able to encompass even block-level security features. Work-groups like the Open Grid Forum's OGSA Data Architecture [3] and CoreGRID's Trust and Security [4] have begun to investigate the challenges related with providing security for grid storage.

In this paper we apply an extended framework to analyze from a systemic point of view the security guarantees provided by the underlying infrastructure technologies and two storage technologies commonly deployed in Data Grid sites, focusing on the typical attacks that can be mounted on the data and meta-data. Our goal is to identify the security gaps and even redundant security features that may affect the Data Grid, so that ongoing research may be focused on fulfilling these needs while keeping a fair balance between security and performance.

The rest of this paper is organized as follows: section 2 introduces a use case based on OGSA Data Working Group's Data Architecture Scenarios [5], which describe a typical Grid system encompassing commonly used data operations ranging from replication to long-term archiving. Section 3 presents and extends the security evaluation framework from [6] so it can be applied for analyzing Grid storage systems. In section 4 we summarize the security guarantees provided by state-of-the-art underlying Grid infrastructures. In section 5 the extended framework is applied to analyze the potential risks and security gaps of two commonly deployed Grid storage technologies. section 6 concludes about the results obtained by the analysis and outlines our future work based on these.

2.   A typical use case for Data Grid's storage services

Using the architectural patterns from [5], Figure 1 presents a typical use case for the Data Grid, where a user (Client 1) accesses a Rendering Grid Service to generate some data and then proceeds to replicate it to three different sites (including a long-term storage). Later, a second user (Client 2) processes the generated data through a Visualization Service, which is in charge of locating an appropriate replica and copying the requested data to a local storage service for better performance. This use case comprises several security-related concerns; to analyze them we extend a framework originally proposed for the security evaluation of storage systems in general.

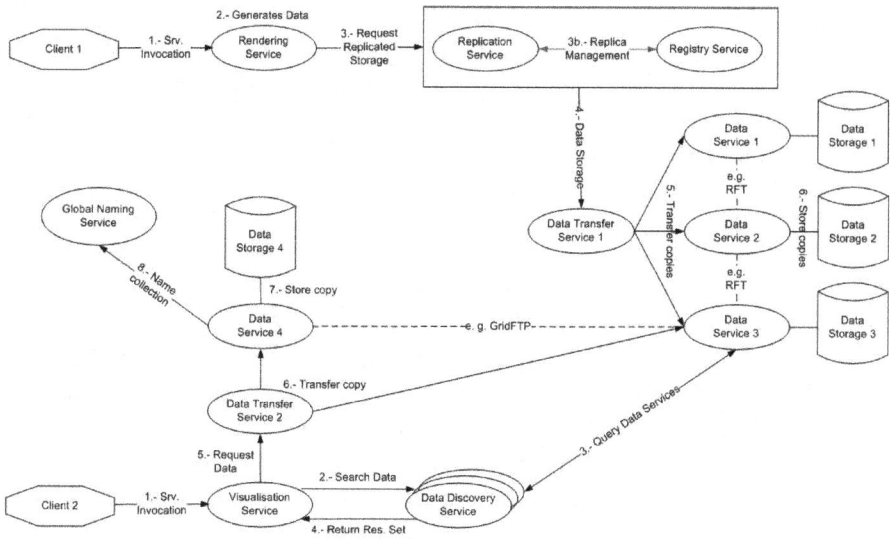

Figure 1. A typical Use Case for Grid Storage Services.

3. An extended framework for evaluating Grid Storage Services security

The commonly accepted security services related with the use case shown in figure 1 include Authentication, Confidentiality, Integrity, Authorization, Auditing, Privacy[1], Availability and Delegation. From the point of view of the Data Grid scenario being studied, its subsystems may become attacked in several ways, however for the purposes of our research the framework proposed by [6] will be used and extended with specific Grid-related features to reflect the main concerns linked with data and meta-data security. To apply this framework we must determine five components: players, attacks, security primitives, granularity of protection, and user inconvenience.

- *Players.* All of the possible players that one has to consider for protecting stored data. Each player is listed with a set of legitimate actions it can perform. Any other action by that player is treated as an attack, and thus the player becomes an *adversary*. A list of players applicable to Grid storage systems includes *(i) owners* (create and destroy data, delegate read and write permission to other players, and revoke another user's read or write privileges on owned data), *(ii) readers* (read data once this permission has been granted by owners), *(iii) writers* (modify data

---

[1]However in in most cases, privacy is seen as a reason for security rather than a security service, as in the case of Grids used in biomedical research [7].

once this permission has been delegated by owners), *(iv) wire* (transfers data among players into the WAN -not within each storage site-), *(v) group servers* (provides Grid-wide Authentication and Authorization - AA- services for other players), *(vi) namespace server* (allow traversal of namespaces, i.e. a file catalog providing Logical File Names -LFNs- and Storage URL -SURL- information), and *(vii) site services* (all players inside the domain of a single site including disk and/or tertiary storage -tape libraries- of data; we aggregate these into a single category because they are controlled by a single administrative authority).

- *Attacks.* The set of possible attacks cited in [6] depends on the architecture of each particular system. A fairly general set of possible attacks that can be mounted on a Grid storage system (data or metadata) includes *(i) by the adversary on the wire* (for instance, an attack mounted on the protocol used to communicate files to the clients), *(ii) by the adversary on the namespace servers* (for instance, an adversary gaining SURL and/or LFN information), *(iii) by a revoked user on the group servers* (for instance where a revoked reader can continue to read files from tertiary storage), *(iv) by the adversary colluding with the group server* (for instance an adversary gaining access to AA services), *(v) by the adversary colluding with the site services* (for instance, one where a filesystem directory is deleted by a user gaining access to Grid files by assuming a valid local user ID), and *(vi) by the adversary colluding with readers or writers* (for instance, a reader passing a copy of a file to an adversary).

  Based on their effects on the data, each of the previous attacks can be further classified into *leak attacks* (where an adversary gains access to some data and compromises its confidentiality and the privacy), *change attacks* (i.e. an adversary that makes *valid* modifications to data, but does not tamper its integrity, only its privacy), and *destroy attacks* (where an adversary makes *invalid* modifications to stored data; this is mainly linked with data's integrity and availability, even though this attack may have been triggered via the underlying authentication and authorization mechanisms).

- *Core security primitives.* Storage systems implement several primitives to enable players to securely perform their functions. These primitives can be categorized into six groups: authentication, authorization, securing data in-transit (over the wire) and at-rest (on storage devices), key management and revocation.

- *Granularity of protection.* To limit the overhead of cryptographic operations, most systems implement optimizations including aggregation of players into groups to simplify authorization, and trading off the security of short-lived keys against the ease of management of long-term keys.

- *User inconvenience.* The level of inconvenience users are willing to tolerate before they become careless and prone to seek ways to circumvent security measures.

Applying the framework presented above, it is possible to identify potential damages caused by attacks that can be mounted on data or metadata from the Grid scenario introduced in section 2. A few examples of potential attacks include adversaries in control of the replication service leaking the generated data from the Rendering Service (i.e. by moving it to the attacker's site); adversaries on the wire performing a leak attack on the transmitted data (i.e. using a network packet sniffer); and it may even be possible for an adversary with full access to storage site services to steal data from disks (leak attack, destroy attack) or re-write the stored data with a previous -and valid- version (change attack).

Damages caused by such attacks can be "combined", thus spreading the negative effects to every Grid subsystem. Our analysis views Data Grid security as a whole system, where if a subsystem is compromised then the negative effects are propagated to others. A property of this systemic view of Data Grid security is that countermeasures can be applied to the *optimal* subsystem (i.e. where overall damage is reduced while performance is maximized), while the final effect is still conveyed to all of them. In the rest of this paper, we use the extended framework to analyze the overall security capabilities and gaps provided by both the underlying state of the art Grid infrastructure, and two widely used grid storage technologies.

4. Capabilities of the underlying Grid security infrastructure

This section summarizes the security capabilities offered by state of the art Grid-related infrastructure (technologies not collocated with the Storage service itself). In particular we will focus on the underlying Grid Security Infrastructure (GSI) and an important set of the Authentication and Authorization Infrastructures (AAI), able to provide an overall security solution to current Data Grid installations. The reviewed infrastructures are summarized at the end of this section to show the protection they offer against most of the attacks mentioned in section 3. In some cases we find that the same security measures are offered by more than one technology. For our research it is important to find which of these security features are also implemented by the Grid Data Storage subsystem, in order to clearly identify not only gaps that may result in a potential attack, but also the redundant mechanisms that should be optimized to keep a balance between security and performance.

4.1   Grid Security Infrastructure

The Grid Security Infrastructure (GSI) [1] is comprised of a set of protocols, libraries, and tools that allow users and applications to securely access Grid resources. The Globus Toolkit [9] is a well-known and widely deployed implementation of GSI. Two mechanisms are defined by GSI: *Secure Conversation -Connectivity layer-* and *Secure Message -Resource layer-*, for *authentication* and *secure communication (integrity and confidentiality)*. In the GSI Secure Conversation approach the client establishes a context with the server before sending any data. This context serves to authenticate the client identity to the server and to establish a shared secret using a collocated GSI Secure Conversation Service. Once the context establishment is complete the client can securely invoke an operation on the service by signing or encrypting outgoing messages using the shared secret captured in the context (through a SSL/TLS channel). The GSI Secure Message approach differs in that no context is established before invoking an operation. The client simply uses existing cryptographic data, such as an X.509 end entity certificate, to secure messages and authenticate itself to the service. Securing of messages in the GSI Secure Conversation approach, i.e. using a shared secret, requires less computational effort than using existing cryptographic data in the GSI Secure Message approach. This allows the client to trade off the extra step of establishing a context to enable more computationally efficient messages protection once that context has been established. For *authorization* purposes GSI can use the SAML standard [10] from OASIS. SAML defines formats for a number of types of security assertions and a protocol for retrieving those assertions even from third-party services, therefore enabling new features like role-based authorization. Finally, GSI provides also a *delegation* capability to reduce the number of times the user must enter his passphrase (single sign-on), this is performed through a *proxy certificate* [11].

4.2   AAI for Grids

The **Virtual Organization Membership Service (VOMS)** [2] is an *Attribute Authority* that exposes attributes and encodes the position of the holder inside the Virtual Organization (VO). A Holder may be a member of several groups, and may hold a special role inside some of his groups. Groups are organized in a tree structure that comprises groups and subgroups, while roles are not hierarchical and are associated to the membership in a group. The internal structure of a VO as defined in VOMS is not a full hierarchical Role Based Access Control (RBAC). However, currently it is the most widely-used attribute authority service, and is a de-facto standard for AA in production Grids.

The **Privilege and Role Management Infrastructure and Standards Validations (PERMIS)** [12] system is an implementation of a hierarchical RBAC mechanism that makes use of a powerful policy engine to take a policy file and then making authorization decisions based on this policy and the Attribute Certificates it receives. It relies on a non-standardized XML policy language and since the roles are internally defined to every policy engine, its use is more appropriate for local sites rather than for VO-oriented environments.

Community Authorization Service (CAS) [13] is an authorization service built on top of GSI. A user requesting access to a resource contacts the CAS server which after a GSI-based authentication, issues a restricted proxy credential with an embedded access-control policy. The user utilizes this credential to connect to the requested resource, and then the resource itself applies its local policy to further restrict this access. With CAS, the ultimate decision about what happens at a Grid resource is removed from the resource provider and put in the hands of the CAS administrator. CAS does not record groups or roles, but only permissions,

Privilege Management and Authorization in Grids (PRIMA) system [14] is an authorization system that makes use of Policy Decision Points and Policy Enforcement Points interactions like the ones described in [15] to focus on access control policies, while user attributes come from external Attribute Authorities like VOMS. This approach uses a VO-global specification of privilege attributes per Role, with local enforcement of privileges using the Grid User Management System (GUMS) [8] identity mapping service.

Grid-aware pluggable authoriZation management (gPLAZMA) [16] is a storage-specific security technology, developed for authorization within dCache [17]. After authentication, gPLAZMA uses PRIMA to query a storage authorization service that calls GUMS for local user mapping. It can operate in a role-based authorization mode.

4.3 Security capabilities as countermeasures

Table 1 summarizes the security capabilities provided by the infrastructure reviewed in this section. The layout of the table is based on the framework proposed by [6] and extended in section 3 to accomplish Data Grid-related needs. Results are categorized by possible attacks (main columns) and types of damage – the Leak, Change, Destroy sub-columns –. Cells marked with an "Y" mean that the system (row) prevents that type of damage caused by this particular attack. Cells marked with an "N" mean that the system does not prevent the damage. If a particular attack does not apply to a system, the cell is marked with a "-". Our goal here is to highlight how this underlying infrastructure's security services can act as countermeasures for the typical attacks that can be mounted on the data and meta-data. From Table 1 we can see that GSI mechanisms are common to all other infrastructure technologies, and therefore in particular the Leak attack is prevented "by default" (it is quite difficult to execute if GSI's Secure Conversation is enabled). There may be however a considerable *performance loss* to take into account if this mechanism is being used into the Grid to move massive amounts of data.

Table 1.   Security capabilities as countermeasures.

Attack	*Adversary on wire (WAN)*			*Adversary on names-pace servers*			*Revoked user on group servers*			*Adversary with group server*			*Adversary with site services[a]*		
Damage	L	C	D	L	C	D	L	C	D	L	C	D	L	C	D
GSI + AAI[b]	Y	Y	Y	Y	Y	Y	Y	Y	Y	N	N	N	N	N	N
GSI+ PRIMA+ gPlazma	Y	Y	Y	Y	Y	Y	Y	Y	Y	N	N	N	Y[c]	Y[c]	Y[c]

[a] Adversary with full control of the site services.
[b] VOMS, CAS, PERMIS.
[c] See discussion about conditions required for this countermeasure.

Some other attacks can be also stopped with GSI+AAI technologies; consider for instance adversaries colluded with the namespace servers, which will be unable to perform any damage (change or destruction) to the data/meta-data, because GSI's mutual authentication and authorization mechanisms based on cryptographic protocols prevent *untrusted* servers from interacting with Grid clients or other services. About the attacks coming from compromised Group servers, even though they cannot be prevented by GSI or related technologies, in practice these are hard to carry out, as they would require colluding with one or more Certification Authorities, Authorization Servers and so on. In the case of the site services and in particular with the storage service subsystem, if it is *GSI+AAI aware* then it will be protected from most of the attacks (this is the particular case of gPlazma), otherwise only leak attacks are likely to be stopped.

Finally, under the assumption of an attacker with *full* control of the site services[2] then even gPlazma and their underlying technologies may not be suf-

---

[2] This is the case of untrusted sites, which we expect to become a serious security problem for the Data Grid.

ficient to protect against leaks (the data into the storage device is not encrypted), changes (re-writing stored data with older, but still valid information) and destruction (low-level formatting the device). Even though there will never be a *total-security solution* for this problem, the security concerns related with Grid storage services are the entry point for the next section, where state of the art storage technologies are analyzed within the extended framework presented in section 3 as a way to provide overall conclusions and research ideas about the security guarantees and gaps associated with them.

5. Security capabilities of Grid Storage Systems

Current state-of-the-art Grid storage systems are hierarchical storage management systems (HSM), managing storage distributed on disk and tape libraries. In most of the cases the interaction with HSMs is made through the so-called Storage Resource Managers (SRMs): middleware software modules whose purpose is to manage in a dynamic fashion what resides on the storage resource at any one time [18].

Our work is currently focused on the most widely deployed grid storage systems in European Grids (and in particular within the EGEE infrastructure), for the time being excluding alternative systems such as the SDSC Storage Resource Broker (SDSC SRB) [27]. The SDSC SRB is a client-server system that exports a unified view of the available datasets while hiding their actual location. Users can store or replicate their data collections across several servers, while maintaining total access control locally. A metadata catalog service supports user queries related to datasets and their properties, including a mapping from logical handles to physical file locations. Long-term preservation and data provenance are important design goals for the SDSC SRB, and we believe that they should be refelected in security capabilities and protocols. These issues will be examined in depth during the course of our work-group's activities. We anticipate that the framework presented in this paper will allow us to characterize this system's security capabilities and pinpoint vulnerabilities.

In the European Grids the most widely used grid storage systems are: *dCache* with *PNFS* [17], *DPM* [21], *CASTOR* [22] and *STORM* [23]. These can be categorized as systems offering storage distribution across more than one grid sites (dCache and DPM) and systems operating within a single site (CASTOR and STORM). Since our analysis focuses on grid distributed storage, we will present in more detail the security capabilities of the former class of systems. Our analysis complements previous works that provided an overview of functional capabilities [25] and a performance evaluation [26].

Our goal is to apply the security framework defined in Section 3 as a tool to determine the potential set of attacks feasible to be performed against the Data Grid storage systems cited here. It is important to note that the applied framework is not intended to allow evaluation of the end-to-end security of a particular system. This requires careful analysis of each component and the particular way of combining them, since any secure system is only as strong as its weakest link. The framework is neither intended as a replacement for such analysis, but simply seeks to allow a high-level comparison among different systems, purposely leaving some secondary details unexamined. Next we present a brief survey of each system, including its security capabilities, followed by a table summarizing potential attacks and damages.

5.1   dCache

dCache/SRM [17] is a grid storage middleware system that combines distributed heterogeneous disk storage systems under a single filesystem tree. It also handles data hot spots, hardware faults and replication for high availability. dCache aims to provide Grid functionalities compliant with definitions of the LHC computing Grid (LCG) Storage Element storage fabric. dCache supports a protocol for local access to data, using PNFS [19], an NFS-like service which allows namespace operations to be performed through a standard NFS2 interface. Actual data transfer is performed through faster channels via a number of protocols, including a native dCap protocol (DCCP), GridFTP, and HTTP. For secure wide-area data access, dCache allows opening files using a URL-like syntax without the PNFS filesystem being mounted, through one of the supported protocols (dCap, GssFTP, GsiFTP and HTTPS).

Each storage element needs to provide status information (availability, load, free space). This is currently achieved using LDAP. For managing storage, dCache supports an SRM interface. Besides namespace operations, it allows to prepare data sets for transfers directly to the client, as well as to initiate 3rd-party transfers between *Storage Elements* (SEs). SRM retries failed transfers and also handlers space reservation and management.

Applications use dCache by linking a user-level library providing POSIX-like file I/O calls. This library supports pluggable security mechanisms, where GssApi (Kerberos) and SSL modules have already been implemented. dCache can also be connected to tertiary storage systems, using custom protocols dependent on the tape system used on every site. Furthermore, it supports autonomous data distribution to various pools using rules/preferences. (e.g. all incoming data are first stored on high-perf disks and later flushed to tape storage). More complex setups consider load-balancing and other run-time factors. There is a file replica manager, that maintains several replicas of each file on different pools according to site or grid-level policies. In any dCache implementation, a node acts as the "admin" node, also known as the dCache server. This node runs PNFS and a number of other dCache services. In addition to the admin server, many file pools may be added. The pool nodes are where files are stored. There is no problem having NFSd or GridFTP running on a pool node.

5.1.1 Security Framework Characteristics.

Players. The following four are involved: *(i)* The PNFS daemon on the admin node is the namespace server, *(ii)* Pool nodes are the storage servers, *(iii)* Door nodes are the group servers providing authentication and authorization based on GSI and VOMS services, and finally *(iv)* Replica managers handle file replication to storage pools.

Trust Assumptions. Seven assumptions were considered: *(i)* Storage servers are authenticated to admin node running PNFS and to clients using dCap or GssApi, however they are trusted with the data (same for disk or tertiary storage), therefore dCache is not protected from attacks in collusion with the site services. *(ii)* Data are protected on the wire to the clients and through the WAN using GssApi or SSL, however namespace protocol (NFS2) data are unprotected on the wire. Upcoming versions will use NFSv4, which can be built on top of a secure RPC framework (using a plugin architecture). Furthermore, file data are not protected on the wire within a single site network, where the NFS protocol is used for namespace operations and local file access. *(iii)* Data are not protected on disk or tapes. *(iv)* Since all authentication and authorization data are present in the group servers, dCache is vulnerable to attacks in collusion with the group server on the door nodes. *(v)* Certificates for access to files are currently being issued for a large time window (e.g. 12 hours) in most implementations. This may allow a revoked user to retain access rights to files within this window if real-time validation is not performed, just as recommended in [20]. *(vi)* The namespace servers map file names and attributes to data on storage pools only available to clients with valid certificates. *(vii)* Since the replica manager has copy, move and delete access to files on storage nodes, dCache is vulnerable to attacks in collusion with the replica manager.

Security Primitives. We have taken the following: *(i)* dCache provides create/read and delete access to a file, but does not allow its modification (i.e. an existing file has to be deleted and rewritten); however, the storage server or the metadata server (admin node running PNFS) may read, modify or delete files on storage nodes. *(ii)* The group server authenticates and authorizes clients using the GSI and VOMS infrastructure.

5.2 DPM: Disk Pool Manager

The Disk Pool Manager (DPM) [21] has been developed at CERN as a disk-only Storage Element, supporting the SRM-compliant Storage Element interfaces, without the complications of multiple modes of access and management of tape storage. DPM offers the following advantages: (i) SRM Interface, (ii) scalability (allows the management of 10+TB distributing the load over several servers), (iii) high performance, and (iv) light-weight management. DPM relies on a MySQL database to store its metadata.

5.2.1   Security Framework Characteristics.

Players.   Three players were considered in the analysis: *(i)* A DPM daemon offers access to a set of filesystems, located on one or more file-server nodes. *(ii)* A SRM service supports the protocol for Grid access to the storage resources, by translating requests to the native DPM protocol. *(iii)* A name service, built over a MySQL database, supports namespace lookup operations.

Trust Assumptions.   Our study considered the following: *(i)* Site services are trusted if clients pass through the AA services (based on GSI and VOMS) and hold valid certificates. *(ii)* Data are protected on the wire to the clients and through the WAN using GssApi or SSL. Within a single site network data are not protected on the wire. *(iii)* Data are not protected on disk or tapes. *(iv)* Certificates for access to files are currently being issued for a large time window (e.g. 12 hours) in most implementations.

Security Primitives.   Two main primitives exist: *(i)* DPM allows create/read and delete access to files, but does not allow direct file modification. However the storage and namespace servers within a site may read, modify or delete files local files. *(ii)* AA in DPM are based on the GSI and VOMS services, described in section 4. Grid IDs are mapped to local user IDs for file access.

5.3   Security Analysis Table

Using the same notation from Table 1, we compare in Table 2 DPM and dCache in terms of their resilience to potential attacks.

As discussed in earlier sections, although both systems rely on GSI+AAI technologies, the use of *non-GSI* aware subsystems (PNFS in the case of dCache and MySQL for DPM) may open the door to attacks to namespace servers that otherwise could have been prevented. Moreover, the surveyed technologies assume that site services are *trustworthy*, therefore an adversary colluding with a site may perform a lot of damage. For both types of attacks (directed to the WAN and performed by a revoked user on the group servers) can be alleviated by the *inheritance* of GSI+AAI security features. On the other hand, this inheritance may provoke unwanted redundant features (i.e. authorization decisions taken by both, local storage systems and Virtual Organizations) resulting in performance issues. Future work will be aimed to further research this topic. For example,

Table 2. Summary of security guarantees provided by Grid Storage Systems.

Attack	Adversary on wire (WAN)			Adversary on names-pace servers			Revoked user on group servers			Adversary with group server			Adversary with site services[a]		
Damage	L	C	D	L	C	D	L	C	D	L	C	D	L	C	D
dCache	Y	Y	Y	N	N	N	Y^b	Y^b	Y^b	N	N	N	N	N	N
DPM	Y	Y	Y	N	N	N	Y	Y	Y	N	N	N	N	N	N

[a] Adversary with full control.
[b] Within period of issued file certificates.

even though dCache does not offer any protection against attacks coming from a revoked user, this countermeasure is achieved thanks to GSI's authentication and authorization functionalities.

6. Conclusions

This paper presents the first part of our research on Grid storage system's security, analyzing the security of state-of-the-art technologies using a framework originally proposed for generic storage systems which we have extended to Grid-specific configurations. Our goal is to describe the potential set of attacks on the data or the meta-data along with the guarantees currently provided by the surveyed technologies, as a way to find out not only the gaps that must be covered, but also the mechanisms that should be optimized due to the redundant security services they are providing at the different Grid layers. Most technologies rely on, or inherit their security features from the underlying Grid Security Infrastructure (GSI) and generally only need to call-out a third-party service for enhanced authorization decisions (e.g. VOMS). GSI provides a wide set of base security capabilities, but still is susceptible to attacks where the adversary has taken control of the groups servers; however this is an unlikely scenario because most Certification Authorities and Authorization servers implement strong security mechanisms for their own protection.

On the other hand, the attacks where the adversary has taken total control over the site services are more dangerous and relevant to our research, because in this case *none* of the surveyed technologies are capable of providing adequate protection. Let us focus, for example, on a scenario where the attacker has taken control of the storage device itself: even though low-level encryption may be enough to protect the assets, what happens with the encryption capabilities provided by upper layers like GSI? Is it feasible to re-use them at the lower-layers to improve performance? Having identified the security gaps related with untrusted site services, our ongoing work will focus on the mechanisms able to manage them while keeping a fair balance between performance and security.

Acknowledgments

We would like to thank Christos Papachristos and Panos Chatziadam for providing us with detailed information about the configuration of storage systems in the context of the HellasGrid Task Force (infrastructure that is part of the EGEE-II: Enabling Grids for E-sciencE project). The work reported in this paper was the result of collaboration between FORTH and INFN, supported in part by the EU-funded CoreGrid Network of Excellence (Contact FP6-004265).

References

[1] V. Welch. Globus Toolkit Version 4 Grid Security Infrastructure: A Standards Perspective. The Globus Security Team. 2005. http://www.globus.org/toolkit/docs/4.0/security/GT4-GSI-Overview.pdf

[2] EU DataGrid, VOMS Architecture v1.1. March, 2007. http://grid-auth.infn.it/docs/VOMS-v1_1.pdf

[3] OGSA-Data Working Group (OGSA-D-WG). March, 2007. https://forge.gridforum.org/sf/projects/ogsa-d-wg

[4] Trust and Security in CoreGRID. April, 2007. http://www.coregrid.net/mambo/content/view/281/275/

[5] D. Berry, et. al. OGSA Data Architecture Scenarios - version 0.15. March, 2007. https://forge.gridforum.org/sf/go/doc14073?nav=1

[6] E. Riedel, M. Kallahalla, R. Swaminathan. A framework for evaluating storage system security. In *Proceedings of the 1st Conference on File and Storage Technologies (FAST)*, Monterrey. CA, USA, January 2002.

[7] BELIEF: Bringing Europe's eLectronic Infrastructures to Expanding Frontiers. March, 2007. http://www.beliefproject.org/

[8] GUMS – The Grid User Management System. April, 2007. http://grid.racf.bnl.gov/GUMS/index.html

[9] I. Foster. Globus Toolkit Version 4: Software for Service-Oriented Systems. In Springer-Verlag LNCS 3779, *IFIP International Conference on Network and Parallel Computing*, pages 2-13, 2005.

[10] Security Association Markup Language (SAML) Specification v.1.0. April, 2007. http://www.oasis-open.org/committees/security/

[11] S. Tuecke, et. al. Request For Comments 3820: Proxy Certificate Profile. Network Working Group, June 2004. http://www.ietf.org/rfc/3820.txt

[12] D. Chadwick, O.Alexander. The PERMIS X.509 Role based privilege management infrastructure. In ACM, *SACMAT '02: Proceedings of the 7th ACM symposium on Access control models and technologies*, pages 135–140, Monterey, California, USA, June 2002. ACM Press

[13] L. Pearlman, et al. A Community Authorization Service for Group Collaboration. In IEEE, *Proceedings of 3rd International Workshop on Policies for Distributed Systems and Networks*. 2002. IEEE Computer.

[14] M. Lorch, et. al. The PRIMA system for privilege management, authorization and enforcement in grid environments. In *Proceedings of the 4th International Workshop on Grid Computing*, Nov. 2003.

[15] J. Vollbrecht, et. al. Request For Comments 2904: AAA Authorization Framework. Network Working Group, August 2000. http://www.ietf.org/rfc/rfc2904.txt

[16] A. Rana. gPLAZMA : Introducing RBAC Security in dCache. In *Computing in High Energy and Nuclear Physics 2006*.

[17] P. Fuhrmann and V. Gulzow. dCache, storage system for the future. In *Europar 2006*, Dresden.

[18] A. Shoshani, A. Sim and J. Gu. Storage Resource Managers: Essential Components for the Grid. In *Grid Resource Management: State of the Art and Future Trends*, 2003. Kluwer Academic Publishers.

[19] Perfectly Normal File System (PNFS). http://www-pnfs.desy.de/

[20] J. Luna, O. Manso and M. Medina. Using OGRO and CertiVeR to improve OCSP validation for Grids. In Springer-Verlag, *Journal of Supercomputing: special issue Technology Deployments in Grid Computing*. Netherlands, March 2007.

[21] Disk Pool Manager. May 2007. http://www.gridpp.ac.uk/wiki/Disk_Pool_Manager

[22] O. BSrring, et. al. Storage Resource Sharing with CASTOR. In IEEE, *Proceedings of NASA Goddard 21st IEEE Conference on Mass Storage Systems and Technologies (MSST2004)*, Apr. 2004.

[23] E. Corso, et. al. Storm, an SRM Implementation For LHC Analysis Farms. In *Computing in High Energy and Nuclear Physics (CHEP 2006)*, Feb. 2006.

[24] F. Schmuck and R. Haskin. GPFS: A Shared-disk File System for Large Computing Centers. In *USENIX Conference on File and Storage Technologies*, pages 231–244, Monterey, CA, Jan. 2002.

[25] G. Stewart, D. Cameron, G. Cowan and G. McCance. Storage and Data Management in EGEE. In *Proceedings of Conferences in Research and Practice in Information Technology*, Volume 68, pages 69–77, 2007.

[26] G.A. Cowan, G. Stewart, and J. Ferguson. Optimisation of Grid Enabled Storage at Small Sites. In *Proceedings of 6th UK eScience All Hands Meeting*, Paper Number 664, 2006.

[27] C.Baru, R. Moore, A. Rajasekar and M. Wan Michael. The SDSC Storage Resource Broker. In *Proceedings of the 1998 Conference of the Centre for Advanced Studies on Collaborative Research (CASCON)*, Toronto, Canada, pages 5–17, 1998.

ANALYSIS OF GRID STORAGE ELEMENT ARCHITECTURES: HIGH-END FIBER-CHANNEL VS. EMERGING CLUSTER-BASED NETWORKED STORAGE

Maciej Brzezniak and Norbert Meyer
Poznan Supercomputing and Networking Center,
61-704 Poznan, Noskowskiego 12/14, Poland
{maciekb,meyer}@man.poznan.pl

Michail D. Flouris, Renaud Lachaiz*, and Angelos Bilas
Institute of Computer Science (ICS)
Foundation for Research and Technology – Hellas (FORTH),
P.O. Box 1385, Heraklion, GR-71110, Greece
{flouris,rlachaiz,bilas}@ics.forth.gr

Abstract   Storage elements that can scale to large capacities and high-performance are an essential component of future GRID infrastructures, especially for supporting an increasing number of data-intensive applications and services. This paper studies two approaches for building scalable networked storage elements: enterprise-level, Fibre-Channel-based Storage (FCS) and commodity, Cluster-based Networked Storage (CNS). First we review the characteristics of FCS, which is currently widely used in high-end enterprise-level installations, discussing various aspects, such as scalability, performance, availability, manageability and security. Then, we compare it with CNS and consider how features of high-end specialized systems may be provided on top of this new architecture. We believe that CNS has a potential for replacing FCS in many application domains; however, there is a need for addressing the feature gap between FCS and CNS at the architectural and storage management layer.

Keywords: Storage systems, storage management, Storage Element

---

*Currently with Joseph Fourier University, Grenoble, France.

1.   Introduction

Recently, there has been a lot of interest in building cost-effective Storage Elements (SEs) that can scale to large capacities, in the range of tens of PBytes, and high-throughput, i.e. tens of GBytes per second. Such storage elements are required to support an increasing number of data-intensive applications and services that impose stringent requirements on modern storage systems. The main challenge in this direction is to scale capacity and throughput without losing important features, such as reliability and availability, flexibility, manageability, and security.

Scalable storage elements traditionally rely on custom, storage-specific components, such as FC (Fibre Channel) or SCSI (Small Computer Systems Interface) controllers, interconnects, and disks. Fiber Channel-based Storage (FCS) systems provide attractive features, however at high cost. Therefore they are mainly used in applications that require strong guarantees and high performance and flexibility such as banking, e-commerce, video-streaming and supercomputing. The centralization points present in these architectures facilitate providing strong reliability guarantees and simplify storage management tools; however, they may eventually limit storage system flexibility, capacity, and performance.

Recently, scalable storage systems have started to evolve through significant architectural changes that will allow them to take advantage of commodity components (CPUs, memory, interconnects, disks). These Commodity-based Networked Storage systems (CNS) will be able to follow technology curves better than specialized storage architectures and offer similar or improved functional and performance characteristics at lower cost. Moreover, their open architecture may allow greater flexibility in closely matching the requirements of users and applications.

FCS systems are built out of custom storage devices, designed and optimized for I/O processing purposes. FCS systems use also storage-specific communication protocols such as Fibre Channel Protocol (FCP). Figure 1 shows a typical FCS setup. Application servers are connected to storage resources through the Storage Area Network (SAN) and FC Host Bus Adapters (HBAs). Typical storage resources are disk matrices, containing disk drives and controller(s) equipped with storage processors (CPUs), cache memory, and XOR engines for calculating RAID checksums. Matrix controllers present to application servers logical volumes, which are virtualized physical drives. There are many potential and actual centralization points in FCS, which may help providing reliability guarantees. However, they can limit important features such as capacity, throughput and increase system cost.

Figure 2 shows the general architecture of a commodity, cluster-based networked storage system (CNS). Typical storage nodes include one or two storage

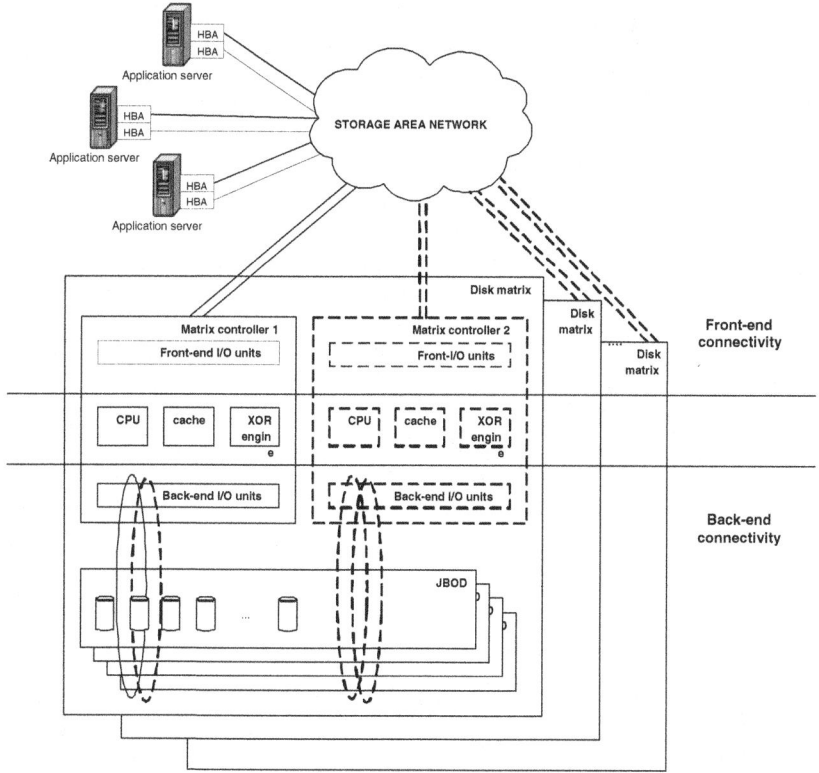

Figure 1. Architecture of FCS.

controllers, each connected to a subset of disks. Depending on the target application domain, the storage node may also include additional CPUs and memory. The exact I/O paths for data and control transfer may vary, depending on the specific node architecture.

CNS is currently being used (mostly) experimentally in various application domains. Cluster-based networked storage systems provide numerous advantages: they benefit from the technology curves for commodity components (CPUs, memory, interconnection), they are more flexible and may adapt to broader application needs, they can scale to larger systems providing higher capacities and performance, they may employ a higher degree of redundancy, and they exhibit lower acquisition costs. Cluster-based storage systems introduce and rely on two architectural characteristics to provide their many advantages. Firstly, they eliminate centralization points in the storage system and move intelligence from hardware to software providing more flexibility. Secondly, they rely on commodity components that address larger markets and may take advantage of economies of scale. These architectural characteristics are also a

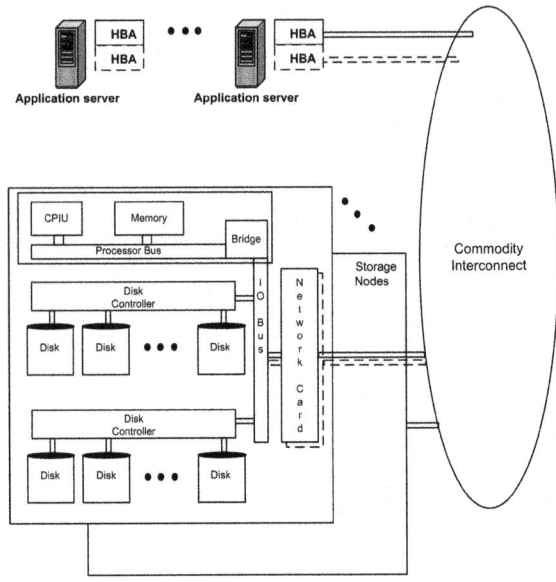

Figure 2.   Architecture of CNS.

source of numerous challenges in building cost-effective, scalable storage systems. For instance, they require extensive system software support for sharing resources and data, reliability and availability, security and management issues.

In this work we examine important features of FCS. The goal is to present today's state-of-the-art in high-end networked storage technology, discuss its most important features and limitations, and examine if and how emerging architectures based on commodity technologies may lead to similar or improved features at a better cost-efficiency. We also try to discover the features that CNS may need to support before replacing FCS in new application domains. In particular, we examine capacity and performance scalability, reliability and availability, manageability and flexibility (virtualization), and security.

Architectural evolutions of the storage systems impacts also Grid systems. Currently, Storage Elements are centralized, custom-technology-based storage systems, whenever large capacities of SEs are required. However, the relatively high costs of custom solutions along with growing CPU speeds of commodity computer systems and rapidly increasing capacities of 'desktop-class' disks may result in a dramatic change to SE architectures.

The rest of this paper is organized as follows. Section 2 discusses the features and limitations of FCS. Section 3 presents CNS features and contrasts them to FCS. Section 4 comments on related work and Section 5 includes our conclusion.

2. Categorization of FCS features

In this section we discuss the main features of FCS using the categories defined in the previous point.

2.1 Capacity and performance scalability

System interconnect network. An important component that may limit storage system scalability is the internal system interconnect. FCS interconnect typically consists of a front-end network and a back-end network (Figure 1). The front-end network connects application servers to matrix controllers. The back-end network inter-connects disks drives and matrix controllers. Each of these networks has different features that impact scalability of the whole storage system. The front-end network consists of application server HBAs, disk matrix front-end I/O ports, and SAN switches. Front-end networks typically are switched (FC-SW, Fibre Channel SWitched) and use star, tree, mesh and tiered topologies. Application servers and storage devices are sometimes connected to multiple, independent SAN fabrics, which improves performance and availability but also increases costs. The overall limitation in FCS front-end network is the relatively high cost of SAN network devices. The back-end network consists of disk drives' I/O interfaces, back-end I/O ports in the matrix controllers, and interconnects. Disks drives in matrices are typically grouped in 14-16-drive JBODs (Just a Bunch Of Disks), enclosed in chassis and connected to at least one matrix controller. The most popular link topology used in back-end network is loop (FC-AL, Fibre Channel Arbitrated Loop). This fact influences the back-end network scalability: practical installations use a maximum of about 40 disk devices per single FC loop in order to avoid link saturation, performance and stability degradation. For performance and availability reasons, disk matrices are equipped with multiple back-end loops, each of which can span 12-20 JBODs. Due to discussed limitations, scaling the back-end network is difficult. Expanding the total system capacity and performance beyond the capacity of a few matrices may be possible, but at a prohibitive cost, due to high prices of controllers and fabric in multi-matrix topologies.

Overall, from an architectural point of view, FCS can reach extreme capacities. The front-end connectivity allows FCS systems to provide thousands of ports and the back-end network allows disk matrices to contain hundreds of disk drives. Thus, given current disk capacities – around 750 GBytes/spindle in early 2007 and 1TByte/spindle announced for the end of 2007 – realistic FCS systems can reach capacities of hundreds of peta-bytes (PBytes). However, cost limitations impose more realistic limits. Large FC-based disk matrices incur very high costs that are prohibitive for many application domains. Using SATA-based matrices (instead of FC-based ones) may improve these costs; however, also at reduced reliability, availability, and performance. Moreover, when the size of FCS network grows significantly, keeping the reliability and performance at a constant level is very difficult and expensive.

Processing and Memory. Processing and memory resources of FCS components are based on high-end, storage-specific architectures. Storage CPUs can offer much better performance in I/O requests processing than general-purpose CPUs with similar clock speeds. However, even such specialized resources can limit the capacity, performance, stability and reliability of the storage system at some point. The demands concerning matrix performance and FC switches throughput may grow during the system life-cycle. Therefore, controller CPU and memory as well as FC switches resources must be over-provisioned by design, which requires additional initial cost. Scaling specialized processing and memory resources in FCS is more complicated and costly than upgrading the commodity CPUs and memory modules. Besides, upgrade options may be reduced due to marketing or economic reasons. From the end-user perspective, the only way to scale processing resources is often the upgrade of the whole component (controller, switch) or adding new components along with system reconfiguration. Both solutions are costly, and may be disruptive to system operation.

Throughput. Data throughput in the FCS system is the product of disk-controller, controller-internal, controller-network, network-core, and network-server throughput. Disk-to-controller throughput is mostly affected by the number of disk-drives in the matrix and the throughput of the back-end network. These parameters should make it possible to accommodate the maximum planned performance by design, since scaling throughput beyond initial planning is not straight-forward. Typically, there are only two ways of scaling it: adding more back-end ports to the controllers or to upgrade link speeds, e.g. from 2Gbit/s to 4Gbit/s. Internal controller throughput should be carefully considered at the system design phase, since it is difficult to upgrade later on. Controller throughput upgrade options are limited to controller's processing and memory resources or replacing whole controllers by more powerful models. Although typical internal controllers' throughput is quite impressive (500-900 MBytes/s) given today's technologies, unfortunately it is static during the matrix life-cycle. Controller-to-network throughput mostly depends on the number of front-end ports used for storage devices in the network and the throughput of each link. Each matrix may employ multiple controllers connected to the same or independent SAN fabrics. Controllers are typically equipped with 1-8 front-end ports. Scaling the front-end connectivity of matrices is possible by adding ports to controllers or by upgrading link speeds. Overall, increasing disk to front-end network throughput beyond discussed limits is often done by increasing the number of matrices, which is usually prohibitive from the point of view of costs and system operation. The front-end network throughput depends on the link speed, the network topology used, and usage of multiple Inter-Switch

Links (ISL). Increasing link speed is very costly since it may require upgrading many components: switches, HBAs and matrices' front-end ports. Another option is to modify the topology of the network in order to eliminate hot-spots, e.g. by migrating from star to mesh or adding more ISLs. However, this approach usually incurs a highly non-linear cost due to the increased number of switches required by such changes. Finally, server-network throughput depends on the type and number of HBAs used in servers and the throughput of links. Typically, servers are connected through one or two FC-SW links (2-Gbit/s or 4-Gbit/s) per fabric. Using more HBAs along with server-side link trunking or using multiple independent fabrics one can increase this throughput. Note however, that the cost of a single HBAs is very high. To sum up, high throughput in FCS storage systems is guaranteed by the usage of storage-specific technologies in storage and network devices along with appropriate network configuration and topology. However, while being high-end, FCS components are relatively costly and have static features.

2.2   Reliability and availability

FCS systems are typically configured to avoid a single point of failure and provide a dual path from any server to any block of data. Additionally, each data block is stored in a redundant manner, i.e. it is replicated on multiple disks or protected by RAID checksums.

Providing dual paths requires replication of resources. Typically, application servers have multiple HBAs and are connected to multiple fabrics. Additionally, particular fabrics may have redundant paths. FC switches have redundant, hot-swappable power supplies, fans, or a fully redundant architecture. Disk matrices may be equipped with multiple controllers, which can have a redundant design themselves. Each disk matrix may connect to multiple independent fabrics. Disks drives are typically hot-swappable. FC and SAS drives are dual-ported and accessible by two controllers using independent back-end links. Single-ported disks can be connected to controllers using passive (and thus fault-tolerant) multiplexers. Finally, firmware upgrade to system components can happen in a non-disruptive manner, e.g. two-step controllers update in matrices.

Avoiding a single point of failure in FCS is sufficient in most practical situations. Techniques of achieving this are standardized and well-documented. However, in some cases, a higher level of redundancy would be useful, but configuring FCS systems in that way may be problematic and may incur significantly higher costs.

Data replication and protection techniques in FCS systems include: RAID support, mirroring and snapshot support as well as matrix cache memory content protection. RAIDs make user data available in the presence of data block damage. Hot-spare features and the use of appropriate RAID levels enable continuous access to data in case of disk drive failure. Apart from RAID support, local and remote data mirroring is used to protect against environmental disasters such as fire and floods. Protecting controller cache contents from failures is very important for data coherency. The issue is quite complex, and it is covered in FCS by techniques such as cache scrubbing, cache coherency techniques, and cache content protection against utility failure, i.e. battery-protection and cache vaulting. Critical configuration data of FCS system are saved to a non-volatile media such as flash cards or selected disk drives in matrices or they may be exported to external media or management databases.

Finally, FCS systems employ detailed component monitoring and events reporting, usually in each component's firmware. Monitoring applies to failures and performance measures (error rate, load, usage, efficiency). It covers various FCS components: switch ports, zones, disk controllers, LUNs, RAIDs, CPUs, caches, disk drives, fans and power supplies. Any problems can be automatically reported by email or SMS alerts and SNMP traps. Active integrity monitoring techniques include periodic disk surface scanning and trial read and write operations to unused areas of disks during low traffic periods.

In summary, the reliability and availability techniques of the FCS systems are well-established and proved. They are supported by fundamental system architecture features: centralization that makes it possible to define semantics during failures as well as redundancy of data paths and blocks, which prevents from possible failure effects. Reliability and availability of FCS is also supported by numerous additional techniques employed in FCS components. However, an important limitation is that these features are achieved at a very high cost – redundancy multiplies the total costs of the system and reliability and availability features must be paid by end-users in the form of a very high purchase price. Another limitation is that higher-than-default levels of resource redundancy are sometimes hard to achieve due to a centralized architecture and static nature of FCS components.

2.3   Security techniques in FCS

Basic security techniques supported in FCS systems are: (a) traffic separation and access control, (b) support for confidentiality of data transfer and data storage.

Traffic separation and access control. A simple technique for access control in SAN networks is LUN masking. A particular disk volume can be mapped to selected servers and the requests from all other servers in the network can be rejected by matrix controller. Additionally, FC switches support zoning that allows to logically separate the data traffic between selected devices in FCS. VSAN is a technique that allows several ports or FCS devices to be grouped together and form a virtual fabric with full fabric functionality. However, the practical effectiveness of the above-mentioned techniques is actually limited, e.g. they can be bypassed by a malicious server with a spoofed address. Overall, these simple security techniques constitute the first line of defense in FCS systems. A second line concerns sharing the FCS fabrics among several organizations. For that purpose access control lists (ACLs) for fabrics, ports, and other fine-grain mechanisms combined with PKI authentication are used. Additionally, monitoring, auditing, event logging, integrity checks and security threat detection techniques may be employed in FCS. Unfortunately, native FCS systems do not support them and external tools are necessary, obviously at additional costs.

Data confidentiality and integrity techniques. An important issue in FCS systems is the lack of the native support for strong security techniques related to data links and data storage. Originally, FCS systems were designed to be dedicated, physically separated infrastructures used by single organizations. However, many security threats originate from the inside of organizations mandating the use of strong data encryption. Real-time encryption of high-volume information accessed at high-throughput is very challenging – it cannot be performed by the application servers because it is computation-intensive and would consume too many computing resources. To deal with encryption performance issues, hardware-based or mixed, i.e. software-hardware-based, encryption solutions are used. However, even these specialized encryption systems have limitations related mainly to performance (not 'at wire speed'), scope of their possible usage (not for all data), cost (e.g. $30,000 per single encryption appliance) and administration overhead (e.g. key loss risk), and finally, mutual compatibility of different vendors products [1].

2.4 Management and flexibility

Actual usability of the storage system strongly depends on the management techniques (called sometimes virtualization techniques) available in it.

Management tools for FCS components cover the network components as well as data storage devices, client hosts, and the data itself. FCS systems components can be controlled, configured and monitored through graphical and text interfaces. They can also generate asynchronous, event-triggered alerts in order to inform system administrators about critical situations. Virtualization techniques for FC switches enable to setup ports, trunking, fabric routing, zoning and name services. Name Services is a mechanism that provides translation between world-wide names (WWNs, physical addresses of FCS devices) and symbolic, human-readable node names. This helps to avoid potential mistakes of a human operator. An important management mechanism is fabric State Change Notification, which allows notification to registered SAN nodes if a change occurs to other specified nodes [2]. Management tools for disk matrices are used for two main purposes: to control the arrangement of the logical data volumes on the physical devices, and to setup and monitor another parameters of matrix operation. It is possible to define RAID volumes: RAID level, stripe size, default serving controller, spare disk assignment as well as to re-size RAID during system operation. Logical volumes-related features include: creation, mapping to hosts and LUN masking. Other mechanisms allow to configure the controllers' collaboration mode: active-active vs. active-passive; cache management policy: for random, sequential and mixed access patterns; cache stripe size and cache write mode: write-back or write-through.

Native FCS virtualization mechanisms support only basic management operations. More complex techniques such as virtual volumes spanning multiple matrix controllers, snapshots, versioning, compression and encryption are available as external software- or hardware-based solutions. A still unsolved issue concerning management and virtualization in FCS is the lack of a complete and standardized approach. Several existing management tools are limited to specific areas of the system, a particular level of the system component and data abstraction, or simply a small set of a vendor's products. This makes management of heterogeneous FCS systems complicated and costly, and the actual scalability hard to achieve. Standardization efforts partially solve this problem [3]. Despite these efforts and existence of extensive management tools for FCS systems, guaranteeing service level agreements (SLAs) in complex FCS setups is still challenging. This is caused by the fact that multiple users and applications may share physical FCS resources, including HBAs, switches, links, storage controllers, caches, and disk drives. Overloading any resource in the I/O path may degrade performance for all applications that share it. Logical separation of FCS components does not solve this issue. Therefore, the only method to provide strong, per-application guarantees is either to use dedicated FCS systems or apply full component redundancy along with careful system design, deployment and testing. On the other hand, this approach incurs prohibitive costs for many application domains. Management automation in FCS systems could significantly reduce associated costs. Activities that can be automated include, for example, using Hierarchical Storage Management (HSM) systems or Information Life-cycle Management (ILM) concepts; however, there is still no complete solution for management automation – HSM systems cover only part of the problem and ILM concepts are far from common practice.

3.　From Fiber-Channel-based to Cluster-Based Networked Storage

One of the main advantages of CNS systems is expected to be the use of scalable, commodity interconnects both for storage and client nodes. Such networks have been demonstrated to scale very well to thousands of nodes at affordable costs [4]. Furthermore, new emerging 10GigE Ethernet networking switches, feature path fail-over functionality, similar to FCS, but at a cost that is constantly dropping [5].

The capacity of a CNS system depends on the maximum capacity of the interconnects used. This specifies the maximum number of storage nodes in the system as well as the maximum number of clients that may access the storage system. Today, a storage node may host up to 32-48 disks [6] resulting in 10's of TBytes per storage node. Given that modern commodity interconnects can scale to thousands of nodes, CNS can practically scale to very large numbers of disks and 100s of PBytes. Finally, adding more clients to a CNS system corresponds to adding more nodes in the interconnect used by the system.

CNS allows both memory and processing resources to scale. Storage nodes can be equipped with one or two CPUs and large amounts of memory without significant increases in base system cost, since this is commodity hardware.

Disk-Controller throughput in CNS can scale by increasing the number of disks in each storage node. In general it is expected that each storage node will hold a small number of disk controllers (1-4) with each controller holding a small number of disks (2-16). This provides a wide range of options in scaling the disk-controller throughput in each installation. Controller-Network and Client-Network: CNS storage nodes use 1-2 network links to connect to the system interconnect (1 or 10 Gigabit Ethernet, Myrinet, Infiniband). The maximum number of links that may be used depends on the bandwidth available in the internal storage node paths. Modern storage nodes can have I/O buses that are able to achieve throughput at the level of 40 Gbits/s full duplex, e.g. two slots of 8x PCI-Express. However, data may have to be staged in the main memory while being transferred from disk to the network (or vice versa). Thus, CNS storage nodes can support multiple network links, e.g. 4x1 Gigabit/s or even 2x10 Gbit/s links. Moreover, as both disk controllers (storage nodes) and clients connect to the system using the same commodity interconnect, similar characteristics apply to client-network throughput scaling.

One of the main advantages of CNS is that it uses a general-purpose interconnect that scales to a large number of nodes in various application areas such as high-performance cluster computing [4]. Although many issues related to interconnects and communication protocols that will be used in CNS systems are not yet clear and are the subject of current research [7], these interconnects will offer significantly more throughput and configuration flexibility at a lower cost compared to traditional FC interconnects. Furthermore, since the same interconnect can be used both for controller-controller and client-controller connectivity, we expect that CNS will, in the long-run, have better scalability characteristics compared to FCS.

3.1   Reliability and availability

The reliability of commodity hardware is not really understood yet. Recent results [8] in large populations of disks indicate that drive failure rates in SCSI, FC, and SATA drives are in reality close. This is counter-intuitive for low-cost drives, compared to the much higher-cost FC and SCSI "enterprise" disks with their much higher MTBFs. This work concludes that there are little differences in failure rates, which may be an indication that disk-independent factors, such as operating conditions, affect failure rates more than component-specific factors. Architecture-wise, a main challenge with CNS is that, unlike FCS, CNS needs to support storage volumes that span (a large numbers of) storage nodes. In FCS systems a volume is typically confined to a single storage controller. This single controller has complete control over all accesses to volume blocks. All accesses to this block can be ordered and thus, it is easy to deal both with consistency issues and failures. Accesses to different blocks are usually ordered and/or made atomic by mechanisms that are external to the FCS system and are usually part of the file system. CNS, on the other hand, needs to support volumes that span multiple storage nodes (controllers). Although CNS may be configured with volumes being confined within a single storage node, this imposes significant limitations to how CNS may be configured and how it may adjust dynamically to the application needs. For instance, if volumes are confined within a single storage node, they may span only a limited (and relatively small) number of disks; replicated blocks may reside only within a single node, requiring replication of all node components to achieve dual path redundancy; accesses to disk blocks are limited to a small number of network links.

Thus, although a CNS system may be configured similarly to FCS, many of the benefits of using CNS derive from its more distributed nature and the ability to distribute volumes across storage controllers. However, this imposes significant challenges that are the subject of current research. Fundamentally, CNS systems need to provide ordering of accesses to distributed copies of a single block and ordering of accesses to different blocks of a volume (and their copies) in the presence of failures. Overall, offering high reliability and availability in CNS systems is the topic of current research. Today research prototypes exist for providing RAID functions across storage nodes, using erasure coding techniques, or stronger voting techniques [10].

3.2   Security

CNS systems use interconnects that may perform similar access control and traffic separation as in FCS systems. Both have been investigated extensively in local area networks and are currently the subject of research in higher-end system area networks. However, the main difference from FCS is that CNS interconnects and nodes tend to be 'general-purpose', as opposed to specialized

FCS interconnects and controllers, and thus are more susceptible to attacks. For instance, given that a CNS system may allow access to the interconnect to large numbers of clients for direct access to storage, 'illegal' or malicious clients may obtain access to the network and thus will be able to send I/O requests to storage nodes. Currently, given that all I/O checks are performed in traditional filesystems, storage nodes reply to all I/O requests, providing access to raw blocks. Such problems and their solutions are currently open research topics [11].

3.3   Management and Flexibility

If a CNS system is configured to provide similar guarantees and semantics to an FCS system, then existing storage management tools can be used on top of CNS systems. However, the real potential of CNS is to provide higher flexibility, reliability, availability, and security compared to FCS systems. In this case, management tools will also need to adapt to new capabilities. Thus management tools should be able to automatically deal with many of the issues that today require human intervention and expertise. Currently, there is very little progress in this area and the role of future research is expected to be significant [12].

4.   Related Work

Recently, there has been a lot of research work in enabling cluster-based networked storage systems. Previous and current work in the area includes: Today, building scalable storage systems that provide storage sharing for multiple applications relies on layering a distributed file-system on top of a pool of block-level storage. This approach is dictated by the fact that block-level storage has limited semantics that do not allow for performing advanced storage functions and especially they are not able to support transparent sharing without application support. Efforts in this direction include distributed *cluster file systems* often based on VAXclusters [13] concepts that allow for efficient sharing of data among a set of storage servers with strong consistency semantics and fail-over capabilities. Such systems typically operate on top of a pool of physically shared devices through a SAN. However, they do not provide much control over the system's operation. Modern cluster file-systems such as the GFS [14] and GPFS [15] are used extensively today in medium and large scale storage systems for clusters. However, their complexity makes them hard to develop and maintain, prohibits any practical extension to the underlying storage system, and forces all applications to use a single, almost fixed, view of the available data. The Federated Array of Bricks (FAB) [10] discusses how storage systems may be built out of commodity storage nodes and interconnects and yet compete (in terms of reliability and performance) with custom, high-end solutions for enterprise environments. Ursa Minor [16], a system for object-based storage bricks coupled with a central manager, provides flexibility with respect to the data layout and the fault-model (both for client and storage nodes). These parameters can be adjusted dynamically on a per data item basis, according to the needs of a given environment. Such fine grain customization yields noticeable performance improvements. Previous work has also investigated a number of issues raised by the lack of a central controller and the distributed nature of cluster-based storage systems, e.g. consistency for erasure-coded redundancy schemes [17] and efficient request scheduling [18].

5.   Conclusions

Our analysis shows that FCS has been fairly successful in providing high scalability and advanced management features, fulfilling stringent requirements on capacity, performance, reliability, availability, and manageability. However, FCS exhibits certain architectural and functional limitations and results in high complexity and cost. For these reasons, the shift towards more commodity architectures for storage elements is an important trend, which is increasingly appealing due to economical and scaling reasons. Although CNS has a significant potential to reduce system cost and eliminate functional limitations, there is still a number of open issues that need to be addressed before CNS prototypes can be deployed in demanding production environments. Several open research issues exist, mostly in the areas of reliability, security and storage management. Although, the shift towards CNS will have an impact on the nature of the storage subsystem in Grid infrastructures, higher level Grid services and architectures should start considering the challenges and opportunities lying ahead.

Acknowledgments

We thankfully acknowledge the support of the European Commission under the Sixth Framework Program through the Network of Excellence CoreGRID (Contract IST-2002-004265). The work at FORTH-ICS was also supported by the European Commission under the Sixth Framework Program through the Marie Curie Excellent Teams Award UNISIX (Contract number MEXT-CT-2003-509595).

References

[1] Storage Magazine, Alan Radding: Is encryption enough?, http://storagemagazine. techtarget.com/magItem/0,291266,sid35_gci1193200,00.html.

[2] SNIA, A SNIA Dictionary of Storage Networking Terminology., http://www.snia.org/ education/dictionary.

[3] SNIA, The SNIA's Storage Management Initiative., http://www.snia.org/smi/home.

[4] Top500 supercomputing sites.

[5] Woven Systems, The Woven Systems EFX 1000 Ethernet Fabric Switch., http://wovensystems.com.

[6] Xyratex Technology Limited., RS-4835-E3-EBD Datasheet., http://www.xyratex.com/products/storage-systems/storage-RS-4835-E3-EBD.asp.

[7] H. bung Chen, G. Grider, and P. Fields, A Cost-Effective, High Bandwidth Server I/O network Architecture for Cluster Systems., in *International Parallel and Distributed Processing Symposium (IPDPS 2007)*, pp. 1–10, IEEE, 2007.

[8] B. Schroeder and C. M. U. Garth A. Gibson, Disk Failures in the Real World: What Does an MTTF of 1,000,000 Hours Mean to You?, in *Proceedings of 5th USENIX Conference on File and Storage Technologies (FAST '07)*, pp. 1–16, San Francisco, CA, USA, 2007.

[9] B. Schroeder and C. M. U. Garth A. Gibson, Disk Failures in the Real World: What Does an MTTF of 1,000,000 Hours Mean to You?, in *Proceedings of 5th USENIX Conference on File and Storage Technologies (FAST '07)*, pp. 17–28, San Francisco, CA, USA, 2007.

[10] Y. Saito, S. Frolund, A. Veitch, A. Merchant, and S. Spence, FAB: Enterprise storage systems on a shoestring, in *Proc. of the ASPLOS 2004*, 2004.

[11] M. W. Storer, K. Greenan, E. L. Miller, and K. Voruganti, POTSHARDS: Secure Long-Term Storage Without Encryption, in *2007 USENIX Annual Technical Conference*, 2007.

[12] A. J. K. Gregory R. Ganger, John D. Strunk, Carnegie Mellon University Report No. CMU-CS-03-178, 2003 (unpublished).

[13] N. P. Kronenberg, H. M. Levy, and W. D. Strecker, ACM Transactions on Computer Systems **4** (1986).

[14] S. Soltis, G. Erickson, K. Preslan, M. O'Keefe, and T. Ruwart, The Global File System: A File System for Shared Disk Storage, 1997.

[15] F. Schmuck and R. Haskin, GPFS: A Shared-disk File System for Large Computing Centers, in *USENIX Conference on File and Storage Technologies*, pp. 231–244, Monterey, CA, 2002.

[16] M. A.-E.-M. et al., Ursa Minor: Versatile Cluster-Based Storage, in *Proceedings of the 4th USENIX Conference on File and Storage Technology*, San Francisco, CA, USA, 2005.

[17] K. A. Amiri, G. A. Gibson, and R. Golding, Highly Concurent Shared Storage, in *Proceedings of 20th International Conference on Distributed Computing Systems (ICDCS'2000)*, edited by IEEE, pp. 298–307, Taipe, Taiwan, R.O.C, 2000, IEEE Computer.

[18] C. R. Lumb, R. Golding, and G. R. Ganger, D-SPTF: Decentralized Request Distribution in Brick-Based Storage Systems, in *Proceedings of the 11th ACM ASPLOS Conference*, Boston, MA, USA, 2004.

TOWARDS UNIFORM AND TRANSPARENT ACCESS TO THE GRID INFORMATION USING THE PALANTIR*

Ivan Rodero, Francesc Guim, and Julita Corbalan
Barcelona Supercomputing Center (BSC)
Technical University of Catalonia(UPC)
Jordi Girona 1-3, 08034 Barcelona, Spain
CoreGRID Institute on Resource Management and Scheduling
ivan.rodero@bsc.es
francesc.guim@bsc.es
julita.corbalan@bsc.es

Abstract   Grids allow large scale resource-sharing across different administrative domains. Those diverse resources are likely to join or quit the Grid at any moment or possibly to break down. Grid monitoring tools have to adapt supporting access information to these heterogeneous and not reliable environments. There is a wide rage of types of resources to be monitored or entities, with different nature, characteristics and so on. These issues make the task of gathering Grid information complex to treat, and it is difficult to provide a generals ways for accessing to all this information. In this paper we propose a set of functionalities that a Grid Information System should provide. We describe the Palantir meta-information system that has been designed for uniform the access to different monitoring and information systems and that implements all the discussed functionalities. Moreover, we present real examples that state how Palantir has been integrated providing the uniform. access to systems with heterogeneous information providers.

Keywords: Grid, metadata model, monitoring systems, information systems, Palantir

*This research work is carried out under the FP6 Network of Excellence CoreGRID funded by the European Commission (Contract IST-2002-004265).

1. Introduction

As other Grid middleware components, monitoring services have to adapt to the characteristics of Grid architecture. They should provide uniform access to information and resources, ways to discover which capabilities it has and how to access it.

In the eNANOS [1] architecture we needed a new component that would allow accessing to all the information related to the entities (a Grid entity is any software or hardware component that is able to provide information) that are involved in our system, i.e: Grid jobs, local processes, resources and so on. This component should integrate and merge information from the bottom part of the Grid, coming from the local components of the centers (such as the eNANOS scheduler) with information coming from the top components of our architecture, in our case from the eNANOS Broker. The nature of the information that it would provide would be much diversified: information from the resource monitoring systems, from the job monitoring systems, performance predictions from predictors etc.

For achieve this goal, our first approach consisted on having a deep study of the available monitoring tools and try to adapt to our requirements the more appropriate one. However, at the best of our knowledge we realized that any of them matched all the requirements that we had. Using our experience in Grid monitoring and information systems obtained in the HPC-Europa project [2], we designed a kind of meta-information system that would implement all the needed functionalities.

The presented system is not intended to substitute any of the other existing monitoring or information tools. It is intended to uniform the access to all the information provided by them. Furthermore, as has been discussed in [2] and [3], most of the HPC centers have already deployed their own site-specific HPC and Grid infrastructure. Therefore, an additional requirement is to keep the autonomy of HPC centers allowing them to use their favorite Information Systems and Information providers.

The goal of this paper is to discuss the need of common and homogenized information protocols, information data models and information access functionalities in the Grid. We propose as a possible solution the Palantir meta-information, and present how the different requirements are provided in its design.

In the first part of the paper we present the motivations that let us to develop the Palantir system. In the second part we present the data model that has been designed for accessing to all the entities information, the architectural components that integrate the system, and finally a description of the main functionalities that will be provided to the Palantir users.

2.   What do we need?

Usually, information systems (IS) do not use to provide all the information that administrator or users want. For example in [2] we stated that the Grid brokers are continuously providing new types of information, and the users and Grid components want this to be available as soon as possible. The IS should provide mechanisms for extend their functionalities and the set of information that they provide.

The Grid information providers (brokers, schedulers, monitoring systems etc.) frequently allow accessing to diversified information with different format and semantics. The IS that are providing access to such information should provide simple and generic APIs for query it. This property of generality is especially important due the information may have different semantic and structure, and new entities may appear in the future. Regarding this access there are two factors that must be taken in consideration:

- The methods that the API provides: they should provide mechanisms for discover the available entity types, its characteristics, the information they provide and the real entities that can provide this information; and mechanism for gather this information of each of this entities instantiations.

- The data model used for conveys the required information. The model should not be linked to a specific kind of entities/resources (such as physical resources like hosts or network, or software resources like applications or jobs).

Related to this issue of how to access the information, there is an important question that the IS should manage itself: where the information is stored?. In the current Grid architectures and systems the user has to know exactly where the information can be retrieved. For instance, if the user "fguim" wants to know the state for the job "grid123@pcmas", he has to know that this information has to be retrieved queering the broker eNANOS that is running on the host "pcmas". This problem may seem quite obvious to solve in some small architectures, however it can become a challenge for users in bigger systems.

Nowadays how to access the information is not only the unique key for the Grid consumers. Controlling to which information the users are accessing is also a mandatory goal when installing the IS to the real enterprises and Grid systems. Security is crucial issue when accessing to the resources information. They should take into account aspects as accounting, user privileges, communication security etc.

It is pretty common that some resource can only be queried by users or applications that have been granted before, for instance only the user that have submitted a job or an administrator can know its performance. Furthermore, the coming Grids markets, like the models proposed by Dr. Buyya [4], needs this support for become a reality.

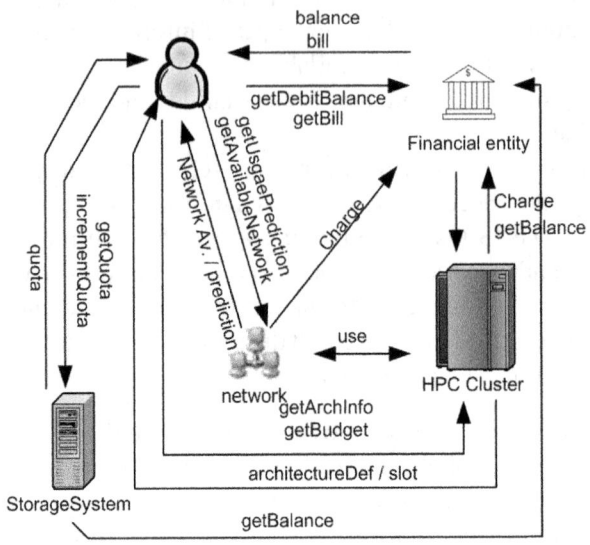

Figure 1. Information workflow in the Grid

The economic Grid is a clear example of an architecture that requires an information system with all the functionalities that we have discussed. Such Grids have to provide access information like bills, resource usage, users, banks accounts etc. It is clear that new entity types may appear and disappear continuously in such environments.

On the other hand each of these entities comes from a very different nature: the bank entities come from the economic namespaces, while the resource usage comes from the computer science domain. In such dynamic and diversified environments the IS must provide a very generic data model. This data model should be able to convey information like the users profile, thread/process/job performance etc.

The coming Grids for the 2010 are supposed to have hundred up to thousands of elements (entities). Each of them may have the role of information provider (IP). At this point, users/applications will not be able to know exactly where the information can be collected. Moreover, they will not know where the information is stored and who is providing it. IS will have to implement mechanism for discover exactly where the information that users are requiring is stored. For example: we can not expect a user will know that the resource consumption for the job "job123@pcmas" has to be queried to the IS "eNANOS@BSC", but the consumption for the job "job124@kadesh" has to be queried to MDS.

Figure 1 exemplifies a situation where a unified mechanism for accessing the information it is required. There are four different components (a financial entity, a StorageSystem, an HPC-Resource and the user) that also have the role of IP. Each of this components may use different IS for publishing its information. When the components have to interact between them, they have to be aware of the format used for querying them, the format of the replies, its semantics etc. Clearly this situation becomes unsustainable when the number of information providers increase.

3.   What can we do?

We carried out a deep study [5] about the more representative information systems available in the research area as a basis of our design: Globus Monitoring and Discovery Service (MDS) [6], GridLab Mercury [7], Network Weather Service (NWS) [8], CrossGrid OMIS Compliant Monitoring service for the Grid [9], and Ganglia [10].

We did not found any of them that exactly match all the requirements that have been discussed before. The main lack was the possibility of extending their functionalities and providing generic and uniform access to all their information.

However, all these IS provide very useful information. As each of these systems is mainly specialized in a specific domain, it is able to provide a high quality data about its namespace (job monitoring, resource monitoring etc.). At this point we the question was: why not unify the access to all these IS?

This question was the base for the Palantir meta-information system designs (see Figure 2). Its main goal is provide a uniform access to the whole Grid information providers.

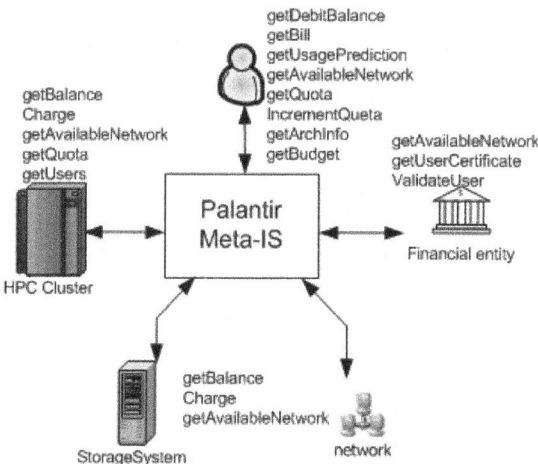

Figure 2.   With a unified protocol

4.   Palantir in the eNANOS system

Currently, we are mainly focused in providing access to all the components that are involved in the eNANOS architecture plus some other IS. This uniform information access will simplify notoriously the collection of data done by all the elements of our system. Figure 3 shows all the information providers that are being currently integrated as a part of the Palantir installation done in our system. Mainly there are four kinds of information providers:

- Resource monitoring IS. (Ganglia)

- Job Monitoring IS. Including both Grid and local job monitoring information (with information such as job / process / thread performance).

- Performance predictors. IS Including NWS and a set of predictor modules that have been designed by our research group.

- Service state information IS (MDS). They will provide information about the state of the services that used by the other components (applications etc.).

- Progress and performance indicators API. It will provide both absolute and relative information about the progress of the applications through a library and a run-time included inside the eNANOS framework [11].

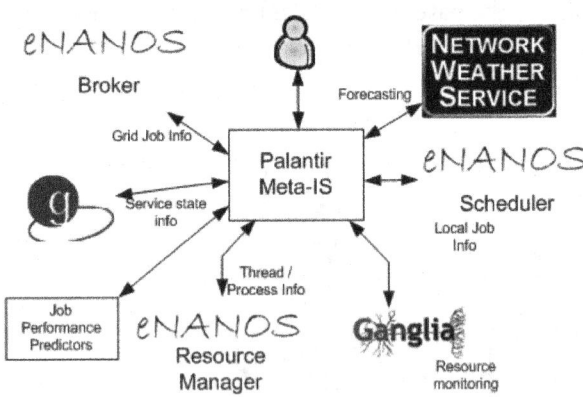

Figure 3.   Palantir in the eNANOS architecture

5.   The Palantir data model

The abstract Palantir data model is composed for two elements: the Entities and the Entity Metrics. The entities represent the conceptual elements of the systems that can contain information suitable to be requested. They are not required to be physical resources. For example, hosts, jobs or applications are considered to be entities. Each entity has associated a set of metrics that contain specific information. For instance the metric elapsed time is a metric that can be associated to the entity job. Each entity type has a set of instantiations: for example the entity host may the instantiations "host1.bsc.es", "host2.bsc.es" etc. The attributes for the entity are (see Figure 4):

- Its name. That must be unique in the system (such as Job, predictor etc).

- Its description. That contains a human readable description of the entity.

- Its key. That, using the XML Schema technology, describes how this entity is identified. For example the key for the host entity may be composed by its hostname or by its IP address (or both).

- Its namespaces. It contains a set of URIs (Uniform Resource Identifier) identifying the semantic spaces to which the entity belongs.

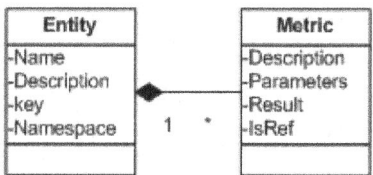

Figure 4.   Abstract Data Model

An entity may have associated a set of metrics; each metric also has a set of predefined attributes:

- Its name. That must be unique to the entities to which it is associated.

- A human readable description of the information that it provides.

- Its parameters. Using also the XML Schema technology defines the parameters that can be provided to Palantir when requiring its content to an instantiation of a given entity. For example the entity Predictor requires the job id as a parameter when querying for its metric JobRunTimePrediction.

- The XML Schema that describes the format of information returned when querying its content. In case that the metric contains a reference to another entity instantiation this will indicated by the Boolean attribute IsRef.

The model presented until this point is the abstract model. However in the systems where Palantir is installed this data model is defined using concrete

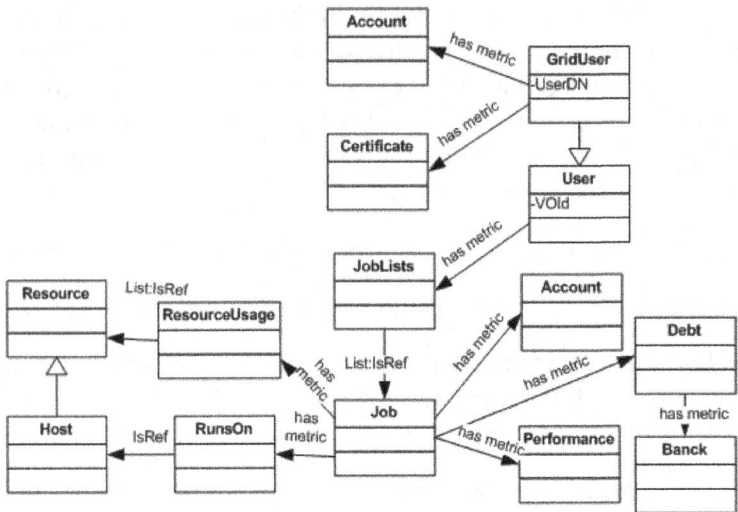

Figure 5.   Palantir Data Model example

entities (not the instantiations). For example the Figure 5 presents a possible Palantir model that could be specified in a system where information about users and its jobs is provided.

Different Palantir systems may be installed in different domains. Each of these installations may have a different concrete model. The concrete model is mainly designed taking into account to which information systems the Palantir is providing access. When a new IS is added to an installation its concrete data model may vary. If this new IS provides new information that it is not included in any of the already defined entities the Palantir administrators can choose one of the three following options:

- Creating new entities that will provide information about the new conceptual elements.

- Extending the definition of an existing entity adding new metrics to it. For example, in case that the new IS provides performance information concerning the running jobs, the metric PerformanceIndicator could be added to the entity job.

- Extending the definition of an existing entity creating a sub entity. The proposed model is a UML like model, and entities may inherit the definition of other entities.

However, this analysis will not always be required when a Palantir will be installed in a particular architecture. There will be a set of predefined entities whom design will be based on a set of IS (Ganglia, NWS etc.) that will available when building a concrete system. Furthermore, future versions may include semi/automatic methods for derive this actions.

6.   The Palantir system architecture

In this section we present the overview of the architecture that allows gathering the information for each of the instantiation of the entities available in a concrete installation of the system.

Figure 6 provides a general view of the system architecture. As can be observed there are three top architectural components: at the top there are the Palantir Access Points that allow the uniform access to the users/applications to the system; the Palantir Gateways are the intermediate layers that control the access to the information providers installed in each of the centers joined to the system; and finally, the bottom components of the system are the information modules. They are the responsible of gathering the required information to the different IP/IS.

6.1   The access points

The first layer is integrated by the Palantir Access Points (AP). These components provide a uniform view to the end-user/application of the whole information that is available in the system. They must know which centers are available to provide information.

When the end-user/application carries out a query to the AP, it redirects it to the appropriate Palantir Gateway or Gateways that are able to provide the required information. An important question to address is how the AP knows to which GW have to connect when the end-user/applications requires information about a given entity. The system distinguishes between two kinds of entities: persistent entities and the temporal entities.

The persistent entities are non-volatile entities that will remain available in the system for a long time. Examples of this kind of entities are: host, cluster, performance predictor, storage system etc. For them the database stores among other data in which Gateway/Gateways its information is stored. For example in Figure 6 the Palantir AP will know that the entity "job21@pcmas" can be queried in the Gateway installed in the BSC Center.

The temporal entities are volatile entities or with a limited amount life time, for example: jobs. The AP identifies the GWs where this information can be gathered analyzing the entity key. If the key is in the composed form, a subset of this key must identify a persistent entity that will be used to find out in which GW the query has to be done. However, as not all the temporal entities will be able to satisfy the above property, a temporary entity can be also identified by a direct links. This directly points to which module/s the information can be retrieved (such: "gw[id='X']/module[id='MDS1']/entity[id='job1']").

The management of this kind of keys should be transparent to the user. As will be presented in the following section, the system provides a set of discovering methods that allow to the clients to retrieve this kind of keys. In this cases the user does not have be aware of what the key means.

The protocol used from the application to this access point is based on the generic protocol presented in the following section. More important is that client does not have to be aware to which information system the final queries are done, abstracting it to the complexity of the underlying systems.

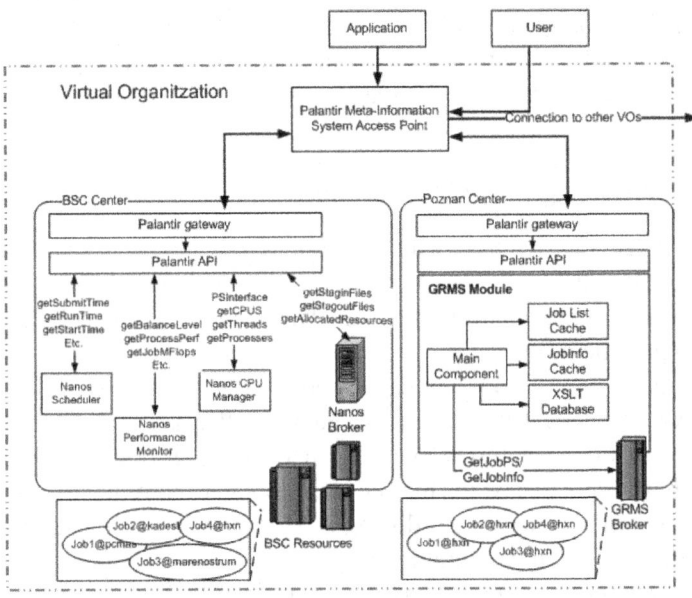

Figure 6.   eNANOS and GRMS modules

6.2   The gateways

The main task of the gateway is choosing the appropriate module that will process a given query. It stores a data base with all the entities that are available on underlying modules. When entity information is required it searches in this database where it can be retrieved. The mechanism used for decide to which modules the information is gathered is exactly the same as the once presented for Access Point.

6.3   Information systems modules

Finally, at the bottom part of the architecture, the modules are responsible of carry out the final queries to the information or monitoring systems that they represent.

At this level, modules must know how the queries have to be done to the systems. For each monitoring or information system that can be queried through the Palantir, a module must be implemented.

6.4   An example: integrating two different job monitoring approaches

Figure 6 shows two different modules that have been developed for accessing the job monitoring information of two different systems [12]. The eNANOS module integrates job information coming form different components of our architecture [1]:

- The eNANOS scheduler provides general information about all the jobs that have been submitted on the local hosts.

- The eNANOS Performance Monitor provides information regarding the progress for the different processes that are running in each host: the achieved MFLOPs, the load balance level etc.

- The NANOS CPUManager provides information about how the different jobs/process/thread are behaving on the resources.

- The eNANOS Broker provides information about the jobs that have been submitted to the Grid: stagein files, stageout files, resources etc.

When the eNANOS module receives a query about a certain job metric it gathers the required information using the different APIs that the presented components provide (such as PSInterface of the CPU Manager, or the getBalanceLevel of the Performance monitor).

On the other hand, the same Palantir architecture allows monitoring the jobs that have been submitted to the GRMS broker [13]. The GRMS Palantir Module access to the GRMS monitoring information using the interface GetJobPS that returns a set of XML documents the monitoring information for a job that has been submitted to the broker. Using XSLT the module transforms these documents to the Palantir protocol format.

In this example, the end-user/application is able to accessing to the job monitoring information that comes from two different systems (with different mechanisms, different interfaces and different formats) using the standard format and protocol proposed in Palantir.

7.   The Palantir protocol and interfaces

The API is divided in three main parts. The first one is a set of methods that allows starting and ending communications between authorized components and the meta-information system. The second set of methods allows discovering which type of features (such as entities types, metrics and entities instantiations) and methods are available. And finally, the third type of methods allows gathering the metric values for the entities instantiations.

7.1   Connecting to the information system

These mechanisms allow the user to be authenticated against the system. The accounting can be used if the underlying systems allow them. However, the security object always will be used for carry out a secure connection. Two main methods will be provided: the StartCommunication opens a secure connection with the system; and the CloseCommunication closes the connection and invalidates the security objects.

```
1   <AvailableEntities    xmlns:xs="http://www.w3.org/2001/XMLSchema">
2     <!— List of resources available —>
3     <Entity name="host">
4       <Description>This resource allows to carry out queries about the resource
              host</Description>
5       <key>
6         <xs:element name="host">
7           <xs:complexType>
8             <xs:choice>
9               <xs:element name="ip" type="xs:string"/>
10              <xs:element name="hostname" type="xs:string" minOccurs="0"/>
11            </xs:choice>
12          </xs:complexType>
13        </xs:element>
14      </key>
15    </Entity >
16    <Entity name="application">
17      <Description>This resource allows to carry out queries about the software
              resource application</Description>
18      <key>
19        <xs:element name="application">
20          <xs:complexType>
21            <xs:choice>
22              <xs:element name="name" type="xs:string"/>
23              <xs:element name="version" type="xs:string" minOccurs="0"/>
24            </xs:choice>
25          </xs:complexType>
26        </xs:element>
27      </key>
28    </Entity >
29  </AvailableEntities>
```

Source 1: GetResourceInstantiation

7.2   Discovering the available features

The meta-information system, as it is providing a wide range of information, and it is using several underlying systems, provides ways to discover how to query it and what information can be gathered. Below are presented all the methods that have been defined for provide these functionalities.

- GetEntitiesTypes: Returns the list of the types of entities available on the system. An example of a returned XML is shown in the Source 1. User can filter the information to be retrieved, for example only entities types that concerns computational resources and forecasting entities.

- GetEntityInstantiation: Returns the list of instances of a provided entity type. For instance, user may know the list of entities of type "host". As the GetEntitiesTypes method, the Palantir client can specify some parameters for filter the instantiations to be retrieved.

- GetMetricInfo: Returns information about a particular metric of a particular entity or resource. For instance, calling getMetricInfo("application", "prediction_job_memory_usage") we could obtain the XML document presented in Source 2.

```
1   <Metric>
2     <Name>prediction_job_memory_usage</Name>
3     <Description>Returns a prediction of the memory that a given application
            will use if executed.
4     </Description>
5     <Parameters>
6       <xs:element name="Parameters">
7         <xs:complexType>
8           <xs:sequence>
9             <xs:element name="AppName"/>
10            <xs:element name="Host"/>
11            <xs:element name="User"/>
12            <!— ETCETERA —>
13          </xs:sequence>
14        </xs:complexType>
15      </xs:element>
16    </Parameters>
17    <!— ETCETERA—>
18    </Filters>
19    <Notifications>
20    <Periodic available="no"/>
21    <Punctual available="yes"/>
22    </Notifications>
23  </Metric>
```

Source 2: Sample of output for the GetMetricInfo

7.3   Getting the entity information

The client can retrieve the metrics values of a given entity instantiation using the GetMetricValue functionality. The input for this method is basically a set of entity instantiations identifiers plus all the metrics that the client wants to know about each of them. Each metric can be parameterized. For instance the metric JobsList for the entity Scheduler can be parameterized as shown in Source 3.

```
1    <Parameters>
2      <JobsMatching >
3        <FilterByDate>
4          <BetweenDates>
5            <StartDate>1136208170544</StartDate>
6            <EndDate>1136380970544</EndDate>
7          </BetweenDates>
8        </FilterByDate>
9        <FilterByState>
10         <State>FAILED</State>
11         <State>SUSPENDED</State>
12        </FilterByState>
13        <SubmissionDate>
14          <BetweenDates>
15            <StartDate>1138886570544</StartDate>
16            <EndDate>1136380970544</EndDate>
17          </BetweenDates>
18        </SubmissionDate>
19      </JobsMatching>
20    </Parameters>
```

Source 3: Parameters for the metric JobLists

8.   Conclusions

In this paper we have discussed the need of a new Grid component that has to provide a uniform access to the whole Grid information. The current Grid architectures are composed by different types of information systems that provide: different access methodology, different format information and semantics. We can not expect users neither applications to know exactly how each of this IP has to be queried. This situation result in unsustainable and non maintainable Grid architectures, where all the information consumers are highly dependant to the changes that the different IP may have. Furthermore, adding new information systems can result in important source redefinitions in the already deployed consumers or, in the worst, cases in a redesign of their internals. This problem will become dramatic if the number of Grid IP and consumer components increases as it is expected.

We also have presented the problematic providing several examples where this component would help to simplify the overall Grid infrastructure and the relations among the different information producers/consumers, and it would make the system more extensible.

As a solution proposal, we have presented the Grid Palantir meta-information systems. We have described how it uniforms the access to different monitoring and information systems and how its functionalities are provided and implemented. It has been shown how it abstracts the access to different data providers, and it has been demonstrated to be useful in situations where a very wide range of information is provided. A real use cases of how this system has been integrated successfully in some architectures have been described.

References

[1] I. Rodero, F. Guim, J. Corbalan, J. Labarta, "eNANOS: Coordinated Scheduling in Grid Environments", Parallel Computing: Current & Future Issues of High-End Computing, G.R. Joubert et al. (Eds.), Parallel Computing (ParCo), pp. 81-88, Malaga, Spain, 13-16 September, 2005.

[2] F. Guim, I. Rodero, J. Corbalan, J. Labarta, A. Oleksiak, J. Nabrzyski, "Uniform job monitoring using the hpc-europa single point of access", International Workshop on Grid Testbeds, in conjunction with CCGrid2006, Singapore, 16-19 May, 2006.

[3] A. Oleksiak, A. Tullo, P. Graham, T. Kuczynski, J. Nabrzyski, D. Szejnfeld, T. Sloan, "HPC-Europa: Towards Uniform Access to European HPC Infrastructures", 6th IEEE/ACM International Workshop on Grid Computing Grid2005, Seattle, USA, 2005.

[4] R. Buyya, "Economic-based Distributed Resource Management and Scheduling for Grid Computing", Ph.D. Thesis, Monash University, Melbourne, Australia, April 12, 2002.

[5] O. Levillain, F. Guim, I. Rodero, J. Corbalan, J. Labarta, "Comparison of several grid monitoring tools", Technical Report UPC-DAC-RR-CAP-2006-22, Computer Architecture Department, Technical University of Catalonia (UPC), Barcelona, Spain, 2006.

[6] K. Czajkowski, S. Fitzgerald, I. Foster, C. Kesselman, "Grid Information Services for Distributed Resource Sharing", Symp. On High Performance Distributed Computing, 2001.

[7] Z. Balaton, G. Gombas, "Resource and Job Monitoring in the Grid", Euro-Par 2003.

[8] R. Wolski, N. T. Spring, J. Hayes, "The network weather service: a distributed resource performance forecasting service for metacomputing", Journal of Future Generation Computer Systems, 1999.

[9] B. Balis, M. Bubak, W. Funika, R. Wismuller, M. Radecki, T. Szepieniec, T. Arodz, M. Kurdziel, "Performance Evaluation and Monitoring of Interactive Grid Applications", LNCS 3241, November 2004.

[10] M. L. Massie, B. N. Chun, D. E. Culler, "The ganglia distributed monitoring system: design, implementation, and experience", Parallel Computing (ParCo), 2003.

[11] I. Rodero, F. Guim, J. Corbalan, J. Labarta, "Design and Implementation of a General-Purpose API of Progress and Performance Indicators", Parallel Computing (ParCo) 2007.

[12] F. Guim, I. Rodero, J. Corbalan, J. Labarta, A. Oleksiak, K. Kurowski, J. Nabrzyski, "Integrating the Palantir Grid Meta-Information System with GRMS", S. Gorlatch et al. (Eds.): Integrated Research in Grid Computing, CoreGRID Integration Workshop, pp. 49-60, Krakow, Poland, 19-20 October, 2006.

[13] K. Kurowski, J. Nabrzyski, J. Oleksiak, "Programming Grid Applications with Gridge", Computational Methods for Science and Technology - OWN 2006.

PEER-TO-PEER METADATA MANAGEMENT FOR KNOWLEDGE DISCOVERY APPLICATIONS IN GRIDS

Gabriel Antoniu
IRISA/INRIA, Rennes Cedex, France
gabriel.antoniu@irisa.fr

Antonio Congiusta
DEIS, University of Calabria, Rende (CS), Italy
acongiusta@deis.unical.it

Sébastien Monnet
IRISA/INRIA, Rennes Cedex, France
sebastien.monnet@irisa.fr

Domenico Talia
DEIS, University of Calabria, Rende (CS), Italy
talia@deis.unical.it

Paolo Trunfio
DEIS, University of Calabria, Rende (CS), Italy
trunfio@deis.unical.it

Abstract   Computational Grids are powerful platforms gathering computational power and storage space from thousands of geographically distributed resources. The applications running on such platforms need to efficiently and reliably access the various and heterogeneous distributed resources they offer. This can be achieved by using metadata information describing all available resources. It is therefore crucial to provide efficient metadata management architectures and frameworks. In this paper we describe the design of a Grid metadata management service. We focus on a particular use case: the Knowledge Grid architecture which provides high-level Grid services for distributed knowledge discovery applications. Taking advantage of an existing Grid data-sharing service, namely JUXMEM, the proposed solution lies at the border between peer-to-peer systems and Web services.

Keywords: Grid, knowledge discovery, metadata management, peer-to-peer.

1.   Introduction

Computational Grids are powerful platforms gathering computational power and storage space from thousands of resources geographically distributed in several sites. These platforms are large-scale, heterogeneous, geographically distributed and dynamic architectures. Furthermore they contain many types of resources such as software tools, data sources, specific hardware, etc. These resources are spread over the whole platform. Therefore, it is crucial to provide a mean for the applications running on Grids to localize and access the available resources in such large-scale, heterogeneous, dynamic, distributed environment.

Each Grid resource can be described by a metadata item (eg., an XML document). Such a metadata document may contain the 1) the description of a particular resource, 2) its localization and 3) information on the resource usage (eg., command line options of a software tool, format of a data source, protocol used to access a particular node, etc.). Thus, given a resource metadata, it is possible to access the resource. All the metadata items, describing the whole set of resources available in a given Grid have to be managed in an efficient and reliable way especially in large-scale Grids.

In this paper we propose a software architecture of a scalable Grid metadata management service. We focus on a particular use case: metadata management for the Knowledge Grid [6]. The Knowledge Grid is a *service-oriented* software distributed framework that aims to offer high-level Grid services for knowledge discovery applications running on computational Grids. The Knowledge Grid services are built on top of existing, low-level Grid services such as GRAM [11], GridFTP [1] or MDS [10].

Within the Knowledge Grid architecture, metadata provides information about how an object (either a data source or an algorithm) can be accessed. It consists of information on its actual location and on its format (for a data source) or its usage (for an algorithm).

As metadata is actually stored as pieces of data (eg., XML files), they may be treated as such. We take advantage of the good properties exhibited by an already existing Grid data-sharing service, JUXMEM [2, 4], to store and retrieve metadata. We then build a distributed and replicated hierarchical index of available metadata.

In the next section we briefly present the architecture of the Knowledge Grid and focus on its metadata management needs. Section 3 presents the JUXMEM Grid data-sharing service that we use to reliably store and retrieve both resource metadata and the distributed replicated index. Section 4 describes our architecture for a metadata management Grid service tailored for the Knowledge Grid and based on JUXMEM. Finally, Section 5 presents ongoing work and concludes this paper.

2. The Knowledge Grid

2.1 Knowledge discovery in Grids

Nowadays, big companies have to deal with daily generated large amounts of data. They need tools to both store this information and retrieve knowledge from it. Computational Grids [13] offering high computational power and large storage resources can be used to store and process large amounts of data. Furthermore their geographically distributed nature fits well with the companies architecture. Indeed companies data sources and computational power may be spread all over the world.

However, performing knowledge discovery over such a distributed and often heterogeneous architecture, using data sources and data mining algorithms spread over thousands of nodes is not a trivial task. Building and running a distributed knowledge discovery application on a Grid requires high-level services. Data sources to be mined have to be located, furthermore their format has to be discovered somehow (they could be relational databases, text files, etc.). As well, data mining algorithms and software tools have to be localized and their usage has to be known. Then the computations (data mining algorithms running over data sources) have to be scheduled over available Grid nodes. A knowledge discovery application can be complex, consisting in numerous sequential or parallel data mining algorithms working on identical or different data sources. Some data mining algorithm may be run with the data produced by another data mining algorithm, leading to task dependencies, etc.

The Knowledge Grid provides high-level services and a user-friendly interface VEGA [8] that allows a user to easily describe a distributed knowledge discovery application, it then takes care of locating the resources (data sources, algorithms, computational nodes), scheduling tasks, and executing the application. Within the Knowledge Grid, the application designer only has to describe an *abstract execution plan*, with VEGA, he can even do it graphically. An *abstract execution plan* defines at high level the algorithms to be executed and the data sources to be mined. The Knowledge Grid services (called K-Grid services for short thereafter) are responsible to locate the resources and services and instantiate the execution plan which becomes an *instantiated execution plan* like the one presented in Figure 1.

An instantiated execution plan contains a set of tasks -with assigned Grid resources- to be done (data transfers and computations). It is executed by the K-Grid services and it may be refined as resources may become available or unavailable in a Grid.

```
<ExecutionPlan type="instantiated">
 <Task label="task1">
  <Program href="minos.cs.icar.cnr.it/software/DB2Extractor.xml"
           title="DB2Extractor on minos.cs.icar.cnr.it"/>
   <Input href="minos.cs.icar.cnr.it/data/car-imports_db2.xml"
          title="car-imports.db2 on minos.cs.icar.cnr.it"/>
   <Output href="minos.cs.icar.cnr.it/data/imports-85c_db2.xml"
           title="imports-85c.db2 on minos.cs.icar.cnr.it"/>
 </Task>
 <Task label="check1">
  <ResourceCheck method="soft"/>
 </Task>
 <Task label="task2">
  <Program href="minos.cs.icar.cnr.it/software/GridFTP.xml"
           title="GridFTP on minos.cs.icar.cnr.it"/>
   <Input href="minos.cs.icar.cnr.it/data/imports-85c_db2.xml"
          title="imports-85c.db2 on minos.cs.icar.cnr.it"/>
   <Output href="abstract_host1/data/imports-85c_db2.xml"
           title="imports-85c.db2 on abstract_host1"/>
 </Task>
 ...
 <Task label="task6">
  <Program href="abstract_host1/software/autoclass3-3-3.xml"
           title="autoclass on abstract_host1"/>
   <Input href="abstract_host1/data/imports-85c_db2.xml"
          title="imports-85c.db2 on abstract_host1"/>
   <Output href="abstract_host1/data/classes.xml"
           title="classes on abstract_host1"/>
 </Task>
 ...
 <TaskLink ep:from="task1" ep:to="check1"/>
 <TaskLink ep:from="check1" ep:to="task2"/>
 <TaskLink ep:from="task2" ep:to="task3"/>
 ...
 <TaskLink ep:from="task5" ep:to="task6"/>
 ...
 <ResourceInstantiation abstractResource="abstract_host1">
   <candidateResource>icarus.cs.icar.cnr.it</candidateResource>
   <candidateResource>telesio.cs.icar.cnr.it</candidateResource>
 </ResourceInstantiation>
</ExecutionPlan>
```

Figure 1.   A sample instantiated execution plan (from [14]).

2.2   The Knowledge Grid architecture

The K-Grid services are organized in a two-layer software architecture: 1) the High-level K-Grid layer and 2) the Core-level K-Grid layer. In its current implementation, the different services composing the Knowledge Grid are Grid services interacting by using the WSRF [9] standard. The organization of the K-Grid services is described by Figure 2. The High-level K-Grid layer includes services to compose, validate and execute distributed knowledge discovery applications. The main services of the High-level K-Grid services are:

- The **Data Access Service (DAS)**, responsible for data sources and mining results publication and search.

- The **Tools and Algorithms Access Service (TAAS)**, responsible for data mining and visualization tools and algorithms publication and search.

- The **Execution Plan Management Service (EPMS)**, allowing to describe a distributed knowledge discovery application by building an execution graph with constraints on resources. It generates an abstract execution plan (resources are not know yet).

- The **Results Presentation Service (RPS)**, offering services for knowledge discovery results presentation;

The services exhibited by the Core K-Grid layer are:

- The **Knowledge Discovery Service (KDS)**, responsible for metadata management. Every resource (nodes, algorithms and tools, data sources and mining results) of the Knowledge Grid is described by a metadata item. In the Knowledge Grid, resource metadata is a XML document stored in a *Knowledge Metadata Repository* (KMR).

- The **Resource Allocation and Execution Management Service (RAEMS)**, responsible to instantiate an abstract execution plan. It uses the KDS service to find resources satisfying the constraints imposed by the abstract execution plan. It is also responsible for the application execution management.

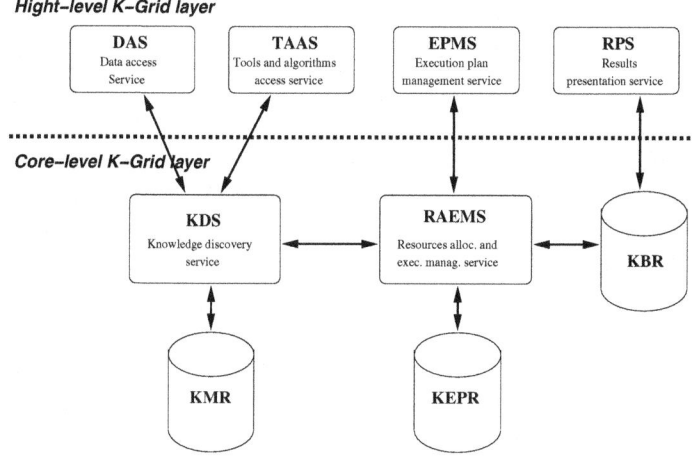

Figure 2. The Knowledge Grid software architecture.

2.3 Current KDS design and limitations

The Knowledge Directory Service (KDS) is responsible for handling metadata describing Knowledge Grid resources. A sample metadata is presented by Figure 3. Such resources include hosts, data repositories, tools and algorithms used to extract, analyze, and manipulate data, execution plans, and knowledge models obtained as result of mining processes.

The metadata information is represented by XML documents stored in a component called Knowledge Metadata Repository (KMR). The functionalities

```
<DataMiningSoftware name="AutoClass">
  <Description>
    <KindOfData>flat file</KindOfData>
    <KindOfKnowledge>clusters</KindOfKnowledge>
    <KindOfTecnique>statistics</KindOfTecnique>
    <DrivingMethod>autonomous knowledge miner</DrivingMethod>
  </Description>
  <Usage>
    ...
    <Syntax>
      <Arg description="executable" type="required" value="/usr/autoclass/autoclass">
        <Arg description="make a classification" type="alternative" value="-search">
          <Arg description="a .db2 file" type="required"/>
          <Arg description="a .hd2 file" type="required"/>
          <Arg description="a .model file" type="required"/>
          <Arg description="a .s-params file" type="required"/>
        </Arg>
        <Arg description="create a report" type="alternative" value="-reports">
          <Arg description="a .results-bin file" type="required"/>
          ...
        </Arg>
        ...
      </Arg>
    </Syntax>
    <Hostname>icarus.cs.icar.cnr.it</Hostname>
    <ManualPath>/usr/autoclass/read-me.text</ManualPath>
    <DocumentationURL>http://ic-www.arc.nasa.gov/ic/projects/...</DocumentationURL>
    ...
  </Usage>
</DataMiningSoftware>
```

Figure 3.   An extract from an XML metadata sample for the AutoClass software (presented in [14]).

of the KDS are mostly used by DAS and TAAS services while publishing and searching for datasets and tools to be used in a KDD application. DAS and TAAS services always interact with a local instance of the KDS, which in turn may invoke one or more other remote KDS instances.

The KDS exports three main operations:

- publishResource, used to publish metadata related to a given resource into the KMR;

- searchResource, for locating resources that match some given search criteria;

- retrieveMetadata, invoked to retrieve metadata associated to a given resource identified by a provided KDS URL.

It should be noted that when a publishResource is performed, only an interaction between a DAS/TAAS service and the local KDS is needed, because each KMR instance stores metadata about resources available on the same Grid node on which the KMR itself is hosted. On the contrary, when a searchResource is invoked, the related query is first dispatched from the DAS/TAAS to the co-located KDS service, which then answers by checking the local KMR, and in turn forwards the same query to remote KDSs with the aim of finding more matches.

The retrieveMetadata receives a KDS URL returned by a previous invocation of the searchResource operation, and uses it to contact the remote KDS on which the resource is available to retrieve the associated metadata document.

It appears clear, thus, that the `searchResource` is the most complex activity performed by the KDS, because it involves interactions and coordination with remote instances of the same service. On the other hand, it should be mentioned that the architecture of the Knowledge Grid does not prescribe any particular mode of interaction and/or protocol between the different KDS instances.

The current implementation, for instance, is adopting to such purpose one of the simplest strategies: the query forwarding is performed by contacting concurrently all of the known remote KDS instances (avoiding loops).

In this paper we propose a new KDS design based on a shared distributed index handled by a Grid data-sharing service and a peer-to-peer technique. This is useful for reducing the number of remote KDS instances contacted when forwarding a search query.

Resources metadata like the one presented by Figure 3 should be stored in a persistent and fault tolerant storage. Furthermore, they may be shared by multiple applications, and sometimes updated. Therefore, it is necessary to maintain the consistency between the different copies that may exist in the Grid. Thus we use a data-sharing service, JUXMEM, which offers transparent access to persistent mutable data, to store the XML files corresponding to pieces of metadata.

3. JUXMEM: a Grid data-sharing service

In this section we present the JUXMEM Grid data-sharing service used in the design of the metadata management Grid service.

3.1 A hierarchical architecture

From the metadata management Grid service perspective, JUXMEM is a service providing transparent access to persistent, mutable, shared data. When allocating memory, a client has to specify in how many sites[1] the data should be replicated, and on how many nodes in each site. This results into the instantiation of a set of data replicas, associated to a group of peers called *data group*. Usually each node runs one single peer. The allocation primitive returns a global *data-ID*, which can be used by the other nodes to identify existing data. To obtain read and/or write access to a data block, the clients only need to use this data-ID.

The data group is hierarchically organized, as illustrated on Figure 4: the *Global Data Group (GDG)* gathers all provider nodes holding a replica of the same piece of data. These nodes can be distributed in different sites, thereby

---

[1]A site is a set of clustered nodes, it can be a physical cluster within a cluster federation, or close from a latency viewpoint.

increasing the data availability if faults occur. The GDG is divided into *Local Data Groups (LDG)*, which correspond to data copies located in a same site.

In order to access a piece of data, a client has to be attached to a specific LDG (to "map" the data). Then, when the client performs the read/write and synchronization operations, the consistency protocol layer manages data synchronization and data transmission between clients, LDGs and GDG, within the strict respect of the consistency model.

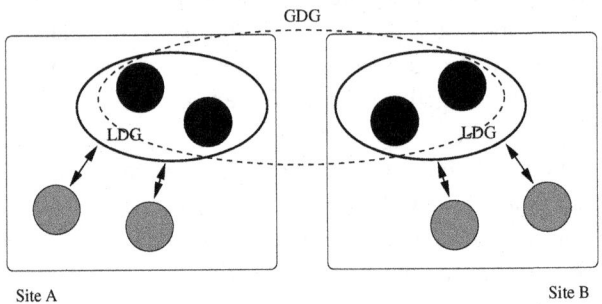

Figure 4.   JUXMEM: a hierarchical architecture.

3.2   JUXMEM **software architecture**

The JUXMEM Grid service is composed of a set of layers presented in Figure 5. The lower layer Juk is the JUXMEM kernel. It relies on JXTA [15] to offer to the uppers layers publish/subscribe operations, efficient communication and storage facilities. Every node involved or using JUXMEM is therefore managed in a peer-to-peer way using JXTA. JXTA is is a set of protocols allowing nodes (Grid nodes, PDA, etc.) to communicate and collaborate in a P2P manner. The implementations of these protocols provide the ability to obtain efficient communications on Grids [5].

Above Juk, a fault-tolerance layer is responsible for hierarchical data replication. It offers the concept of *Self-Organizing Group* (SOG), a SOG is a replication group that is able to adapt itself in case of dynamic changes (by creating new replicas or removing old ones), this provides the ability to keep fault tolerance guarantees even in presence of failures.

The upper layer is responsible for data consistency management, it serves data access requests, manages locks and maintain pending requests lists.

A multi-protocol architecture.   The layers presented above are built as interchangeable software modules. Therefore, it is possible for each data item stored by the Grid data-sharing service to specify a particular consistency protocol or a particular SOG implementation.

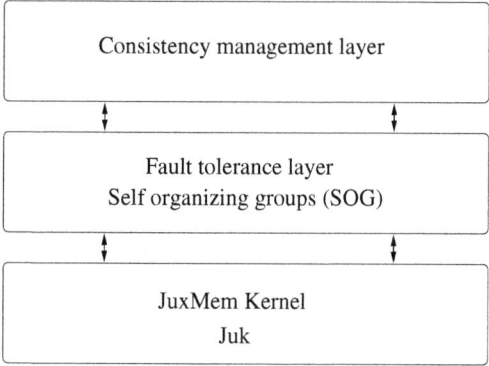

Figure 5.   JUXMEM layered software architecture.

The JUXMEM service can not be used in its current design to manage metadata, but additional features must be provided. Data stored in JUXMEM is accessible (localizable) *only* by using its associated data-ID. Metadata items have to be localizable using only names and attributes. The following section presents our approach to build a metadata management service using the JUXMEM data-sharing service.

4.   A Grid metadata management service

From the Knowledge Grid viewpoint, the Grid metadata management service consists of a particular design and implementation for the KDS service and the KMR repository. The service presented below serves requests from the TAAS and the DAS High-level K-Grid services but also from the RAEMS Core K-Grid service (see Figure 2).

Our approach relies on the use of the JUXMEM Grid data-sharing service prototype presented in the previous section. Metadata items are stored within the Grid data-sharing service.

4.1   Metadata storage and retrieval

Requirements.   Resources metadata should remain available in the Grid. Therefore they should be stored in a *fault tolerant* and *persistent* manner. This may provide the ability to access metadata information in spite of failures and disconnections. Furthermore, some metadata should be *updatable*. In the Knowledge Grid use case, a piece of metadata may describe the result of a knowledge discovery task, this result may be refined later which leads to metadata modifications. If a resource location is changing, it should also be reflected by updating the associated metadata. Finally, metadata has to be localizable by providing name, attributes and constraints upon the described resource.

Storing metadata in a Grid data-sharing service.   To achieve high availability of metadata despite failures we store them in the JUXMEM Grid datasharing service. Each metadata item describing a resource is though replicated and associated to one unique ID as described in Section 3. This ID can then be used to retrieve metadata information stored in the Grid data-sharing service. Availability and consistency (eg., in case of concurrent updates) is then also managed by the Grid data-sharing service. The metadata items that will not be updated (e.g. describing a large data source that will not be updated and will not be moved) can take advantage of JUXMEM multi-protocol feature by using a very simple and efficient consistency protocol without synchronization operations. Thus, JUXMEM is used as a *fault-tolerant*, *distributed* and *shared* KMR (see Section 2) and JUXMEM's data-IDs are used as KDS URLs.

Locality.   Metadata information is strongly linked with the resource it describes. Therefore if the resource becomes unavailable, its corresponding metadata information would become useless (it can also become misleading). Therefore, regarding JUXMEM hierarchical architecture, metadata information should be stored within the site containing the resource it describes (i.e. over one unique JUXMEM LDG). If all the nodes of the site fail (due to a power failure in a computer room for instance) the resources metadata of this site become unavailable but it is also the case of the described resources. Thus, we choose to store metadata information in the described resources' site using only one JUXMEM LDG per metadata item. However notice that LDG are reliable self-organizing groups, ie. the failure of a node does not lead to the loss of metadata items.

4.2   Fault-tolerant distributed indexes

While looking for metadata information using the `searchResource` operation, applications[2] can provide information like a name (eg., a data source name "clientdata1" or an algorithm name "J48") or a set of attributes and constraints as the one in the "Description" section of the metadata presented in Figure 3. An accurate description of the kind of requests the KDS service should be able to serve is given in [14].

Therefore it is necessary to have a mean to find a metadata identifier (which then permit to retrieve the metadata information itself) using names and attributes that represent the resource described by the metadata.

---

[2]In our current use case the applications are the DAS, TAAS and RAEMS K-Grid services.

Distributed indexes.   Usual approaches rely on the use of a centralized indexing system. It can be either a relational database like MySQL [17] or a LDAP [12] server (used in previous Knowledge Grid implementations). We use distributed indexes: in each site composing the Grid, we maintain a *site index* of the published resources metadata within this site. This site index contains tuples consisting of the resource name, attributes (as a byte vector) and the resource metadata identifier (its JUXMEM data-ID).

Fault tolerance.   There again we rely on the JUXMEM data-sharing service: the site indexes are data item that can be stored in JUXMEM. Therefore they are automatically replicated for fault tolerance. Notice that a site index only contains information of its own site, furthermore it does not contain the whole metadata information but only metadata item names and some relevant attributes. Thus, a site index size remains limited.

Index sharing.   The WSRF KDS instances serving publishResource and searchResource requests are clients of the JUXMEM service. In each site it is possible to have multiple KDS services having mapped the site's index as illustrated in Figure 6. The KDS are responsible for parsing the index, finding the metadata identifier, fetching the metadata (using the identifier) and sending back the retrieved metadata to the requester (either DAS, TAAS or RAEMS). These tasks are achieved by interacting with the JUXMEM service. It is important to notice that the site index is a data item stored by JUXMEM and mapped by the multiple KDS: the consistency of the shared index is ensured by the grid data-sharing service while new publications occur.

The shared site indexes allows KDS instances to retrieve *locally* (on their node) KDS URLs of metadata describing resources spread over their site nodes.

4.3   Big picture

4.3.1   Metadata publication.   Metadata publications done by the DAS and the TAAS are made through the publishResource operation provided by KDS. When a KDS receives such a request:

1 It stores the corresponding XML file within JUXMEM,

2 locks the index to ensure no concurrent publish occurs,

3 updates it, adding the new resource metadata index entry (attributes and JUXMEM data-ID of the XML file).

The KDS then releases the lock upon the index. To allow the other KDS to continue serving search requests while an update occurs, we use a particular consistency protocol allowing read operations concurrent to a write operation.

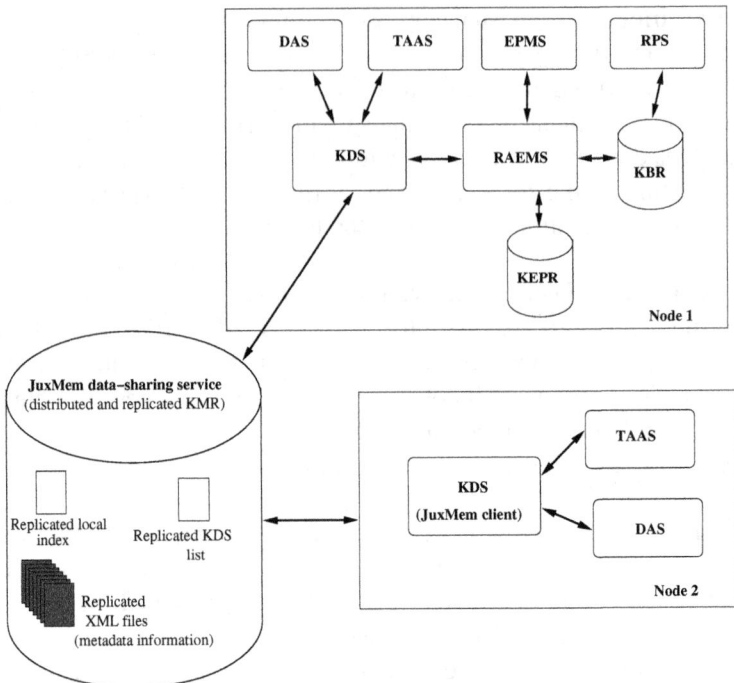

Figure 6. In each site KDS interact with the JUXMEM service to access 1) the local index, 2) the KDS list, and 3) the metadata information itself.

Such a protocol is available in JUXMEM, it is described and evaluated in details in [3]. Note that the publication of a site resource affects only the index stored in this site and used by the local KDSs, furthermore resources metadata are also stored on intra-site JUXMEM providers (in LDGs). Therefore a publish operation does not imply inter-site communications.

4.3.2   Metadata search.   When K-Grid services need to search a particular resource metadata, they request the KDS running on the same node or a randomly chosen remote KDS within their own site[3]. The KDS receiving such a request search in its mapped (in its local memory) site index. If the resource is found, it gets the corresponding XML file using the data-ID stored in the site index. In this case the resource is available within the same site. If a corresponding resource can not be found in the site index, the KDS forwards it to one randomly chosen KDS in each other site involved in the Grid using JXTA peer-to-peer communication layers as illustrated by Figure 7. To achieve this, a

---

[3] A round robin policy could also be used.

partial list of KDS instances is stored and maintained within the JUXMEM Grid data-sharing service. This list is replicated hierarchically in the whole platform using the GDG/LDG hierarchy presented in Section 3.

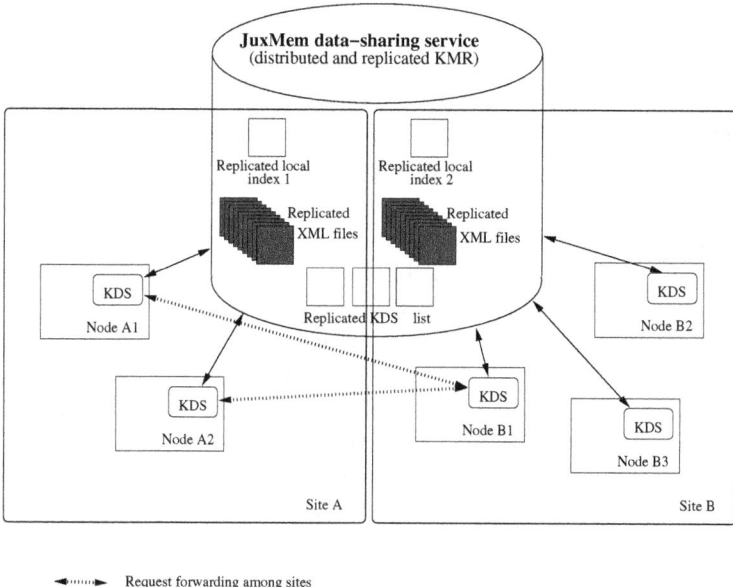

Figure 7. Among sites, KDS cooperate using the hierarchically replicated KDS list.

At initialization, a KDS maps its site index and the KDS list, it can then add itself into this list. If a KDS does not answer to a request (either publish or search), it is removed from this list. The KDS list is not expected to be frequently updated as Grid nodes are assumed more stable than peers in peer-to-peer systems.

4.4 Technical concerns

From a technical view point our solution implies integrating the JUXMEM and the Knowledge Grid research prototypes. JUXMEM entities are managed in a peer-to-peer manner, using Sun Microsystems JXTA protocols, while the entities involved in the Knowledge Grid service use the WSRF Grid standard.

The junction between the two different sets of protocols is done by the new KDS implementation: KDS instances are part of both the JUXMEM platform, as clients of the JUXMEM Grid service, and they serve WSRF requests from the Knowledge Grid services (publishResource and searchResource).

The KDSs are also responsible to parse the distributed index. The distributed nature of the index implies a cooperation between the KDS instances distributed in different sites all over the Grid. This cooperation is made in a peer-to-peer manner, taking advantage of the Grid data-sharing service to store, manage and share a neighbor list (the KDS list).

5.   Conclusions

Metadata data management in large scale, heterogeneous, geographically distributed and dynamic architectures such as computational Grids is an important problem. Providing an efficient and reliable metadata management service allows applications to easily access heterogeneous resources spread over thousands of nodes.

The solution we presented in this paper takes advantage of already existing work in Grids. By integrating the JUXMEM Grid data-sharing service in the design of a metadata management service for the Knowledge Grid, XML metadata files are stored on a fault tolerant and consistent support, and are kept close to the resources they describe. The proposed two-level index hierarchy allows the applications to get resources located in their own site if they exist or in remote ones otherwise, enhancing locality.

The integration of the two research prototypes is in progress, and we plan to evaluate this solution on a real Grid platform such as Grid'5000 [16, 7]. The format of the distributed index should then be further investigated, using binaries trees for instance. The peer-to-peer cooperation between KDS instances should also be enhanced, for instance by selecting several KDSs for inter-site cooperation.

Acknowledgements

This research work is carried out under the FP6 Network of Excellence CoreGRID funded by the European Commission (Contract IST-2002-004265).

References

[1] B. Allcock, J. Bester, J. Bresnahan, A. L. Chervenak, C. Kesselman, S. Meder, V. Nefedova, D. Quesnel, S. Tuecke, and I. Foster. Secure, Efficient Data Transport and Replica Management for High-Performance Data-Intensive Computing. In *Proc. 18th IEEE Symposium on Mass Storage Systems (MSS 2001)*, San Diego, USA, 2001.

[2] G. Antoniu, M. Bertier, E. Caron, F. Desprez, L. Bougé, M. Jan, S. Monnet, and P. Sens. GDS: An Architecture Proposal for a Grid Data-Sharing Service. In *Future Generation Grids*, V. Getov, D. Laforenza, A. Reinefeld (Eds.), pages 133–152, Springer, 2006.

[3] G. Antoniu, L. Cudennec, and S. Monnet. Extending the entry consistency model to enable efficient visualization for code-coupling grid applications. In *Proc. 6th IEEE/ACM International Symposium on Cluster Computing and the Grid (CCGrid 2006)*, pages 552–555, Singapore, 2006.

[4] G. Antoniu, J.-F. Deverge, and S. Monnet. How to bring together fault tolerance and data consistency to enable grid data sharing. *Concurrency and Computation: Practice and*

Experience, 18(13):1705–1723, 2006.

[5] G. Antoniu, M. Jan, and D. A. Noblet. Enabling the P2P JXTA Platform for High-Performance Networking Grid Infrastructures. In *Proc. 1st International Conference on High Performance Computing and Communications (HPCC'05)*, pages 429–440, Sorrento, Italy, 2005.

[6] M. Cannataro and D. Talia. The Knowledge Grid. *Communications of the ACM*, 46(1):89–93, 2003.

[7] F. Cappello, E. Caron, M. Dayde, F. Desprez, E. Jeannot, Y. Jegou, S. Lanteri, J. Leduc, N. Melab, G. Mornet, R. Namyst, P. Primet, and O. Richard. Grid'5000: A Large Scale, Reconfigurable, Controlable and Monitorable Grid Platform. In *Proc. 6th IEEE/ACM International Workshop on Grid Computing (Grid'05)*, Seattle, USA, 2005.

[8] A. Congiusta, D. Talia, and P. Trunfio. VEGA: A Visual Environment for Developing Complex Grid Applications. In *Proc. 1st International Workshop on Knowledge Grid and Grid Intelligence (KGGI 2003)*, pages 56–66, Halifax, Canada, 2003.

[9] A. Congiusta, D. Talia, and P. Trunfio. Distributed data mining services leveraging WSRF. *Future Generation Computer Systems*, 23(1):34–41, 2007.

[10] K. Czajkowski, S. Fitzgerald, I. Foster, and C. Kesselman. Grid Information Services for Distributed Resource Sharing. In *Proc. 10th IEEE International Symposium on High-Performance Distributed Computing*, pages 181–184, San Francisco, USA, 2001.

[11] K. Czajkowski, I. Foster, N. Karonis, C. Kesselman, S. Martin, W. Smith, and S. Tuecke. Resource Management Architecture for Metacomputing Systems. In *Proc. IPPS/SPDP: Workshop on Job Scheduling Strategies for Parallel Processing*, pages 62–82, 1998.

[12] J. Hodges and R. Morgan. Lightweight Directory Access Protocol (v3): Technical Specification. IETF Request For Comment 3377, Network Working Group, 2002.

[13] C. Kesselman and I. Foster. *The Grid: Blueprint for a New Computing Infrastructure*. Morgan Kaufmann Publishers, 1998.

[14] C. Mastroianni, D. Talia, and P. Trunfio. Metadata for managing grid resources in data mining applications. *Journal of Grid Computing*, 2(1):85–102, 2004.

[15] B. Traversat, A. Arora, M. Abdelaziz, M. Duigou, C. Haywood, J.-C. Hugly, E. Pouyoul, and B. Yeager. Project JXTA 2.0 Super-Peer Virtual Network. http://www.jxta.org/project/www/docs/JXTA2.0protocols1.pdf, 2003.

[16] Grid'5000. http://www.grid5000.org.

[17] MySQL. http://www.mysql.com.

III

GRID WORKFLOW AND FAULT TOLERANCE

TAXONOMIES OF THE MULTI-CRITERIA GRID WORKFLOW SCHEDULING PROBLEM*

Marek Wieczorek
Institute of Computer Science, University of Innsbruck
Technikerstraße 21a,
A-6020 Innsbruck, Austria
marek@dps.uibk.ac.at

Andreas Hoheisel
Fraunhofer FIRST, Berlin, Germany
Kekuléstraße 7,
D-12489 Berlin, Germany
andreas.hoheisel@first.fraunhofer.de

Radu Prodan
Institute of Computer Science, University of Innsbruck
Technikerstraße 21a,
A-6020 Innsbruck, Austria
radu@dps.uibk.ac.at

Abstract   The workflow scheduling problem which is considered difficult on the Grid becomes even more challenging when multiple scheduling criteria are used for optimization. The existing approaches can address only certain variants of the multi-criteria workflow scheduling problem, usually considering up to two contradicting criteria being scheduled in some specific Grid environments. A comprehensive description of the problem can be an important step towards more general scheduling approaches. Based on the related work and on our own experience, we propose several novel taxonomies of the multi-criteria workflow scheduling problem, considering five facets which may have a major impact on the selection of an appropriate scheduling strategy: scheduling process, scheduling criteria, resource model, task model, and workflow model. We analyze different existing workflow scheduling approaches for the Grid, and classify them according to the proposed taxonomies, identifying the most common use cases and the areas which have not been sufficiently explored yet.

Keywords: Grid, workflows, multi-criteria scheduling, taxonomy

---

*This work is partially funded by the European Union through the IST-034601 Edutain@Grid and FP6-004265 CoreGRID projects.

1.   Introduction

Scheduling of computational tasks on the Grid is a complex optimization problem which may require different scheduling criteria to be considered. Usually, execution time is applied as the most important criterion. In some other cases, the global efficiency (job throughput) should be maximized by the Grid system. In market models (especially in business Grids), economic cost optimization is also considered. Other possible criteria include quality of results, reliability of service, etc. In a multi-dimensional parameter space, it is in general not possible to find a solution that is "best" with respect to all the metrics at the same time. There are several existing approaches to the problem of multi-criteria workflow scheduling on the Grid, most of them addressing two specific criteria (usually execution time and economic cost), by applying some specific approaches invented for specific cases. Our goal is to analyze the general problem of Grid workflow scheduling, by discovering regularities and irregularities between different problem variants. We aim at providing a study which can be used as a basis to move towards a scheduling approach addressing different problem classes for multiple scheduling criteria. The rest of the paper is organized as follows. In Section 2, we formally describe the problem which we want to address. Section 3 provides our contribution to the state of the art. We introduce several taxonomies of the workflow scheduling problem for different aspects, considering both different problem variants and different approaches used to solve the problem. At the end of the section, we summarize the performed case study, by classifying several existing workflow scheduling approaches according to the taxonomies introduced previously. Finally, Section 5 concludes the paper and provides a short roadmap for the future work.

2.   Grid workflow scheduling problem

We define Grid workflow scheduling as the problem of assigning different Grid services to different workflow tasks. Every workflow is a *directed graph* (digraph) $w \in \mathcal{W}, w = (\mathcal{V}, \mathcal{E})$ consisting of a set of nodes $\mathcal{V}$ and a set of edges $\mathcal{E}$, where nodes and edges represent tasks $\tau \in \mathcal{T}$ and data transfers $dt \in \mathcal{D}$ (as we explain in Section 3.5, the mapping between the sets $\mathcal{V}, \mathcal{E}$, and the sets $\mathcal{T}$, $\mathcal{D}$ can differ, depending on the current workflow model). In some workflow representations applied in the related work cited by us, workflow elements may have special semantics that defines complex workflow constructs (loops, parallel loops, if/switch conditions). Workflows expressed in such formalisms (e.g., Petri Nets [26], BPEL [47], AGWL [23]) can be systematically reduced during the runtime to simple Directed Acyclic Graphs (DAG), for instance by means of loop unrolling and by predicting and evaluating the conditions [35]. In case of any full-ahead workflow scheduling approach, such conversion has to be performed globally for the whole workflow each time when the scheduling is triggered. The set S contains all the *services* that are available for scheduling in the Grid and that implement different workflow tasks. In order to run a workflow, every task of the workflow has to be mapped to a service that implements the task. For every task $\tau_i \in T$, there is a set $S_i = \{s_{i1}, ..., s_{ip_i}\} \subset S$ of the services which implement the task τ_i, where p_i may differ for different i. A *schedule* is defined as a function $sched_w : T \mapsto S$, where $sched_w$ assigns to each task $\tau_i \in T$ a service $s \in S_i$, creating a complete *schedule* (mapping) of the workflow w. Set SC contains all possible schedules for all workflows $w \in W$. The *cost model* for workflows is described by n multiple *scheduling criteria* $C_i, 1 \le i \le n, n \in \mathbb{N}^+$, for instance by execution time, economic cost, and quality of results. The *partial cost functions* $cost_i : S \mapsto \mathbb{R}, 1 \le i \le n$, defined for each scheduling criterion C_i, assign to each service $s_j \in S$ its *partial cost* c_i^j (e.g., "execution time of 5 minutes", "economic cost of 5\$", "quality of results 100%"). In the remainder of this paper, we will sometimes refer to the cost of a service $s \in S$ which is mapped to a task $\tau \in T$ (i.e., where $sched_w(\tau) = s$) as the *cost of the task* τ. Similarly to the partial cost functions, the *total cost functions* $cost_i^{tot} : W \times SC \mapsto \mathbb{R}, 1 \le i \le n$ assign to a workflow $w \in W$ scheduled by $sched_w \in SC$ its *total costs* c_i^{tot}, calculated based on the partial costs of the services mapped to the workflow tasks. The optimization goal is to find a schedule $sched_w$ with the *best possible* total costs $c_i^{tot}, 1 \le i \le n$. As we describe in Section 3.2, the total costs can be evaluated in different ways.

3. Taxonomies in workflow Grid scheduling

When analyzing the problem of workflow scheduling, several important *facets* (e.g., resource model, criteria model) of the problem have to be considered, as they may strongly influence the decision as to which scheduling approach is most appropriate in the given case. Each facet describes the scheduling problem from a different perspective. In this section, we will analyze in detail 5 different facets of the problem:

- scheduling process
- scheduling criteria
- resource model
- task model
- workflow model

For every facet, we propose a certain *taxonomy* which classifies different scheduling approaches into different possible *classes*. The classes are distinguished either with respect to different variants of the scheduling problem (e.g., multiple workflows, user-oriented scheduling), or with respect to the way the problem is approached (e.g., full-ahead planning, advance reservation based). We describe the classes using the RDF notation *subject-predicate-object*, which we extend in some cases to distinguish between different *sub-classes* of the problem. The proposed taxonomies can by no means be considered to be exhaustive, as our attempt is to create a model only for a certain subset of the general workflow scheduling problem (i.e., for the multi-criteria workflow scheduling on the Grid). We illustrate the derived taxonomies by providing examples of approaches for different classes, which partially come from the related work. Some of those examples are taken from [20], which provides a more complete analysis of the scheduling problem on the Grid.

3.1   Taxonomy of scheduling process

Different classes of Grid workflow scheduling can be distinguished with respect to different properties of the scheduling process (see Fig. 1). In this section, we will analyze both the information processed by the scheduler, and the way in which this information is being processed.

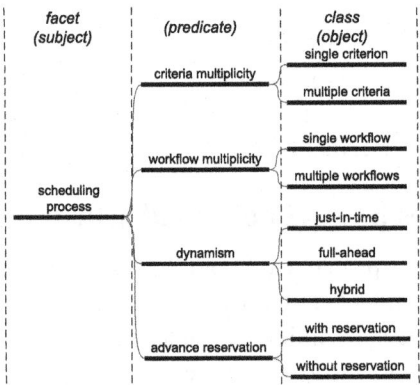

Figure 1.   Taxonomy of workflow scheduling process

Criteria multiplicity   This classification is essential from the point of view of the current work. Multiple criteria make the scheduling much more difficult, as they represent multiple and often contradicting optimization goals which require multi-objective scheduling techniques. From this point of view, the scheduling processes can be divided into two classes:

- *Single criterion.* The optimization is done for one criterion only (usually, for execution time).

- *Multiple criteria.* The scheduler tries to optimize multiple scheduling criteria.

There exist several workflow scheduling approaches which consider more than one criterion (e.g., [21, 59, 57, 58, 45, 8, 44]), and many of them consider the trade-off between execution time and economic cost. Vienna Grid Environment [8] proposes a scheduling approach for multiple criteria (*Quality of Service parameters*), usually for execution time and economic cost. It applies a general multi-criteria scheduling approach, by using an optimization technique based on integer programming [43] to optimize a weighted goal function combining different QoS parameters.

Some other criteria are the main focus for the Grid-wide optimization (see Section 3.2) and for the pipelined workflows (see Section 3.5). In Instant Grid [27], a simple resource ranking model based on the number of CPUs and the last known load is created dynamically, in order to optimize the profit of the Grid. In [45], the scheduling of pipelined workflows is optimized with respect to the throughput and the latency of workflow execution.

Workflow multiplicity The optimization process performed by a workflow scheduler usually considers a single workflow only, but it can also attempt to optimize the execution of multiple workflows at a time. Therefore, we can distinguish the following two classes of workflow scheduling processes:

- *Single workflow.* The execution of a single workflow is optimized within a single scheduling process.
- *Multiple workflows.* The execution of multiple workflows can be optimized within a single scheduling process.

Only few existing scheduling approaches can optimize the execution of more than one workflow at a time. The work presented in [63] distinguishes three different approaches to the problem, the first one based on a sequential scheduling of multiple graphs (DAGs), the second one which incorporates also backfilling to fill gaps in the schedule, and the third one based on an initial merging of multiple DAGs into a single DAG. The paper concentrates on the third approach, and distinguishes four different merging schemes. It also proposes an approach to increase fairness of scheduling, by trying to equalize the slowdown of different DAGs being scheduled (the slowdown is defined as the difference in the expected execution time for the same DAG when scheduled together with other workflows and when scheduled alone).

Dynamism Workflow scheduling is a process which prepares workflows for an actual execution, therefore scheduling and execution should be considered together, and the time relation between them may differ for different scheduling approaches. In [18], three different types of workflow scheduling are distinguished: *full-plan-ahead, in-time local scheduling*, and *in-time global scheduling*. The first approach is fully static, as it schedules the whole workflow before the actual execution starts. On the other extreme, the second approach can be considered as dynamic, as tasks are scheduled dynamically, only when they are going to be executed. The first approach combines the two former approaches by performing full-ahead planning every time a new scheduling decision needs to be made. Based on this classification, we distinguish the following three classes of scheduling processes:

- *Just-in-time scheduling* (in-time local scheduling). The scheduling decision for an individual task is postponed as long as possible, and performed before the task execution starts (fully dynamic approach).

- *Full-ahead planning* (full-plan-ahead). The whole workflow is scheduled before its execution starts (fully static approach).

- *Hybrid.* The scheduling approach combines the two aforementioned approaches.

Just-in-time scheduling is represented by many simple scheduling heuristics like Min-min, Max-min, Suffrage, and XSuffrage. These approaches are also applied to schedule parameter sweep workflows on the Grid [13]. Two typical example approaches which fall into the second class are presented in [42] and [57]. In Vienna Grid Environment [8], both a full ahead scheduling approach and a just-in-time scheduling approach are applied (referred to as *static planning* and *dynamic planning*, respectively). The static planning can be applied only if the *meta data* for performance prediction is known in advance. The hybrid approach proposed in [19] combines the just-in time scheduling and the full-ahead planning by partitioning the workflow into subworkflows and by performing full-graph scheduling of the individual subworkflows in a just-in-time manner. Another hybrid approach presented in [60] achieves the same goal by triggering rescheduling when the state of the Grid changes (i.e., when some resources appear or disappear). Rescheduling of applications is the most widely used method to make full-ahead planning more dynamic. To trigger rescheduling of an application, certain acceptance criteria defined for the application execution are needed, as well as a monitoring system which can control the fulfillment of these criteria. An example of such acceptance criteria are the *performance contracts* proposed in [52], which define the expectation concerning the execution time of the applications, and which are applied in the GrADS system [17, 6].

Advance reservation   When scheduling a workflow, we should take into consideration the environment in which the workflow will be executed. Most of the Grid environments are based on local resource managements with standard queuing systems which can give only a guarantee that a task submitted to the Grid will be executed at some time point. Many of the systems (e.g., Pegasus [19]) are based on DAGMan [16] which is a simple workflow processor which processes workflows and sends workflow tasks to local queuing systems. This simple model can be extended by applying *advance reservation*, which is a limited or restricted delegation of a particular resource capability over a certain time interval to a certain user. If an environment supports advance reservation, then the user can know in advance when his task may start, not relying on the best-effort policy of the local queuing system. Therefore, we can distinguish the following two types of scheduling:

- *With reservation.* Advance reservation is supported and considered by the scheduler.
- *Without reservation.* Advance reservation is not considered by the scheduler, or not supported by the environment.

When considering queuing systems, the Grid scheduler should be aware if the queues on resources have finite or infinite length (capacity). In case of the finite-length queues, it is possible that queues become full and some jobs are lost, which may cause the need for their resubmission. Different advance reservation models for workflow Grid scheduling are proposed in [44, 54, 62]. In [44], different algorithms for resource provisioning are proposed, which reserve time slots on resources based on the economic cost and the execution time criteria. The approach presented in [54] proposes a workflow scheduling approach based on so-called *progressive* reservation. The introduced approach optimizes the profit both of the user (minimal execution time) and of the environment (best possible resource usage and fairness) by putting some limitations on the amount of resources reserved for a single user at a time, and shows some advantage over the approach based on simple *attentive* reservations which does not impose any fairness policy. In [62], an advance reservation model is proposed based on the concept of *Application Spare Time*. The spare time is assigned to every workflow task, based on the deadline defined by the user for the whole workflow, in order to guarantee the feasibility of the workflow execution, when the actual task execution times differ to a certain extent from the predicted times. Two different approaches for spare time allocation are proposed: *recursive allocation* and *Critical Path based allocation*.

3.2   Taxonomy of scheduling criteria

The scheduling criteria may be characterized by various properties (e.g., workflow structure dependence, calculation method) which determine the optimization goal and the way in which the total cost of a workflow is calculated for the given criterion. When scheduling workflows on the Grid, it is always important to take into consideration the type of criteria used as the optimization objectives in the given case. For instance, one scheduling algorithm will be applied when minimizing the execution time of a workflow, and another one will be applied when maximizing the quality of the results produced by a workflow. The scheduling criteria may also differ with respect to the Grid actor (e.g., resource consumer, environment) for whom the optimization goal is defined. The proposed taxonomy of scheduling criteria, considering both the properties of a single criterion and the joint properties of groups of criteria, is depicted in Fig. 2.

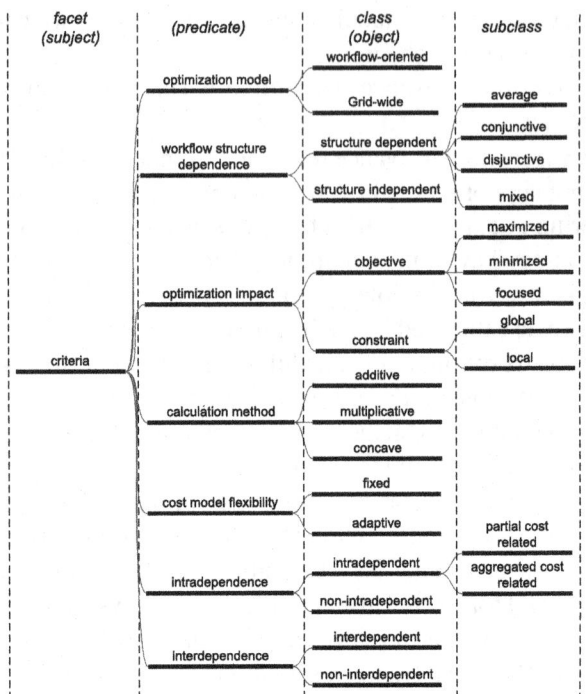

Figure 2.   Taxonomy of workflow scheduling criteria

Optimization model   Considering workflow scheduling as an optimization process, we can distinguish two different perspectives from which the criteria can be defined:

- *Workflow-oriented.* The optimization criterion is defined for the user who executed the workflow (e.g., execution time, economic cost).
- *Grid-wide.* The optimization criterion is defined for the Grid environment (e.g., resource usage, fairness of execution).

Most of the related work proposes approaches based on the former perspective. The latter perspective is common for local resource management systems (e.g., PBS [3], Sun Grid Engine [46], LSF [1], Maui [15]), and is also applied for workflow scheduling, for instance in [63] where fairness of multiple workflow executions is considered as one of the optimization goals. Dynamic cost models based on Grid Economy and on other negotiation-based strategies, which are described more in detail later in this section, can be used to equilibrate between the requirements of the user and of the Grid. *Market equilibrium* which is the goal of any economy-based technique is a desirable state from the point of view of the Grid environment. Some study is conducted in [31, 33, 32] to compare the influence which different negotiation strategies have on resource utilization on the Grid.

Workflow structure dependence   Whereas tasks in a task batch are independent, workflows contain dependencies between tasks which determine a certain
workflow structure. For some scheduling criteria (e.g., for execution time), the
structure has to be considered when calculating the total cost, while for some
others (e.g., for economic cost) the structure can be neglected. This leads us to
two distinct classes of criteria:

- *Structure dependent* (e.g., execution time).
- *Structure independent* (e.g., economic cost).

Most of the existing workflow scheduling approaches only optimize execution
time which is a structure dependent criterion. Some multi-criteria workflow
scheduling approaches (e.g., [21, 59, 57, 58, 8]) also consider economic cost
which is structure independent. Some other scheduling criteria can belong to
either of the two classes, depending on the way the user defines them. Let us
denote by *quality of results* any kind of qualitative description (for instance,
expressed in percentage) of the results produced by alternative services (this
quality will usually be higher for an expensive commercial application than for
its open-source equivalent). To calculate the quality of the final results, the
user can either simply multiply the quality of the results produced by individual
workflow tasks, or can also consider the dependencies between different tasks
and the order in which the partial results are produced, defining in this way a
structure dependent function which calculates the quality of results.

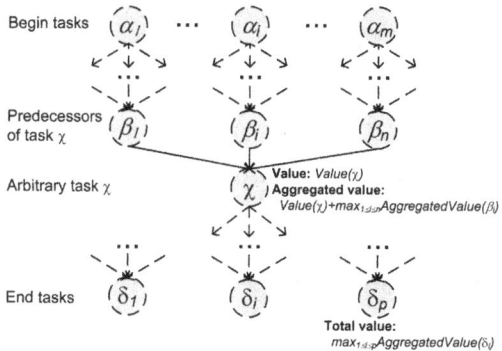

Figure 3.   Recursive calculation of aggregated costs for a structure dependent criterion

Within the class of structure dependent criteria, we can distinguish several
sub-classes, depending on the way in which the partial costs are aggregated in
the workflow. Let us consider as an example the calculation of execution time.
In order to calculate the total execution time, we calculate the *aggregated costs*
(execution times) for all workflow tasks $\tau \in \mathcal{T}$ in a workflow $w \in \mathcal{W}$, and use
the maximum aggregated cost as the total cost (execution time) of the workflow.
A calculation scheme for such a structure dependent criterion is depicted in

Fig. 3, where the aggregated cost for the task γ is calculated based on the partial cost of the task γ and on the aggregated costs of the tasks $\beta_i, 1 \leq i \leq n$. The aggregated costs are calculated recursively, so the same scheme would also apply for the tasks $\beta_i, 1 \leq i \leq n$. The aggregated cost function will be denoted $acost : \mathcal{T} \times \mathcal{W} \times \mathcal{SC} \mapsto \mathbb{R}$. In case of execution time, the aggregated costs of the predecessors are aggregated by finding the *maximum* cost among them. This type of aggregation function is called *disjunctive function*, as it simulates the logical OR operation and gives outputs no smaller than the largest argument. For some other criteria (e.g., for quality of results), the aggregation function can calculate the mean (or weighted mean) over the arguments. Such function is referred to as *averaging function*. Many different averaging functions are proposed in the literature ([51, 36]). For our taxonomy, we chose four averaging functions which seem to be most relevant from the point of view of workflow scheduling:

- *Averaging. Averaging functions* give outputs which lie between the greatest and the smallest elements of the input (e.g., mean, weighted mean).

- *Conjunctive. Conjunctive functions* simulate the logical AND and give outputs no greater than the smallest element of the input (e.g., minimum).

- *Disjunctive. Disjunctive functions* simulate the logical OR and give outputs no smaller than the largest element of input (e.g., maximum).

- *Mixed. Mixed aggregation functions* exhibit different behavior in different regions of the workflow (e.g., maximum for the end tasks, average for the other tasks).

This classification shows some similarities to the classification of calculation methods which is introduced in the later part of this section. However, an aggregation function can only be defined for the structure dependent criteria, and it applies only to a part of the cost calculation procedure (i.e., to the aggregation of the predecessor costs).

Optimization impact   Scheduling criteria may have different impact on the optimization process. If the goal of the process is to find the best possible cost for a certain criterion (e.g., to minimize the total cost), then we can say that the criterion has an *optimization objective*. If the optimization process is constrained by a constant limit established for a certain criterion (e.g., by a budget limit or a time deadline), then we can say that there is an *optimization constraint* assigned to the criterion. Obviously, there may exist a constraint (or multiple constraints) defined for a certain criterion which has an optimization objective. Therefore, the optimization impact of workflow scheduling criteria can be divided into two classes:

- *Objective.* An optimization goal to find the best possible cost for the given criterion (e.g., to minimize the execution time).

- *Constraint.* A restriction imposed on the results of an optimization process (e.g., a time deadline, a budget limit).

In most of the existing workflow scheduling approaches (e.g., [42, 19, 34, 37]), there is an optimization objective defined for execution time (time minimization). A common way to deal with a multi-criteria scheduling [50] is to define an optimization objective for one criterion, and to establish constraints for all the other criteria. The scheduling techniques presented in [59, 57, 58, 21] apply this approach to the problem of bi-criteria scheduling, by defining a constraint for one of the two scheduling criteria (either execution time or economic cost) and by minimizing the other one.

When considering a criterion for which an optimization objective is defined, we should also consider the optimization goal connected with the objective. For instance, when optimizing the execution time of a workflow, the goal is to *minimize* the total time. On the other hand, when optimizing the quality of results or the security and reliability of execution, the goal is to *maximize* the total cost. We can also imagine that the scheduling criterion is the ratio between the costs for two contradicting criteria (e.g., between the memory usage and the execution time). In such a case, the goal will be to obtain a total cost which is possibly close to a certain goal value (i.e., the optimization objective is *focused* on a certain goal cost). We will distinguish three different variants of scheduling objectives:

- *Maximized.* The optimization goal is to maximize the total cost (e.g., for quality of results).

- *Minimized.* The optimization goal is to minimize the total cost (e.g., for economic cost).

- *Focused.* The optimization goal is to achieve a certain total cost (e.g., for memory usage/execution time ratio).

Some approaches (e.g., [8]) distinguish *global constraints* and *local constraints*:

- *Global constraint.* A constraint defined for the whole workflow.

- *Local constraint.* A constraint defined for a single workflow task.

Calculation method Another classification can be done with respect to the operation used for the cost calculation. For instance, addition is performed to combine the individual economic costs of tasks, when calculating the total workflow cost. The same operation is used to calculate the total execution time of a workflow, with a difference that the partial costs are added up taking into consideration also the structure of the workflow (see Fig. 3). There exist a large number of criteria for which it is convenient to express costs as real numbers from the range $[0, 1]$ (e.g., quality of results, probability of failure, availability rate, security). For these criteria, we usually multiply the partial costs of the workflow tasks to calculate the total cost of the workflow. To make the picture more complete, we also mention the class of *concave* criteria, proposed in [56]. The total cost of a concave criterion is equal to the minimal cost among all the individual costs (e.g., bandwidth in pipelined execution or in networks). Therefore, at least three important classes of criteria should be distinguished:

- *Additive* (e.g., economic cost, execution time).
- *Multiplicative* (e.g., quality of results).
- *Concave* (e.g., bandwidth).

Cost model flexibility   A simple cost model assumes that the partial costs of services are a fixed input for scheduling and cannot be changed. This model is widely accepted in the Grid, so it is applied in most of the existing Grid workflow systems. However, there is an increasing interest in more *adaptive* flexible cost models, where the costs can be negotiated or established through some economy-based mechanisms before the application is executed. From this point of view, we have the following two cost models for scheduling criteria:

- *Fixed*. The partial costs of services are given as a fixed input for scheduling.
- *Adaptive*. The partial costs of services are dynamically adjusted through certain mechanisms (e.g., auctions or negotiations).

This classification is similar to the classification based on *intradependence*, which is introduced later in this section. The difference is that for the intradependent criteria, costs are calculated internally by the scheduler using some deterministic functions, while in case of the adaptive cost models discussed here, costs are either determined externally by a Grid broker or result from negotiations between different actors of the Grid.

Adaptive pricing have been extensively studied in the past (although usually not for workflow scheduling), and different models have been proposed. An important class of such models originates from human economy, so the common name to refer to them is *Grid Economy*. Many Grid Economy models have been enumerated and discussed in [11, 10], where a Grid architecture realizing them has also been proposed. In the *commodities market model*, prices are established centrally based on the current demand and supply rate, with the goal of achieving *market equilibrium*. In the *tender/contract-net model*, the consumer announces its requirements, and the service providers respond with the their offers. The *auction model* supports one-to-many negotiation, between a service provider and many consumers. Different auction models (English auction, first-price auction, Vickrey auction, Dutch auction) are known in the literature. The other economic models mentioned in [11] include the *posted price model*, the *bargaining model*, the *bid-based proportional resource sharing model*, the *community/coalition/bartering/share holders model*, and the *monopoly/oligarchy model*.

The Grid Economy models are usually applied to determine the economic cost of services or resources, where the cost can either represent real money or be applied just a useful abstraction introduced for instance for the sake of a fair balance between the demands of different users of the Grid. Different types of resources are treated as individual and interchangeable commodities [55]. The scheduling approach proposed in [49] uses the commodities market model to determine the cost of resource usage in context of non-workflow streaming applications. The approches based on a single market and on multiple markets are compared in this work. The work presented in [55] compares the economic models based on the commodities market and on the second-price Vickrey auctions, showing the superiority of the former approach in terms of the economic factors like price stability, market equilibrium, consumer efficiency, and producer efficiency. The introduced market model called "The First Bank of the G" is an extension of the Scarf's algorithm known in economy. A real workflow scheduling approach based on an economic model is introduced in [14], in which the first-price auction model is applied. Workflows are scheduled in a full-ahead manner, and the scheduling is performed together with bidding for resources. The distance of individual tasks from the end of the workflow determines how *urgent* each task is; the more urgent tasks are given higher prices during the auction in order to increase the possibility of meeting the deadline defined for the workflow.

Other negotiation-based techniques are common for *agent systems*. The automatic negotiation techniques introduced in such systems are developed especially for computer environments rather then originate from human economy. A good introduction to the problem of automatic negotiation is presented in [28]. According to this work, a negotiation strategy can be described by the *negotiation protocol*, *negotiation objects* (objectives for which the negotiation is performed), and the *decision making model* (the negotiation strategy). Three groups of negotiation strategies are distinguished: the *game theoretic techniques* based on the extensively studied strategies known in game theory, the *heuristics* based on more intuitive techniques which lack solid theoretical grounds, and the *argumentation-based techniques* in which the negotiating parties can exchange between each other any kind of *feedback* rather than only simple *counter-proposals*. The work presented in [31, 33, 32] proposes non-workflow scheduling techniques using heuristic-based negotiation strategies. The heuristics are implemented through special *utility functions* which determine the behavior of the negotiating parties. For instance, some utility functions can make a negotiator "tough" (i.e., unwilling to change its initial proposals), while some other functions can make it "conceding" (i.e., apt to accept counter-proposal). The authors examine different scenarios in which *job users* and *resource providers* apply different negotiation strategies, comparing the ratio of agreements successfully created within a limited time, the achieved *utility value*, and the duration of the negotiation process.

Intradependence   The notion of intradependence of scheduling criteria has a major impact on the workflow scheduling. For some criteria, scheduling decisions made for some workflow tasks may change the costs of some other tasks. A good example of such a criterion can be the economic cost in a special progressive price model. A common practice in the market is to introduce a dependence between the size of an order and the price for an individual item (usually, the larger the order, the lower the price). If this is the case, then we can say that the scheduling decisions depend on one another within a scheduling criterion. Also for execution time, the scheduling decisions made for some tasks may influence the aggregated costs of some other tasks (because tasks consume resources whose amount is limited). On the other hand, the scheduling decisions made for criteria like reliability, quality of results, or the economic cost calculated in a simple price model does not seem to show any intradependence. From this point of view, we will distinguish two classes of criteria:

- *Intradependent* (e.g., economic cost in a progressive price model, execution time).
- *Non-intradependent* (e.g., quality of results, economic cost in a simple price model).

Within the class of intradependent criteria, which is the most difficult one for scheduling, we can also distinguish two subclasses. For instance in the aforementioned progressive price economic cost, decisions made for individual workflow tasks may influence the *partial costs* for some other tasks. For a change in execution time, a scheduling decision made for a workflow task does not always change the execution times of other tasks, however it usually influences the way in which the *aggregated costs* are calculated. In this way, we can distinguish two types of intradependence:

- *Partial cost related.* The partial costs of workflow tasks are influenced by the scheduling decisions made for some other workflow tasks (e.g., economic cost in a progressive price model).
- *Aggregated cost related.* The aggregated costs of workflow tasks are influenced by the scheduling decisions made for some other workflow tasks (e.g., execution time).

Interdependence   When considering multiple scheduling criteria, we may observe that some of them strongly depend on others, whilst some others are mutually independent. For example, when optimizing the execution time of a workflow, also the availability and the reliability of services should be taken into consideration, as highly unstable resources on which a service is deployed may provide longer execution times than its more reliable counterparts. On the other hand, the economic cost of a service usage does not have any influence on the execution time, so it can be considered irrelevant from the point of view of this criterion. This observation is of major importance for scheduling, since when considering a group of criteria where some criteria depend on some other criteria, the multi-criteria optimization problem can often be reduced to the optimization of a goal function being a simple product. Therefore, when considering groups of criteria, we will distinguish the following two disjoint classes:

- *Interdependent* (e.g., execution time and availability).

- *Non-interdependent* (e.g., execution time and economic cost).

A workflow scheduling approach based on the idea of interdependent criteria reduction is proposed in the Instant-Grid [27]. The two criteria (number of CPUs and the last known load) are used to calculate a special *quality* value for each resource, based on which the scheduler selects the most appropriate mapping for each workflow task (the Grid-wide optimization perspective applied).

3.3 Taxonomy of Grid resources

Characteristics of the resources on which tasks are executed are especially important from the point of view of *performance-oriented scheduling*, in which the scheduling goal is to optimize the amount of useful work compared to the time and resources used (usually, the execution time or the job throughput optimization). The scheduler has to take into consideration the type of resources used for execution, and the way in which the resources handle the execution of tasks. The proposed taxonomy of Grid resources from the point of view of workflow scheduling is shown in Fig. 4.

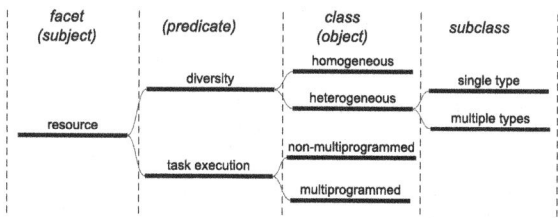

Figure 4. Taxonomy of Grid resources

Diversity One of the main characteristics of the Grid resources is their *heterogeneity*. Therefore, most of the existing Grid environments belong to the second one of the following two classes:

- *Homogeneous.* Multiple resources have identical static and dynamic characteristics (i.e., same type, same performance, same load, etc.).

- *Heterogeneous*. Multiple resources have diverse characteristics (i.e., different types, different performance, different load, etc.).

Heterogeneity can be understood as the existence of diverse characteristics (e.g., CPU speed, RAM size) within a group of resources of the same type (e.g., computational resources). At the extreme, we can take into consideration even the dynamic resource characteristics, and also call the identical resources which have different CPU loads or different amounts of free memory heterogeneous. On the other hand, heterogeneity can be considered only as the distinction between different resource types (e.g., computational resources, network resources, storage resources). We will distinguish two types of heterogeneity:

- *Single type*. The resources of the same type (e.g., computational resources) differ with respect to their characteristics (e.g., CPU speed, RAM size).

- *Multiple types*. The resources differ with respect to their types (e.g., computational, storage, and network resources).

The existing workflow scheduling approaches we are aware of address the former variant of the problem, although the characteristics of some types of resources (e.g., network bandwidth, storage size) are sometimes included in the description of the computational resources (e.g., [25]).

Much effort has been put into addressing multiple types of resources on the Grid. Stork [30] aims at "making data placement a first class citizen in the Grid", by handling data transfers tasks in a similar way as execution tasks. The concept of Open Grid Service Architecture (OGSA) [24] has been introduced to describe the Grid as a service-oriented environment where heterogeneous resources are treated in a uniform way as so-called *Grid Services*. The MetaScheduling-Service (MSS) [53] developed within the VIOLA project aims at co-allocation of different types of resources (currently, compute resources and network resources) in multiple administrative domains.

Task execution   Resources can be divided into two categories, according to the way they can be used by multiple tasks:

- *Non-multiprogrammed*. The scheduler can schedule at most a single task to be executed on a resource at the same time.

- *Multiprogrammed*. The scheduler can schedule multiple tasks to be executed on a resource at the same time.

The resources from these two classes are sometimes referred to also as *disjunctive* and *cumulative*, respectively [4]. Most of the existing Grid environments consist of parallel machines being managed by local resource managers which allow only for disjunctive access to the resources (external load on the resources can always be the case). Therefore, all the Grid workflow scheduling approaches which we are aware of address the non-multiprogrammed resource model. In [41], a scheduler called O-OSKAR is proposed, which schedules workflows of general (not necessarily computational) activities on multiprogrammed resources. The problem is approached as a Meta-CSP (Meta-Constraint Satisfaction Problem), and solved using an algorithm called ISES [2].

3.4   Taxonomy of workflow tasks

Workflow tasks may differ with respect to their requirements and characteristics which have to be taken into consideration when scheduling a workflow. The proposed taxonomy of tasks is depicted in Fig. 5.

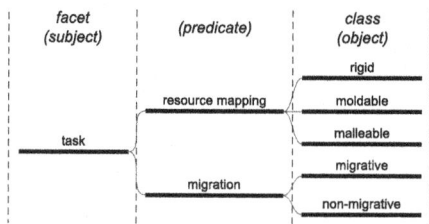

Figure 5.   Taxonomy of workflow tasks

Resource mapping   In a similar way as a single resource can be used by multiple tasks at a time (see Section 3.3), also a single task may require multiple resources to be used (e.g., parallel MPI and PVM programs). We can distinguish three classes of tasks, with respect to its resource mapping requirements:

- *Rigid.* A task requires a fixed number of resources to be used (usually, one resource).
- *Moldable.* A task requires multiple Grid resources to be used, and the number of resources required by the task is not known *a priori* but determined before the execution starts.
- *Malleable.* A task requires multiple Grid resources to be used which may be added or withdrawn from a job according to the current system state.

The processing speed of a task (referred to as the *processing speed function*) is usually a nonlinear function of the number of processors allocated to the task. Most of the existing workflow scheduling approaches assume that tasks belong to the first class. The other two classes are much more difficult for scheduling, as a new dimension is added to the task allocation problem. Many of the existing algorithms for moldable and malleable tasks proceed in two steps [39]: the first step aims at finding an optimal *allocation* for each task, and the second step determines a *placement* for the allocated tasks, that is the actual processor set to execute each task that minimizes the total completion time. *Mixed task and data parallel application* are considered often as cases of moldable and malleable tasks (e.g., [40, 39], [12], [45, 25]).

A typical algorithm which deals with the problem of workflow scheduling of moldable tasks in homogeneous environments is the Critical Path and Area-based algorithm (CPA) [40]. This algorithm aims at finding the best compromise between the length of the critical path, and the *average area T_A* which measures the mean processor-time area required by the application. Formally, $T_A = \frac{1}{R} \sum_{i=1}^{N} (t(\tau_i, N_p(t_i)) \cdot N_p(t_i))$, where R denotes the total number of resources, N the total number of tasks, $\tau_i, 1 \leq i \leq N$ a task, $N_p(\tau_i)$ the number of resources allocated to the task τ_i, and $t(\tau_i, N_p(\tau_i))$ the execution time of the task τ_i executed on $N_p(\tau_i)$ resources. In [39], CPA is extended to the Heterogeneous Critical Path and Area-based algorithm (HCPA) designed for heterogeneous environments. To adapt the algorithms to the heterogeneous environments, the following two modifications are introduced: (i) a novel "virtual" cluster methodology for handling platform heterogeneity is applied in the allocation step, and (ii) a novel task placement step is introduced, to determine whether the placement step of heuristics for homogeneous platforms is adapted to the heterogeneous case.

Another approach to the problem of scheduling of moldable tasks in workflows is proposed in [12]. The authors show a way in which a typical list scheduling algorithm for heterogeneous environment can be adjusted for moldable tasks. The authors propose a new M-HEFT algorithm which extends the existing Heterogeneous Earliest Finish Time (HEFT) algorithm [61] with respect to the way in which the *cost values* (expected execution times) for different tasks are calculated. The cost values are used in the algorithm to determine the scheduling order and to find the best mapping for each task. Since a single task may use different numbers of CPUs of a compound Grid site, the values are estimated for different *configurations* of different Grid sites (e.g., for different numbers of CPUs of a cluster). In the simplest version of the proposed algorithm (called M-HEFT1), the cost values are estimated for a single 1-processor configuration of each site. Vienna Grid Environment [8] applies heuristics to determine the number of processors required to execute an MPI job within the user-specified time constraints.

The work presented in [25] addresses the problem of distributed database query scheduling on the Grid. The authors enumerate three common approaches to the problem based on three different kinds of parallelism: *independent, pipelined,* and *partitioned* (or *intra-operator*). In context of the taxonomies proposed by us, the first type of parallelism assumes that all tasks are rigid, the second type is related to the *pipelined workflows* (see Section 3.5), and the third type, which is exploited in the proposed approach, assumes that all tasks are moldable. Distributed queries in the problem under consideration are defined as tree-like DAGs consisting of different basic tasks (*operators*), which are originally described as *single-node plans* (where *node* refers to a computational node), and which are subsequently converted to *multi-node plans* (in which individual operators can be mapped to multiple computational nodes) by the proposed algorithm. The parallelization of single-node plans is done by incrementally increasing the number of computational nodes mapped to the *costlies* (i.e., most time consuming) parallelizable operators.

The problem of scheduling of malleable tasks in a parallel environment is addressed in [7]. The authors provide a theoretical analysis of the problem of scheduling of independent tasks, and propose a scheduling algorithm that solves the problem in linear time when all the processing speed functions are convex, and in polynomial time when the speed functions are concave. The GrADS projects [6] applies a dynamic performance tuning of malleable tasks by applying so-called *MPI Swapping*. In this approach, the resources are grouped into two sets, the *active* set and the *inactive* set, where only the first set contains resources which can be used by applications. During the execution, the resources are systematically moved between the sets, depending on the current performance measurements.

The requirement of multiple resources for a task is connected with the concept of *co-allocation*, i.e., the simultaneous allocation of resources in multiple sites. In the KOALA Grid Scheduler [38], co-allocation is done by the Co-allocator (CO) which is responsible for finding the execution sites with enough idle processors for the tasks. In the MetaScheduling-Service (MSS) [53], developed within the VIOLA project, heterogeneous resources are co-allocated across multiple administrative domains.

Migration Dynamic scheduling can be implemented more effectively in environments where preemption and migration are enabled. With respect to these properties, we will distinguish two classes of tasks:

- *Migrative.* Task execution can be checkpointed at a certain resource, preempted, migrated, and resumed on another resource (assuming that the operating systems on the resources support migration).

- *Non-migrative.* Task migration is not enabled.

Task migration is rarely applied in the real Grid, due to well-known problems with the implementation of reliable and effective task migration. All existing implementations are restricted only to specific platforms, and impose strict prerequisites on the tasks which can be migrated [5]. The only Grid workflow system we are aware of which supports task migration is GrADS [6].

3.5 Taxonomy of workflow model

The taxonomy depicted in Fig. 6 differentiates workflows with respect to their representation and behavior.

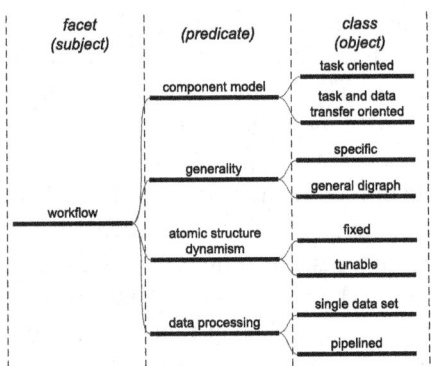

Figure 6.   Taxonomy of workflow model

Component model   From the scheduling point of view, workflows may differ with respect to the way computational tasks and data transfers are represented in them. We can distinguish two classes of workflow models:

- *Task oriented.* Computational tasks are represented as graph nodes. Data transfers are represented as graph edges.

- *Task and data transfer oriented.* Both computational tasks and data transfers are represented as graph tasks.

The existing Grid workflow scheduling approaches are based predominantly on the former model. There are only few workflow representations which support the latter model (e.g., Karajan [29] and Stork [30]). In Vienna Grid Environment [8], the low level workflow representation denotes both tasks and data transfers as workflow nodes. However, in the high level representation used for requirement specification and scheduling, there are no separate *VGE services* representing data transfers. The distributed query workflows used in [25] include also special workflow nodes called *exchange operators* which involve communication between other workflow nodes.

Generality   Although the workflow model specified by us in Section 2 is the directed graph (digraph), many existing workflows have a well-defined structure which can be described by a simpler model being a subset of the general digraph model (e.g., a master-worker workflow with well-defined parallel sections of identical tasks). For specific workflow models, there may exist some specialized algorithms which produce better results than any general-purpose digraph scheduling algorithm. Therefore, we will distinguish the following two workflow models:

- *Specific.* The workflow structure has certain regularities, so it can be described by a well-defined subset of the general digraph model (e.g., parameter sweep applications).

- *General digraph.* The workflow is a general digraph defined in Section 2.

Many existing approaches are based on a specific workflow model. The work presented in [45] considers a pipelined workflow model based on a sequence of data parallel tasks. The workflows used to model distributed database queries in [25] are based on a special tree-like structure constructed according to certain restricted composition rules. The regular structure of the workflows considered in [19] allowed to introduce the idea of workflow partioning which consists in converting the workflow to a sequence of subworkflows. The dynamic scheduling of the parameter sweep applications considered in [34] is approached by a special prioritization policy which gives higher priority to the tasks whose so-called *children's ancestors* have already been finished. In [13], several heuristics for dynamic scheduling of parameter sweep applications (Min-min, Max-min, Suffrage) are compared, and a new heuristic called XSuffrage is proposed. In the Abstract Grid Workflow Language (AGWL) [23] used in ASKALON [22], the workflows are expressed by means of hierarchical embedded structures (loops, parallel loop, conditionals, etc.), which is appropriate for a broad range of scientific workflows. For scheduling purposes, the workflows expressed in AGWL are converted to the general digraph model [35]. The general digraph model of workflows is addressed for instance in [42, 63, 37, 21, 59].

Atomic structure dynamism   Apart from task mapping, also changing the basic workflow structure can be considered as a scheduling method. Workflow nodes (atomic workflow elements) can be added to or removed from a workflow, or can be grouped together to form new atomic elements, with the aim to increase the profit of the user or of the Grid. We will say that an approach is designed for workflows with a *tunable* atomic structure, if it may modify the workflow structure (for optimization purposes) within the scheduling process, in contrast to the approaches which modify the workflow structure only as a consequence of a normal workflow execution (e.g., through loop unrolling or user interactions). We also impose an additional restriction on this group, by assuming that it contains only those approaches which add/remove/modify nodes, not those which just add/remove/modify dependencies. The reason for this is to exclude the approaches based on workflow clustering (i.e., on an auxiliary partition of the workflow to a set of non-atomic subworkflows), which is a standard scheduling approach. We introduce the following two workflow classes:

- *Fixed.* The atomic workflow structure is not changed during the scheduling process (some additional dependencies can be added or removed).

- *Tunable.* Atomic nodes can be added, removed, or modified during the scheduling process.

In K-WfGrid [48], workflows are created on demand and semantically tuned by the components called Workflow Composition Tool (WCT) and Automatic Application Builder (AAB) before the tasks are mapped to services. Also in PEGASUS [19], the workflows are first converted from an *abstract* to a *concrete* form. Three different restructuring techniques are involved in this process. Firstly, data sets which are produced by workflows running in the Grid can be reused in the subsequent workflow executions, which makes the execution of some workflow tasks unnecessary. Secondly, the *granularity* of a workflow is increased by combining (clustering) several tasks and treating the result as a single unit for mapping and scheduling. The third restructuring technique consists in clustering together several tasks scheduled to multi-processor systems, and running them together as one schedulable unit, possibly in a master/slave fashion. The last two approaches aim at decreasing the scheduling overheads. In the approaches designed for pipelined workflows (e.g., [45]), tasks in the original sequence can be *replicated* (several instances of the same task may process different data sets in parallel), in order to increase the overall throughput.

Data processing   This classification distinguishes two different types of workflow processing, which are addressed in different scheduling approaches. When considering the amount of data processed by an individual workflow, we can identify the following two workflow models:

- *Single data set.* The workflow is executed once, for a single set of input data.
- *Pipelined.* The workflow is executed many times, for multiple data sets which are processed by the workflow as a stream.

Most of the existing Grid approaches address the first of the aforementioned classes. The second class is common in several application domains, including digital signal processing, image processing, and computer vision. The approach presented in [45] addresses the problem of scheduling of pipelined computations with the goal of optimizing the latency and the throughput of execution. The applications consist of a sequence of data parallel tasks which can be mapped onto a parallel machine in a variety of ways, employing different combinations of task and data parallelism.

In [49], the authors analyze the problem of scheduling of pipelined (*streaming*) applications, and give several reasons why the classical scheduling algorithms are not well suited to the problem addressed by them. Although they define the problem for workflow scheduling, they provide only a solution for scheduling of single processing units.

3.6   Classification of the existing Grid systems

To summarize the material presented in this section, in Table 1 we show a survey of different existing scheduling approaches, classified according to the

Table 1.   Survey of Grid workflow scheduling approaches

Yu, Shi [60]	*Subhlok, Vondran* [45]	*Radulescu et al.* [40]	*N'Takpé, Suter* [39]	*Mika et al.* [37]	*Yu, Buyya, et al.* [57]	*Ma, Buyya* [34]	Instant-Grid [27]	K-WfGrid [26, 48]	*Gounaris* [25]	ASKALON [22, 35, 54, 23]	*Sakellariou, Zhao* [42, 62, 63]	*Tsiakkouri et al.* [21]	*Singh et al.* [44]	PEGASUS [18]	*Chien et al.* [14]	*Casanova et al.* [13]	*Casanova et al.* [12]	*Vienna Grid Environment* [8]	GrADS [6, 17]	Paper/System
	+				+		+	+				+	+					+		multiple criteria
+		+	+	+	+	+		+	+	+	+	+	+	+	+	+	+	+	+	execution time
					+							+	+					+		economic cost
	+						+	+										+		other criteria
							+			+	+			+						multiple workflows
						+	+								+		+			just-in-time
+	+	+	+	+	+	+		+	+	+	+	+	+	+	+		+	+	+	full-ahead
+															+				+	hybrid
+					+					+	+		+					+		advance reservation
+	+	+	+	+	+	+		+	+	+	+	+	+	+	+	+	+	+	+	workflow-oriented
							+			+										Grid-wide
+	+	+	+	+	+	+	+	+	+	+	+	+	+	+		+	+	+	+	fixed cost model
															+					adaptive cost model
+			+	+	+	+	+	+	+	+	+	+	+	+	+	+	+	+	+	heterogeneous resources
																				multiprogrammed resources
	+	+	+						+				+	+			+	+	+	moldable tasks
																			+	malleable tasks
																			+	migrative tasks
+	+	+	+	+	+	+	+	+		+	+	+	+	+	+	+	+	+	+	task oriented
									+											task and data transfer oriented
	+					+			+	+				+		+				specific workflow model
+		+	+	+	+		+	+		+	+	+	+	+	+		+	+	+	general digraph model
	+							+						+				+		tunable workflows
+		+	+	+	+	+	+	+	+	+	+	+	+	+	+	+	+	+	+	single data set workflows
	+																			pipelined workflows

proposed taxonomies. In this survey, we concentrate only on the workflow scheduling approaches dedicated for the Grid, although the term "Grid" may not be explicitly mentioned in all of them. In order to make the comparison more concise, we do not show there the classifications introduced by us for scheduling criteria (except for optimization model and cost model flexibility). Instead, we just state explicitly whether the compared approach considers execution time, economic cost, or other kinds of criteria. Several times, groups of multiple approaches are described in a single table row. It was done when the approaches were proposed by the same authors and were logically related (e.g., were developed within the same project).

4.   Conclusions

The presented study shows that multi-criteria scheduling on the Grid is a complex problem for which multiple variants can be distinguished based on different possible aspects. Obviously, it is not feasible in general to develop a single scheduling approach which works efficiently for all classes of the problem. For instance, it is rather unlikely that a scheduling approach which works well for workflows consisting of rigid tasks running on non-multiprogrammed resources will work equally good for a pipelined workflow processing a stream of video data, containing moldable tasks which can share the same resources. Therefore, when developing any general scheduling strategy, the first step should be to identify the set of problem classes which can be approached in a similar way.

There exist some multi-criteria workflow scheduling approaches, most of them considering execution time as the most important scheduling criterion. In most of the cases, the scheduling process performed for the criteria is workflow-oriented. The existing workflow scheduling approaches are usually based on full-ahead planning. Most of them are designed for task oriented general digraphs and on the data processing model based on a single data input set. The pipelined workflows, which are characteristic only for some specific areas (e.g., for multimedia systems) have considerably different behaviors and require different scheduling techniques.

There are almost no workflow scheduling approaches which are based on an adaptive cost model for criteria. Such cost models present a very promising research direction, as they can lead towards scheduling techniques applicable in utility Grids with paid access to resources, and which can address the challenges like Service Level Agreements (SLAs). Advance reservation can be applied as a logical extension of such models. There is still a large research potential for scheduling of malleable tasks, and for the multiprogrammed resource model, although it is not certain whether the latter problem class has any significant practical meaning (we are not aware of any workflow scheduling research for the Grid which addresses this problem). Another interesting research area is related with the heterogeneity model based on multiple resource types. Also workflow tuning and task migration as optimization methods seem to be underrepresented among the existing scheduling approaches.

The current study shows that the Grid workflow scheduling problem is still not fully addressed by the existing work. We believe that the presented taxonomies will facilitate development of scheduling approaches capable of dealing with some of the distinguished problem classes. In the future, we are planning to invent a generic scheduling approach for two or more criteria, exploring different types of criteria. An economic model provided for multiple consumers and providers, incorporating price negotiation and advance reservation, seems to be most appropriate for our goals. Starting from simple cases (bi-criteria scheduling), we will try to move towards more complicated problem classes, considering different types of intradependence, and different characteristics of tasks and workflows.

References

[1] Platform Computing Inc. Platform LSF. http://www.platform.com/Products/Platform. LSF.Family/.

[2] A. O. A. Cesta and S. Smith. A Constrained-Based Method for Project Scheduling with Time Windows. *Journal of Heuristics*, 8:109–136, 2002.

[3] Altair Engineering, Inc. PBS Professional. http://www.altair.com/software/pbspro.htm.

[4] P. Baptiste, C. Le Pape, and W. Nuijten. *Constraint-based Scheduling: Applying Constraint Programming to Scheduling Problems*, volume 39 of *International Series in Operations Research and Management Science*. Kluwer Academic Publishers, Norwell, MA, 2001.

[5] J. Basney, M. Litzkow, T. Tannenbaum, and M. Livny. Checkpoint and migration of unix processes in the condor distributed processing system. Technical Report Technical Report 1346, April 1997.

[6] Berman, F. et al. New Grid Scheduling and Rescheduling Methods in the GrADS Project. *International Journal of Parallel Programming*, 33:209–229(21), June 2005.

[7] J. Blazewicz, M. Machowiak, J. Weglarz, M. Kovalyov, and D. Trystram. Scheduling Malleable Tasks on Parallel Processors to Minimize the Makespan: Models and Algorithms for Planning and Scheduling Problems. *Annals of Operations Research*, 129:65–80(16), July 2004.

[8] I. Brandic, S. Benkner, G. Engelbrecht, and R. Schmidt. QoS Support for Time-Critical Grid Workflow Applications. In *E-SCIENCE '05: Proceedings of the First International Conference on e-Science and Grid Computing*, pages 108–115, Washington, DC, USA, 2005. IEEE Computer Society.

[9] I. Brandic, S. Pllana, and S. Benkner. Amadeus: A Holistic Service-oriented Environment for Grid Workflows. *gccw*, 0:259–266, 2006.

[10] R. Buyya, D. Abramson, and S. Venugopal. The Grid Economy. In M. Parashar and C. Lee, editors, *Proceedings of the IEEE*, volume 93 of *Special Issue on Grid Computing*, pages 698–714. IEEE Press, New Jersey, USA, Mar 2005.

[11] R. Buyya, H. Stockinger, J. Giddy, and D. Abramson. Economic Models for Management of Resources in Peer-to-Peer and Grid Computing. Technical Report 0108001, Economics Working Paper Archive at WUSTL, 2001. available at http://ideas.repec.org/p/wpa/wuwpco/0108001.html.

[12] H. Casanova, F. Desprez, and F. Suter. From Heterogeneous Task Scheduling to Heterogeneous Mixed Parallel Scheduling. In M. Danelutto, D. Laforenza, and M. Vanneschi, editors, *Proceedings of the 10th International Euro-Par Conference (Euro-Par'04)*, volume 3149 of *Lecture Notes in Computer Science*, pages 230–237, Pisa, Italy, August/September 2004. Springer.

[13] H. Casanova, A. Legrand, D. Zagorodnov, and F. Berman. Heuristics for Scheduling Parameter Sweep Applications in Grid Environments. In *Proceedings of 9th Heterogeneous Computing Workshop (HCW)*, pages 349–363, Cancun, Mexico, May 2000.

[14] C.-H. Chien, P. H.-M. Chang, and V.-W. Soo. Market-Oriented Multiple Resource Scheduling in Grid Computing Environments. In *AINA '05: Proceedings of the 19th International Conference on Advanced Information Networking and Applications*, pages 867–872, Washington, DC, USA, 2005. IEEE Computer Society.

[15] Cluster Resources, Inc. Maui Cluster Scheduler. http://www.clusterresources.com/pages/products/maui-cluster-scheduler.php.

[16] DAGMan (Directed Acyclic Graph Manager). http://www.cs.wisc.edu/condor/dagman/.

[17] H. Dail, O. Sievert, F. Berman, H. Casanova, A. YarKhan, S. Vadhiyar, J. Dongarra, C. Liu, L. Yang, D. Angulo, and I. Foster. Scheduling in the Grid Application Development Software Project, 2003.

[18] E. Deelman, J. Blythe, Y. Gil, and C. Kesselman. Workflow Management in GriPhyN. *Grid Resource Management, State of the Art and Future Trends.* pages 99–116, 2004.

[19] E. Deelman, G. Singh, M.-H. Su, J. Blythe, Y. Gil, C. Kesselman, G. Mehta, K. Vahi, G. B. Berriman, J. Good, A. Laity, J. C. Jacob, and D. Katz. Pegasus: a Framework for Mapping Complex Scientific Workflows onto Distributed Systems. *Scientific Programming Journal*, 13(2), November 2005.

[20] F. Dong and S. G. Akl. Scheduling Algorithms for Grid Computing: State of the Art and Open Problems. Technical Report 2006-504, School of Computing, Queen's University, Kingston, Ontario, January 2006.

[21] H. Z. E. Tsiakkouri, R. Sakellariou and M. D. Dikaiakos. Scheduling Workflows with Budget Constraints. In S. Gorlatch and M. Danelutto, editors, *In Proceedings of the CoreGRID Workshop "Integrated research in Grid Computing"*, pages 347–357, Nov. 2005.

[22] T. Fahringer, R. Prodan, R. Duan, F. Nerieri, S. Podlipnig, J. Qin, M. Siddiqui, H.-L. Truong, A. Villazon, and M. Wieczorek. ASKALON: A Grid Application Development and Computing Environment. In *6th International Workshop on Grid Computing (Grid 2005)*, Seattle, USA, Nov. 2005. IEEE Computer Society Press.

[23] T. Fahringer, J. Qin, and S. Hainzer. Specification of Grid Workflow Applications with AGWL: An Abstract Grid Workflow Language. In *Proceedings of IEEE International Symposium on Cluster Computing and the Grid 2005 (CCGrid 2005)*, Cardiff, UK, May 9-12, 2005. IEEE Computer Society Press.

[24] I. Foster, C. Kesselman, and S. Tuecke. The Anatomy of the Grid: Enabling Scalable Virtual Organizations. *International Journal of Supercomputing Applications*, 15(3), 2002.

[25] A. Gounaris, R. Sakellariou, N. Paton, and A. Fernandes. A novel approach to resource scheduling for parallel query processing on computational grids. *Distributed and Parallel Databases*, 19:87–106(20), May 2006.

[26] A. Hoheisel. User tools and languages for graph-based Grid workflows: Research Articles. *Concurr. Comput. : Pract. Exper.*, 18(10):1101–1113, 2006.

[27] A. Hoheisel and H. Rose. Konzept für das Scheduling von Workflow-Aktivitäten in Instant Grid. Technical report, Fraunhofer Institut für Rechnerarchitektur und Softwaretechnik, June 2006.

[28] N. R. Jennings, P. Faratin, A. R. Lomuscio, S. Parsons, C. Sierra, and M. Woodlidge. Automated Negotiation: Prospects, Methods and Challenges. *International Journal of Group Decision and Negotiation*, 10(2):199–215, 2001.

[29] Java CoG Kit Karajan Guide. http://www.cogkit.org/current/manual/workflow.pdf.

[30] T. Kosar and M. Livny. Stork: Making data placement a first class citizen in the grid, 2004.

[31] J. Li and R. Yahyapour. A Negotiation Model Supporting Co-Allocation for Grid Scheduling. In *Proceedings of 7th IEEE/ACM International Conference on Grid Computing (Grid'06)*, Barcelona, Spain, 2006. IEEE Computer Society Press.

[32] J. Li and R. Yahyapour. Learning-Based Negotiation Strategies for Grid Scheduling. In *IEEE Int'l Symposium on Cluster Computing and the Grid (CCGrid 2006), Singapore*, pages 567–583. IEEE Press, 2006.

[33] J. Li and R. Yahyapour. Negotiation Strategies for Grid Scheduling. In *The First International Conference on Grid and Pervasive Computing (GPC2006)*, volume 3947 of *Lecture Notes in Computer Science*, pages 42–52, Tunghai University, Taiwan, 2006. Springer-Verlag.

[34] T. Ma and R. Buyya. Critical-Path and Priority based Algorithms for Scheduling Workflows with Parameter Sweep Tasks on Global Grids. In *Proceedings of the 17th International Symposium on Computer Architecture and High Performance Computing (SBAC-PAD 2005)*, Rio de Janeiro, Brazil, Oct. 24-27 2005. IEEE Computer Society Press.

[35] M. Mair, J. Qin, M. Wieczorek, and T. Fahringer. Workflow conversion and processing in the askalon grid environment. *2nd Austrian Grid Symposium*, 2007.

[36] C. F. Mela and D. R. Lehmann. Using fuzzy set theoretic techniques to identify preference rules from interactions in the linear model: an empirical study. *Fuzzy Sets Syst.*, 71(2):165–181, 1995.

[37] M. Mika, G. Waligóra, and J. Weglarz. Workflow Management in GriPhyN. *Grid Resource Management, State of the Art and Future Trends.* pages 295–318, 2004.

[38] H. Mohamed and D. Epema. The Design and Implementation of the KOALA Co-Allocating Grid Scheduler. In *European Grid Conference*, volume 3470 of *Lecture Notes in Computer Science*, pages 640–650. Springer-Verlag, 2005.

[39] T. N'Takpé and F. Suter. Critical path and area based scheduling of parallel task graphs on heterogeneous platforms. In *Proceedings of the 12th International Conference onParallel and Distributed Systems, ICPADS 2006*, Minneapolis, Minnesota, USA, July 2006. IEEE Computer Society Press.

[40] A. Radulescu, C. Nicolescu, A. J. C. van Gemund, and P. P. Jonker. CPR: Mixed task and data parallel scheduling for distributed systems. In *Proceedings of the 15th International Parallel and Distributed Processing Symposium (IPDPS)*, pages 39–41, San Francisco, USA, Apr. 2001. IEEE Computer Society Press.

[41] M. D. Rodriguez Moreno, D. Borrajo Millán, and D. Meziat Luna. *Representing and Planning tasks with time and resources*. PhD thesis, Universidad de Alcalá, Spain, Dec. 2003.

[42] R. Sakellariou and H. Zhao. A Hybrid Heuristic for DAG Scheduling on Heterogeneous Systems. In *IPDPS*, 2004.

[43] A. Schrijver. *Theory of Linear and Integer Programming*. Wiley, 1987. SchRI a 87:1 1.Ex.

[44] G. Singh, C. Kesselman, and E. Deelman. Application-Level Resource Provisioning on the Grid. *e-science*, 0:83, 2006.

[45] J. Subhlok and G. Vondran. Optimal Use of Mixed Task and Data Parallelism for Pipelined Computations. *Journal of Parallel and Distributed Computing*, 60:297–319(23), March 2000.

[46] Sun Microsystems, Inc. Grid Engine. http://gridengine.sunsource.net/.

[47] T. Andrews, et al. Business Process Execution Language for Web Services. Technical report, BEA Systems, et al., May 2003.

[48] The K-WfGrid project. http://www.kwfgrid.net.

[49] L. Tian and K. M. Chandy. Resource allocation in streaming environments. In *Proceedings of 7th IEEE/ACM International Conference on Grid Computing (Grid'06)*, Barcelona, Spain, 2006. IEEE Computer Society Press.

[50] V. T'kindt and J. Billaut. *Multicriteria Scheduling*. Springer Verlag, Berlin, 2002.

[51] A. Čaplinskas and J. Gasperovič. Techniques to Aggregate the Characteristics of Internal Quality of an IS Specification Language. *Informatica*, 16(4), 2005.

[52] F. Vraalsen, R. A. Aydt, C. L. Mendes, and D. A. Reed. Performance Contracts: Predicting and Monitoring Grid Application Behavior. *Lecture Notes in Computer Science*, 2242:154–166, 2001.

[53] O. Wäldrich, W. Ziegler, and P. Wieder. A Meta-Scheduling Service for Co-allocating Arbitrary Types of Resources. Technical Report TR-0010, Institute on Resource Management and Scheduling, CoreGRID - Network of Excellence, December 2005.

[54] M. Wieczorek, M. Siddiqui, A. Villazon, R. Prodan, and T. Fahringer. Applying Advance Reservation to Increase Predictability of Workflow Execution on the Grid. In *E-SCIENCE '06: Proceedings of the Second IEEE International Conference on e-Science and Grid Computing*, page 82, Washington, DC, USA, 2006. IEEE Computer Society.

[55] R. Wolski, J. S. Plank, J. Brevik, and T. Bryan. Analyzing Market-Based Resource Allocation Strategies for the Computational Grid. 15(3):258–281, Fall 2001.

[56] X. Xiao and L. M. Ni. Internet QoS: A Big Picture. *IEEE Network*, 13(2):8–18, Mar. 1999.

[57] J. Yu and R. Buyya. A Budget Constrained Scheduling of Workflow Applications on Utility Grids using Genetic Algorithms. In *Proceedings of the 15th IEEE International Symposium on High Performance Distributed Computing (HPDC 2006)*, Paris, France, June 2006. IEEE, IEEE CS Press.

[58] J. Yu and R. Buyya. Scheduling Scientific Workflow Applications with Deadline and Budget Constraints using Genetic Algorithms. *Scientific Programming Journal*, 14(1), 2006.

[59] J. Yu, R. Buyya, and C. K. Tham. QoS-based Scheduling of Workflow Applications on Service Grids. In *Proceedings of the 1st IEEE International Conference on e-Science and Grid Computing (e-Science 2005)*, Melbourne, Australia, Dec. 2005. IEEE, IEEE CS Press.

[60] Z. Yu and W. Shi. An Adaptive Rescheduling Strategy for Grid Workflow Applications. In *Proceedings of the 21st IPDPS 2007*, Long Beach, USA, Mar 26 -30 2007. IEEE Computer Society Press.

[61] H. Zhao and R. Sakellariou. An Experimental Investigation into the Rank Function of the Heterogeneous Earliest Finish Time Scheduling Algorithm. In *Euro-Par*, pages 189–194, 2003.

[62] H. Zhao and R. Sakellariou. Advance Reservation Policies for Workflows. In *Proceedings of the 12th International Workshop on Job Scheduling Strategies for Parallel Processing*, volume 4376 of *Lecture Notes in Computer Science*, pages 47–67, Saint-Malo, France, June 2006. Springer-Verlag.

[63] H. Zhao and R. Sakellariou. Scheduling Multiple DAGs onto Heterogeneous Systems. In *15th Heterogeneous Computing Workshop (HCW'06)*, Rhodes, Greece, April 2006. IEEE Computer Society Press.

REAL-WORLD WORKFLOW SUPPORT IN THE ASKALON GRID ENVIRONMENT*

Radu Prodan, Thomas Fahringer, Farrukh Nadeem, and Marek Wieczorek
Institute of Computer Science, University of Innsbruck, Technikerstraße 21a, A-6020 Innsbruck
radu@dps.uibk.ac.at
tf@dps.uibk.ac.at
farrukh@dps.uibk.ac.at
marek@dps.uibk.ac.at

Abstract   We present the approach taken by the ASKALON project to support various runtime phases of a real world hydrological application in the Austrian Grid environment. We describe techniques for performance prediction, scheduling, advance reservation, and scalability analysis and illustrate a variety of experimental results that validate each of our technique.

Keywords: Scientific workflows, performance prediction, scheduling, advance reservation, performance analysis, hydrological application.

*This work is supported by the European Union through IST-004265 CoreGRID and IST-034601 edutain@grid projects.

1.   Introduction

Scientific workflows emerged as one of the most attractive paradigm for programming Grid infrastructures. As a consequence, numerous efforts among which the ASKALON project [2] are currently developing integrated environments to support the development and execution cycle of scientific workflows on dynamic Grid environments.

In this paper, we illustrate a case study of using ASKALON for porting and executing a hydrological application in a real Grid environment. First of all, the application is specified by the user at a high-level of abstraction using a UML modelling tool or an XML-based specification language (see Section 2). In combination with the XML language, a resource manager shields the user from the complexity of the underlying Grid infrastructure through advanced functionality such as resource discovery and matchmaking, and semi-automatic deployment of software components. A performance prediction service presented in Section 4 estimates the execution time of individual activities of different Grid sites using a well-defined training phase based on a reduced set of experiments. A scheduling service (see Section 5) uses optimisation heuristics to map entire or partial workflows onto the Grid such as the predicted execution time is minimised. Optionally, to increase predictability of executions in dynamic environments like the Grid, the scheduler negotiates with the resource manager advance reservation slots for individual activities. Finally, an enactment engine service executes the workflow on the Grid according to the given schedule and investigates the most severe sources of performance overheads and the scalability of the execution compared to the fastest local Grid site available (see Section 6).

2.   Invmod

Invmod [10] is a hydrological application designed at the University of Innsbruck for calibration of parameters of the Water Balance Simulation Model ETH (WaSiM-ETH) hydrological application developed at the Swiss Federal Institute of Technology Zurich [4]. Invmod uses the Levenberg-Marquardt algorithm to minimise the least squares of the differences between the measured and the simulated runoff for a determined time period. We re-engineered the monolithic sequential Invmod application into a Grid-enabled scientific workflow consisting of two levels of parallelism as depicted Figure 1: (1) each iteration of the outermost parallel section called *random run* performs a local search optimisation starting from an arbitrarily chosen initial solution; (2) alternative local changes are examined separately for each parameter to be calibrated, which is done in parallel in the innermost parallel section of wasim_b activities. The number of sequential iterations in the inner loop is variable and depends on the actual convergence of the optimisation process.

3. UML Workflow Modelling

ASKALON offers to the end user the privilege of composing workflows through a graphical modelling tool based on the UML standard that combines Activity Diagram modelling elements in a hierarchical fashion. We have implemented this graphical service as a platform-independent workflow editor in Java based on the Model-View-Controller paradigm comprising three main components: graphical user interface, model traverser, and model checker. The drawing space consists of a tabbed panel that can contain several diagrams. The model traverser provides the possibility to walk through the model, visit each modelling element, and access its properties (for instance, element name). We use the model traverser for the generation of various model representations; for instance, an XML representation serves as input for the ASKALON Grid environment. The model checker is responsible for the correctness of the model.

To efficiently model the Invmod workflow introduced in Section 2 in UML, ASKALON introduces two standard constructs (see Figure 2): (1) *parallel*

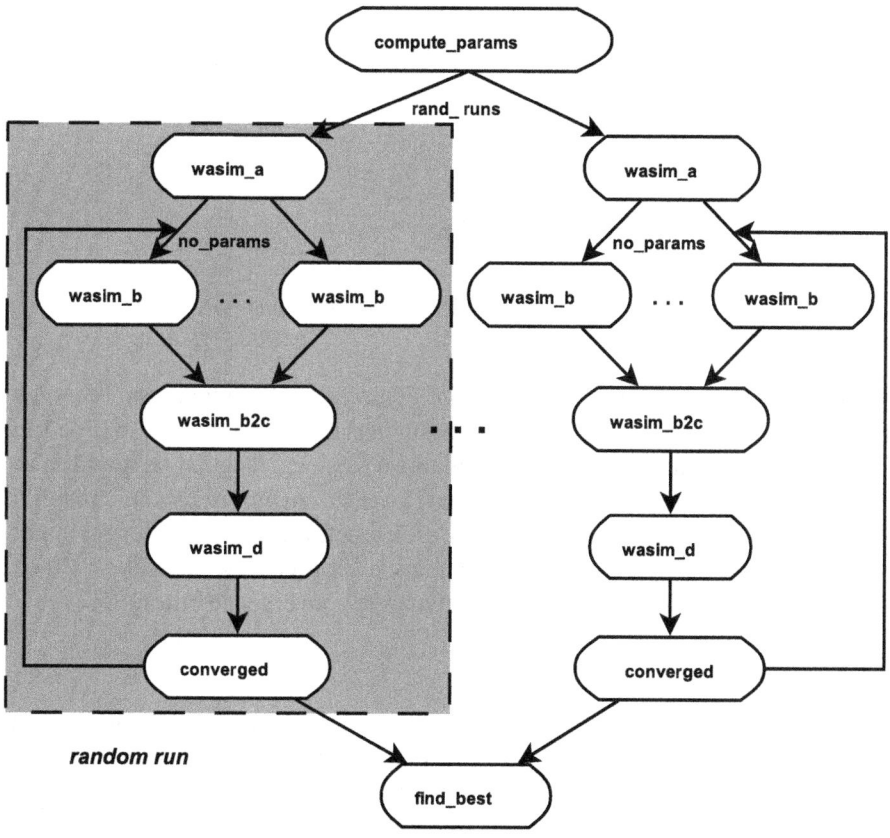

Figure 1. The unrolled Invmod workflow.

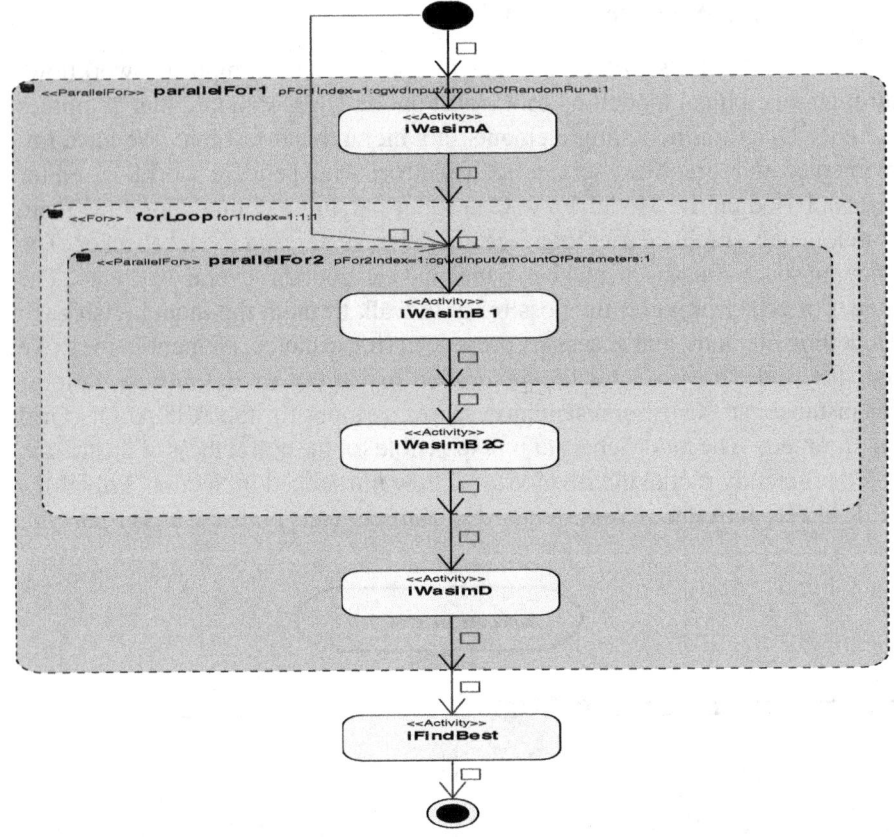

Figure 2.   The Invmod compact UML representation in ASKALON.

loops for expressing the large number of outer parallel random runs (denoted through rand_rans as degree of parallelism in Figure 1 and parallelFor1 in Figure 2) and the inner parameter calculations (denoted through no_params as degree of parallelism in Figure 1 and parallelFor2 in Figure 2); (2) *sequential loops* (denoted as forLoop in Figure 2) for repetitive invocation of the inner parameter calibration steps which contains a loop carried dependency (and therefore cannot be parallelised) and a dynamic convergence criterium.

4.   Performance Prediction

The purpose of the prediction service is to support optimised scheduling and ultimately high performance executions in heterogeneous Grid environments. We employ a prediction model based on historical data collected through a well-defined *experimental design* and *training phase*. Specifically in our work, the general purpose of the experimental design phase is to set a strategy for experiments to get the maximum performance information (execution time) to support its prediction later in minimum numbers of experiments.

We consider the Grid as consisting of a number of homogeneous parallel computers with heterogeneous parallel architectures and underlying processors. The factors affecting the response variable which we currently consider are the problem range p incorporating the set of value instances for each parameter variable, the Grid size g comprising all the Grid sites (i.e. parallel computers), and the average machine size m including all different processor numbers on a Grid site. An experiment is an execution of the application for a certain problem size, on a certain Grid site, using a well-defined machine size.

To reduce the experimental space from $p \times g \times m$, we introduce a *Performance Sharing and Translation (PST)* mechanism based on the experimental observation of inter- and intra-platform performance relativity of embarrassingly parallel applications (our pilot applications) across different problem sizes.

Inter-platform PST specifies that the performance behaviour $P_g(A, p)$ of an application A for a problem size p relative to another problem size r on a Grid site g is the same as that of the same problem sizes on another Grid site h: i.e. $\frac{P_g(A,p)}{P_g(A,r)} \simeq \frac{P_h(A,p)}{P_h(A,r)}$.

Similarly, *intra-platform PST* specifies that the performance behaviour of an embarrassingly parallel application A on a Grid site g for a machine size m relative to another machine size n for a problem size p is similar to that for another problem size q, i.e. $\frac{P_g(A,p,m)}{P_g(A,p,n)} \simeq \frac{P_g(A,q,m)}{P_g(A,q,n)}$.

Inter-platform PST assumes a problem size of one, therefore in our notation $P_g(A, p) \equiv P_g(A, p, 1)$.

We choose one Grid site (the fastest based on previous runs) as the reference site and make a full factorial set of experiments on it. Later, we make one single experiment on each of the other Grid sites and use the reference values to calculate the predictions for other platforms using inter-platform PST and thus minimise problem size combinations with the Grid size. Similarly, to minimise machine size combinations with the Grid size, we make a full factorial of experiments with one reference machine size and later make one single experiment each for each of the other machine sizes to translate the reference performance values for other machine sizes using intra-platform PST.

By means of inter-platform PST, the total number of experiments reduces from $p \times m \times g$ to $p \times m + (g - 1)$ for parallel computers, and from $p \times m$ to $p + g - 1$ for single processor machines. By introducing intra-platform PST, we reduce total number of experiments for parallel machines (Grid sites) further to a linear complexity of $p + (m - 1) + (g - 1)$.

We analysed the scalability of our experimental design strategy by varying the problem size from 10 to 200 for fixed values of the remaining factors: 10 Grid sites with machine size 20 and 50 single processor machines. We observed

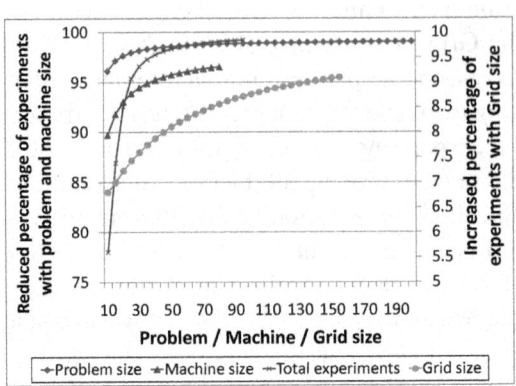

Figure 3.   Experiment reduction with problem, machine, and Grid size.

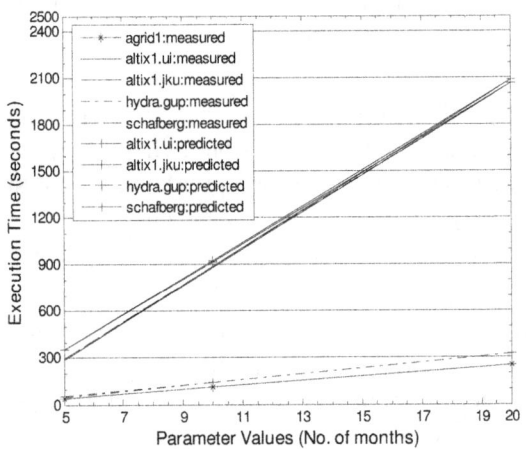

Figure 4.   Relative values of `wasim_b2c`.

a reduction in the total number of experiments from 96% to 99%, as shown in
Figure 3. A reduction from 77% to 97% in the total number of experiments was
observed when we varied the machine size from one to 80 for fixed factors of
10 parallel machines, 50 single processor Grid sites and problem size of five.
From another perspective, we observed that the total number of experiments
increased from 7% to 9% when the Grid size was increased from 15 to 155 for
the fixed factors of five parallel machines with machine size of 10 and problem
size 10. We observed an overall reduction of 78% to 99% when we varied all
factors simultaneously: five parallel machines with machine size from 1 to 80,
single processor Grid sites from 10 to 95, and problem size from 10 to 95.

We comparatively show in Figure 4 the predicted results using the inter-
platform PST method versus the measured values for the `wasim_b2c` activity

Table 1.   A subset of the Austrian Grid testbed.

Rank	Site	Architecture	Size	Processor	Ghz	Mgr.	Location
1	pc2201	NOW, Ethernet	8	Pentium 4	1.8	Torque	Innsbruck
2	pc2509	NOW, Ethernet	8	Pentium 4	1.8	Torque	Innsbruck
3	hydra	COW, Ethernet	6	Athlon	1.6	Torque	Linz
4	pc450	NOW, Ethernet	8	Pentium 4	1.8	Torque	Innsbruck
5	agrid1	NOW, Ethernet	8	Pentium 4	1.8	Torque	Innsbruck
6	pc338	NOW, Ethernet	8	Pentium 4	1.8	Torque	Innsbruck
7	altix1	ccNUMA, Altix	8	Itanium 2	1.6	PBS	Linz
8	schafberg	ccNUMA, Altix	10	Itanium 2	1.6	PBS	Salzburg

in the Austrian Grid testbed depicted in Table 1. The lowest curve represents the execution values on the base Grid site whose values are used in the PST mechanism. Every two curves of measured and predicted values are very much similar, however, we can see that they are closest to each other near the reference problem size (i.e. the one used for the single measurement on the target Grid site) and the difference increases with the distance from the reference problem size. Due to this reason and whenever possible, we take the reference problem size as close as possible to the target value. We observed that the average variation in the predicted values from the measured value, if made on the basis of maximum available value, is at the most 10% which yields 90% accuracy in the prediction. As we get more data during the actual runs, the probability of finding closer parameter values other than the one calculated in the training phase increases which further improves the prediction accuracy.

5.   Scheduling

The ASKALON scheduler applies best-effort heuristic algorithms to achieve good workflow mappings onto the Grid. We currently consider three types of optimisation heuristics: (1) simple *myopic* heuristics, like Condor matchmaking [7], look only at single activities which are mapped onto the best resource available; (2) *full-graph* heuristics such as *genetic* [6] or *Heterogeneous Earliest Finish Time (HEFT)* [12] algorithms optimise the entire predicted workflow makespan. The full-graph algorithms receive as input a Directed Acyclic Graph (DAG) (where each DAG node represents a workflow activity) generated primarily by unrolling the workflow sequential and parallel loops and by eliminating the conditional activities, as we formally presented in [6]. Since such DAGs can get rather huge, we also propose (3) *partitioning*-based heuristics as a hybrid mechanism that schedules in advance a sub-workflow of a certain depth.

5.1   Heterogeneous Earliest Finish Time Algorithm

HEFT [12] is a list scheduling algorithm adjusted for heterogeneous environments. The
algorithm consists of three distinct phases: the *weighting
phase*, the *ranking phase*, and
the *mapping phase*. During the
weighting phase, to each activity N is associated a weight
calculated as the average value
of the predicted execution times
$T_N(R)$ on every individual resource R (i.e. processor) avail-
able on the Grid: $\overline{W}(N) = \underset{\forall R \in Grid}{avg} \{T_N(R)\}$. In the exam-

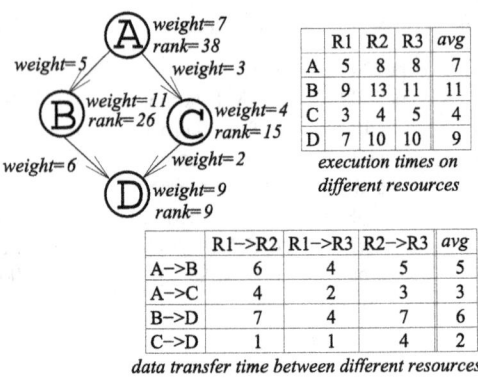

	R1	R2	R3	avg
A	5	8	8	7
B	9	13	11	11
C	3	4	5	4
D	7	10	10	9

execution times on
different resources

	R1->R2	R1->R3	R2->R3	avg
A->B	6	4	5	5
A->C	4	2	3	3
B->D	7	4	7	6
C->D	1	1	4	2

data transfer time between different resources

Figure 5.   HEFT weights and ranks.

ple depicted in Figure 5, the Grid consists of three processors and, therefore, the
weight of the activity A is calculated as: $\overline{W}(A) = \frac{T_A(R1)+T_A(R2)+T_A(R3)}{3} = \frac{5+8+8}{3} = 7$. Similarly, the weight associated to a data dependency is calculated
as the average of the predicted data transfer times on all interconnection links
available between Grid sites. The ranking phase is performed by traversing the
workflow graph upwards and assigning a rank value to each activity. The rank
value of an activity is equal to the weight of the activity plus the maximum rank
value of the successors, including the communication to the current activity (if
any): $\overline{R}(N) = \underset{\forall(N,Succ)}{max} \{\overline{W}(N) + \overline{W}(N, Succ) + \overline{R}(Succ)\}$. For example,
the rank of activity A is calculated as: $\overline{R}(A) = max\{\overline{W}(A) + \overline{W}(A, B) + \overline{R}(B), \overline{W}(A) + \overline{W}(A, C) + \overline{R}(C)\} = max\{7 + 5 + 26, 7 + 3 + 15\} = 38$.
The list of workflow activities is then sorted in a descending order according
to their ranks, i.e. A, B, C, and D. Finally in the mapping phase, the ranked
activities are mapped onto the processors that deliver the earliest completion
time, i.e. A onto $R1$, B onto $R1$, C onto $R3$, and D onto $R1$.

5.1.1   Experiments.
We converted the Invmod workflow into a DAG by
unrolling the sequential loops within each parallel random run using historical
information about the number of iterations available from previous executions.
A typical result of such a conversion is a strongly imbalanced workflow in
which one of the outermost parallel loop iterations is significantly longer than
the others because of slower convergence of the optimisation algorithm for the
corresponding random run. In our case, the converted DAG consists of 100
parallel iterations, one of which contains 20 sequential iterations of the inner

optimisation loop, while the other 99 iterations only contain 10 iterations each (see Figure 6). This means that one parallel iteration needs approximately twice the execution time of the others.

Figure 7 illustrates the predicted makespan delivered by each scheduling algorithm for the imbalanced Invmod workflow in the Grid testbed depicted in Table 1. As expected, the myopic algorithm provides the worst results which are approximately 32% worse than HEFT. The genetic algorithm produces quite good results, however, worse than HEFT since

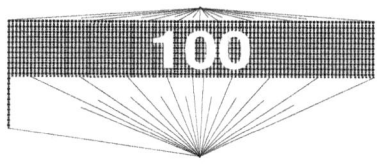

Figure 6. Invmod converted DAG.

does not consider in the optimisation process the execution order of parallel activities scheduled on same processor. In addition, we applied incremental scheduling using with 10, 20, and 30 partitioning layers and compared the results against the full-ahead workflow scheduling consisting of 44 layers. For such strongly imbalanced workflows, the activities belonging to workflow execution paths that are much longer than the critical schedule path should be given priority which is well handled by the entire workflow scheduling strategy based on optimisation heuristics like HEFT and genetic algorithm. Therefore, scheduling strategies based workflow partitioning deliver worse results than those based on full workflow analysis, although they are still better than the one found by the myopic algorithm. The genetic algorithm takes two orders of magnitude longer than the others to converge to good solutions (see Figure 8). We performed experiments with and without prediction information to measure the importance of the performance prediction service. With prediction information, the results are between 33% and 50% better.

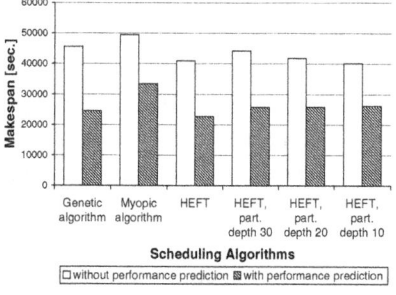

Figure 7. Schedule makespan.

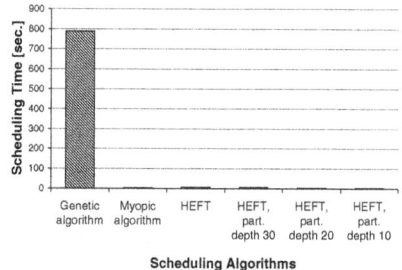

Figure 8. Scheduling algorithm time.

5.2   Advance Reservation

To support advance reservation, we modified the *mapping* phase of the HEFT algorithm by assigning to each activity a list of resources instead of a single resource only. The list is ordered according to the increasing completion time so that the first element on the list is always the best one. In the example depicted in Figure 5, the resource order for the first activity A is: $\{R1, R2, R3\}$. Finally, we introduced to the algorithm a new fourth phase which we called the *reservation phase* in which the scheduler negotiates with the resource manager one resource from the mapping list of each activity. The reservations are performed in a retry loop which handles situations when a negotiation fails for some reason (e.g. the offer is timed out or taken by another user). We developed two reservation strategies: attentive and progressive.

The *attentive* reservation offers a requested slot only if it is available, otherwise generates alternative offers according to the available slots close to the requested time frame. While generating alternative offers, it tries to keep the reserved segments as minimum as possible by proposing alternative options which are overlapping or adjacent to the existing reserved slots, i.e. it tries to find slots during or immediately before or after an existing reservation for all the available processors in a Grid site.

The *progressive* reservation is an extension of the attentive algorithm that considers fairness as well. This method attempts to fairly distribute available resource capacity among competing clients instead of allowing a single client reserve the entire capacity available on a Grid site. The earliest time when a reservation can be made depends on the number and duration of the reservations already made by the client and is done by introducing a new restriction on the number of processors of a Grid site which can be offered to a user at once.

As output, the scheduler returns an execution plan and the reservations performed for each activity.

5.2.1   Experiments.   We performed several experiments, each of which consisting of 10 workflows executed in sequence at 60 seconds time interval. Reservations were performed for individual processors which gave to users exclusive access over the allocated time periods. In order to challenge this particular experiment, we simulated the execution of the workflows in a highly dynamic Grid environment by altering the actual execution time randomly up to 50% from the predicted values to count for possible inaccurate predictions, queuing system delays, security latencies, or external load. Therefore, the workflow execution does not necessarily follow the schedule and the reservations. To ameliorate this behaviour, the scheduler can request for either short reservations, which are 20% longer than the predicted execution time, or for long reservations which are twice as long.

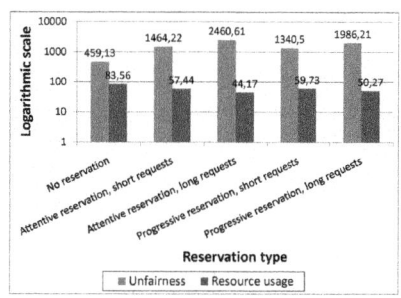

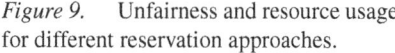

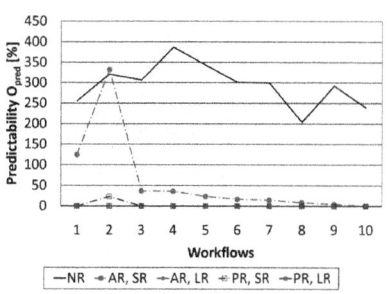

Figure 9. Unfairness and resource usage for different reservation approaches.

Figure 10. Predictability for different reservation approaches.

We first evaluated the reservation *unfairness* by calculating the standard deviation of execution times over all workflows W scheduled within an experiment: $t_{avg}(W) = \frac{\sum_{\forall w \in W} t_{act}(w)}{|W|}$, $\rho(W) = \sqrt{\frac{1}{|W|} \sum_{\forall w \in W} (t_{act}(w) - t_{avg}(W))^2}$. A high value of ρ indicates that some workflows took significantly longer than others, which means a low resource allocation fairness. Obviously, the progressive approach gives always a better fairness than the attentive approach (see Figure 9).

Figure 10 compares the predictability of different reservation approaches calculated as the relative overhead O_{pred} derived from inaccurate predictions that underestimate execution times and, therefore, exceed the reservations: $O_{pred}(w) = \begin{cases} \frac{t_{act}(w) - t_{pred}(w)}{t_{pred}(w)}, & t_{pred}(w) < t_{act}(w); \\ 0, & t_{pred}(w) \geq t_{act}(w). \end{cases}$ The highest prediction error (200%–400%) is obtained by the scheduling without reservations. The attentive reservations with short reservation requests do not provide good predictability either as they fill the resources with tight time slots which allow a very small error margin for which any exceeding time slot can be very costly (see workflow with label 2). The progressive approach provides much better predictability because the reservations do not fill the time space too tightly so that a delayed activity can easily find an "emergency" slot. Long reservation requests eliminate entirely the problem of wrong predictability and no activities are delayed anymore.

In addition, we also measured the *resource usage* U_R as a ratio between the aggregated time when resources were effectively used and the overall available execution time (number of available resources multiplied by the total time during which all experiments were performed): $U_R = \frac{\sum_{\forall A \in W} t_A}{t_{total} \cdot |R|}$, where $|R|$ represents the number of resources available. The best usage (more than 80%) is achieved for the approach without reservations (see Figure 9). For the reservations with short reservation requests, the usage is more than 25% lower for

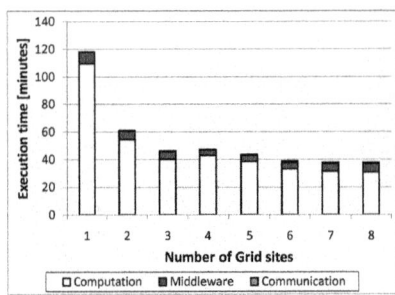

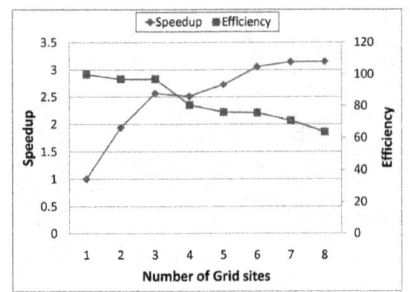

Figure 11.   Scalability.   *Figure 12.*   Speedup and efficiency.

both attentive and progressive reservation policies. Applying the long reservation requests provides an additional loss of more than 10% which decreases the resource usage to less than 50%.

6.   Scalability analysis

The ultimate goal of our work is to study whether through our techniques we can really gain performance by executing the Invmod workflow in the Austrian Grid environment. The workflow execution is coordinated by the ASKALON enactment engine after receiving a complete schedule. We selected a problem size consisting of 100 parallel random runs. We first executed each problem size on the pc2201 reference Grid site, which is the fastest cluster from the Grid testbed for this 32 bit application. Then, we incrementally added new sites to the execution testbed (in the order given by the rank column in Table 1) to investigate whether we can improve the performance of the application by increasing the available computational resources. During the experiments the Grid was idle, while access to processors was granted by the local queuing system. For each execution, we scheduled the activities using the HEFT algorithm without reservations and measured the execution time and the most significant communication and Grid middleware (comprising scheduling and resource management) overheads.

We calculated the workflow *speedup* as the ratio between the fastest single site execution time T_{seq}^g (pc2201 in Innsbruck) and the current Grid execution time T: $S = \dfrac{\min\limits_{\forall g \in Grid}\{T_{seq}^g\}}{T}$. In addition to the speedup, we computed the *efficiency* of each execution as the speedup normalised against the number of the Grid sites used, where each Grid site g is weighted with the speedup of the corresponding single site execution time: $E = \dfrac{S}{\sum_{\forall g \in Grid} S_g}$, where: $S_g = \dfrac{\min\limits_{\forall g' \in Grid}\{T_{seq}^{g'}\}}{T_{seq}^g}$. The efficiency formula becomes therefore: $E = \frac{T^{-1}}{\sum_{\forall g \in Grid}(T_{seq}^g)^{-1}}$. The fastest Grid site has a weight of one, whereas the slowest Grid site has the smallest weight (i.e. closest to zero).

Figure 11 shows that the Invmod execution time improves by increasing the number of Grid sites. The speedup curve is not linear because of the increasing Grid middleware overheads and a larger load imbalance beyond four aggregated sites (see Figure 12). The largest Grid middleware overhead is achieved for one single Grid site due to the large number of requests that have to be served by the GRAM gatekeeper which becomes a bottleneck. This overhead first decreases with the number of Grid sites and increases again beyond five sites due to the distributed nature of the environment controlled by one centralised engine. Beyond six sites, the middleware overhead represents one fifth of the overall execution time which produces a rather low increase in performance and decreases the efficiency. Since the schedule is performed by the HEFT algorithm such that the data dependent activities are scheduled on the same sites, the time spent in communication is negligible in all experiments despite the rather large size of the data dependencies (gigabytes). Despite the large middleware overhead, we obtained a very good efficiency over 60%.

7. Conclusions

We presented techniques used in the ASKALON project to support prediction, scheduling, and performance-oriented execution of a hydrological application in the Austrian Grid environment. The workflow is first expressed at a high-level of abstraction using a novel graphical tool based on the UML modelling standard and advanced constructs such as parallel and sequential loops.

A performance prediction services employs a well-defined experimental design to extract the maximum amount of information needed for prediction with a reduced number of training runs. While there have been some attempts to get reactive training set for performance prediction of Grid application through analytical benchmarks and templates [3] [9], to our knowledge we are the first to attempt a proactive training phase with proper experimental design.

A scheduling service uses global optimisation heuristics to find good mappings onto the Grid that minimise the execution time. To our knowledge, our scheduler is the only one to effectively employ the HEFT algorithm for real applications in a real Grid environment.

An resource manager supporting advance reservation assists the scheduler in increasing execution predictability in dynamic environments like the Grid. In contrast to other existing approaches [1] [5] [8], we provide a customisable negotiation mechanism and compare two different reservation approaches among which the progressive approach shows promising results with respect to different evaluation metrics.

Finally, an enactment engine supported by a systematic performance analysis service tries to go beyond existing monitoring tools [11] and identify the major sources of overhead that may occur in distributed Grid executions.

References

[1] Erik Elmroth and Johan Tordsson. A grid resource broker supporting advance reservations and benchmark-based resource selection. In *PARA*, volume 3732 of *LNCS*, pages 1061–1070. Springer Verlag, 2004.

[2] Thomas Fahringer, Radu Prodan, Rubing Duan, Jürgen Hofer, Farrukh Nadeem, Francesco Nerieri, Jun Qin Stefan Podlipnig, Mumtaz Siddiqui, Hong-Linh Truong, Alex Villazon, and Marek Wieczorek. Askalon: A development and grid computing environment for scientific workflows. In I. J. Taylor, E. Deelman, D. B. Gannon, and M. Shields, editors, *Scientific Workflows for Grids*, Workflows for e-Science, chapter Frameworks and Tools: Workflow Generation, Refinement and Execution. Springer Verlag, 2007. ISBN: 978-1-84628-519-6.

[3] Michael A. Iverson, Füsun Özgüner, and Lee C. Potter. Statistical prediction of task execution times through analytic benchmarking for scheduling in a heterogeneous environment. *IEEE Transactions on Computers*, 48(12):1374–1379, 1999.

[4] K. Jasper and J. Schulla. Model description WaSiM-ETH. Technical report, Institute for Climate Research, ETH Zurich, 2000. pp. 166.

[5] Andrew Stephen McGough, Ali Afzal, John Darlington, Nathalie Furmento, Anthony Mayer, and Laurie Young. Making the grid predictable through reservations and performance modelling. *Journal of Computers*, 48(3):358–368, 2005.

[6] Radu Prodan and Thomas Fahringer. *Grid Computing. Experiment Management, Tool Integration and Scientific Worflows*, volume 4340 of *LNCS*. Springer Verlag, 2007.

[7] Rajesh Raman, Miron Livny, and Marvin H. Solomon. Matchmaking: Distributed resource management for high throughput computing. In *High Performance Distributed Computing Symposium*, pages 140–147, 1998.

[8] Thomas Röblitz and Alexander Reinefeld. Co-reservation with the concept of virtual resources. In *International Conference on Cluster Computing and the Grid*, pages 398–406. IEEE Computer Society Press, 2005.

[9] Warren Smith, Ian T. Foster, and Valerie E. Taylor. Predicting application run times with historical information. *Journal of Parallel and Distributed Computing*, 64(9):1007–1016, 2004.

[10] Dieter Theiner and Peter Rutschmann. An inverse modelling approach for the estimation of hydrological model parameters. In *Journal of Hydroinformatics*. IWA Publishing, 2005.

[11] Serafeim Zanikolas and Rizos Sakellariou. A Taxonomy of Grid Monitoring Systems. *Future Generation Computing Systems*, 21(1):163–188, 2005.

[12] Henan Zhao and Rizos Sakellariou. An experimental investigation into the rank function of the heterogeneous earliest finish time scheduling algorithm. In *Euro-Par Conference*, pages 189–194, 2003.

A PRACTICAL APPROACH FOR A WORKFLOW MANAGEMENT SYSTEM

Simone Pellegrini, Francesco Giacomini, and Antonia Ghiselli
INFN CNAF Viale Berti Pichat, 6/2 - 40127 Bologna, Italy
simone.pellegrini@cnaf.infn.it
francesco.giacomini@cnaf.infn.it
antonia.ghiselli@cnaf.infn.it

Abstract   A variety of grid middlewares and workflow languages causes the existence of many workflow management systems (WfMS). Formalisms used to represent workflows vary from simple Directed Acyclic Graphs (DAG) to more complex (non deterministic) Petri Nets. Therefore a workflow description is strictly bound to a particular WfMS and to the computational resources that WfMS address, as far as no cooperation among WfMSs exists. This might be critical in scientific workflows where a large amount of resources is usually needed. In this paper we propose a WfMS that aims at language independence and Grid middleware abstraction dealing with interoperability as proposed in the reference model of the Workflow Management Coalition (WfMC). The main goal of such WfMS is to provide an effective solution to run complex scientific workflows (legacy or not) taking full advantage of the distributed and etherogeneous nature of the Grid. A Petri Net formalism has been chosen as internal representation due to its formal behavioral description and the existence of several analysis tools. Our proposed WfMS will be implemented on top of the gLite Grid middleware provided by the EGEE project because of its stability and large adoption.

Keywords: Grid, workflow management, interoperability, Petri Net, EGEE/gLite

1.   Introduction

The evolution of the Grid towards a *service-oriented* architecture enables scientists to build complex applications as *workflows*. WfMSs allow the composition and execution of such distributed applications at a high abstraction level; a workflow language, usually graph based, is used to specify dependencies (control and data flow) between tasks. Several WfMSs exist both in scientific and in business environments. This underlines the research interest in this field.

Unlike business WfMSs, scientific ones lack a recognized standard; as a consequence several workflow languages exist. Apart from the syntax, these languages differ for the formalism used to express the workflow model. Most of the graphical workflow languages are based on DAGs where the *control flow* can be described in terms of *sequence, parallelism* and *choice*. More powerful than DAGs, formalisms such as *Petri Nets* and π-*Calculus* allow to define *iteration* (also know as *loop* or *cycle*). As a consequence of that variety of languages and formalisms, WfMSs are *incompatible*. Furthermore a WfMS usually address a small set of computational resources and without interoperability scientific workflows cannot fully take advantage from the distributed, heterogeneous nature of the Grid. The Workflow Management Coalition (WfMC) encourages WfMSs standardization in its *reference model* which defines a set of APIs (called WAPI) and interfaces numbered from 1 to 5 in order to achieve *interoperability*. In particular, interface 4 describes different levels of workflow coordination/co-operation. Unfortunately the WfMC has so far failed its standardization scope and no WfMS formally follows its reference model.

In this paper we propose a *generic* WfMS architecture that abstracts from the underlying grid middleware and deals with workflow interoperability. As we will see in detail, the definition of a grid abstraction layer makes it possible to build a middleware-independent workflow engine. A Petri Net formalism is used as the internal representation due to its *formal semantics*. Petri Nets capture both the control and data flow of the workflow, they formally describe its state evolution and they are Turing-complete. Workflow interoperability is addressed using language translators and model converters.

The implementation of our WfMS will rely on the gLite Grid middleware. gLite exposes several Grid *services* with a good level of reliability and the amount of managed resources allows users to execute complex and large workflows. The Job Description Language (JDL) is the *lingua-franca* of the gLite middleware, it is used for job and also workflow (expressed as DAGs) descriptions. DAGs are executed by Condor DAGMan [1] which provides a *basic* support for workflow management. In fact, DAGMan pratically lacks failure recovery and that limits expressiveness in workflow design. With this work

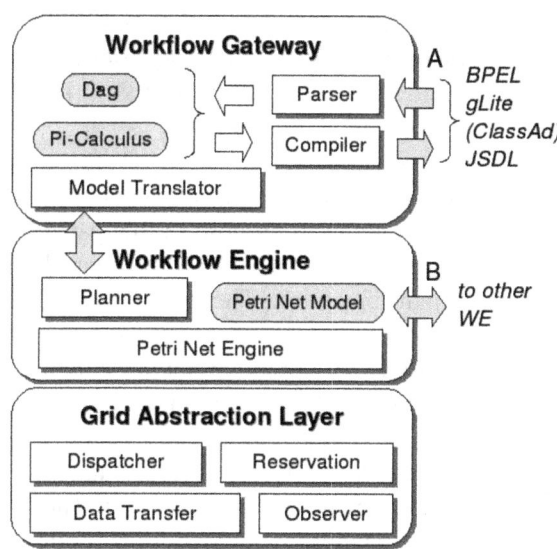

Figure 1. The WfMS Architecture, interfaces *A* and *B* will be explained in more detail in Sect. 4.

we want to improve workflow support in gLite allowing users to keep all the advantages of using a full feature WfMS.

In Sect. 2 we will go along describing in details at the engine architecture, defining the layers and how they interact. In Sect. 3 we will focus on the interoperability problem and in Sect. 4 we will show some details related to the implementation of such WfMS, concluding with the description of how we intend to progress with this work in the future in Sect. 5.

2. Workflow Architecture Overview

In this section we propose a generic WfMS architecture that aims at Grid middleware *independence*, as proposed in [2], and at *multi-language* support. The use of a layered architecture makes it possible to abstract both from a particular Grid infrastructure and a workflow language in order to provide portability and multi-language compatibility.

An outline of such architecture is shown in Fig. 1. At the bottom lies the basic Grid infrastructure: a collection of *computational* and *storage* resources. These resources are transparent to users thanks to a so called *Grid middleware* which acts as a mediator that provides a consistent and homogeneous access to them.

Since *multiple* Grid infrastructures still exist, a *Grid Abstraction Layer* is introduced in order to abstract high level Grid functionalities such as job submission, data transfer, job state observation and resource reservation. This makes it possible to *decouple* the workflow engine from the underlying grid architecture allowing workflows to use a large set of Grid infrastructures and therefore resources.

The workflow engine is the main component of the WfMS; it basically submits *tasks* to the Grid taking care of their dependencies and the overall workflow execution. The engine we are going to propose in this paper executes workflows represented in term of Petri Nets. Petri Nets have been chosen as *internal* model because of their formal semantics. The structure of a Petri-Net-model is formally defined by a set of *places*, a set of *transitions* and a set of *arcs* connecting places to transitions and vice versa (but not place to place or transition to transition). The *High Level Petri Nets* (HLPN) model extends classical Petri Nets with features that make them more suitable for workflow representation; an introduction to theoretical aspects of HLPN can be found in [3](in our paper we always refer to HLPN when the Petri Net term is used). The dynamic behavior of the net is described by using *tokens* which are associated to places; tokens enable transitions, make them *fire* and as a consequence they flow through the network. From a workflow perspective, a transition is associated to a task execution (job submission) and a token represents data that flows between tasks. An outline of a Petri-Net-based workflow engine can be described using the state chart diagram shown in Fig. 2. The engine needs to select enabled transitions, submits relative tasks to the Grid and monitors their execution; when a task ends the net state is updated, data (tokens) are moved and new transitions are selected to fire. The workflow execution continues until all the submitted jobs terminate and there is no further enabled transition. Unlike a formal Petri Net model, where transitions are *atomic* operations, we have also to deal with a transition *failure* (referred to a task failure). In scientific workflow, tasks are tipically operations which take raw data in input and produce refined data as output. As far as tasks are usually *idempotent*, the common failure recovery strategy (which is also used by DAGMan) consists in a task re-submission. However, in ordert to achieve at business workflows compatibility, we have to deal with different failure recovery strategies (i.e. rollback, choose an alternative task). This is made possible by pushing out of the engine the failure management: when a failure is recognized, it is handled by the workflow itself as shown in Fig. 2. Failure management could be explicity done by the user during the process design; or as a result of a workflow refinement discussed in [4].

The top layer aims at language *independence*. The basic idea is to make the workflow engine compatible with a large set of workflow languages. A pluggable system of parsers provides support for several languages in order to allow *collaboration* between WfMSs and support for *legacy* workflows. As we will see in more detail in the next section this layer has the responsibility

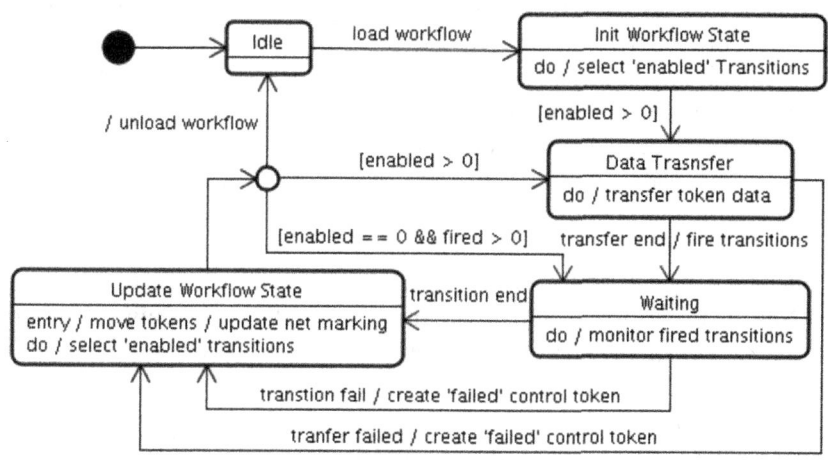

Figure 2.   The Workflow engine behavior

to extrapolate the semantics behind a workflow description and translate it in terms of a Petri Net. On the other side the gateway makes it possible to transfer parts of a process to a different WfMS.

Our interest is to build such WfMS in term of a *micro-kernel* pattern as proposed in [5]. A micro-kernel pattern [6] aims at the separation of a minimal functional core such as job submission, monitoring and data movement from extended functionality providing *extensibility*. That means advanced workflow features such as planning, scheduling strategies and QoS management should be built on top of the kernel API. A micro-kernel pattern provides *modularity* and *extensibility* which are fundamental properties for systems like a WfMS, where a standard is not well defined yet and they must be able to adapt easily to changing requirements.

3.   Workflow Interoperability

As shown in Fig. 1 there are two kinds of interaction we would like to investigate: the first one (*A*) is about translation between different workflow description languages; the second one (*B*) is about synchronization between different workflow engines. Both aspects are part of the interoperability interface described in the WfMC's reference model [7].

As previously said many workflow languages exist due to the lack of a strong standard. However, *translation* from one language to another is often possible; what is needed is a language *parser*, a *model translator* and a *compiler*, as shown in the top layer of Fig. 1. Parsers have the responsibility to extract the workflow semantics from a description, expressed using a workflow language.

As explained before, workflows can be described in terms of DAGs, Petri Nets, π-Calculus or Activity Diagrams, albeit with different expressivity levels (e.g. a DAG cannot describes an iteration of tasks). Conversion between these formalisms is provided by the model converter which represents the critical part of such process. In fact is not always possible to rapresent one model in terms of a different one; for example a Petri Net cannot always be converted in term of a DAG. Finally compilers translate the model into a specific (usually different from the initial) language description.

A debate exists around the best formalism to use for workflow description; Petri Nets and π-Calculus are widely used for workflow modeling. As far as both the formalisms are Turing-complete, the choice relies on the way these models deal with *workflow patterns*. Workflow patterns are a collection of well-known problems, and solutions, related to the support of process-oriented applications [8]. According to [9], Petri Nets outperform other formalisms in workflow description thanks to their formal semantics; also several *analysis techniques* exist in order to determine the properties (*correctness*, *deadlocks* and *boundary*) of a process design. As previously said, Petri Nets provide mechanisms for model conversion. DAGs can be simply represented in terms of Petri Nets; also π-Calculus based models (such as BPEL) can be translated in terms of Petri Nets; the semantics of such translation is discussed in [11]. This choice is also compatible with the one done by other CoreGRID partners like the Fraunhofer FIRST which introduced an XML based language called GWorkflowDL [10] that allows the representation of *abstract* and *concrete* workflows using Petri Nets. Fraunhofer FIRST also works, since several years, on a workflow enactment engine called GWES in which we would like to contribute with our work.

Compilers come into stage when a workflow model, or a part of it, needs to be represented using a specific language. For example a part of a process, usually a sub-workflow, can be transferred to a different WfMS; the internal Petri Nets representation must be converted in a language description the third-party WfMS understands. Unfortunately this kind of conversion is not always possible, for example there is no explicit semantics for translating a Petri Net in terms of π-Calculus formalism. A set of specific language compilers are needed in order to achieve at compatibility with *legacy* WfMSs.

Interoperability as described in the WfMC's reference model needs an engine level synchronization mechanism identified with letter *B* in Fig. 1. A runtime support for the interchange of various types of control information and transfer of workflow relevant and/or application data between different WfMSs. Synchronization can be useful even when several instances of the same workflow engine want to collaborate; it can be useful when we want to use the WfMS as *distributed* service to increase its performances.

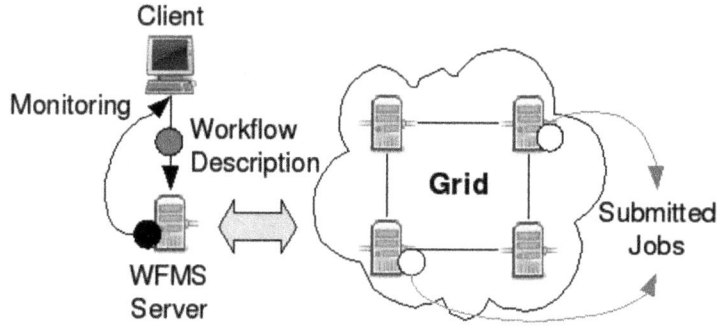

Figure 3. The WfMS deploy scenario 1

4. Implementation

The implementation will rely on the gLite middleware developed within the EGEE project, due to its maturity and its large adoption. Job submission in gLite is done by the Workload Management System (WMS) [12]; it comprises a set of Grid middleware components responsible for the distribution and management of tasks across Grid resources. The core component of the WMS is the Workload Manager (WM) whose purpose is to accept and satisfy requests for job management, expressed via a ClassAd-based Job Description Language (JDL). The WMS also supptorts the execution of single workflows expressed as DAGs. Job monitoring in the WMS is provided by the Job Logging and Bookkeeping Service (LB).

Many scientific workflows are expressed as JDL DAGs. As first step, our purpose is to provide a mechanism that allows those legacy processes to take advantage of the WfMS. Thanks to a JDL *parser* the DAG model can be extracted and then converted (using the *model converter*) into a Petri Net the WfMS can execute. Subsequently we would like also to investigate the integration of the BPEL workflow language providing a π-Calculus to Petri Net model translator as proposed in [11].

Initially the WfMS will run as a separate process on a dedicated server, as shown in Fig. 3. In this scenario the client sends the workflow description to the WfMS server, which executes it submitting jobs to the the Grid. The WfMS server also allows the client to monitor the workflow execution. This kind of solution is simple to realize but has some disadvantages: as far as a workflow could run for several days a failure in the WfMS server could cause the loss of the entire process and data. To avoid that the server must provide high *reliability* and recovery tools.

Later we will investigate an alternative solution that takes effort of the Grid environment to run users' workflows. In fact the Grid provides computational

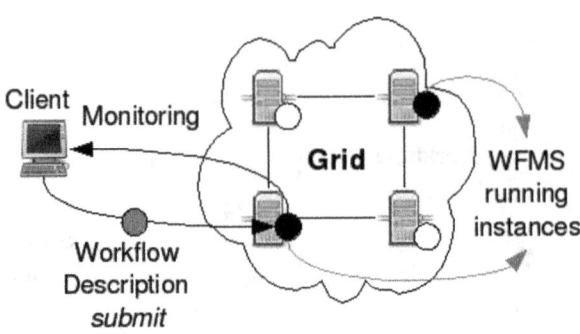

Figure 4.   The WfMS deploy scenario 2

resources and mechanisms that helps failover management which makes run of the WfMS as a Grid job a strategic choice. Grid is a batch system where users send jobs and waits for their termination; a WfMS is also a sort of *complex job* which can be submitted to the Grid within the workflow description. As shown in Fig. 4, the client submits a workflow using the Grid middleware; a new WfMS instance will start on a Grid node (selected by the WMS) and it will use the Grid Abstraction Layer for job submission and monitoring.

As a consequence of these considerations, the WfMS must easily adapt to environment changes. Therefore during the development stage we will not focus on the system itself but in defining a set of basic functions, according to the micro-kernel pattern, which the WfMS will rely on, making changes simpler.

5.   Conclusions and Future Work

In this paper we introduced a WfMS architecture with the intent to be compatible with the roadmap of the CoreGRID project. The main focus will be on language conversion and interoperability between WfMSs using language and model translators; Grid middleware independence will be satisfied thanks to a layered architecture. The combination of these features makes it possible for users to run their legacy workflows (usually written in different languages) on a large set of computational resources. In fact, coordination of workflows among several heterogeneous WfMSs is one of the main challenges in today WfMS research.

The WfMS we are proposing is quite simple compared to other WfMSs like Triana or GWES; for example it lacks QoS management, advanced planning techniques and so on. However, one of the pourposes of this work is to introduce a generic *lightweight* WfMS core with basic functions where advanced functionalities can be easily and *dynamically* integrated thanks to the micro-kernel architecture. A WfMS for researchers who want to investigate high level aspects related to workflows management without taking care of low level problems such us job submission, data transfer and so on.

References

[1] Condor DAGMan, http://www.cs.wisc.edu/condor/dagman/

[2] D. Colling et al.: *Adding Instruments and Workflow Support to Existing Grid Architectures*, International Conference on Computational Science (3), 2006.

[3] Kurt Jensen: *An Introduction to the Theoretical Aspects of Colored Petri Nets*, Lecture Notes in Computer Science (Springer), 1994.

[4] A. Hoheisel and U. Der: *Dynamic workflows for Grid applications*, in: Proceedings of the Cracow Grid Workshop '03 (Cracow, Poland, 2003).

[5] Dragos A. Manolescu: *An extensible Workflow Architecture with Object and Patterns*, TOOLSEE 2001.

[6] Douglas Schmidt et al.: *Pattern-Oriented Software Architecture*, Siemens AG, pages 171-192, 2000.

[7] D. Hollingsworth: *Workflow management coalition: The workflow reference model*, Document TC00-1003, Workflow Management Coalition, 1994.

[8] Workflow Patterns, http://www.workflowpatterns.com.

[9] W.M.P. van der Aalst: *The Application of Petri Nets to Workflow Management*, The Journal of Circuits, Systems and Computers, pages 21-66, 1998.

[10] Martina Alt et al.: *A Grid Workflow Language Using High-Level Petri Nets*, Lecture Notes in Computer Science (Springer), CoreGRID Technical Report Number TR-0032, 2006.

[11] Christian Stahl: *A Petri Net Semantics for BPEL*, Humboldt University Berlin, 2004.

[12] P. Andreetto et al.: *Practical Approaches to Grid Workload and Resource Management in the EGEE Project*, Conference for Computing in High-Energy and Nuclear Physics (CHEP 04), Interlaken, Switzerland, 27 Sept - 1 Oct 2004.

SECURE AND FAULT TOLERANT DISTRIBUTED FRAMEWORK WITH MOBILITY SUPPORT

Lukáš Hejtmánek
Institute of Computer Science,
Masaryk University,
Botanická 68a, 602 00 Brno,
Czech Republic
xhejtman@mail.muni.cz

Abstract   In this paper, we propose an architecture of distributed data storage framework that incorporates fault tolerance, mobility support, and security. Main goal of our system is to provide equal opportunities for both connected and disconnected clients. Consequence is that mutual exclusion may not be involved. Data storage systems without mutual exclusion suffer from update and name conflicts. We avoid the update conflicts using immutable data storage. Mutable data is provided via either file versioning or Redo Logs. The name conflicts are automatically resolved without user's guidance, the file names are automatically changed to non-conflicting names, the directories are represented implicitly and thus we avoid conflict names connected to directories. Because the file names may be changed by the system, each file version is assigned an immutable globally unique identifier using which the file version can be accessed. Security model is based on certificates and VOMS attributes. This system is suitable for use within Grid VOs and it also supports services provided simultaneously to different VOs. Our prototype implementation exhibits very favorable performance so that it could be used as robust, secure, highly reliable and high performance Storage Elements.

Keywords: Distributed data storage, logistical networking, security, fault tolerance, disconnected operations

1. Introduction

Large scale distributed systems consisting of thousands of nodes have serious problems with failures. If such systems have a large number of components (disks in disk arrays) and their total capacity is in the order of petabytes, then according to [27], they face component failure once a day. Fault tolerance can be achieved using some kind of redundancy. The redundancy can be achieved in a number of ways, starting with replication that is space but not CPU consuming, and ending with space conserving error correction codes [14] which require a lot of CPU power and furthermore, data modification is a quite complex and expensive operation. However, error correction codes are not commonly used in large scale distributed systems because firstly they are expensive to update and secondly, failure is the rule rather than an exception. In our approach, we opted for replication, with data stored in multiple identical copies. It is CPU conservative and it does not require extensive updating operations.

On the other hand, even simple a replication brings complexity into the architecture of distributed systems. Replication of read only data is trivial, whereas replicating mutable data brings problems with the consistency of the replicas. There are several approaches to dealing with replication and this consistency problem. We can divide replication into a primary backup approach and a state machines approach [24]. Primary backup approach refers to storing data on a fixed replica and this fixed replica distributes data to the other replicas. In the state machines approach data is stored directly to all replicas. It also means that replication is client driven whereas primary backups can be both client driven or server driven. The primary backup approach has a fundamental problem with a single point of failure. If a primary copy (i.e., the node that spreads data to the other replicas) is not accessible (e.g., due to network partitioning) then data updating is not possible. The state machines approach has a problem with data synchronization in network partitioning, as data updates in distinct network partitions may lead to different data states on particular nodes—we call this situation an *update conflict*. We can see that these two approaches represent a trade off between low availability (conflict avoidance) and low coherency (conflict resolution). A combination of the state machine and primary backup approaches is called the multiple-primary backup. In this case, we define a set of primary servers that are kept consistent using the sate machines approach and they collectively spread data to other replicas. This approach does not contain a single point of failure and users do not need to upload data to all replicas. In this case, consistency is limited similarly to the state machines approach.

All the above presented approaches may be combined with two other concepts: pessimistic and optimistic replication [16]. Using pessimistic replication, data is spread synchronously to all replicas (and replicas are locked meantime, i.e., we mutually exclude concurrent updates). Using optimistic replication, data is spread asynchronously to all replicas and no exclusion is needed. Even these approaches represent yet more trade off between low availability (pessimistic replication) and low coherency (optimistic replication).

Data redundancy on storage servers is not a panacea for failures. When network failure occurs between the client and the distributed storage system, data redundancy on storage servers does not help. Therefore, we need to include the clients into replication system where the clients act as partial replicas of the storage servers. To completely conceal network failures, the client's replica has to provide all operations needed by the client, with the exception that only locally satisfiable requests can be completed. The same functionality can be also used to support a client's mobility. Mobility (or disconnected operations support) refers to the ability of a frequent connection and disconnection of the client and mainly the ability to work with data even when no connection is available. An example of such a system is CVS [3] where the users may check out files, disconnect from the network, work with files, connect to the network and commit changes. However, this mobility involves one fundamental problem connected to the fact that there is no upper limit on the duration of the disconnection. Without this limit, we cannot use any kind of mutual exclusion for conflict avoidance because prospective locks are either potentially held forever or prematurely released. Another challenge connected to mobility support is how to provide equal opportunities for connected and disconnected clients (with the obvious exception that disconnected clients cannot access arbitrary data but only data marked as accessible in disconnected mode), e.g., the disconnected clients may create new files and create new directories. These operations usually require mutual exclusion to avoid the creation of multiple directory entries of the same name. In this paper, we provide an approach to dealing with these problems and we provide a distributed framework with unrestricted mobility support.

Our aim is to build a large scale distributed storage system that provides (1) fault tolerance, i.e., it provides data replication, (2) mobility support, i.e., the system provides disconnected operations and mainly offers equal opportunities to both connected and disconnected clients, and (3) reasonable security model with properly authenticated and authorized users. We expect that our work can be highly usable in Grid environments as secure, robust, highly reliable and high performance Storage Elements [6].

The rest of this paper is organized as follows. In the Section 2, we discuss the design principles of our proposed distributed data storage framework. Section 3 describes some preliminary experiments. In the Section 4, we discuss related work. Concluding remarks are given in Section 5.

2.   Design Principles

Our goal is to provide a storage architecture where data is highly available and coherent. As we stated above, these two requirements are contradictory except in one case—immutable data storage, where data can be written only once and read many times (WORM, write once read many). For this reason, we have chosen a storage substrate that provides Write Once Read Many semantics of data storing. On this storage substrate, we aim to build a mutable data storage system that preserves data availability and data coherency. This concept of conflicts avoidance applies equally to mobility support as it does not involve mutual exclusion.

2.1   Immutable Data Block Substrate

In essence, our storage framework works with files. Files are decomposed into data blocks and metadata. The metadata contains references to data blocks and basically represents the files, it is equivalent to the well known UNIX I-node, the main difference being that data blocks are distributed across many storage nodes instead of being stored on a local disk.

Replicating read only data blocks does not pose any problem. We can adopt replication strategies mentioned in the introduction which would provide higher availability and low data consistency: data inconsistency is an issue of concurrent updates of data. In dealing with immutable data, data consistency is not an issue. We use the multiple-primary backup approach for data replication. This means that users may upload a data block to any storage node and may request the storage node to replicate the data block to another storage node.

Such an approach has two advantages. Firstly, the user does not need to upload data blocks to all replicas which could overload his network connection which can have lower bandwidth than network connection between storage servers. Secondly, there is no single point of failure as a client may contact any storage node. Because data blocks cannot be updated, the data coherency is automatically provided. We enforce strict ordering of data and metadata, i.e., we add references in metadata to data blocks if the data blocks are completely stored on storage servers. Consequently, a referenced data block (which may be a replica of another data block) always exists on the storage server.

We need metadata replication for two reasons. The first is that the clients can cache metadata so that the clients do not overload metadata servers and the cached metadata is basically a replica of metadata. And the second is that files are not accessible without metadata, thus non replicated metadata forms a crucial single point of failure. However, replicating metadata is not without its problems. We have stated that metadata contains references to data blocks. If we replicate data blocks, we add more references to the corresponding metadata. This means that creation (or deletion) of data blocks changes metadata, and consequently, the metadata is no longer read only which means that it cannot be easily replicated. On the other hand, using simple consistency vectors[1], we can easily detect metadata changes and in particular all of the metadata can always be merged into a single file. This is due to the fact that metadata can be seen as a set of data blocks. We can merge metadata using a standard union operation to all the sets. The only problem here is to distinguish between the addition and removal of a data block, but this can be solved using the above mentioned consistency vectors.

Using the principles outlined above, we are able to provide distributed and replicated immutable data storage. While immutable storage is quite suitable for distribution and replication, it is quite unsuitable for users. Therefore, we show the way how to provide mutable distributed and replicated data storage on top of immutable substrate.

2.2 Mutable Data Storage with an Immutable Data Block Substrate

Providing a mutable file system on top of the immutable storage substrate involves creating a new file whenever a block is changed. The new data blocks must be added to the corresponding metadata which results in a change in the metadata. In the previous subsection, we stated that mutable metadata does not pose a problem, while the mutation of metadata is caused by addition or removal of replicated data blocks. This property does not hold for mutations caused by file updates. Concurrent updates of the same file may cause update conflicts that may be difficult to resolve (user guidance may be required). Consequently, immutable metadata is needed to avoid update conflicts (immutable metadata with the exception of adding or removing data blocks replica). However, the immutable metadata imposes immutability also on files.

For immutable metadata, we can use the same approach as for the read only data blocks. Updating the file results in new metadata. Such approach basically creates a form of file versioning. Each set of metadata for a particular file corresponds to a particular file version. Taken together, we present the so called *versioned files* that are mutable files consisting of immutable file versions. File versions are represented by immutable metadata that references immutable data blocks. Every update of a versioned file results in a new file version, i.e., in new data blocks and in new metadata. We can use a replication strategy that provides high availability of data but must deal with update conflicts. Using such a strategy, we provide high availability of data which avoids update conflicts

---

[1]We use the term *consistency vectors* instead of the standard term *version vectors* [13] as we use the term version for file versioning. A mutable object is assigned a serial number. We increase the serial number with each object modification and we also maintain the previous serial numbers. Using serial numbers of the object and their history, we are easily able to detect changes in replicated objects.

by read only data and we still provide mutable files. To avoid an explosion of version numbers of versioned files, we use open-close semantics. This means that the new file version is created only after the file is closed.

However, two problems still remain: (1) These principles do not deal with name conflicts—i.e., conflicts caused by the creation of multiple directory entries with the same name. We could use directory versioning which solves the problem but this is characterized by an explosion of number of directory versions. Changing any directory entry increases a number of directory versions up to the root directory. (2) Another problem is how to represent non-versioned mutable files. A new file version is usually created after the file is closed which makes it impossible to (read/write) share files between parallel applications. Both problems are addressed in the following sections.

2.2.1   Name Conflicts.   There are many approaches to dealing with name conflicts but basically we can divide them into two groups: (1) conflict avoidance and (2) conflict resolution. Name conflicts can be avoided by using either a mutual exclusion or a read only approach. We have stated that versioning is not suitable for directories due to versions explosion. On the other hand, mutual exclusion is not suitable for mobility unless we impose an upper limit to the duration of the disconnected state. Consequently, we must use one of the conflict resolution strategies.

Name conflicts that arise from file name operation such as create and rename are solved using automatic renaming. Such a conflict is detected either when the new name is created or when the client switchs from the disconnected mode to the connected mode. During this transition, data and metadata are synchronized with storage servers. If the client created a new file name, it is created on the storage servers too and it may cause a name conflict. The conflicting name is automatically changed. For instance, three conflicting names testfile.txt are automatically resolved into two new names testfile.txt#1 and testfile.txt#2 (one of the files keeps the original conflicting name). The consequence of this approach is that the file name cannot be used as an immutable file identifier. Thus, beside file name, each file (and each file version) is assigned a globally unique identifier that can be used to access the file instead of using the file name.

Replication of versioned files leads to special name conflicts. We distinguish versions via numbering them and we use a deterministic algorithm to assign file version numbers[2]. This algorithm runs at each replica (storage server) and is local to that replica. It may happen (after concurrent updates of the same file version) that two instances of the algorithm, each running on different replica,

---

[2]We increment the last version by one to get the new last version. The increment is made locally on the replica thus it is possible that two or more replicas assign the same number to different file versions.

assign the same version number to file versions with different content. We solve such name conflict by using our replica synchronization algorithm [8]. This algorithm does not involve mutual exclusion which would cause the non-availability of data or metadata, but it is still able to guarantee identical version numbers for the same file version on all replicas.

Similarly, name conflicts may arise from directory name operations such as create and rename. Also in this case, these conflicts are usually avoided using mutual exclusion. We avoid directory name conflicts via implicit directory representation. This means that we use a flat directory structure and a full path is an attribute of a file. The downside of this approach lies in the absence of authorization information bound to directories. Authorization information can be associated with files only and the user cannot create directories exclusively for himself. On the other hand, we believe that extended ACLs for files can mostly substitute ACLs for directories, this is discussed in more details in Section 2.4.

2.2.2   Non Versioned Mutable Files.   Our system does not support mutable files in their natural way. We simulate mutable files via versioned files. However, versioned files with open-close semantics cannot be shared between applications that update the file in parallel. We represent mutable files as versioned files but with changed semantics. Within this changed semantics, the new file version is created either (1) after predefined timeout, or (2) after predefined amount of new data, or (3) after the mutable file is closed. It is clear that using this extended semantics, the number of file versions rapidly grows. To avoid an explosion of version numbers, we remove obsolete versions, i.e., file versions which are completely overwritten by newer versions.

If storage servers are reachable, the client checks before each read or write operation whether a new file version is available. If it is available, the client downloads and uses the new metadata (file version). Using this approach together with the extended access semantics described above, updates are distributed among other online clients within a predefined timeout.

To avoid disk space wastage caused by a potentially large number of file versions and also due to the fact that file updates are usually small compared to the overall size of the file, we store initial file versions and then we store only updated records, i.e., the differences from the previous file version. This approach is the well-known log structured file system approach that use Redo Logs [15] which is a log of immutable update records. Each update record contains information about the update, the offset in file, and the length of the update.

However, using this concept of Redo Logs, we do not guarantee that the updates are instantly visible to all other participants. And because the files are mutable and we do not use mutual exclusion, update conflicts may arise after the concurrent modification of the same area of the same file. The conflicting updates are resolved automatically so that one of conflicting updates prevails the others are lost. We do not explicitly specify which update prevails and which one is lost. Neither do we guarantee that subsequent updates have the same order for all participants except two cases. The first case is, if all subsequent updates have been distributed in the same way through the network and the second is if a time period between two subsequent updates is higher than the time period required to distribute updates between all participants. If such behavior is not acceptable then the application level mutual exclusion should be used.

2.3   Metadata Handling

We store metadata on metadata servers. Metadata can be replicated and replication is done per versioned file (or its equivalent—non versioned mutable file). Replication of metadata is driven by a dynamically elected replication coordinator which is responsible for coordinating the replication for a single update of a single file. Further updates and different files can be coordinated by another coordinator. Replication runs asynchronously to updates. Our replication algorithm can be found in [8].

Metadata servers are distributed across a network. Metadata is spread among metadata servers using virtual distributed search tree P-Grid [1]. We have chosen this peer-to-peer system because it is possible for the clients to gain routing tables from the metadata servers and from which the clients are able to predict where the metadata is stored. This prediction is precise if the set of metadata is stable (without any metadata server connects or disconnects) which should be the case most of the time.

As stated above, we do not explicitly represent directories. Path names are an attribute of files but we use path and file name as a key to the P-Grid system to find file location. This approach is problematic for directory content listing because files of a single directory may be spread among many metadata servers. Thus, for directory listing, the client must contact all metadata servers. Solving this problem is one of our future tasks.

2.4   Security

We can say that file systems internally decompose files into data and metadata. In terms of UNIX-like file systems, we have I-nodes (metadata) and data blocks that are referenced by these I-nodes. Assuming that a user does not have direct access to raw storage media, the user cannot access data without knowing a particular I-node, therefore access control is usually made at this level. Once users are allowed to access the I-node, they are then granted access to the data. However, if we split metadata and data into two independent services, we must require access control verification at both services. We then face the problem of how to force a user to pass access control on both services in a defined order and how to verify that both services have granted or denied access.

The issues have been reduced to the following problems. We are given a set of services. We need to force a client to obtain a token from the services in a defined order given by service providers. We require that no service is skipped by the client and that the client cannot skip a service using an old token. Further, we require that the verification of a token is always local and no service is required to contact a third party during the verification process. The second problem is how to provide cacheable time limited metadata to the clients. The metadata manager issues metadata to the client, so the client may cache metadata for an unlimited period, potentially, which makes authorization irrevocable. Since the size of the metadata is not insignificant, the creation of a signature can take significant period of time. Signed metadata must be valid only to the particular user and only for a specified time period. Signature must be certifiable offline. The solution to these problems is presented in [9]. This solution extends network storage stacks from logistical networking so that each part of the network storage stacks authenticates and authorizes the user. User authentication is based on PKI, authorization is based on ACLs.

As we do not explicitly represent directories, we cannot bind ACLs with them. ACLs bound to directories basically serve as shortcuts for setting appropriate ACLs to individual files. For instance, we may deny entry to a directory instead of denying access to the individual files. Thus, we can simulate directory ACLs by file ACLs except in two cases: (1) we cannot deny the creation of new files in a directory and (2) we cannot hide the subdirectories (which is usually done by denying directory listing). Neither we can deny entry into a directory but if we deny access to all files and set all files to be invisible (both possible using an appropriate file ACL) in a subtree beginning in this directory, the result is the same. Taken together, we believe that the inability to bind ACLs with directory does not impose a real problem.

3. Experiments

Our prototype implementation utilizes the IBP protocol from the Logistical Networking concept [2]. Using the IBP protocol, we build an immutable data blocks storage substrate. We are using our own implementation of the components of the Logistical Networking with an extended security model as described in [9] where also performance tests related to the extensions can be found. The IBP servers are implemented in C language. The IBP servers allow to store data blocks and allow modification of these data blocks but the latter feature is not utilized in our system. The metadata (called eXnodes in the Logistical Networking) is represented by XML files. The metadata is stored at metadata managers which are implemented in Java language. The client side of both IBP and metadata interfaces is implemented also in Java language.

Our experiments have been focused on file storage and file retrieval and their performance on high speed networks. We have used a single client equipped with 10 Gbps fibre optics network card, 8 GB RAM, and two dual-core Intel Pentium Xeon processors. We have used eight storage servers, each equipped with 1 Gbps metallic network card, 8 GB RAM, and two dual-core Intel Pentium Xeon processors. The storage servers use disk array consisting of two 320 GB SAS disks organized as software RAID 0. We are able to store data into a single file at 139 MB/sec (1112 Mbps), and to read data from a single file at 178 MB/sec (1424 Mbps). Using `iperf` [10] network performance tool, we are able to achieve 750 Mbps between the client and any storage server using a single TCP stream. This limited transfer rate is caused by the network interface card at storage servers. However, using multiple TCP streams simultaneously from the client to all the storage servers, we can achieve aggregate rate of 5.6 Gbps. This special setup has been used to demonstrate that our system allows to utilize extensively the storage servers in parallel.

Table 1.   A single file upload and download transfer rate and RAM and CPU usage. The usage and transfer rate is measured at the client.

Block Size	File Size	Transfer Rate	RAM	CPU
32 MB	156 GB	3656 Mb/sec down 3392 Mb/sec up	756 MB	90%
2 MB	9.7 GB	2488 Mb/sec down 2000 Mb/sec up	90 MB	50%

We did several tests to evaluate our prototype implementation. The first simple tests evaluated overall performance of storing and retrieving large files from and to client's memory only to eliminate client's local disk performance. We evaluated transfer speed for file upload and download, CPU usage, and RAM usage for two data block sizes: 2 MB and 32 MB. We expect that the latter size will likely be used. Each file comprised 10,000 data blocks. The results can be seen in Table 1. We can see that using 32 MB blocks, we are able to saturate available network bandwidth up to 65% (for download) and up to 60% (for upload). Using 2 MB blocks the bandwidth saturation is lower due to higher overhead when manipulating smaller data blocks. We can also see that larger data blocks require a lot of memory. To achieve such high transfer rates, the client must allocate at least two data blocks for each storage server, thus 512 MB is occupied by data blocks cache for the 32 MB data blocks and 32 MB for the 2 MB data blocks. Rest of the memory is occupied by the Java application itself. In the case of 2 MB data blocks, we can see lower CPU usage because the smaller blocks require more messages to be sent. This is because CPU is idle during the message sending process.

We stated that mutable files are represented by the Redo Log. It may happen that the Redo Log size is not negligible. The whole Redo Log is traversed and processed when the file is opened. Therefore, we have evaluated relation of the Redo Log size and the duration of file opening. The results can be found in Figure 1. We can see that up to 1,000 update records, the duration of file open is negligible. Assuming 32 MB blocks, 32 GB file is opened within 1 second. There is optimization possible as we could merge individual update records into a bigger single update record. This optimization is left as a future work.

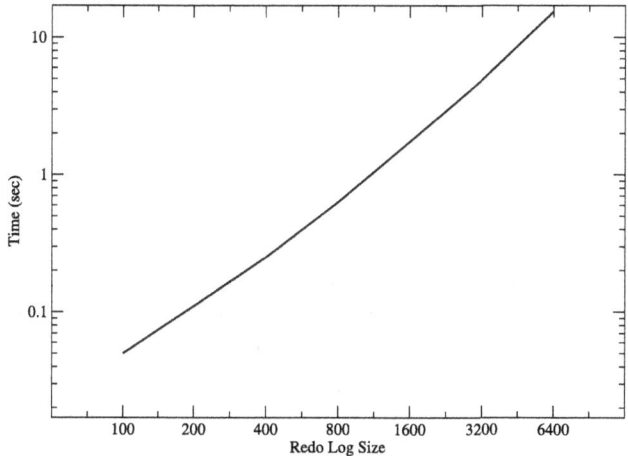

Figure 1.   Duration of the file open operation for varying number of update records in the redo log.

We have not evaluated latency of replicated data blocks because the storage servers have relatively slow network connection to each other compared to the connection to the client. Thus data replication should be originated directly from the client and under such conditions, storing of two replicas of a file takes exactly once more time than a single replica of the file.

On the other hand, metadata replication is handled by our distributed algorithm and for this reason, we evaluated performance of distribution of the metadata updates. The results can be found in Figure 2. We can see that our algorithm scales well and that distribution of the metadata updates takes about 10% of time of data distribution. The distribution process runs asynchronously to update operation. The Figure illustrates time limit within which the metadata updates are distributed to all the replicas.

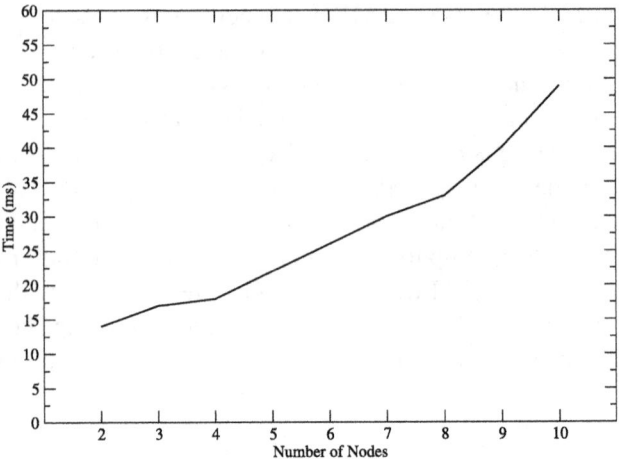

Figure 2.   Latency of file update distribution among specified number of replicas.

Our prototype implementation has shown feasibility of our system. Our preliminary experiments have manifested that our system provides high performance distributed data storage. The clients can access the storage servers in parallel to utilize available network bandwidth. The experiments have also shown that some parts of the system will need optimization in future, such as opening of mutable files consisting of a large number of the update records.

4.   Related Work

There exist many different distributed storage systems incorporating different approaches to the data storage problem. There are standard distributed file systems with POSIX access semantics such as AFS [18], NFSv4 [20], GPFS [19], Lustre [4] which, however, do not contain support for mobility and their support for replication is very limited (AFS—read only replication, NFSv4—incomplete specification, no complete implementation, GPFS—fixed number of replicas, Lustre—no replication of metadata servers).

The Coda [17] file system was one of the first file systems that presented disconnected operations. Compared to AFS, the Coda also provides read write optimistic replication. Replication granularity is per volume rather than per file. Volume is a set of files belonging to particular directory subtree. Coda also distinguishes between connected and disconnected mode, and it reports conflicting updates to the user. The security of the Coda file system is based on user IDs and group IDs.

In addition to these distributed file systems there exist experimental distributed storage systems which have either POSIX access semantics or access via special API.

Ceph [25] file system is replicated, scalable, and high performance distributed file system. It decomposes files into data blocks and metadata. Data blocks are stored to object storage devices (OSD). Data blocks are organized into placement groups and using CRUSH (Controlled Replication Under Scalable Hashing [26]) are mapped to OSDs. Compared to our system, this approach has the disadvantage, in that if we add more OSDs, some of the existing data blocks may be required to migrate to the new OSDs. Replication uses a primary copy approach using a monitor which coordinates the election of the primary copy holder. The monitor impose a single point of failure, on the other hand a monitor is not required if the primary copy holder is reachable. Ceph does not support mobility or file versioning. Security is based on time limited capabilities issued and signed by metadata servers.

Ivy [12] is a read write peer-to-peer file system. It uses DHash [5] peer-to-peer block storage substrate, and all data is stored as a value into a distributed hash using data checksum as its key. DHash provides replication of immutable data blocks. A mutable file system is provided via a log that forms a linked list of immutable log records. The user processes his own log and all publicly available logs and searches for the most recent changes. Compared to our system, Ivy provides only open-close access semantics. It does not explicitly support file versioning but it supports snapshots. It does not support mobility.

Eliot [21] is another peer-to-peer file system built on immutable peer-to-peer storage. It uses Charles [22] reliable and fault tolerant block storage substrate. But it uses only a single mutable metadata service which degrades Eliot fault tolerance.

The large scale storage system, OceanStore [11], provides file versioning (old versions are read only), disconnected operations and replication. However, performance is limited due to slow file lookup and also due to protocols for the Byzantine agreement. Compared to our system, the client is not allowed to predict data location and speed up metadata manipulation.

The Google file system [7] is an application level replicated distributed file system used for the well known Google search engine. Its architecture is based on a single master server (which imposes a single point of failure) and multiple chunk servers. The architecture is optimized for fast reading and appending files. Compared to our system, it does not provide file versioning or mobility support. Our system also supports replication of our equivalent to the Google's master server.

The L-Store [23] application level distributed file system closely resembles our distributed data storage system. It is also based on IBP [2] protocol. It supports replication of both data and metadata. Compared to our system, it does not provide file versioning or mobility support. Its security model requires online communication between a metadata server and an IBP server which makes it less robust compared to our security model.

5.   Conclusions

We have designed a reliable, fault tolerant, and secure framework for distributed data storage with mobility support. The framework offers equal opportunities for both connected and disconnected clients which requires the system not to involve mutual exclusion. Systems without mutual exclusion suffer from update and name conflicts. We avoid the update conflicts using immutable data storage. Mutable data is provided via either file versioning or Redo Logs. The name conflicts are automatically resolved without manual guidance of a user, the file names are automatically changed to non-conflicting names, the directories are represented implicitly. Thus we avoid conflicts in directory naming. Security model is based on certificates and VOMS attributes. This makes the system suitable for use within Grid environments with the VO concept and it also supports services provided simultaneously to different VOs.

We have designed and implemented a prototype implementation and performed preliminary performance evaluation. This evaluation shows that even the prototype implementation exhibits very favorable performance so that it can be used as secure and high performance Storage Element service.

Acknowledgments

This research is supported by a research intent "Optical Network of National Research and Its New Applications" (MŠM 6383917201) and by the CESNET Development Fund project 172/2005. I would also like to thank to Ludìk Matyska and to Petr Holub for stimulating discussions and help with the work described in this paper.

References

[1] Karl Aberer, Philippe Cudré-Mauroux, Anwitaman Datta, Zoran Despotovic, Manfred Hauswirth, Magdalena Punceva, and Roman Schmidt. P-Grid: A Self-organizing Structured P2P System. *SIGMOD*, 32(3):29–33, 2003.

[2] M. Beck, T. Moore, and J. S. Plank. An end-to-end approach to globally scalable network storage. *SIGCOMM Comput. Commun. Rev.*, 32(4):339–346, 2002.

[3] Brian Berliner. CVS II: Parallelizing software development. In *Proceedings of the USENIX Winter 1990 Technical Conference*, pages 341–352, Berkeley, CA, 1990. USENIX Association.

[4] Cluster File Systems, Inc. Selecting a Scalable Cluster File System, 2005. Cluster File Systems, Inc. Whitepaper.

[5] Frank Dabek, M. Frans Kaashoek, David Karger, Robert Morris, and Ion Stoica. Wide-area cooperative storage with CFS. In *SOSP '01: Proceedings of the eighteenth ACM*

symposium on Operating systems principles, pages 202–215, New York, NY, USA, 2001. ACM Press.

[6] EGEE. Site Access Control Architecture DJRA3.2. 2005. `https://edms.cern.ch/document/523948`.

[7] Sanjay Ghemawat, Howard Gobioff, and Shun-Tak Leung. The Google File System. In *SOSP '03: Proceedings of the nineteenth ACM symposium on Operating systems principles*, pages 29–43, New York, NY, USA, 2003. ACM Press.

[8] Luká Hejtmánek and Ludìk Matyska. Distributed Data Storage with Strong Offline Access Support. In *The Second International Multi-Conference on Computing in the Global Information Technology Challanges for the Next Generation of IT & C*, pages 1–6. IEEE Computer Society Press, 2007.

[9] Luká Hejtmánek, Ludìk Matyska, and Michal Procházka. Secure logistical networking in virtual organizations. Technical Report 2/2007, CESNET, z.s.p.o, February 2007.

[10] Iperf. `http://dast.nlanr.net/Projects/Iperf`.

[11] John Kubiatowicz, David Bindel, Yan Chen, Patrick Eaton, Dennis Geels, Ramakrishna Gummadi, Sean Rhea, Hakim Weatherspoon, Westly Weimer, Christopher Wells, and Ben Zhao. OceanStore: An Architecture for Global-Scale Persistent Storage. *SIGPLAN Not.*, 35(11):190–201, November 2000.

[12] Athicha Muthitacharoen, Robert Morris, Thomer M. Gil, and Benjie Chen. Ivy: A Read-/Write Peer-to-Peer File System. *SIGOPS Oper. Syst. Rev.*, 36(SI):31–44, 2002.

[13] D.S. Parker, G.J. Popek, G. Rudisin, A. Stoughton, B.J. Walker, E. Walton, J.M. Chow, D. Edwards, S. Kiser, and C. Kline. Detection of Mutual Inconsistency in Distributed Systems. *IEEE Transactions on Software Engineering*, SE-9(3):240–247, 1983.

[14] J. S. Plank. A tutorial on Reed-Solomon coding for fault-tolerance in RAID-like systems. *Software – Practice & Experience*, 27(9):995–1012, September 1997.

[15] Mendel Rosenblum and John K. Ousterhout. The Design and Implementation of a Log-Structured File System. *ACM Transactions on Computer Systems*, 10(1):26–52, 1992.

[16] Yasushi Saito and Marc Shapiro. Replication: Optimistic Approaches. Technical Report HPL-2002-33, HP Laboratories Palo Alto, 2002.

[17] M. Satyanarayanan, James J. Kistler, Puneet Kumar, Maria E. Okasaki, Ellen H. Siegel, and David C. Steere. Coda: A highly available file system for a distributed workstation environment. *IEEE Transactions on Computers*, 39(4):447–459, 1990.

[18] Mahadev Satyanarayanan. Scalable, Secure, and Highly Available Distributed File Access. *IEEE Computer*, 23(5):9–21, May 1990.

[19] Frank Schmuck and Roger Haskin. GPFS: A Shared-Disk File System for Large Computing Clusters. In *Proc. of the First Conference on File and Storage Technologies (FAST)*, pages 231–244, Berkeley, CA, USA, 2002. USENIX Association.

[20] S. Shepler, B. Callaghan, D. Robinson, R. Thurlow, C. Beame, M. Eisler, and D. Noveck. RFC 3530: Network File System (NFS) version 4 Protocol, April 2003. `http://www.ietf.org/rfc/rfc3530.txt`.

[21] C. A. Stein, Michael J. Tucker, and Margo I. Seltzer. Building a Reliable Mutable File System on Peer-to-Peer Storage. In *SRDS '02: Proceedings of the 21st IEEE Symposium on Reliable Distributed Systems (SRDS'02)*, page 324, Washington, DC, USA, 2002. IEEE Computer Society.

[22] Lex Stein, Michael J. Tucker, and Margo I. Seltzer. Reliable and fault-tolerant peer-to-peer block storage. Technical Report HU-TR-04-02, Harvard CS, 2002.

[23] Alan Tackett, Bobby Brown, Laurence Dawson, Santiago de Ledesma, Dimple Kaul, Kelly McCaulley, and Suyra Pathak. QoS issues with the L-Store distributed file system, 2006. Advanced Computint Center for Research and Education, Vanderbilt University, Whitepaper.

[24] Andrew S. Tanenbaum and Maarten Van Steen. *Distributed Systems: Principles and Paradigms*. Prentice Hall PTR, Upper Saddle River, NJ, USA, 2001.

[25] S.A. Weil, S.A. Brandt, E.L. Miller, D.D.E. Long, and C. Maltzahn. Ceph: A Scalable, High-Performance Distributed File System. In *Proceedings of the 7th Symposium on Operating Systems Design and Implementation (OSDI)*, pages 307–320. USENIX, 2006.

[26] Sage A. Weil, Scott A. Brandt, Ethan L. Miller, and Carlos Maltzahn. Grid resource management—CRUSH: controlled, scalable, decentralized placement of replicated data. In *SC '06: Proceedings of the 2006 ACM/IEEE conference on Supercomputing*, page 122, New York, NY, USA, 2006. ACM Press.

[27] Qin Xin, Ethan L. Miller, Thomas Schwarz, Darrell D. E. Long, Scott A. Brandt, and Witold Litwin. Reliability mechanisms for very large storage systems. In *MSS '03: Proceedings of the 20th IEEE/11th NASA Goddard Conference on Mass Storage Systems and Technologies (MSS'03)*, page 146, Washington, DC, USA, 2003. IEEE Computer Society.

IMPROVEMENT ON FAULT-TOLERANCE AND MIGRATION FACILITIES WITHIN THE GRID COMPUTING ENVIRONMENT - INTEGRATION WITH THE LOW-LEVEL CHECKPOINTING PACKAGES

Gracjan Jankowski, Radoslaw Januszewski, and Rafal Mikolajczak
Poznan Supercomputing and Networking Center,
61-704 Poznan, Noskowskiego 12/14, Poland
gracjan@man.poznan.pl
radekj@man.poznan.pl
Rafal.Mikolajczak@man.poznan.pl

Jozsef Kovacs
Computer and Automation Research Institute of the Hungarian Academy of Sciences
1111 Budapest Kende u. 13-17. Hungary
smith@sztaki.hu

Abstract   The paper describes the integration of a low-level checkpointing package with the GRID computing environment. The presented integration provides both fault-tolerant and job-migration facilities. The integration has been performed as proof-of-concept implementation of some concepts of Grid Checkpointing Architecture (GCA) that is being developed within the CoreGRID project. The individual components constituting the proof-of-concept implementation and their mutual relationships are presented. The described integration of a low-level checkpointing package with the GRID environment allows the Grid Resource Broker to recover user's jobs in case of failure. Thanks to the migration facilities the job can be recovered even if the physical node that originally hosted the job is no longer available.

Keywords: Checkpointing, fault tolerance, load balancing

1.   Introduction

One of the most common benefits of checkpointing technology is the high-level of fault tolerance offered by the environments that can take advantage of that technology. In case of any failure the checkpointed application can be recovered to the point where the last checkpoint was taken. Additionally, the checkpointing technology can serve as a basis for the implementation of a job migration mechanism which in turn can be utilized to improve the load-balancing and job preemption capabilities. The job migration can also be useful when after failure the original physical node is no more available . To date, there have been a few low-level checkpointing packages [1] [2] and each of the checkpointing packages offers different functionality and interface. Because of technical issues the checkpointing packages impose some limitations on applications that are to be checkpointed. The support for distributed applications is especially difficult - a significant problem is how to make consistent checkpoint of multiple cooperating processes and simultaneously not to lose the just in-transit messages. Thus, the conclusions are the following: so far not every application can be checkpointed, if one checkpointing package is able to deal with the given application, another package may not. Even if there are more than one checkpointing packages that are able to deal with the given application, the interfaces to the checkpointing functionality are likely to differ. Consequently, due to these features the integration of low-level checkpointing packages with the GRIDs is a difficult and not yet accomplished task.

Nevertheless, the possibility of achieving a higher level of fault-tolerance of the computing systems together with the introduction of unique features such as jobs migration makes the checkpointing technology a very attractive technique from the point of view of the GRID environment. Generally, there are two ways of introducing the checkpointing functionality to the GRID environment - it is either putting all functionality in the GRID application, so it is up to the application to store and restore its state [15], or taking some existing checkpointing packages and designing a service that will expose its functionality to the GRID. In our work we focus on the second approach, therefore, just to make the checkpointing packages available to the GRID environment we work on the Grid Checkpointing Architecture [3] [4] which aims to define novel, GRID-embedded components and associated design patterns that will allow the GRIDs to utilize a variety of the existing and future low-level checkpointing mechanisms in a conscious way.

To better understand the domain that GCA is dealing with and to check the feasibility of the developed concepts we are preparing a series of proof-of-concept environments that implement the different parts of GCA. In the paper we are going to present one of such proof-of-concept environments. The presented environment was prepared to prove the possibility of integrating the low-level checkpointing package with the Local Resource Manager and with the Grid Resource Broker. The involved individual components and the proposed architecture are described adequately in section 2 and 3. Relying upon the architecture described in section 3, the two scenarios of experiments have been realized. The user-driven and workflow-driven scenarios are described in section 4. The proposition of further extensions to the presented concept are briefly mentioned in section 5. The final conclusions that arise from the performed tests are presented in section 6.

The described integration has been prepared as derivative of another integration presented at CoreGRID Industrial Conference 2006 in Sophia-Antipolis in France [14] in the form of a live Demo Case. Comparing to that Demo Case in the integration presented in this paper, the technology used to provide user interface has been changed and the job migration capability has been added.

2. Involved components

The main functional components involved in the integration are: the low-level checkpointer, the Execute Manager, the Local Resource Manager and the Grid Resource Broker. This section provides a short overview of the implementations of the actual components used during the integration. The mutual relations between these components and their role within the considered proof-of-concept environment are described in the next section.

2.1 Low-level checkpointer - AltixC/R

The low-level checkpointer utilized during the integration is AltixC/R [6] [7]. It is a kernel-level checkpointing package designed by PSNC for Altix systems equipped with IA64 processors and running under the SGI ProPack environment (i.e. Linux-based environment prepared by SGI). The most recent version works with the Linux kernel 2.6. The required kernel-level functionality is provided in the form of a dynamically loaded kernel module, so it is easy to use and install. Contrary to some non kernel-level checkpointers, there is no assumption on the availability of source codes or the programming tools that were used to write the programs to be checkpointed. The package is able to checkpoint multi-process and multi-threaded programs that communicate through the signals, shared files or the System V IPC objects. A unique feature of the package is virtualization of some global system keys and identifiers (for example, PIDs are virtualized). Thanks to that, when the program is recovered, it is cheated that the identifiers have not changed, even though due to technological reasons, they are very likely to have changed.

2.2   Execution Manager - WS GRAM

The Execution Manager is meant to provide the Grid Resource Broker with the uniform interface to a variety of underlying Computing Nodes. Thanks to that the interface to different types of clusters (which are accessed through the Local Resources Managers) and even to single computing machines is similar and well abstracted in the form of the Execution Manager imposed protocol. In the considered integration we have used the WS GRAM [8] as the Execution Manager. WS-GRAM stands for Web Services Grid Resource Allocation and Management and is a part of the Globus Toolkit. According to the Globus Toolkit website [9], the WS GRAM component of the toolkit comprises a set of WSRF-compliant Web Services [10] to locate, submit, monitor, and cancel jobs on the GRID computing resources.

2.3   Local Resource Manager - Torque

The component that provides access to local computing resources is named Local Resource Manager (LRM). The actual LRM used in the presented integration is Torque [11] which is an open source implementation of the manager that provides control over jobs distributed among Computing Nodes of the cluster. In the simplest scenario the cluster together with management infrastructure can be scaled down to one node.

2.4   Grid Resource Broker - GRMS

The Grid Resource Broker is a component that is able to coordinate resources allocation and job submissions in the GRID environment. This is also the component that the end users interact with in order to submit, monitor and control their jobs. The user interface to the Grid Resource Broker can vary from the specialized GUI or the CLI tools to the WWW or the WAP-based pages. The Grid Resource Broker used in the presented integration is the Grid Resource Management Service (GRMS) [12] which is a part of the GRIDGE Grid Toolkit [13] being a set of integrated, ready to use GRID services. The GRMS supports building and deploying resource management systems for large scale distributed computing infrastructures. Comparing to other similar products, a unique feature of GRMS is the ability to deal with jobs defined as a set of tasks with precedence relationships where the execution of a child task can be triggered by any status of a parent task. It is noteworthy that during the integration activity we have experienced an active support from the GRMS development team.

2.5   User Interface - GRMS command line interface and GridSphere portal interface

As it was stated above, modern Grid Resource Brokers can cooperate with a variety of user interfaces. The two used in the described integration are the GridSphere portal interface [16] and the GRMS command line interface. The GridSphere is a portal framework that allows developing portlets providing interface to GRID infrastructure. The GRMS command line interface provides the end user with a set of commands to interact with the GRMS resource broker. Both the GRMS resource broker and GRMS command line interface are closely connected and developed by the same development team.

2.6   Images sharing - NFS

In the case of jobs migration the mechanism for exchanging the checkpoint images between nodes is needed. In the considered proof-of-concept environment, the Network File System (NFS) together with smart images naming policy has been used to provide access to the images on different nodes.

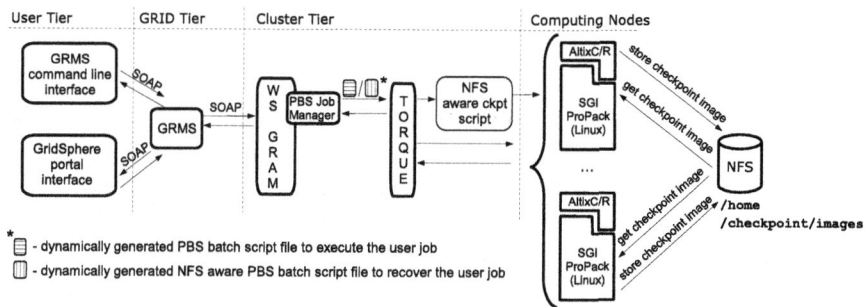

Figure 1.   Architecture

3.   Testbed architecture details

The outline of the architecture of the described proof-of-concept environment is depicted in Figure 1. The components presented there correspond to the ones introduced in section 2, but in some cases they are presented together with internal subcomponents that are not mentioned in section 2. The figure has been divided into four parts that represent the division of the architecture from the deployment point of view. The next part of the section describes the architecture. First, the lowest level components are presented and then the higher level ones.

From the point of view of the presented architecture, the most low-level component is NFS to which the checkpoint images are saved and from which the images are fetched during the recovery stage. With the help of NFS technology, the shared disk space that constitutes the images repository is mounted on each node to the same mount point. Therefore, thanks to bright images naming policy each node is able to locate and access the desired image if it is required (for example during the recovery stage).

The component that in Figure 1 takes advantages of the NFS technology is AltixC/R checkpointing package. The checkpointing package provides dynamically loaded kernel modules and the command line tools that allow for taking checkpoints and recovering users' jobs. The AltixC/R package has to be deployed on each Computing Node on which the checkpointing functionality should be available. The AltixC/R assumes that the checkpointing functionality is exposed only to locally logged users, so it does not expose any interface to the GRID or Cluster environment.

In Figure 1 it is shown that the jobs are submitted to the Computing Node through the TORQUE LRM. The TORQUE has the support for low-level checkpointers but by default the support is disabled. To enable the support the TORQUE has to be recompiled and the following line has to be added to the src/include/pbs_config.h file.:

```
#define MOM_CHECKPOINT 1
```

The TORQUE allows for employing the third-party checkpointing packages by means of special checkpointing script and additional arguments passed to the qsub[1] command. The checkpointing script has to be customized for each checkpointing package by a person who has adequate knowledge about the checkpointer, the TORQUE itself and the way the TORQUE executes the script. The qsub command of syntax qsub –c c=<time> <PBS batch script> submits the job defined within the <PBS batch script> file to the cluster. The arguments –c c=<time> determine that every <time> minutes the checkpointing script will be executed. The assumption is that the checkpointing script is available on the Computing Node to which the job will be submitted. The path to the script is defined within the TORQUE-related configuration files of the Computing Nodes. For example, in our testing environment the file /var/spool/torque/mom_priv/config that resides on the Computing Node contains the following line that indicates the checkpointing script location.:

```
$checkpoint_script home/fujisan/bin/mom-checkpoint.sh
```

The most important arguments passed to the checkpointing script are:

---

[1]qsub command submits the user job to the cluster to be executed, what job will be executed is defined within the user provided PBS batch script.

PID of the PBS batch script that represents the job that is to be checkpointed, JOB ID assigned by the TORQUE to the job and Unix like USER ID of the owner of that job. These arguments are available in the checkpointing script through the $1, $2 and $3 variables. These variables and knowledge about locally available low-level checkpointing package should be enough to write the checkpointing script that successfully takes checkpoints of the user's job.

To resume a job in this environment, the user has to prepare the dedicated PBS batch script and resubmit the job. The resubmitted PBS batch script is finally executed on the assigned Computing Node. The assumption is that this time, instead of executing the user's job from the beginning, the PBS batch script uses the locally available checkpointing package to recover the job. Of course, the image of the being recovered job has to be available. In the presented environment the filesystem used to store the images was exported using the NFS and is mounted at the same point on each node. The exact path and the name of the image can be devised relying on the assumed image naming policy. Our naming policy uses the job ID to assemble the image name, therefore in the same directory multiple images of different jobs were placed. The mentioned policy resulted in only one image for each running job, so only the most recent image of the checkpointed was available. If the checkpointing package is installed on all nodes within the TORQUE managed cluster, the job will be recovered even if the originally utilized node is not available (for example, because of failure). The TORQUE is not aware that a given PBS batch script recovers a job. The recovering PBS batch script is treated as any others. It is submitted to any currently available node according to the local scheduling policy. The knowledge how to recover the given job is embedded into the PBS batch script. It certainly uses locally available checkpointing package and NFS to recover the user job. In the described environment all the user actually has to know to write the recovering PBS batch script is the path to the "recover" command and to the checkpoint image (to establish the latter, knowledge of images naming policy is also required).

At this point the local resource manager is able to checkpoint and to recover jobs that are submitted by users directly to the TORQUE. However, as it is shown in Figure 1, the cluster managed by TORQUE is further exposed to the GRID environment. The element that links the cluster with the GRID is WS GRAM which is able to transform the SOAP messages to the dynamically generated PBS batch scripts and submit them to TORQUE. The part of the WS GRAM that is responsible for preparing and submitting the PBS batch script is the PBS Job Manager. The problem is that by default the PBS Job Manager is not able to submit the job with the additional "-c c=<time>" parameter and cannot prepare the PBS batch script that recovers the job using locally available checkpointing package. Therefore, to achieve this functionality the PBS Job Manager had to be adjusted. The PBS Job Manager is written in the

Perl language and the source file resides in the pbs.pm file that is a part of the Globus Toolkit. The WS GRAM accepts job executing requests in the form of job description defined as special xml file. Even though the format of this file does not contain any checkpointing-related elements explicitly, it allows for customizing the job description through the <extensions> xml element. So, we defined the following xml elements as the <extension>'s children: <ckpt_id>, <checkpointable>, <period>, <recovery> and <grms_id>. The detailed description of these elements is omitted. However, as the adjusted PBS Job Manager is passed the whole job descriptor, it extracts from it the newly defined checkpointing-related elements and relying on them prepares the adequate PBS batch script.

The next crucial element in Figure 1 is GRMS. The GRMS is the Grid Resource Broker which, relying on the request received from the user, finds the adequate Computing Resource and submits the user's job to it. The GRMS submits the job to the Computing Resource with the help of the WS GRAM service. In order to submit the job, the GRMS prepares the aforementioned job descriptor and sends it to the selected WS GRAM. In the described proof-of-concept environment the GRMS has been extended with the ability to prepare job descriptors that contain the previously defined checkpointing-related elements. As the GRMS itself accepts its own xml job descriptors provided by the users, this descriptor has also been extended with the additional checkpointing-related elements.

As it is shown in Figure 1, we used two kinds of user interface to test the environment. The first type of interface is the GRMS provided command line interface which allowed us to submit jobs to the GRID and to indicate that the given jobs have to be executed on Computing Resource equipped with the checkpointing functionality. The second, more convenient kind of interface, is the GridSphere-based web site (see Figure 2). The engines of both kinds of interfaces communicate with the GRMS resource broker with the help of the SOAP protocol.

4.   Demo scenario

Relying on the proof-of-concept environment described in the previous section, we have performed a set of tests and experiments. The two of them are described in this section. The outline of both scenarios is similar. The user submits to the GRID a POV-Ray based job by means of a command line or GridSphere-derived interface. After the Grid Resource Broker allocates an appropriate Computing Resource and submits the job to it, failure of the computing infrastructure is simulated. Next, depending on the scenario, user-driven or workflow-driven recovery action is performed. The scenarios utilize the POV-Ray application in the form of the example user's job due to the following

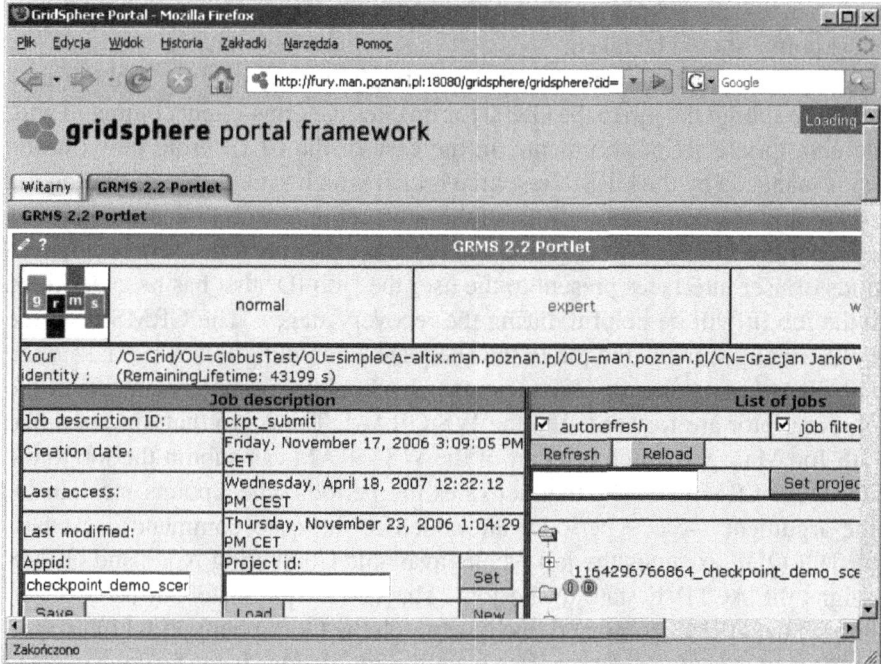

Figure 2.   Part of GridSphere GUI

reasons: it can be checkpointed and recovered with the help of AltixC/R check-pointing package[2], it is a time consuming, computing demanding application and the intermediate and final results are easily readable for people.

4.1   User-driven recovery scenario

Using the term "user-driven recovery scenario", we mean that when the failure occurs, the recovery action has to be triggered by the user and not by the system itself. The scenario begins with the user dealing with the GridSphere or command line interface.

In order to submit the job to the GRID, first the user, with the help of the favorite plain text editor (in case of CLI) or with the help of the web-based wizard (in the case of GridSphere portal) prepares a job descriptor that corresponds to the being submitted job. The crucial elements of the descriptor are the following: location of the POV-Ray application, the input parameters and files, and where the result files are to be stored. Additionally, to utilize the checkpointing technology, the descriptor has to contain elements implying that

---

[2]Each checkpointing package is able to checkpoint only finished set of applications.

the job is to be checkpointed and defining the period of time in which the next checkpoints should be taken.

When all parameters are set, the user simply has to click the "Submit job" button to submit the job to the GRID (or invokes the grms-client command with the appropriate set of arguments, in the case of the CLI). From now on, the job is managed by the GRMS resource broker which is in charge of finding the Computing Resource that fulfills all the job's requirements (including the one related to the checkpointing functionality). Just after the job is submitted, both kinds of user interfaces present to the user the "job ID" that has been assigned to the job (it will be helpful during the recovery stage). The GRMS resource broker finally submits the job to the adequate Computing Resource (i.e. to the WS GRAM component). Of course, the checkpointing-related elements of the job descriptor are forwarded to the WS GRAM. Thanks to that, the modified PBS Job Manager which is a part of the WS GRAM can submit the job to the TORQUE LRM in a way that activates the periodic checkpoints mechanism (the arguments –c c=<period> are added to the qsub command). At last, the TORQUE executes the job on any available Computing Node and GRMS assigns the ACTIVE state to the job. The current job state can be obtained through the GRMS command line or through the GridSphere portal interface.

The next step of the test scenario is failure simulation. It can be done in a few ways. However, we just find out the Computing Node where the job is executed and then kill the process that constitutes the job. When the job fails, its state changes into FAILED, from the GRMS point of view. If the user notices this change (for example, in the web interface) he or she would like to recover the job to the point where the last checkpoint was taken. To do so, the failed job has to be submitted again but additional elements in the job descriptor have to be specified. The new elements in the job descriptor indicate that the job is to be recovered instead of being executed from the beginning, and they point out the original "job ID" of the job. The job descriptor is submitted to the GRMS resource manager in a usual way. Relying on above-mentioned new job descriptor elements, the GRMS resource manager submits the job to the same Computing Resource (i.e. to WS GRAM) that handled the original job. As the additional job descriptor elements are also passed to the PBS Job Manager, it dynamically generates the PBS batch script that utilizing the previous "job ID" and with the use of checkpointing package and NFS is able to recover the job to the point of the last checkpoint. Thanks to NFS, shared home directories and smart image path naming policy, the job can be successfully recovered, even if TORQUE assigns to it a Computing Node which is different from the one used originally.

4.2   Workflow driven recovery scenario

The workflow driven scenario is even more attractive because the job failures are automatically detected and handled by the GRMS. This functionality has been achieved thanks to the GRMS feature that allows for managing complex workflows. The workflow consists of a number of tasks and an individual task can be triggered by status changes of other tasks. The tasks constituting the workflow and control flow between them, which is in fact not very complicated one, is depicted in Figure 3.

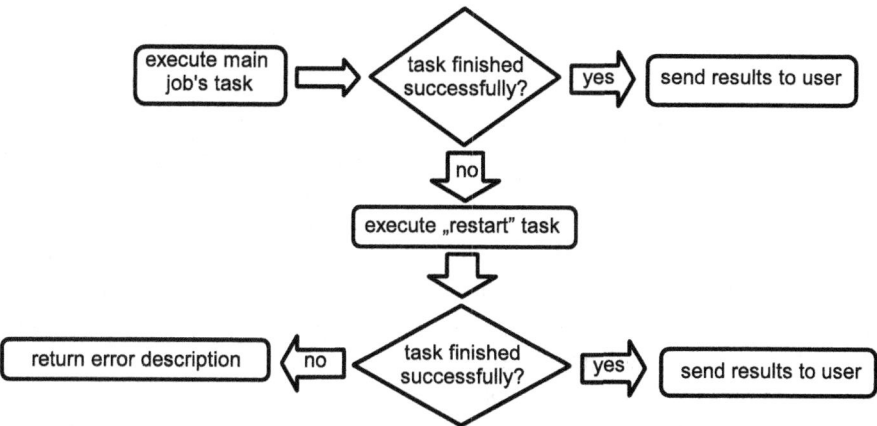

Figure 3.   Auto-recovery workflow

When the state of the task under which the POV-Ray is running changes to FAILED, the workflow manager automatically triggers the task that recovers the failed job. The drawback of this approach is a complex job descriptor which has to be prepared by the user to define individual tasks in the workflow and their mutual relationships.

When the job descriptor is ready, the job is submitted to the GRMS resource broker in the same way it was done in the previous scenario. After the job achieves the ACTIVE state, the failure is simulated exactly the way it was done in the previous case in the user-driven scenario. However, this time the failure simulation does not crash the whole job. The GRMS resource broker detects the failure and automatically submits the request that recovers the job to the WS GRAM. When the recovered job finally finishes, the scenario results can be validated simply by displaying the image produced by the POV-Ray application.

5.   Further work

The work described in the paper focuses on improving fault-tolerance and load-balancing level of GRID with the help of low-level checkpointing packages. The presented migration facilities have been implemented on the Local Resource Manager level. In such environment the job can migrate in the area of a single cluster. The future work encompasses extension of the presented proof-of-concept environment with the migration performed between clusters. In other words, the extended version of the environment assumes that the GRMS resource broker is able to recover the job even if, due to a failure, the previously used WS GRAM is unusable. Therefore the significant component of the next proof-of-concept environment will be the data management service that will allow for sharing the checkpoint images between distant clusters.

6.   Conclusions

The proof-of-concept environment described in the paper has been developed as a part of the work on GCA [3] [4]. Nevertheless, the presented environment is not the implementation of GCA as such. The environment has been utilized to check the feasibility of the ideas that GCA is based on. So far, the results of the tests and experiments that have been performed are promising and prove the sanity of the most recent GCA assumptions. In particular, the possibility of conscious interacting of the Grid Resource Broker with the Computing Resource equipped with a low-level checkpointing package has been confirmed. It has also been proved that the knowledge of the given low-level checkpointing package allows for providing scripts or programs that generalize the low-level checkpointing interface to the more abstract form exposed to the higher layers of the system. Simultaneously, the described proof-of-concept environment was able to improve the fault-tolerance level of the GRID computing environment. Even though failures were simulated, the workflow- and user-driven recovery procedures were able to recover the computing process to the point of the most recent checkpoint. Thanks to that, no significant computing cycles wasting took place and potential time or CPU cycles limitations imposed on the computing process can be fulfilled.

7.   Acknowledgments

This research work is carried out under the FP6 Network of Excellence CoreGRID funded by the European Commission (Contract IST-2002-004265).

References

[1] A survey of Checkpoint/Restart Implementations, Eric Roman, Lawrence Berkley National Laboratory, CA.

[2] http://www.checkpointing.org

[3] Gracjan Jankowski, Jozsef Kovacs, Norbert Meyer, Radoslaw Januszewski and Rafal Mikolajczak, Towards Checkpointing Grid Architecture, PPAM2005 proceedings.

[4] Gracjan Jankowski, Rafal Mikolajczak, Radoslaw Januszewski, Jozsef Kovacs, Attila Kertesz, Maciej Stroinski, Grid Checkpointing Architecture - Integration of low-level checkpointing capabilities with GRID, CoreGRID Technical Report TR-0075. Usenix Winter 1995 Technical Conference, New Orleans, LA, January, 1995.

[5] http://desktop.psnc.pl/

[6] Gracjan Jankowski, Radoslaw Januszewski, Rafal Mikolajczak, Checkpoint/Restart mechanism for multiprocess applications implemented under SGIGrid Project, CGW2004.

[7] http://checkpointing.psnc.pl/

[8] http://www.globus.org/toolkit/docs/4.0/execution/wsgram/

[9] http://www.globus.org/toolkit/

[10] http://www.oasis-open.org/committees/tc_home.php?wg_abbrev=wsrf

[11] http://www.clusterresources.com/pages/products/torque-resource-manager.php

[12] http://www.gridlab.org/WorkPackages/wp-9/

[13] http://www.gridge.org/

[14] http://www.coregrid.net/mambo/content/view/262/288/

[15] https://forge.gridforum.org/sf/projects/gridcpr-wg

[16] http://www.gridsphere.org/

TOWARDS AUTOMATED DIAGNOSIS OF APPLICATION FAULTS USING WRAPPER SERVICES AND MACHINE LEARNING*

Juergen Hofer and Thomas Fahringer
Distributed and Parallel Systems Group,
Institute of Computer Science, University of Innsbruck, Austria
juergen|tf@dps.uibk.ac.at

Abstract   With increasing size and complexity of Grids manual diagnosis of individual application faults becomes impractical and time-consuming. Quick and accurate identification of the root cause of failures is an important prerequisite for building dependable systems. Examples of causes are unsatisfied dependencies, deployment or configuration problems, expired credentials, quota limits or disk crashes. We describe a technique for application-specific fault diagnosis based on models built of indicators, symptoms and rules. Tailor-made wrapper services then apply this knowledge to reason on root causes of failures. In addition to user-provided diagnosis models we show that given a set of classified past fault events it is possible to extract new models through learning that are able to correctly diagnose faults appearing in unseen contexts. Our approach was implemented as part of the Otho Toolkit that 'service-enables' legacy applications via synthesis of wrapper services for the Grid.

Keywords: Grid services, legacy applications, fault diagnosis, reliability, Grid dependability, service oriented architectures, Grid tools, machine learning

---
*This work is partially funded by the European Union through the IST FP6-004265 CoreGRID and IST FP6-031688 EGEE-2 projects.

1. Introduction

A portion of todays applications used in High-Performance and Grid environments belongs to the class of batch-oriented programs with command-line interfaces. They typically have long lifecycles that surpass multiple generations of Grid and Service environments. Service Oriented Architectures and Web services became a widely accepted and mature paradigm for designing loosely-coupled large-scale distributed systems and can hide heterogeneity of underlying resources. As re-implementation of application codes is frequently too expensive in time and cost, their (semi-)automatic adaptation and migration to newer environments is of paramount importance. We suggest an approach with tailor-made wrapper services customized to each application. Mapping the functionality of applications to wrapper services requires not only to map input and output arguments, messages and files but also to ensure that the applications behavior is well-reflected. Occurrence of faults needs to be detected and diagnosed and then propagated via the services interface, such that clients may react appropriately to prevent larger system failures. In order to recover from failures in many cases their root causes such as unsatisfied dependencies, deployment or configuration problems, expired credentials, quota limits or disk crashes have to be identified. With increasing complexity of Grids - growing in size and heterogeneity - this tasks becomes increasingly difficult. Several abstraction layers conveniently shield the user from lower level issues. However these layers also hide important information required for fault diagnosis. Users or support staff are forced to drill down through layers for tracking possible causes. For larger number of failures it then quickly becomes impractical and time-expensive to manually investigate on individual causes by hand.

Related Work. Monitoring and failure detection systems [10, 12, 22] are important Grid components however they discriminate faults no further than into generic task-crashes and per-task exceptions. On the other hand a variety of systems has been suggested for building fault tolerant applications and middleware [11, 14] which could benefit from accurate and detailed diagnosis of faults and their causes. Common approaches for fault diagnosis start from formal system specifications [1, 13, 19] or from its source code [4, 15] to derive test cases. Instead neither source code availability nor a formal system specification are prerequisites to our approach. Fault diagnosis in Grids however still is a largely manual time-consuming task. Automation efforts include an approach for fault localization through unit tests [5] that however requires manual implementation of test cases and frameworks for verification of software stacks and interoperability agreements such as [21]. Instead we use a model-based description and to automatically generate diagnosis code. The use of machine learning has been successfully applied to many kinds of different classification problems [3, 20], e.g. to classify software behavior based on execution data [2] or to locate anomalies in sets of processes via function-level traces [17]. We apply machine learning to semi-automatically create models that allow services to diagnose faults of wrapped applications.

Synthesizing Wrapper Services using the Otho Toolkit. In previous work we discussed the semi-automatic transformation of legacy applications to services for integration in service-oriented environments [7]. Our focus lies on resource-intensive, non-interactive command-line programs as typically used in High-Performance and Grid environments. We presented the *Otho Toolkit* as *service-enabler* for *Legacy Applications* ($\mathcal{LA}$). Based on formal $\mathcal{LA}$ descriptions it generates tailor-made wrapper services, referred to as *Executor Services* ($\mathcal{XS}$). They provide a purely functional interface hiding technical details of the wrapping process on a certain execution platform, the *Backend* $\mathcal{BE}$. Input and output arguments, streams and consumed and produced files are mapped to the $\mathcal{XS}$ interface. Multiple views on the same $\mathcal{LA}$ can be defined to reflect different needs and to ease usage of complex interfaces. The Otho Toolkit generates wrapper service source codes including a build system. Multiple service environments can be targeted and the services may be equipped with application-specific features and generic extensions[1].

2. Diagnosing Application Faults

Normally software has been extensively tested before released to production. Nevertheless in large-scale deployments and complex environments such as Grids applications are likely to fail[2]. Common reasons are improper installations or deployments, configuration problems, failures of dependent resources such as hosts, network links, storage devices, limitations or excess on resource usage, performance and concurrency issues, usage errors, etc. Our goal is to provide a mechanism to automatically identify and distinguish such causes. The fault diagnosis process consists of the tasks of error detection, hypothesizing possible faults, identification of actual fault via analysis of application, application artifacts and environment and finally reporting of diagnosis results. As prototype application we chose the raytracer POV-Ray [29], an open-source general-purpose visualization application and the GNU Linear Programming Toolkit (GLPK) [27] a software package for solving linear programming and mixed integer programming problems.

Building Fault Diagnosis Models. Instead of requiring a full formal system specification we provide a set of easy-to-use elements for building fault diag-

---

[1]Currently supported are WSRF-Services with Globus Toolkit [26], Web services with Apache Axis and Apache Axis [24], JBoss EJBs [28] and ASG services [25]. Examples for features are filetransfer, resource usage accounting, support for MPI/OpenMP or parameter sweeping. Available extensions include components for Grid credential management, monitoring and filesystem operations.

[2]In accordance with Laprie [16] we define a *fault* as the hypothesized or identified cause of an error, e.g. due to a hardware defect; an *error* as a deviation from the correct system state that, if improperly handled or unrecognized, may lead to a system *failure* where the delivered service deviates from specified service.

nosis models. They allow developers to describe cases in which their programs may fail and users to describe cases in which their programs have failed in the past. As no knowledge on formal system specification techniques is required we believe our approach is practical and more likely to be applied in the community of Grid users. The diagnosis models are rule-based case descriptions that allow services to perform automated reasoning on the most-likely cause of failures of the wrapped application. Results are then reported to clients. Such diagnosis models are constructed as follows: **(1) Indicators** are externally visible and monitorable effects of the execution of a certain application. We distinguish boolean-valued predicates, e.g. the existence of a certain file or directory, indicators returning strings (StringInd) such as patterns in output, error or log-files, indicators returning reals (RealInd) and indicators performing counting operations (CountInd) such as the number of files in a directory. A few examples are given below

$$(\exists file) file \qquad extract\_stdout(regexp) \qquad exitCode()$$
$$(\exists file) dir \qquad extract\_file(file, regexp) \qquad wall\_time()$$
$$(\exists regexp) pattern\_stdout \qquad count\_pattern\_stdout(regexp)$$
$$(\exists file)((\exists regexp) pattern\_file) \qquad count\_files(regexp)$$

Next to the set of predefined indicators we allow the use of custom user-provided indicators specific to certain applications, e.g. to verify functional correctness via result checks, error rates, data formats, etc. In some cases runtime argument values are needed as parameters for indicators, e.g. to refer to an output file named via a program argument. Formally we use the $\Theta(argname)$ notation to refer to runtime arguments. **(2) Symptoms** are sets of indicators describing an undesirable situation, more concretely the existence of a fault. They are comparisons of indicators with literal values or comparative combinations of indicators evaluating to boolean values.

$$symptom \vdash CountInd|RealInd\{< | \leq | = | \geq | >\}\{r|r \in \mathbb{R}\}$$
$$symptom \vdash CountInd|RealInd\{< | \leq | = | \geq | >\}CountInd|RealInd$$
$$symptom \vdash StringInd\{= | \neq\}\{s|s \in string\}$$
$$symptom \vdash StringInd\{= | \neq\}StringInd$$
$$symptom \vdash Predicate|\neg symptom|symptom \wedge symptom$$

Examples for symptoms are the existence of a coredump file, occurrence of the string 'Segmentation fault' in stderr, certain program exit codes, output values or number of output files above or below some threshold, etc. **(3) Rules** built on the basis of symptoms allow to reason about fault types. We define rules as implications of the form $(s_1 \wedge s_2 \wedge \ldots \wedge s_n) \Rightarrow u$. Example diagnosis rules for the POV-Ray application are given below.

exit=0 $\wedge \exists file(\Theta(\text{sceneout})) \wedge \neg \exists pattern\_stdout("Failed") \Rightarrow done\_successful$
exit=249 $\Rightarrow failed\_illegal\_argument$
exit=0 $\wedge \exists file(\Theta(\text{sceneout})) \wedge filesize(\Theta(\text{sceneout})) = 0 \quad \wedge$
$\qquad \exists pattern\_stdout("Disk quota exceeded.") \Rightarrow failed\_quota$
exit=0 $\wedge filesize(\Theta(\text{sceneout})) = 0 \Rightarrow failed\_disk\_quota\_exceeded$

exit=0 $\wedge \neg \exists file(\Theta(\text{sceneout}))$ $\wedge$
$\quad \exists pattern\_stdout(\text{"File Error open"}) \Rightarrow \text{failed\_file\_writing\_error}$
exit=0 $\wedge \exists pattern\_stdout(\text{"Got 1 SIGINT"}) \Rightarrow \text{failed\_received\_sigint}$
gramExit=1 $\wedge \exists pattern\_gram\_log(\text{'proxy is not valid long enough'}) \wedge$
$\quad \Rightarrow \text{failed\_proxy\_expires\_soon}$
gramExit=1 $\wedge \exists pattern\_gram\_log(\text{'couldn't find a valid proxy'}) \wedge$
$\quad \exists pattern\_gram\_log(\text{'proxy does not exist'}) \Rightarrow \text{failed\_no\_proxy}$
gramExit=1 $\wedge \exists pattern\_gram\_log(\text{'proxy does not exist'}) \Rightarrow \text{failed\_proxy\_expired}$

The second rule e.g. states that the return code 249 unambiguously identifies an illegal argument fault. Failures caused by exceeded disk quota are recognized by an apparently successful return code however in combination with a zero-size outputfile and a certain error message. **(4) Models.** Finally a set of rules builds a fault diagnosis model. The rules are meant to be evaluated post-mortem, i.e. immediately after the execution terminated, in the specified ordering. If no rule evaluates to true, the fault cannot be identified. Depending on the desired behavior the diagnosis can continue the evaluation if multiple rules are satisfied. The fault is then considered to belong to all found classes. For practical reasons we developed a simple XML-based syntax for representing fault diagnosis models as those shown above.

```
<fdiag>
  <cause name="successful" status="DONE">
    <exitCode value="0" />
    <fileExists name="|sceneout|" />
    <not><regexpStdout value="Failed" /></not>
  </cause>
  <cause name="illegal argument" status="FAILED">
    <exitCode value="249" />
  </cause>
</fdiag>
```

This example lists two root causes each named and tagged with a post-execution status value. A set of indicators sequentially evaluated with logical conjunction can be given. Elements may be negated by adding a 'not' tag.

Service States. Executor Services ($\mathcal{XS}$) always reside in one of a finite well-defined set of states. The corresponding finite state machine is shown in Figure 1. The faulty states $F1, \ldots, Fn$ are replaced by a finite set of fault classes specific to each application. The transition from F to $F1, \ldots, Fn$ is triggered after fault diagnosis. All other transitions are triggered by the $\mathcal{XS}$ based on actions it performs (e.g. job submission) or events it receives (e.g. a state-change notification from a resource management system).

Implementation. Wrapper services, and especially our synthesized tailor-made Executor Services $\mathcal{XS}$, already possess detailed knowledge on the application structure and behavior, control its execution and lifecycle and are aware of input and output arguments, messages and files. Moreover they have the necessary proximity to the execution host for fault investigation. Therefore we chose to address and implement the fault diagnosis as part of the Otho Toolkit

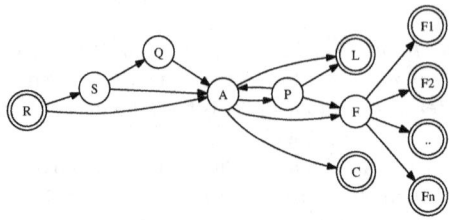

Figure 1. $\mathcal{XS}$ as FSM. Ready (R), Submitted (S), Queued (Q), Active (A), Suspended (P), Cancelled (L), Completed (C), Failed (F). Faults: F1, F2, ... Fn

and the $\mathcal{XS}$ it synthesizes. All indicators were implemented as generic Bash and Python scripts. We extended Otho Toolkits $\mathcal{LA}$ description with the fault diagnosis syntax as shown above. The Otho Toolkit then translates the formal model into source code that evaluates each case using the generic indicator scripts. The $\mathcal{XS}$ executes this script immediately after the application. The script evaluates the diagnosis model rule by rule. Indicator results are cached to prevent redundant evaluations of re-occurring indicators.

```
<definitions name="PovrayImage" ... >                     <simpleType name="FaultClass">
 <types>                                                    <restriction base="xsd:string">
  <schema ...>                                               <enumeration value="DISKQUOTA" />
   <element name="executePovrayImageRequest">                <enumeration value="SIGKILL" />
    <complexType>                                            <!-- also: ILLEGALARGUMENT,
     <sequence>                                                    SIGINT, SUCCESS, ..." -->
      <element name="scenepov" type="xsd:string"/>          </restriction>
      <element name="width"    type="xsd:int"/>            </simpleType>
      <!-- ... -->                                         </schema>
     </sequence>                                           </types>
    </complexType>
   </element>                                               <portType name="PovrayImage">
   <!-- ... -->                                              <operation name="createResource"> ..
                                                             <operation name="execute"> ..
   <simpleType name="Status">                                <operation name="getStatus"> ..
    <restriction base="xsd:string">                          <operation name="getFaultDiagnosis"> ..
     <enumeration value="READY" />                           <operation name="getStdOut">
     <enumeration value="SUBMITTED"/>                         <!-- also: getStdErr, cancel, suspend,
     <enumeration value="QUEUED" />                                resume, destroyResource, .. -->
     <!-- also: ACTIVE, SUSPENDED                           </portType>
         FAILED, CANCELED, COMPLETED" -->                   <!-- .. -->
    </restriction>                                         </definitions>
   </simpleType>
```

Figure 2.   Parts of $\mathcal{XS}$ Interface for Propagation of Fault Diagnosis Results

If the $\mathcal{XS}$ executes the $\mathcal{LA}$ via job submission to a resource management systems the $\mathcal{LA}$ and the fault diagnosis script are submitted as one job to ensure execution on the same resource. The fault diagnosis capabilities and states need to be represented in the service interface. Figure 2 shows parts of the WSDL for the Axis2 [24] $\mathcal{XS}$ platform. The request type contains the input argument values for the wrapped $\mathcal{LA}$. Operations allow to query state, fault diagnosis via fault classes and other artifacts and information. Obviously the interface differs depending on the concrete service platform. E.g. Axis2 webservices use a job identifier whereas WSRF GT4 services rely on stateful resource properties.

3. Semi-Automated Learning of Fault Diagnosis Models

With increasing utilization variety and frequency of faults will increase. Our hypothesis is that given a set of past classified fault events it is possible to learn models that are able to correctly classify unseen novel faults.

Phases. The process of learning and improvement in the context of the Otho Toolkit and $\mathcal{XS}$ is depicted in Figure 3. In the bootstrapping phase an initial set of services is created and deployed by the Otho Toolkit. At runtime each fault is analyzed and added to the knowledge base as new fault event. At the end of the bootstrapping phase the collected fault events are tagged with class labels. This is a manual step done by users, service provider or developers. Now the classified training set is used as input to the machine learning procedure that creates new models which enable the classification of unseen fault events that are similar to past faults. The updated or newly learned model is then fed into the Otho Toolkit that creates and redeploys an improved revision of the $\mathcal{XS}$. Additional events are then again collected, learning is re-triggered, followed by synthesis and redeployment and so forth.

Fault Events. For each detected fault event a tuple of the form $(I \cup T) \times (S \cup F)$ is generated automatically. It contains all relevant information characterizing a certain fault incidence specific to a given application. A set of boolean or numeric indicators $i_i \in I$ such as existence, modification, size, open for reading/writing as detailed above and a set of boolean indicators $t_i \in T$ whether certain regular expression-based patterns (error messages, codes) can be found, are applied to a given set of artifacts created during applications runs. Those

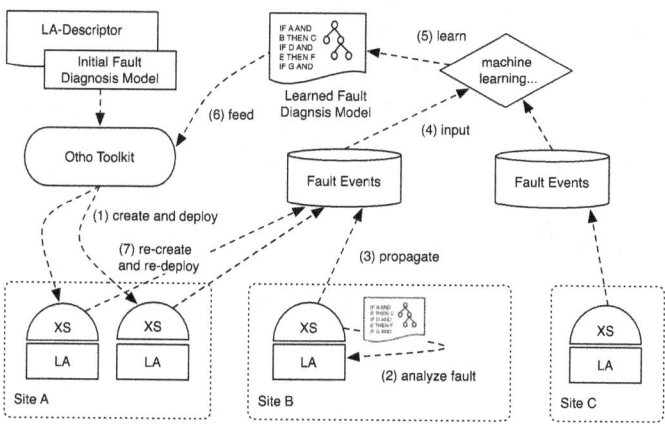

Figure 3. Applying Fault Diagnosis and Learning of Improved Models

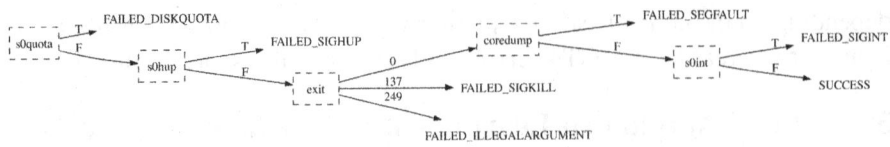

Figure 4.   Decision Tree Classifier learned during Evaluation

artifacts include the standard input/output files associated with each process of and application and the execution environment by $s_i \in S$, i.e. stdout, stderr, system log and log files of resource management system and application-specific input and output files $f_i \in F$. The latter set has to be provided by the user and may be a function of the program arguments. To each tuple the class label is attached for use as training set for machine learning.

Classification Models and Algorithms.   We selected a set of well-known supervised machine learning techniques for classification problems [6, 18, 31]. All of them require a training set containing examples with class labels and induce a model (classifier) that can then be used to assign unseen examples to a set of classes. *OneR (OR)* is an algorithm that produces one-level classification rules based on single attributes. A classification rule consists of an antecedent that applies tests to reason about the consequent. *DecisionStump (DS)* produces simple one-level decision trees. Decision trees follow the divide-and-conquer principle where the problem space is partitioned by outcome of tests until all examples belong to the same class. *Logistic (LG)* is a statistical modeling approach based on logistic regression where coefficients are estimated using the maximum log-likelihood method. *BayesNet (BN)* is a statistical modeling approach producing Bayesian networks in forms of directed acyclic graphs with probabilities over relevant attributes. *DecisionTable (DT)* denotes an algorithm that produces a table consisting of relevant attributes, their values and the prediction class. Finally *J48* is an improved version of the C4.5 decision tree machine learning algorithm. Figure 4 contains an example for a specific decision tree classifier learned from the dataset 'failed/succ cleaned' during the evaluation of the J48 algorithm as described below. Each node represents a certain indicator, branches are tests and leaf nodes are the fault classes. The root node in this particular decision tree classifier is a boolean $pattern\_exists$ indicator searching for the string 'disk quota exceeded' in stdout ('s0'). If the first two tests are false but the exitCode indicator test evaluates to '137' the fault diagnosis will yield the class label 'Failed_Sigkill. Naturally the model is specific to a certain application, training set and learning technique.

Evaluation.   To evaluate the machine learning techniques for suitability to our approach we used our implementation as part of the Otho Toolkit and the $\mathcal{XS}$ it synthesizes. All learning techniques described above were implemented based on [30]. We deployed both applications on the AustrianGrid [23] and injected

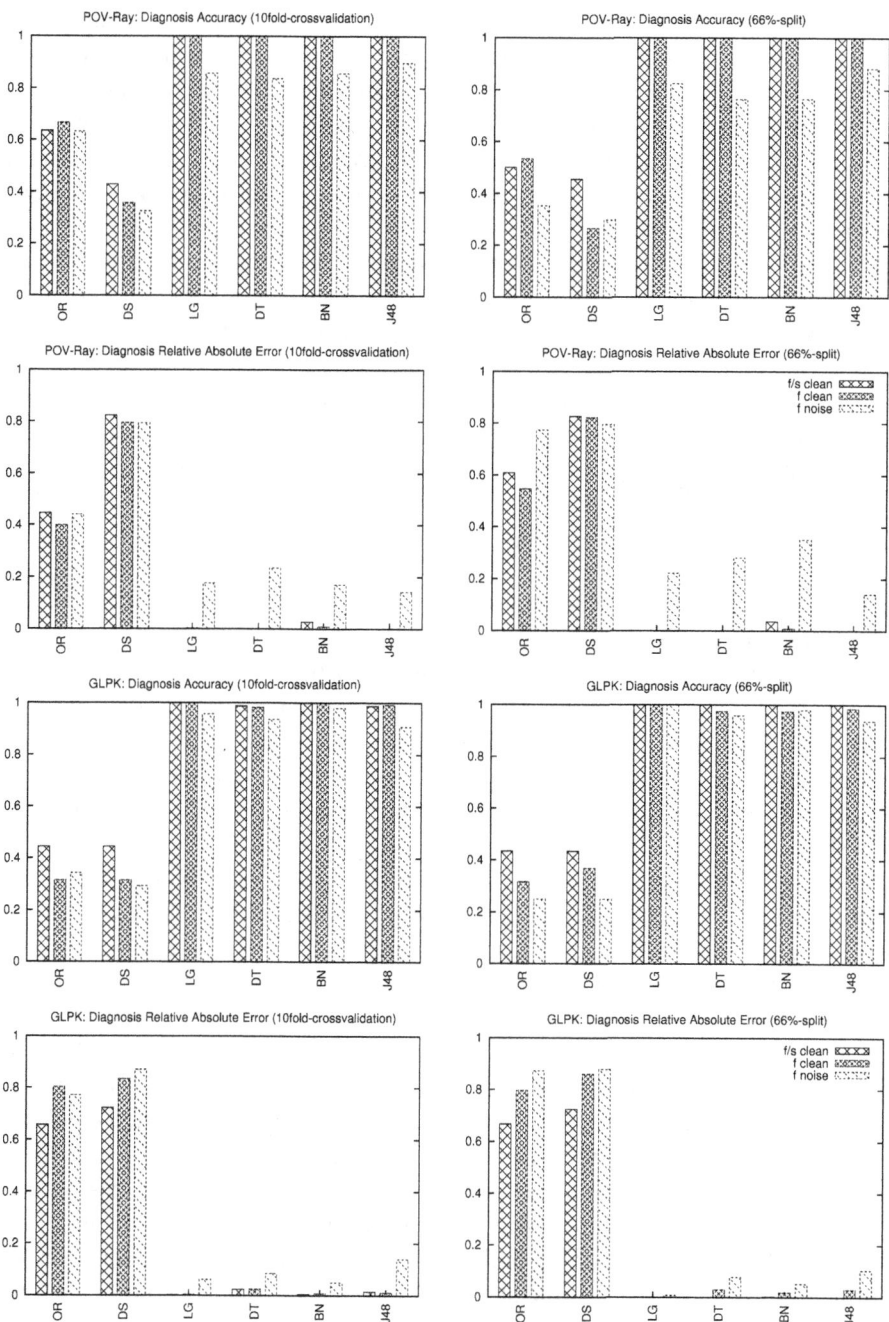

Figure 5.   Evaluation of Machine Learning Algorithms for POV-Ray

several types of faults. After each failure the fault event capturing was started. The result of each indicator evaluation was recorded in a repository. We attached to each tuple a class label. The resulting training set was used in its raw state ('failed noise'), in a cleaned state ('failed clean') and to allow our classifier to also identify correct behaviour with added successful runs ('failed/succ clean'). The performance or accuracy of classifier is commonly evaluated in terms of their success rates which is the proportion of true and false predictions. We also show the relative absolute error $\text{RAE} = \sum_{i=1}^{n} |p_i - a_i| / \sum_{i=1}^{n} |a_i - \overline{a}|$ as a commonly used metric. An important issue is the question on which set of instances to learn from and which set to evaluate against, as classifiers tend to show better performance if evaluated against the training set than against unseen examples. Therefore we applied three evaluation techniques. First we used the full dataset ('ts') for learning and evaluation. Second we used two-third for learning one-third for evaluation ('66-sp'). Third we used 10-fold cross-validation ('10-cv') where metrics are averaged from ten iterations with 9/10 of examples used for training and 1/10 for evaluation. The set of examples not used for training represent unseen fault cases.

Discussion.   Figure 5 plots the accuracy and error rates of our experiments for 10-cv and 66-sp. In general it can be observed that prediction accuracy for the GLPK application case study were better than those for the POV-Ray application in most cases. The overall quality apparently strongly depends not only on the machine learning technique but also on the concrete application, the indicators used and the corresponding structure of the training set. The second observation is that even on the cleaned datasets the algorithms OR and DS show significantly lower prediction accuracy than LG, DT, BN and J48. For POV-Ray using 10-fold cross-validation DS has an accuracy of only 0.429 and OR of 0.635 on the succ/failed compared to an observed 0.837 lower bound accuracy for the other algorithms. Both methods produce rather simplistic classifier clearly unsuited to capture complex fault events. Nevertheless for trivial diagnostics, e.g. exit code unambiguously identifies fault case, they may be useful as part of meta-models. The remaining four algorithms LG, DT, BN and J48 show comparable performance without significant differences among each other. For the cleaned datasets 'failed/succ cleaned' and 'failed cleaned' all four provide outstanding performance, correctly classifying up to 100% of unseen instances. For instance for the POV-Ray application J48 has on the 'failed uncleaned' raw dataset slightly better performance of 0.898 compared to 0.837 of DT and 0.857 of BN and LG on average on the unseen data. During evaluation we observed that the statistical models BN and LG tend to capture also noise, whereas J48 tree pruning prevented such undesired behavior.

4. Conclusion

With increasing size and complexity of Grids manual diagnosis of application faults becomes impractical and time-consuming. We developed a model-based mechanism allowing users, support staff or application developers to formulate precise, rule-based fault diagnosis models evaluated immediately after program termination. Such diagnosis models are used to provide accurate and reliable reports. Our approach was implemented as part of application wrapper services synthesized by the Otho Toolkit. In addition we suggest the use of machine learning to create fault diagnosis models from past classified fault events. Our evaluation showed that the learned diagnosis models were able to classify novel fault situations with high accuracy. The overall performance however depends on the dataset quality. We observed significant perturbation caused by noisy or falsely labeled examples. Ideally developers, service providers and knowledgeable users therefore regularly remove unclean examples from the training set. As part of future work we plan to use a larger set of applications to get access to a larger variety of faults. Exploration of clustering algorithms is also planned as they allow to partition a set of instances automatically into groups without the need for a priori labelling. Moreover we intend to investigate on overheads and scalability of our fault diagnosis and machine learning approach.

References

[1] J.-R. Abrial, S. A. Schuman, and B. Meyer. A specification language. In R. McNaughten and R.C. McKeag, editors, *On the Construction of Programs*. Cambridge University Press, 1980.

[2] J. Bowring, J. Rehg, and M. J. Harrold. Active learning for automatic classification of software behavior. In *Proc. of the Int. Symp. on Software Testing and Analysis (ISSTA 2004)*, July 2004.

[3] M. Chen, A. Zheng, J. Lloyd, M. Jordan, and E. Brewer. Failure diagnosis using decision trees. In *Proc. of Int. Conf. on Autonomic Computing (ICAC)*, York, NY, May 2004.

[4] Richard DeMillo and Aditya Mathur. A grammar based fault classification scheme and its application to the classification of the errors of tex. Technical Report SERC-TR-165-P, Purdue University, 1995.

[5] A. N. Duarte, F. Brasileiro, W. Cirne, and J. S. A. Filho. Collaborative fault diagnosis in grids through automated tests. In *Proc. of the The IEEE 20th Int. Conf. on Advanced Information Networking and Applications*, 2006.

[6] Jiawei Han and Micheline Kamber. *Data Mining: Concepts and Techniques*. Morgan Kaufmann, 2001.

[7] Jürgen Hofer and Thomas Fahringer. Presenting Scientific Legacy Programs as Grid Services via Program Synthesis. In *Proceedings of 2nd IEEE International Conference on e-Science and Grid Computing*, Amsterdam, Netherlands, December 4-6 2006. IEEE Computer Society Press.

[8] Jürgen Hofer and Thomas Fahringer. Specification-based Synthesis of Tailor-made Grid Service Wrappers for Scientific Legacy Codes. In *Proceedings of 7th IEEE/ACM Inter-*

national Conference on Grid Computing (Grid'06), Short Paper and Poster*, Barcelona, Spain, September 28-29 2006.

[9] Jürgen Hofer and Thomas Fahringer. The Otho Toolkit - Synthesizing Tailor-made Scientific Grid Application Wrapper Services. *Journal of Multiagent and Grid Systems. IOS Press*, 3(3), 2007.

[10] Yuuki Horita, Kenjiro Taura, and Takashi Chikayama. A scalable and efficient self-organizing failure detector for grid applications. In *6th IEEE/ACM Int. Workshop on Grid Computing (Grid'05)*. IEEE Computer Society Press, 2005.

[11] S. Hwang and C. Kesselman. A flexible framework for fault tolerance in the grid. *Journal of Grid Computing*, 1(3):251–272, September 2003.

[12] Soonwook Hwang and Carl Kesselman. Gridworkflow: A flexible failure handling framework for the grid. In *12th IEEE Int. Symp. on High Performance Distributed Computing (HPDC'03)*, Seattle, Washington, June 2003. IEEE.

[13] Cliff Jones. *Systematic Software Development using VDM*. Prentice Hall, 1990.

[14] George Kola, Tevfik Kosar, and Miron Livny. Phoenix: Making data-intensive grid applications fault-tolerant. In *Proc. of 5th IEEE/ACM Int. Workshop on Grid Computing*, pages 251–258, Pittsburgh, Pennsylvania, November 8 2004.

[15] D. R. Kuhn. Fault classes and error detection in specification based testing. *ACM Transactions on Software Engineering Methodology*, 8(4):411–424, 1999.

[16] J.-C. Laprie. Dependable computing and fault tolerance: Concepts and terminology. In *Proc. of 15th Int. Symp. on Fault-Tolerant Computing*, 1985.

[17] A. V. Mirgorodskiy, N. Maruyama, and B. P. Miller. Problem diagnosis in large-scale computing environments. In *Proc. of ACM/IEEE Supercomputing'06 Conference*, 2006.

[18] T. M. Mitchell. *Machine Learning*. McGraw-Hill, Boston, 1997.

[19] Frank Ortmeier and Wolfgang Reif. Failure-sensitive Specification - A formal method for finding failure modes. Technical report, University of Augsburg, January 12 2004.

[20] A. Podgurski, D. Leon, P. Francis, W. Masri, M. Minch, J. Sun, and B. Wang. Automated support for classifying software failure reports. In *Proc. of 25th Int. Conf. on Software Engineering*, pages 465–475, Portland, Oregon, 2003.

[21] S. Smallen, C. Olschanowsky, K. Ericson, P. Beckman, and J.M. Schopf. The inca test harness and reporting framework. In *Proc. of the ACM/IEEE Supercomputing'04 Conference*, Nov 2004.

[22] P. Stelling, I. Foster, C. Kesselman, C. Lee, and G. von Laszewski. A fault detection service for wide area distributed computations. In *Proc. 7th IEEE Symp. on High Performance Distributed Computing*, pages 268–278, 1998.

[23] AustrianGrid. http://www.austriangrid.at.

[24] Apache Axis2. http://ws.apache.org/axis2/.

[25] EU Adaptive Services Grid (ASG). http://asg-platform.org/.

[26] Globus Toolkit. http://www-unix.globus.org/toolkit/.

[27] GNU Linear Programming Kit (GLPK). http://www.gnu.org/software/glpk/.

[28] JBoss J2EE Application Server. http://www.jboss.com.

[29] POV-Ray. http://www.povray.org.

[30] Weka. http://www.cs.waikato.ac.nz/ml/weka.

[31] Ian H. Witten and Eibe Frank. *Data Mining: Practical Machine Learning Tools and Techniques with Java Implementations*. Morgan Kaufmann, 2000.

IV

SERVICE LEVEL AGREEMENT

USING SLA FOR RESOURCE MANAGEMENT AND SCHEDULING - A SURVEY

Philipp Wieder
Central Institute for Applied Mathematics
Research Centre Jülich,
52425 Jülich, Germany
ph.wieder@fz-juelich.de

Jan Seidel, Oliver Wäldrich, and Wolfgang Ziegler
Department of Bioinformatics
Fraunhofer Institute SCAI
53754 Sankt Augustin, Germany
{jan.seidel, oliver.waeldrich, wolfgang.ziegler}@scai.fraunhofer.de

Ramin Yahyapour
IRF, University Dortmund
44221 Dortmund, Germany
ramin.yahyapour@udo.edu

Abstract   Service Level Agreements are used to establish agreements on the quality of a service between a service provider and a service consumer. The roles of service provider and service consumer may be realised in different shapes ranging from individuals to institutions, software agents or other systems acting on behalf of physical entities or steered by those. This paper gives an overview of state-of-the-art Grid software using Service Level Agreements in the domain of scheduling and resource management. We provide an introduction to the different areas where Service Level Agreements are used in Grid environments, the technologies used, and what should be accomplished followed by descriptions of the systems that already implement and use Service Level Agreements.

Keywords: Grid, Service Level Agreements, resource management, scheduling, QoS

1. Introduction

Service Level Agreements (SLA) are used in different domains and on different levels to establish agreements on the quality of a service (QoS) between a service provider and a service consumer. SLAs can be based on general agreements, e.g. framework agreements, that govern the relationship between parties, may include also legal aspects and may set boundaries for SLAs. However, this paper addresses the usage of SLAs on a lower, technical level and focuses on agreements dealing with properties of services and resources in the area of resource management and scheduling (RMS).

The remainder of the paper is organised as follows. Section 2 presents a number of typical use cases in the RMS area. Two existing frameworks for SLAs are introduced in Section 3, WSLA and WS-Agreement. The latter is quite commonly used in the Grid landscape and we therefore describe in Section 4 RMS systems already using WS-Agreement or planning to use it in the near future. Section 5 concludes the paper and gives a brief outlook on future work.

2. Use Cases

In this section we present three classes of use cases where SLAs are either already used in the Grid RMS environment or will be used in near future.

2.1 Resource Reservation

For a presentation with live demonstration of an application the necessary compute resource to run the application has to be available at the time of the presentation. In an normal cluster environment where the nodes of the cluster are used under a space-sharing policy, i.e. giving each user for the time of his job exclusive access to the part of the resources needed for the job-execution, the probability of finding a free slot that matches the requirements of a user immediately is low, thus his job usually will be queued and executed later. For a presentation with a fixed schedule this is not acceptable. Thus, the presenter needs to reserve the resources in advance to be sure that they can be used for the demonstration at the time foreseen. This reservation can be expressed as a Quality of Service and an SLA is created for the reservation is fixed. In the VIOLA project [11] this is done by the MetaScheduling Service (MSS), which negotiates the time-slot with the scheduler of the cluster and initiates the reservation of the nodes requested by the user.

2.2 Agreement on multiple QoS Parameters

In an environment consisting of several clusters potentially operated in different administrative domains SLAs might be used for co-allocation or the resource allocation for workflows. A typical use-case is the co-allocation of multiple compute resources together with network links with a dedicated QoS between these resources to run a distributed parallel application. The user specifies his request and the resource orchestrator starts negotiating with the local scheduling systems of the compute resources and the network RMS (NRMS) in order to find a suitable time-slot, where all required resources are available at the same time. Once a common time-slot is identified the orchestrator requires the reservation of the individual resources. Again, this reservation can be expressed as a QoS and an SLA is created for the reservation. In the VIOLA project this is done by the MSS, which negotiates the time-slots with the different schedulers of the clusters and the NRMS and initiates the reservation of the all resources by the user. Another use-case is a workflow spanning across several resources. The only difference to the use-case described before is the type of temporal dependencies: While for the distributed parallel application the resources must be reserved for the same time, for the workflow use-case the resources are needed in a sequence given by the workflow.

2.3 Grid Scheduler interoperation

As there is no single orchestrating service or Grid scheduler in a Grid spanning across countries and administrative domains we have to deal with multiple instances of independent Grid schedulers. Using resources from different domains requires co-ordination across multiple sites. There are two approaches either directly trying to negotiate with respective local scheduling systems or negotiation with the respective local orchestrator. The former solution requires local policies allowing a remote orchestrator to negotiate with local schedulers, which is in general not the case. In the second case there is one access point to the local resources, which then negotiates on behalf of the initiation orchestrator. As the second approach also has a better scalability than the first one the OGF Grid Scheduling Architecture Research Group (GSA-RG) decided to consider this approach for the definition of a Grid Scheduling Architecture. For the communication between the different orchestration services or Grid schedulers a language and a protocol to create SLAs was selected to achieve the necessary interoperability while at the same time resulting SLAs at the end of the negotiation process, that can be composed by the initiating orchestrator into one single agreement vis-à-vis his client.

3. Service Level Agreement Frameworks

This section introduces two existing frameworks for SLA specification and monitoring: Web Service Level Agreement (WSLA) developed by IBM (completed in March 2003) and Web Service Agreement (WS-Agreement) developed in a working group of the Open Grid Forum (OGF). While the WSLA specification [14] can still be downloaded at the WSLA web-page it was not widely adopted and seems to be superseded by WS-Agreement to some extent now.

3.1   WS-Agreement

The Web Services Agreement Specification [1] from the Open Grid Forum (OGF) describes a protocol for establishing an agreement on the usage of Services between a service provider and a consumer. It defines a language and a protocol to represent the services of providers, create agreements based on offers and monitor agreement compliance at runtime. An agreement defines a relationship between two parties that is dynamically established and dynamically managed. The objective of this relationship is to deliver a service by one of the parties. In the agreement each party agrees on the respective roles, rights and obligations. A provider in an agreement offers a service according to conditions described in the agreement. A consumer enters into an agreement with the intent of obtaining guarantees on the availability of one or more services from the provider. Agreements can also be negotiated by entities acting on behalf the provider and / or the consumer. An agreement creation process usually consists of three steps: The initiator retrieves a template from the responder, which advertises the types of offers the responder is willing to accept. The initiator then makes an offer, which is either accepted or rejected by the responder. WS-AgreementNegotiation which sits on top of WS-Agreement furthermore describes the re/negotiation of agreements. An agreement consists of the agreement name, its context and the agreement terms. The context contains information about the involved parties and meta-data such as the duration of the agreement. Agreement terms define the content of an agreement: Service Description Terms (SDTs) define the functionality that is delivered under an agreement. A SDT includes a domain-specific description of the offered or required functionality (the service itself). Guarantee Terms define assurance on service quality of the service described by the SDTs. They define Service Level Objectives (SLOs), which describe the quality of service aspects of the service that have to be fulfilled by the provider. The Web Services Agreement Specification allows the usage of any domain specific or standard condition expression language to define SLOs. The specification of domain-specific term languages is explicitly left open.

3.2   Web Service Level Agreement (WSLA)

WSLA [13] is a framework developed by IBM for specifying and monitoring Service Level Agreements (SLA) for Web Services. The framework is able to measure and monitor the QoS parameters of a Web Service and reports violations to the parties specified in the SLA. In a Web Service environment, services are usually subscribed dynamically and on demand. In this environment, automatic SLA monitoring and enforcement helps to fulfil the requirements of both service providers and consumers. WSLA provides a formal language based on XML Schema to express SLAs and a runtime architecture which is able to interpret this language. The runtime architecture comprises several SLA monitoring services, which may be outsourced to third parties (supporting parties) to ensure a maximum of objectivity. The WSLA language allows service customers and providers to define SLAs and their parameters and specify how they are measured. The WSLA monitoring services are automatically configured to enforce an SLA upon receipt.

The SLA management life cycle of WSLA consists of five distinct stages:

Negotiation / Establishment: In this stage an agreement between the provider and the consumer of a service is arranged and signed. An SLA document is generated.

SLA Deployment: The SLA document of the previous stage is validated and distributed to the involved components and parties.

Measurement and Reporting: In this stage the SLA parameters are computed by retrieving resource metrics from the managed resources and the measured SLA parameters are compared against the guarantees defined in the SLA.

Corrective Management Actions: If an SLO has been violated, corrective actions are carried out. These actions can be to open a trouble ticket or automatically communicate with the management system to solve potential performance problems. Before all actions regarding the managed system the Business Entity of the service provider is consulted to verify if the proposed actions are allowable.

SLA Termination: The parties of an SLA can negotiate the termination the same way the establishment is done. Alternatively, an expiration date can be specified in the SLA.

4. Usage of SLAs for Resource Management and Scheduling

4.1 Schedulers with WS-Agreement implementations

A number of projects already started implementing and using WS-Agreement for the definition of SLA. The projects are in different stages and not all build their implementation on the version 1.0 of WS-Agreement that has become a proposed recommendation in May 2007. However, it may be expected that all of the implementations move to this version within the next months.

4.1.1 VIOLA MetaScheduling Service (MSS).

Description: In the VIOLA project an optical testbed was implemented between multiple partners in Germany. The main goals were the test of advanced network architectures, development of software for user-driven dynamical provision of bandwidth and test of parallel applications. The project ended April 2007 but the MSS will be further developed in a number of other projects.

Grid ecosystems: Grid applications in VIOLA were run on three Linux-based PC-Clusters, a SUN-Cluster and a Cray X-D1 with a total peak performance of 900 GFLOPS. The VIOLA Grid is based on UNICORE. A single instance of a MetaScheduling Service integrated into the UNICORE middleware is able to perform co-ordinated CPU and network bandwidth reservation between the clusters in the Grid, enabling distributed applications on these systems [12].

WS-Agreement implementation: The VIOLA MetaScheduling Service MSS is responsible for negotiation of resource allocation with the local scheduling systems. It is implemented as a Web Service receiving a list of resources pre-selected by a resource selection service. The resource reservation is based on WS-Agreement. Network resources are reserved through a WS-Agreement Interface with the Adapter of the NRMS ARGON [8]. Resource reservations are negotiated through adapters with local scheduling systems also using WS-Agreement. Furthermore, the negotiation between the MSS and the UNICORE Client is based on WS-Agreement. When a UNICORE Client wants to make a reservation, it sends the resource request to the MSS as a WS-Agreement template. The MetaScheduling Service then negotiates a potential start time for the Job and requests reservation of the network and computational resources. After successful completion of this reservation the MSS sends an End Point Reference (EPR) of the created WS-Agreement back to the UNICORE Client.

4.1.2 AssessGrid openCCS.

Description: AssessGrid is a European project, which started in April 2006. AssessGrid introduces risk management and assessment to Grid computing to facilitate a wider adoption of Grid technologies in business and society. Risk assessment helps providers to make decisions on suitable SLA offers by relating the risk of failure to penalty fees. Similarly, end-users get knowledge about the risk of an SLA violation by a resource provider that helps to make appropriate decisions regarding acceptable costs and penalty fees. A broker is the matchmaker between end-users and providers. The broker provides a time / cost / risk optimised assignment of SLA requests to SLA offers.

Grid ecosystems: AssessGrid uses a distributed RMS called Computing Center Software (CCS or openCCS). CCS provides interfaces to UNICORE and Globus Toolkit 4 [6].

WS-Agreement implementation: In CCS a Grid-wide resource broker provides transparent access to Grid resources by querying resource providers on behalf of end-users. For the end-user the broker acts as a pre-selector of Grid resource providers. The WS-Agreement protocol is currently being implemented for openCCS. The major negotiable SLA parameters in openCCS are: General parameters like number of nodes, amount of memory, job runtime, Deadline for job completion, Policies on security or migration, and Fault tolerance requirements. A negotiator module is responsible for negotiating SLAs with external contractors using the WS-Agreement-Negotiation protocol. The negotiator defines the price, penalty and risk in the SLA according to policies. The risk is included in the SLA as an additional attribute. The Risk Assessor evaluates current monitoring information as well as aggregated statistical information to assess the risk for an SLA violation. WS-Agreement is used in the communication of the user with the broker, the user with the provider and the broker with the provider. The user interface modifies the SLA template of the broker or provider based on the user prerequisites such as hardware architecture and available libraries and sends it back to the broker or provider in order to receive SLA offers. Offers are presented to the end-user by the broker with price, risk of failure and penalty attributes. The end-user then either agrees or rejects such an offer.

4.1.3   ASKALON.

Description: ASKALON is a Grid project of the Distributed and Parallel Systems Group at the University of Innsbruck. The main goal is to simplify the development and optimisation of applications that can utilise a Grid for computation. ASKALON is used to develop and port scientific applications as workflows in the Austrian Grid project. The developers designed an XML-based Abstract Grid Workflow Language (AGWL) to compose job workflows.
Grid ecosystems: A resource manager remotely deploys software e.g. by using the Globus Toolkit middleware with the GridFTP protocol and the Globus Resource Allocation Manager (GRAM).
WS-Agreement implementation: SLAs can be made with the Grid resource for a specified time-frame by using the GridARM Agreement package. GridARM ensures that a defined capacity and capability is available in the agreed time-frame including parameters like number of CPUs. The agreement management consists of two parts: The AgreementNegotiator and the AgreementService. The AgreementNegotiator works as an agreement factory service. During the agreement negotiation process with the client, multiple agreement offers are created based on the information provided by the client as an AgreementTemplate. The client can accept one or more of the offers or reject all of them. The AgreementService manages particular agreements. After the negotiation process is finished, all interaction addressing e.g. agreement access and updates is done by interacting with the AgreementService using an EPR. In ASKALON, the client (consumer) always creates agreement templates and is therefore always the agreement initiator. The provider creates one or more offers which are accepted or rejected by the client.

4.1.4   Community Scheduler Framework (CSF).

Description: CSF [3] is an open source implementation of an OGSA-based meta-scheduler. It is developed by Platform Computing Inc. and the Jilin University. CSF is a set of modules that can be assembled to create a meta-scheduling system that accepts job requests and executes them using available Grid compute services. Grid level scheduling algorithms can for example include scheduling across multiple clusters within a VO, co-scheduling across multiple resource managers, scheduling based on SLAs and economic scheduling models.

Grid ecosystems: CSF supports the Globus Toolkit's Grid Resource Allocation and Management (GRAM) service. It is included in Globus Toolkit 4.0.

WS-Agreement implementation: CSF claims to support the WS-Agreement specification, however we are not aware of an implementation using WS-Agreement so far.

4.1.5   AgentScape.

Description: The Intelligent Interactive Distributed Systems (IIDS) group of the Vrije Universiteit Amsterdam develops the AgentScape framework that provides mobile agents access to computing resources on heterogeneous systems across the Internet [7].

Grid ecosystems: The negotiation of resource access for applications is based on WS-Agreements. A mediator called domain coordinator (DC) in AgentScape represents multiple autonomous hosts and communicates with the mobile agent on behalf of these nodes. Agents can negotiate their options with DCs of multiple domains, being able to select the DC that provides the best offer.

WS-Agreement implementation: The WS-Agreement based negotiation infrastructure of AgentScape allows agents to negotiate terms of conditions and quality of service of resource access with domain coordinators. Hosts providing resources are aggregated into virtual domains. The DC represents the hosts within a virtual domain in the negotiation process. The WS-Agreement interaction model is extended to allow a more sophisticated negotiation. In this extended negotiation model, hosts provide an agreement interface to their DC. The DC aggregates templates offered by hosts into composed templates and makes these available to agents. Agreement requests made by agents based on composed templates are received by the DC. The DC then negotiates an agreement with the hosts with the requested resources. The additional accept/reject interaction sequence allows agents to enter into negotiations with multiple providers and compare received offers. Resources that can be requested and used by agents include CPU time, communication bandwidth, amount of memory, disk space, web services that the agent is allowed to access and the number of calls of a web service that the agent is allowed to do. After the negotiation phase, a host manager monitors and controls the resource usage to ensure that agreements are met.

4.2 Schedulers planning WS-Agreement implementations

The Grid Scheduling Architecture research group (GSA-RG) of the Open Grid Forum and the research group for the Definition of a Grid scheduling architecture of the CoreGRID Institute on Resource Management and Scheduling address the overall architecture of scheduling in the Grid, the components and their interaction. In the GSA-RG a number of projects and groups are represented that have developed and maintain most of the systems described before. One of the outcomes of the work in the GSA-RG is considering WS-Agreement for the communication between Grid schedulers. The developers of the two systems described below are also participating in the GSA-RG and decided to join the effort of implementing WS-Agreement to provide interoperability with other Grid schedulers and to create a testbed to perform a number of demos and experiments.

4.2.1 Grid Resource Management System (GRMS).

Description: GRMS [5] is an open source meta-scheduling system, which is developed at the Poznan Supercomputing and Networking Center. It is a part of the Gridge Toolkit. GRMS allows developers to build and deploy resource management systems for large scale distributed computing infrastructures. The main goal of GRMS is to manage the process of remote job submission to various batch queueing systems, clusters or resources. GRMS supports dynamic resource selection, mapping and scheduling.

Grid ecosystems: The Gridge Toolkit components were tested with different version of the Globus Toolkit and other Grid middleware solutions. GRMS Service is a web service implemented in Java. GRMS can be used in conjunction with various queuing systems, such as Condor, PBS and LSF.

WS-Agreement implementation: GRMS developers are active in the OGF GSA-RG and plan to extend GRMS to support the evolving proposal for a Grid Scheduling Architecture.

4.2.2 GridWay.

Description: GridWay [4] is a meta-scheduler developed by the Distributed Systems Architecture Group at the University of Madrid. GridWay performs job execution management and resource brokering transparently to the end user. It furthermore adapts job execution to changing Grid conditions by providing e.g. fault recovery mechanisms, dynamic scheduling, on-request migration and opportunistic migration.

Grid ecosystems: GridWay provides interfaces to remote resources through Globus GRAM and therefore supports all remote platforms and resource managers (for example fork, PBS and LSF) compatible with Globus. GridWay supports the usage of the Job Submission Description Language (JSDL) as well as GridWay Job Template files.

WS-Agreement implementation: The GridWay meta-scheduler could be extended or used as a building block for more complex architectures that implement SLAs or advanced reservation. Gridway developers are active in the OGF GSA-RG and plan to support the evolving proposal for a Grid Scheduling Architecture.

4.2.3   CATNETS.

Description: CATNETS is a project of several universities and research centers across Europe with the objective to determine the applicability of a decentralized economic self-organization mechanism for resource allocation in application layer networks (ALN), which include Grid systems. The name CATNETS is based on an economic self-organization approach of a free market, the Catallaxy. CATNETS simulates the ALN environment by an economy, where the resources are for example processor time or storage space, while the economic actors are computers or web services. The application service and compute resource allocation of Application Layer Networks is broken down into two types of interrelated markets: A Grid resource market, where computational and data resources are traded and a service market where application services are traded. These services provide particular application functionality, e.g. query execution or molecule docking. In these separate markets complex services buy basic services, which buy raw resources. In this Catallaxy approach, the market is self-organizing which means that no centralized broker is required.

Grid ecosystems: In the prototype implementation the middleware is implemented as a set of simple, specialised agents using the light-weighted agents platform of the Decentralised Information Ecosystem Technologies (DIET) project. The agents provide for example access to markets, negotiations, object discovery and communication. The management of local resources is based on the WS-Resource Framework offered by Globus Toolkit 4. Middleware is further implemented using JXTA technology.

WS-Agreement implementation: WS-Agreement is used in the implementation of both the service market and the resource market. CATNETS defines separate bidding language for the service and the resource market, which are used by agents to submit bids for services or resources. These languages are mapped onto WS-Agreement via domain-specific schemes. The offers are encoded in XML using WS-Agreement and JSDL. In the resource market basic services can submit sell orders to the order books with WS-Agreement and the resource services can submit buy orders to the order books. After submission of all bids to the auctioneer, the allocation and the corresponding prices are determined, which results in an agreement. The activity on the service market is quite similar. The WS-Agreement implementation of CATNETS is technically integrated into the Triana workflow engine which allows visualisation of Agreement Templates and Offers. It also enables the workflow to be paused until an Agreement Offer has been confirmed.

4.3 Scheduler planning to use other SLA technology

4.3.1 eNanos Resource Broker.

Description: In the eNanos project [9] of the Barcelona Supercomputing Center a general purpose OGSI-compliant Grid resource broker is developed and maintained.

Grid ecosystems: The eNanos Grid resource broker [9] is implemented on top of Globus Toolkit (GT) and supports both GT2 and GT3. The broker focuses on resource discovery and management as well as dynamic policies management for job scheduling and resource selection. It utilises some of the Globus Toolkit services such as the Grid Security Infrastructure (GSI), the Grid Resource Allocation and Management (GRAM), Data Management Services and the Information Services, Monitoring and Discovery System (MDS).

Service Level Agreement implementation; The eNanos Grid resource broker provides dynamic policy management and multi-criteria user requirements. The user multi-criteria file is an XML document is composed of requirements and recommendations and can be used in policy evaluation. A requirement (hard attribute) is a restriction for the resource filtering and a recommendation (soft attribute) can be used to create a resource ranking for policy evaluation. Extending the Grid resource broker to include an SLA component is currently under discussion.

4.3.2 Grid superscalar.

Description: GRID superscalar [2] is a Grid programming environment developed and maintained at the Barcelona Supercomputing Center [10]. With GRID superscalar a sequential application composed of tasks of a certain granularity is automatically converted into a parallel application where the tasks are executed in different servers of a computational GRID. GRID superscalar provides automatic deployment of tasks. It sends and compiles code in the remote workers and the master.

Grid ecosystems: The current version is built on top of Globus 2.4, Globus 4.0 ssh/scp. For file transfer, security, etc. the Globus functionality is used.

Service Level Agreement implementation; When a task is ready for execution the scheduler tries to allocate a resource. In this case the broker receives a request and checks if a resource fulfils the constraints of this task. If more than one resource fulfils the constraints, the resource with minimum file transfer and execution time is selected. Extending Grid superscalar to include an SLA component is currently under discussion.

5.   Outlook

There are already a number of schedulers either using an SLA implementation to provide dedicated QoS for the user's applications. Others plan to provide an implementation of it in the near future, either for interoperability reasons and/or to provide a guaranteed level of service. Recent public discussions at the OGF GRAAP working group and at the 5th Meeting of the CoreGRID Institute on Resource Management and Scheduling point out that SLAs will play a stronger role in the domain of Grid RMS. WS-Agreement is now a proposed OGF recommendation for the expression and creation of SLAs. We expect that more Grid level schedulers or brokers will now adopt to using SLAs for two reasons: (i) interoperability with other Grid level schedulers and brokers and (ii) using a standardised interface for negotiating QoS between users and service providers.

Acknowledgments

Some of the work reported in this paper is funded by the German Federal Ministry of Education and Research through the VIOLA project under grant #01AK605L. This paper also includes work carried out jointly within the CoreGRID Network of Excellence funded by the European Commission's IST programme under grant #004265.

References

[1] A. Andrieux et al.   Web Services Agreement Specification (WS-Agreement), May 2007.   Open Grid Forum, Grid Forum Document GFD.107, available at <http://www.ogf.org/documents/GFD.107.pdf>.

[2] R. M. Badia, R. Sirvent, J. Labarta, and J. M. Perez. *Programming the GRID: An Imperative Language Based Approach*. American Scientific Publishers, January 2006.

[3] CSF - Community Scheduler Framework, 2007.   Web site, 15 June 2007 <http://www.globus.org/grid_software/computation/csf.php>.

[4] Gridway, 2007. Web site, 15 June 2007 <http://www.gridway.org/>.

[5] GRMS - Grid Resource Management System, 2007. available at the Gridge web site, 15 June 2007 <http://www.gridge.org>.

[6] A. Keller. openCCS: Computing Center Software. Technical report, Paderborn Center for Parallel Computing, 2007.

[7] D.G.A. Mobach, B.J. Overeinder, and F.M.T Brazier. A WS-Agreement Based Resource Negotiation Framework for Mobile Agents. *Scalable Computing: Practice and Experience*, 7 (1):23 – 36, 2006.

[8] M. Pilz et al.   ARGON - Allocation and Reservation in Grid-enabled Optic Networks.   VIOLA Project Report B2.4.1, VIOLA, March 2006.   <http://www.viola-testbed.de/fileadmin/VIOLA/reports/B2-4-1-allocation.pdf>.

[9] I. Rodero, J. Corbal‡n, R.M. Badia, and J. Labarta. eNANOS Grid Resource Broker. In *Proceedings of the European Grid Conference 2005*, volume 3470 of *LNCS*, pages 111 – 121, Amsterdam, Netherlands, February 2005. Springer.

[10] GRID superscalar, 2007. Web site, 15 June 2007 <http://www.bsc.es/grid/gridsuperscalar>.

[11] VIOLA – Vertically Integrated Optical Testbed for Large Application in DFN, 2007. Web site, 15 June 2007 <http://www.viola-testbed.de/>.

[12] Ph. Wieder, O. Wäldrich, and W. Ziegler. A meta-scheduling service for co-allocating arbitrary types of resources. In *Proceedings of the 6th International Conference, Parallel Processing and Applied Mathematics, PPAM 2005,*, volume 3911 of *LNCS*, pages 782 – 791, Poznan, Poland, September 2005. Springer.

[13] Web Service Level Agreements (WSLA) Project. Web site, 15 June 2007<http://researchweb.watson.ibm.com/wsla/documents.html/>.

[14] WSLA Language Specification, Version 1.0, January 2003, IBM Corporation, 2003. Web site, 15 June 2007 <http://www.research.ibm.com/wsla/WSLASpecV1-20030128.pdf>.

MANAGING VIOLATIONS IN SERVICE LEVEL AGREEMENTS

Omer F. Rana
School of Computer Science/Welsh eScience Centre
Cardiff University, UK
o.f.rana@cs.cardiff.ac.uk

Martijn Warnier, Thomas B. Quillinan, and Frances Brazier
Department of Computer Science,
VU University Amsterdam, The Netherlands
warnier@cs.vu.nl
tb.quillinan@few.vu.nl
frances@cs.vu.nl

Dana Cojocarasu
Norwegian Research Center for Computers and Law
University of Oslo, Norway
d.i.cojocarasu@jus.uio.no

Abstract   A Service Level Agreement (SLA) represents an agreement between a service user and a provider in the context of a particular service provision. SLAs contain Quality of Service properties that must be maintained by a provider. These are generally defined as a set of Service Level Objectives (SLOs). These properties need to be measurable and must be monitored during the provision of the service that has been agreed in the SLA. The SLA must also contain a set of penalty clauses specifying what happens when service providers fail to deliver the pre-agreed quality. Although significant work exists on how SLOs may be specified and monitored, not much work has focused on actually identifying how SLOs may be impacted by the choice of specific penalty clauses. The participation of a trusted mediator may be necessary to resolve conflicts between involved parties. The main focus of the paper is on identifying particular penalty clauses that can be associated with an SLA.

Keywords: Service Level Agreements, violations, penalty clauses, WS-Agreement

1.   Introduction

A Service Level Agreement (SLA) represents an agreement between a client and a provider in the context of a particular service provision. SLAs may be between two parties, for instance, a single client and a single provider, or between multiple parties, for example, a single client and multiple providers. SLAs generally specify performance related properties, generally referred to as Quality of Service (QoS) terms, that must be maintained by a provider during service provision. These properties need to be measurable and must be monitored during the provision of the service that has been agreed in the SLA – and are referred to as Service Level Objectives (SLOs). The SLA must also contain a set of penalty clauses when service providers fail to deliver the pre-agreed quality. Although significant work exists on how SLOs may be specified and monitored [10], not much work has focused on actually identifying how SLOs may be impacted by the choice of specific penalty clauses. The participation of a trusted mediator may be necessary to resolve conflicts between involved parties. Automating this conflict resolution process clearly provides substantial benefits. Different outcomes are possible. These include monetary penalties, impact on potential future agreements between the parties and the enforced re-running of the agreed service. While it may seem reasonable to penalise SLA non-compliance, there are a number of concerns when issuing such penalties. For example, consider a service provider violation in a multi-provider SLA: determining whether the service provider is the only party that should be penalised, or determining the type of penalty that are applied to each party would be required. Enforcement in the various legal systems of different countries can be tackled through stipulating a 'choice of law clause', that is, a clause indicating expressly which countries' laws will be applied in case a conflict between the provider and the client would occur. Specific 'legal templates' [4] can be used to further refine such clauses. This paper focuses on identifying particular penalty clauses that can be associated with an SLA and on identifying how penalty clauses impact the choice of SLOs. The next section discusses the types of violations that can be used in SLAs. Section 3 discusses the type of penalties that can be used. An example from resource sharing in an electronic market (based on work in the CATNETs project [4]) is presented in Section 4 and a mapping to the WS-Agreement specification is proposed in Section 5. The paper ends with discussions and conclusions.

2.   Types of Violations

An SLA can go through a number of stages once it has been specified. Assuming that the SLA is initiated by a client application, these stages include: discovering providers; defining the SLA; agreeing on the terms of the SLA (in addition to the penalties if the SLOs are not met); monitoring SLA violations;

terminating an SLA; enforcement of penalties for SLA violation. Monitoring plays an important role in determining whether an SLA has been violated, and determining the particular penalty clause that should be invoked as a consequence.

Monitoring SLA violations begins once an SLA has been defined. A copy of the SLA must be maintained by both the client and the provider. It is necessary to distinguish between an 'agreement date' (forming of an SLA) and an 'effective date' (subsequently providing a service based on the SLOs that have been agreed). For instance, a request to invoke a service based on the SLOs may be undertaken at a time much later than when the SLOs were agreed. During provision it is necessary to determine whether the terms agreed in the SLA have been complied with during provision. In this context, a monitoring infrastructure is used to identify the difference between the agreed upon SLO and the value that was actually delivered during service provisioning – which is 'trusted' by both the client and the provider.

From a legal perspective, monitoring is a prerequisite for contract enforcement. In the present context, the consequences of breaching the agreed SLOs is a basic requirement. In addition, service clients base the reputations of, and their trust in, service providers largely on the supported monitoring infrastructure. In the context of SLAs three types of monitoring infrastructures can be distinguished: a trusted third party (TTP); a trusted module at the service provider; and a module on the client site. In most typical situations a TTP module provides all the necessary functionality for a monitoring service.

One of the main issues that the provider and the consumer will have to agree during the SLA negotiation is the penalty scheme. It is also necessary to define what constitutes a violation. Depending on the importance of the violated SLO and/or the consequences of the violation, the provider in breach may avoid dispatch or obtain a diminished monetary sanction from the client. As both the service provider and the client are ultimately businesses (rather than consumers), they are free to decide what kind of sanctions they will associate to the various types of SLA breaches, in accordance with the importance of the SLO that was not fulfilled. According to the Principles of European Contract Law [3], the term 'unfulfilment' is to be interpreted as comprising: (1) defective performance (parameter monitored at lower level); (2) late performance (service provided at the appropriate level but with unjustified delays); (3) no performance (service not provided at all). Based on these descriptions we define the following broad categories:

- 'All-or-nothing' provisioning: provisioning of a service meets all the SLOs – that is, all of the SLO constraints must be satisfied for a successful delivery of a service;

- 'Partial' provisioning: provisioning of a service meets some of the SLOs – that is, some of the SLO constraints must be satisfied for a successful delivery of a service;

- 'Weighted Partial' provisioning: provision of a service meets SLOs that have a weighting greater than a threshold (identified by the client).

Monitoring can be used to detect whether an SLA has been violated. Typically such violations result in a complete failure – making SLA violations an 'all-or-nothing' process. In such an event a completely new SLA needs to be negotiated, possibly with another service provider, which requires additional effort on both the client and the service provider. Based on this all-or-nothing approach, it is necessary for the provider to satisfy all of the SLOs. This equates to a conjunction of SLO terms. An SLA may contain several SLOs, where some (for example, at least two CPUs) may be more important than others (for example, more then 100 MB hard disk space). During the SLA negotiation phase, the importance of the different SLOs for the client must be established. Clients (and service providers) can then react differently according to the importance of the violated SLO. In the WS-Agreement specification [1], the importance of particular terms is captured through the use of a 'Business Value'. Weighted metrics can also be used to ensure a flexible and fair sanctionatory mechanism in case an SLA violation occurs. Thus, instead of terminating the SLA altogether it might be possible to renegotiate, for example, with the same service provider, the part of the SLA that is violated. Again, the more important the violated SLO, the more difficult it will be to renegotiate (part of) the SLA.

3. Penalties

The use of penalty clauses in SLAs leads to two concerns: what types of penalty clauses can be used; and how, if at all, can these be included in SLAs. The 'burden of proof' and the interest in demonstrating that the agreed SLOs have been violated lie with the main beneficiary of the service, that is, in the service client. An important issue that should be considered when designing 'penalty schemes' is that behind the imposition of any contractual sanctions lies the idea that faulty behaviour of a provider should be deterred. As such, it is always possible for the service provider to contest its liability in the unwanted result (SLA breach) and claim that a 'force majeure' situation occurred. Although the situation is impossible to be dealt with through automatic enforcement, monitoring the message exchanges among the provider and the client can indicate whether the SLA violation was the consequence of a 'misconduct' from the provider (either intentional or negligent). The parties are advised to stipulate either in the SLA or in the associated Collaboration Agreement how they choose to deal with the situation where the provider's faulty behaviour cannot be documented, and a 'force majeure' situation did occur. A penalty clause in an SLA may consist of the following:

- a decrease in the agreed payment for using the service, that is, a direct financial sanction;

- a reduction in price to the consumer, along with additional compensation for any subsequent interaction;

- a reduction in the future usage of the provider's service by the consumer;

- a decrease in the reputation of the provider – and subsequent propagation of this value to other clients.

During the negotiation phase, client and provider can agree on a direct financial sanction. Usually, the amount to be paid depends on the value of the loss suffered by the client through the violation (that should be covered entirely) and if agreed, a fix sum of money that has to be paid as 'fine' for the unwanted behaviour. Due to the potential difficulties in proving and documenting the financial value of the loss, during the negotiation phase the parties may choose an 'agreed payment for non performance', that is, a fixed sum of money that will have to be paid upon non-performance, regardless of the fact that no financial loss was suffered by the client. The service provider can deposit the negotiated fine in escrow with a TTP, who acts as a mediator, before the service provision commences. Escrow is a bond, deed, deposit, etc., kept in the custody of a third party, taking effect, or made available, only when a specified condition has been fulfilled[1]. On successful completion of the service provision (based on the SLA) the TTP returns the deposit to the service provider. Otherwise, the client receives the deposit as compensation for the SLA violation. Notice that a trusted monitor is required for this, as a client can never prove by itself that an SLA was (partially) violated. For automated use, a micro-payment [7] system is required – such as Paypal. Another possibility is that a client reduces its usage of services from a provider that violated an SLA. If the economic position of the client is strong enough, this can be a valid strategy. A third kind of penalty clause can lead to a change in the reputation of a provider [9, 12]. In such a system the reputation of service providers that violate SLAs will drop. In this case special care needs to be taken that the reputation of a service provider is correctly determined. Both reputation building, using dummy clients that 'praise' a service provider, and slandering reputations, where dummy clients (unjustly) complain about a service provider, form serious threats in reputation based systems. In the negotiation phase of the SLA, both service provider and client can agree on the reputation mechanism to use.

---

[1] from *Concise Oxford English Dictionary, Revised 10 Edition.*

4.   Resource Sharing Use Case

Consider a market of computational service providers, where each provider may use a combination of resources to meet a particular set of metrics of interest to a client. In a service market, the parameters of interest may be of three types: latency (time it takes to get a result back from the provider), execution time (total time it takes to execute a service at the provider), and execution cost (the monetary value associated with running a service by the provider). The resources (R) that may be used by the provider are defined as a four tuple – consisting of: number of CPUs (C), primary memory (M), disk storage (D), and time interval (δt) – δt represents the interval between the start time and the end time over which the resource is available. A resource provider is required to define their capacity using these four parameters. Generally a client does not care what resources are used, as long as their application performance constraints are met. Conversely, a service provider needs to identify which resources need to be used to achieve these metrics. Two types of SLAs co-exist in this scenario – an SLA between an application client and the service provider, and an SLA between a service provider and one or more resource owners. In this example we use only four parameters to characterise access to a resource – however this model can be expanded to include additional attributes that have been specified within the Common Information Model (CIM) [6]from DMTF.

The SLA between the service provider and the resource owner may be defined using the terms: $(C, M, D, \delta t) = R$ – and may be offered by a single provider, or it may be the aggregate capability of a group of providers. Properties of each R_i are published in a registry service—the resource owner being responsible for updating these values in the registry. The registry may also contain an aggregate resource description, describing the combined capability of multiple providers. After having discovered a provider to interact with, a client asks the provider for an SLA template. The template contains those parameters that the provider understands and can monitor. Depending on the type of description scheme being used, the client now adds constraints associated with parameters that have been identified in the SLA. This 'offer' is now sent to the provider—who may either agree with the request, or make a counter offer. A negotiation process is initiated, which eventually results in either an agreement or a failure. An example of an SLA in this context would be: $SLA_1 = (2, 512MB, 2GB, (20071001190000), (20071001191000))$— indicating a request for a resource with 2 CPUs, 512MB of RAM, 2GB of disk on October 1, 2007 from 19:00 to 19:10. Such a scenario also occurs in many data centre applications today [13].

The SLA between the client and the service provider is often harder to specify, as it can contain application specific terms as SLOs. As outlined in [5], given an SLO of 'average response time' to be less than 10 seconds, the configuration with CPU assignment of 20% fails to meet the SLO, but a CPU assignment of 90% meets the SLO but the system is over-provisioned (as only 50% is needed to meet the SLO). Therefore, identifying the types of provisioning that is needed to ensure that the SLO is not violated, but that excessive resources are not used to address a particular SLO requirement is important. A mapping is needed between the requirements identified in an SLA between a client and a service provider, and one between a service provider and a resource.

It is necessary when specifying an SLO to also specify the penalty that would be incurred by a provider if the SLO was not met. Often a gradual structure of penalties is defined, whereby SLO violations incur fines, and a certain number of violations within a particular time period (such as a week or a month), gives a client the right to terminate access to the service. A penalty identifies the compensation that would be made to a service client if the SLO has been violated. Examples of penalty clauses that may be associated with an SLA between a service provider and a resource owner may be as follows [2]:

- If 90% of the number of requested CPUs, and 90% of requested memory have been delivered, then these SLOs have not been violated. For provisioning below 90% of CPU and memory, and for each percent, the provider must incur a penalty of α monetary units.

- If 90% of the number of requested CPUs and 90% of the requested RAM and 80% of the requested disk have not been delivered, then for each deviation from 90% (for CPU and RAM) and 80% for disk, the penalty to the provider is β monetary units.

For an SLA between a client and a service provider, a service execution time may be used as the SLO, then the penalty clause would be written as:

- If 90% of the execution times are not in the 2 second range, then for each deviation from the 98% of between 2 and 5 seconds, the penalty to the provider is β monetary units, and for each percent of the 98% of execution times more than 5 seconds, the penalty is γ, and for other percents that are more than 5 seconds, the penalty is α monetary units.

A service provider must evaluate the penalty it would incur from the client if a resource owner was not able to achieve their SLOs.

5. Mapping to WS-Agreement

The WS-Agreement specification [1] provides an XML schema to represent the top-level structure of an agreement between two parties. This includes concepts such as an agreement identifier, guarantee terms in an agreement etc. A simple protocol is provided which allows offers, acceptance and rejection of an agreement to also be captured. An 'Agreement Factory' is used as an interface to create a new instance of an agreement, with the use of 'creation constraints' as an optional description of the types of agreements that a provider is willing to accept. An important factor in this discussion is the use of the 'Business Value' (BV) and 'Preference' specification made available in WS-Agreement. A BV allows a provider to assess the importance of a given SLO to a client. Similarly, a provider may indicate to a client the confidence that a provider has in meeting a particular SLO. Based on the specification, a BV may be expressed using a `penalty` or `reward` type. The penalty is used to indicate the likely compensation that will be required of a provider if the SLO with which the penalty is associated is not met. We may weigh the importance of an SLO with reference to other SLOs that constitute an agreement. Notice that a BV list consists of both a penalty *and* a reward – to enable a provider to assess the risk/benefit of violating a particular SLO. `Preference` is used in the BV list to provide a more detailed sub-division of a business value for different alternatives that may exist. Essentially, `Preference` allows a service provider to consider different possible alternatives for reaching the same overall SLO requirement. For instance, in the example of section 4, if a client requests access to a particular number of CPUs, it is possible to fulfil this requirement based on CPUs from one or more resource owners. `Preference` allows the provider to chose between the available options to improve its own revenue or meet other constraints that it has (provided this is not prohibited by the service provision agreement or other agreements between the parties involved).

A `Penalty` in WS-Agreement may be associated with one or more SLOs, and occurs when these SLO(s) are violated. According to the WS-Agreement specification, assessment of a violation needs to be monitored over an `AssessmentInterval` – which is defined either as a time interval or some integer count. Essentially, this means that a penalty can only be imposed if an SLO is violated within a particular time window, or if a certain number of service requests/accesses fail. `ValueUnit` identifies the type of penalty – in this case a monetary value – that must be incurred by the service provider if the violation occurs. In the current WS-Agreement specification, the concept of a `ValueExpr` is vague – being an integer, float or a 'user defined expression'. This implies that a user and provider may determine a dynamic formula that dictates the penalty amount depending on the particular context in which the WS-Agreement is being used.

```
<wsag:Penalty>
    <wsag:AssesmentInterval>
        <wsag:TimeInterval>xs:duration</wsag:TimeInterval> |
        <wsag:Count>xs:positiveInteger</wsag:Count>
    </wsag:AssesmentInterval>
    <wsag:ValueUnit>xs:string</wsag:ValueUnit>
    <wsag:ValueExpr>xs:any</wsag:ValueExpr>
</wsag:Penalty>
```

In WS-Agreement the ability to also specify a Reward, in addition to a penalty, provides an incentive mechanism for a provider to meet the SLO. Based on the example in Section 4, a penalty clause for the SLA between the client and the service provider would be as indicated below – specifying that four incorrect invocations of a service would lead to a penalty of $500.

```
<wsag:AssesmentInterval>
     <wsag:Count>4</wsag:Count>
 </wsag:AssesmentInterval>
<wsag:ValueUnit>US Dollar</wsag:ValueUnit>
<wsag:ValueExpr>500</wsag:ValueExpr>
```

The extent to which terms and conditions specified in WS-Agreements are legally binding is currently the subject of research [4]. One basic element is that agreements need to be confirmed by both parties. As such, penalties in a WS-Agreement, for example, cannot be one-sided. The WS-Agreements needs to be confirmed by the client. The lack of this confirmation makes WS-Agreement restricted in the context of legal perspective, as explored by Mobach et al. [11].

6. Discussion & Conclusions

The use of penalties in SLAs has obvious benefits for both clients and service providers. Monetary sanctions and reputation-based mechanisms can both be used as, pre-agreed, penalties. It has been shown how the WS-Agreement specification can be used to specify penalties and rewards, in the context of a particular resource sharing scenario.

A particular focus has been discussion of the types of violations that can occur in SLOs during provisioning. Based on European legal contract law, we identify three types of violations that may lead to penalties – an 'all or nothing', 'a partial' or a 'weighted partial' violation of a contract. An observation in this work is that flagging a violations incurs a cost for the client (as well as the provider). It is therefore in the interest of the client to continue with service provision, even if some of the SLOs are not being observed fully – a trade-off discussed in this paper. A key contribution of this work is a model that demonstrates how a client may provide weighting to certain SLOs over others, the legal basis on which this model is based (as outlined in Section 3) and subsequently how this approach can be used alongside WS-Agreement.

Acknowledgements

This research is in part supported by the NLnet Foundation, http://www.nlnet.nl and in part is funded by the NWO TOKEN program. Part of this work is also supported by the European Commission Future and Emerging Technologies programme under the IST-2006-027004 "S3MS" and the IST-FP6-003769 "CATNETS" projects.

References

[1] A. Andrieux, K. Czajkowski, A. Dan, K. Keahey, H. Ludwig, T. Nakata, J. Pruyne, J. Rofrano, S. Tuecke, and M. Xu. Web Services Agreement Specification (WS-Agreement). *GRAAP Working Group at the Open Grid Forum*, September 2006.

[2] ARAD Automatic Real-time Decision-making, 2002. available at:http://www.haifa.il.ibm.com/projects/software/arad/papers/ARAD-May-2002.pdf.

[3] M. J. Bonell. The UNIDROIT Principles of International Commercial Contracts and the Principles of European Contract Law: Similar Rules for the Same Purposes?, 1996.

[4] M. Boonk, F. Brazier, D. de Groot, M. van Stekelenburg, A. Oskamp, and M. Warnier. Conditions for Access and Use of Legal Document Retrieval Web Services. In *Proceedings of the Eleventh International Conference on Artificial Intelligence and Law (ICAIL'07)*. ACM Press, 2007.

[5] Y. Chen, S. Iyer, X. Liu, D. Milojicic, and A. Sahai. SLA Decomposition: Translating Service Level Objectives to System Level Thresholds. *HPL-2007-17*, 2007.

[6] DMTF, "Common Information Model". See Web site at: http://www.dmtf.org/standards/cim/. Last accessed: June 2007.

[7] R. Hauser, M. Steiner, and M. Waidner. *Micro-payments Based on IKP*. IBM TJ Watson Research Center, 1996.

[8] L. Joita, O. F. Rana, P. Chacin, I. Chao, F. Freitag, L. Navarro, and O. Ardaiz. Application Deployment on Catallactic Grid Middleware. *IEEE DS-Online*, 7(12), 2006.

[9] S. D. Kamvar, M. T. Schlosser, and H. Garcia-Molina. The eigentrust algorithm for reputation management in p2p networks. In *Proc. of the 12th Int. World Wide Web Conference*, Budapest, Hungary, May 20-24 2003. ACM Press.

[10] A. Keller and H. Ludwig. The WSLA Framework: Specifying and Monitoring Service Level Agreements for Web Services. *Journal of Network and Systems Management*, 11(1):57–81, 2003.

[11] D. G. A. Mobach, B. J. Overeinder, and F. M. T. Brazier. A WS-Agreement Based Resource Negotiation Framework for Mobile Agents. *Scalable Computing: Practice and Experience*, 7(1):23–36, 2006.

[12] P. Resnick, K. Kuwabara, R. Zeckhauser, and E. Friedman. Reputation systems. *Communications of the ACM*, 43(12):45–48, 2000.

[13] E. Wustenhoff. Service Level Agreement in the Data Center. *Sun Microsystems Professional Series*, April 2002.

OPERATING VIRTUAL ORGANIZATIONS USING BIPARTITE SERVICE LEVEL AGREEMENTS

Hubert Hérenger, René Heek, and Roland Kübert
High Performance Computing Center Stuttgart (HLRS), Allmandring 30, 70569 Stuttgart, Germany
{herenger,heek,kuebert}@hlrs.de

Mike Surridge
IT Innovation Centre, 2 Venture Road, Southampton, SO16 7NP, UK
ms@it-innovation.soton.ac.uk

Abstract   Virtual Organizations are evolving as a means of inter-domain collaboration. The reason for building Virtual Organizations can be summarized as sharing resources and enabling collaboration between service providers from different organizational units. Within this paper we will show that bipartite Service Level Agreements can be used as a basic principle for the management and operation of Virtual Organizations. We show that our approach to build Virtual Organizations on top of bipartite Service Level Agreements leads to agile and dynamic Virtual Organizations, in contrast to most of the well-established models which regard Virtual Organizations as rather static in nature.

Keywords: Virtual Organizations, bipartite, Service Level Agreements, lifecycle, federation

1.   Introduction

The term Virtual Organization (VO) is mentioned in the Grid community for the first time in [1] and is described as a mechanism for controlled resource sharing. But neither this definition of the term VO nor any other single definition is accepted in general. The Next Generation Grids Expert Group defines a VO as "an abstraction for resource sharing and collaboration action across multiple administrative domains" [2]. Although this is an intuitive definition, it seems to be very unspecific. In contrast, the NextGRID project has developed a very specific understanding of a VO that will be presented in this chapter. We will give an overview of NextGRID VOs in general before explaining the different types of Virtual Organizations that have been identified. We then give an explanation of a VO's lifecycle, whose understanding is of utmost importance for the following explanations. In the following text, we call entities participating in a VO "members" or "services", regardless of them being service providers, service consumers or a hybrid service both providing and consuming services.

2.   NextGRID SLA Management

Before introducing the SLA and VO specific parts of our work we want to give a brief overview on the relevant components in the NextGRID Architecture [5].

2.1   Bipartite Service Level Agreements

Service collaboration is in general achieved using Service Level Agreements, where an SLA is a legally binding contract between two or more parties. From an organizational point of view in most of the time, one of the parties can be seen as a service consumer while the other parties can be seen as service providers.

In NextGRID, it has been decided to only employ bipartite SLAs, i.e. SLAs which are established between two partners. This provides important architectural simplifications when seeking to implement a managed Grid. However, it also means that VO must be realised without using multi-party SLAs. The focus of this paper is to show how this can be achieved, using the concept of SLA federation which is also described.

NextGRID SLAs must adhere to the NextGRID SLA Schema shown in Figure 1. The top-level structure is modeled after the WS-Agreement structure [10], while the metrics use some of the elements defined in the WSLA specification [11]. Principally, NextGRID SLAs consist of three building blocks: the SLA's name, a context part and a terms part. The name may be used to uniquely identify an SLA. The context contains information about all parties participating in an SLA; there may only be one service customer and one service provider,

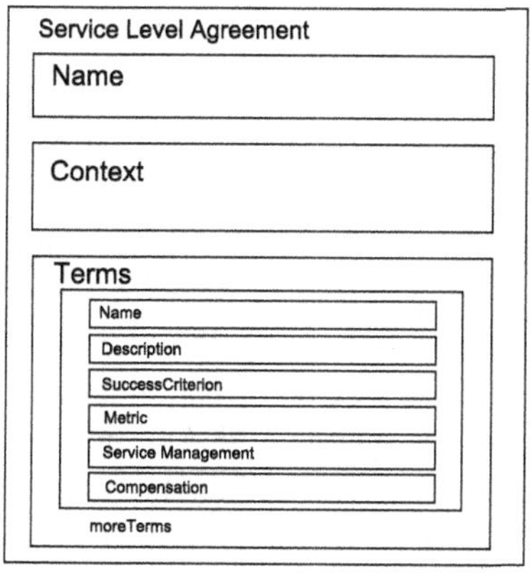

Figure 1. Structure of a NextGRID SLA

regardless of their organizational state, but there may be additional supporting parties defined. Be aware, that the restriction of the context information is what we have called previously a bipartite SLA. In contrast to the other elements, which set the scope of an SLA, terms can be seen as the content of an SLA, describing desired qualities, lifetimes and payment issues.

Applying basic federation primitives to established bipartite SLAs in order to infer new bipartite SLAs results in some additional input to bipartite SLAs peculiar to federation mechanisms. We introduced a new property which controls the allowance of federation from an already established bipartite SLA. This is due to the fact that legal implications might force a service provider to inhibit deduction of new SLAs through usage of basic federation principles from SLAs the service provider has previously negotiated. Furthermore, this property can be employed to reduce the derivation depth of inferred SLAs.

```
<Metric name="FederationAcceptance" defn="cc:FederationAcceptanceType">
  <Target unit="boolean" dialect="http://www.w3.org/TR/xquery/">
   <SuccessMeasure>
    True
   </SuccessMeasure>
  </Target>
</Metric>
```

Figure 2. Metric for controlling federation

Figure 2 shows the metric controlling the allowance of federation. If the *SuccessMeasure* is set to *False*, the federation of SLAs from the SLA encapsulating this metric is not allowed.

2.2   NextGRID Negotiation Protocol

The negotiation of an SLA in NextGRID has to follow a specific protocol. The NextGRID Negotiation Protocol is a so-called Discrete-Offer-Protocol which can also be seen as a one-phase negotiation. Using this protocol, a customer sends a request for an "offer", called a "bid", to a service provider's negotiator component. This bid is based on information received during a discovery phase. The negotiation component checks the provider's SLA repository to see if he has a template for an SLA which corresponds to the bid received from the customer. Determining exactly when an SLA template matches a certain bid is entirely up to the service provider or rather the negotiation component. If an SLA template has been selected by the negotiator, the customer's contact details are filled in, all necessary adaptions in regard to the bid are performed and the resulting SLA offer is sent to the customer; if no template has been selected by the provider, the customer will receive an information that he cannot obtain an offer for the previously sent bid. If the customer receives an offer, he has the chance to review it. If he agrees with the offer, he will send an acceptance message to the service provider's negotiator, otherwise he will send a reject message. An acceptance message from the customer means that the offer has now been turned into a bipartite SLA. Further information on the NextGRID negotiation protocol and related aspects is given in [5], [6] and [7].

3.   Federation Principles

It was previously mentioned that every interaction between two services in a NextGRID VO is governed by a bipartite SLA. Federation principles help to reduce the number of bipartite SLAs which are directly established between two partners by providing a mechanism for deriving new bipartite SLAs based on already established bipartite SLAs. If a new bipartite SLA is created using federation principles, we refer to this SLA as being an inferred SLA. Three basic federation principles have been identified ([12], [13]).

3.1   Encapsulation

Encapsulation is the act of providing a service to a consumer using a second service, with no direct interaction between the consumer of the first service and the provider of the second service.

Figure 3.   Resource Encapsulation

As can be seen in Figure 3, there is no direct relationship between the consumer (SC) and the service provider b (SP b) since the SLAs established by service provider a (SP a) between SC and SP a and SP a and SP b are not related. However, the effect is to federate resources from SP a and SP b in order to provide service to the consumer (SC).

3.2 Orchestration

Orchestration arises when a common consumer of two services requires them to interact directly with each other. The basic scenario is for a consumer (SC) to invoke one of two services (SP a) passing it an instruction that causes it to invoke the other (SP b). Figure 4 shows the basic orchestration scenario.

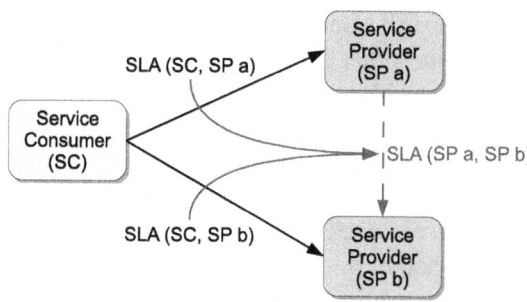

Figure 4.   Resource Orchestration

The effect of orchestration is the same as encapsulation: to federate resources and to make them available to the consumer. The difference is that federation is initiated by the consumer, while in encapsulation it is initiated by the first service provider and may be completely hidden from the consumer. In an orchestration, the consumer already has bipartite SLAs established between himself and the two corresponding service providers, and it is possible to derive the bipartite SLA governing the orchestrated interaction from the already existing SLAs.

3.3 Sharing

Sharing arises when a consumer a (SC a) shares his access to service (SP) with another service consumer b (SC b). This does not federate resources, as in the encapsulation or orchestration principles, but rather federates consumers as shown in Figure 5.

Common to both resource orchestration and sharing is the fact that all collaborating parties are aware of federation taking place.

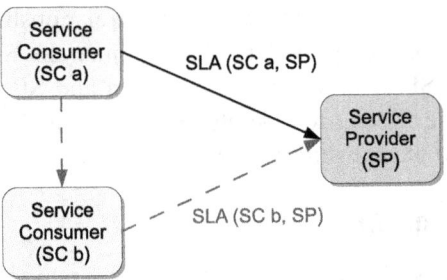

Figure 5.   Resource Sharing

4.   Virtual Organizations

The NextGRID project defines a VO as follows [8]: "A NextGRID VO is defined by a set of bipartite Service level Agreements (SLAs) established between VO members such that all VO members are connected directly or indirectly through bipartite SLAs. The boundary of a VO is either defined by SLA paths combined with SLA visibility, unique VO IDs or membership management services. Having established at least one bipartite SLA with some VO member, the customer of a VO is a member of the respective VO as well. Any pair of VO members can directly interact if a corresponding bipartite SLA is available, no matter whether this SLA is negotiated or inferred."

The difference between negotiated and inferred SLAs lies therein that negotiation is a complex process and can take up a long time, whereas the step of inferring new bipartite SLAs can be done much faster and with less overhead.

4.1   Types of Virtual Organizations

It is obvious that many forms of Virtual Organizations exist. Two main types which represent two extremes in a very wide range of possibilities emerged from early work on Grids. The "Big VO" arose naturally in early work on scientific Grids [1], and are also found in some industrial collaborations such as the supply chains for large engineering projects. The "Fast VO" came out of early work on Web Service Grids [3]. Since then a wider range of possibilities has been identified that have both "Big" and "Fast" characteristics to varying degrees, and work to classify these is ongoing [4].

The "Fast VO" is characterized by the fact that service providers do not collaborate directly with other VO members. Instead, they provide services to customers, who may initiate the federation of services from different providers (and hence collaboration between service providers) as required for their applications. In a "Fast VO" service providers normally have bipartite Service Level Agreements (SLA) with their customers but not with each other, making it easy to set up short-lived collaborations as required.

Since NextGRID management is based on bipartite SLAs [5], it is trivial to implement "Fast VO" using the NextGRID architecture. However, the NextGRID architecture must be able to support a wide range of Grids including more traditional "Big VO" configurations. Architectural experiments were therefore carried out to find and validate a way to do this.

A "Big VO" is characterized by the fact that every VO member has a negotiated bipartite SLA established with each other VO member. Obviously, this type of VO requires the negotiation of $n(n-1)/2$ bipartite SLAs in a VO consisting of n members. While this number of negotiated SLAs might be acceptable for smaller "Big VO"s , this VO type does not scale well since the number of negotiated SLAs lies in $\mathcal{O}(n^2)$ in general. Figure 6 shows an exemplary Virtual Organization of the "Big VO" type with 6 members and the maximum of 15 negotiated bipartite SLAs. Henceforth, SLAs are plotted as tuples in the remaining figures for ease of readability.

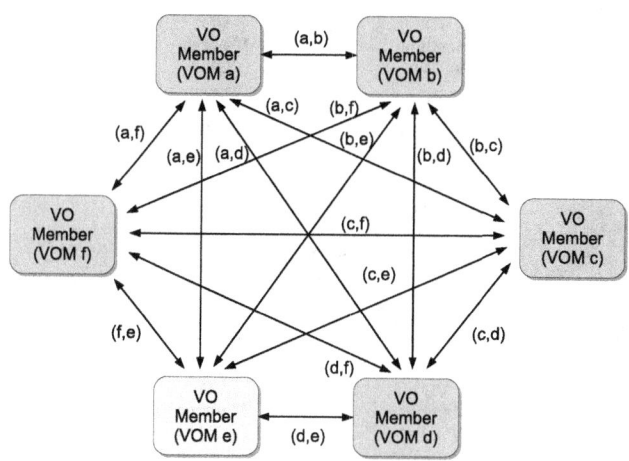

Figure 6. An exemplary "Big VO"

One solution to limiting the excessive growth in the number of negotiated bipartite SLAs is service federation [8]. Through the use of service federation, the number of negotiated SLAs can be reduced dramatically. Even more so if nested service federation is allowed, because then it is only necessary to have a chain of negotiated SLAs connecting all VO Members in a line. This reduces the necessary number of negotiated SLAs to $n-1$, resulting in a general number of negotiated SLAs which lies in $\mathcal{O}(n)$. This, however, comes with the price of building a huge dependency tree on the negotiated SLAs. Cancelling a negotiated SLA leads to the cancellation of all SLAs inferred from the originally negotiated SLA. This ensures that rights, which have been originally granted through the negotiated SLA, are revoked when the original SLA is cancelled.

Of course, this does not prevent renegotiations. Furthermore, it is often desired to have a central management instance in a Virtual Organization.

This leads to yet another way of building a "Big VO" on top of bipartite SLAs by introducing an additional VO member which manages all interactions (Figure 7). The introduction of such a central management instance limits the number of negotiated bipartite SLAs to $n - 1$ as well, but additionally resolves the problem of building a huge dependency tree on the negotiated SLAs. If a negotiated SLA is canceled, only collaboration with the VO member connected through this SLA is lost. As every VO member must have a negotiated bipartite SLA established with the central management instance, access to any other VO member can be achieved by applying basic service federation. To gain access to any other VO member, only one federation step is required. Thereby, the federated bipartite SLAs are directly inferred from negotiated SLAs and thus have not to be negotiated.

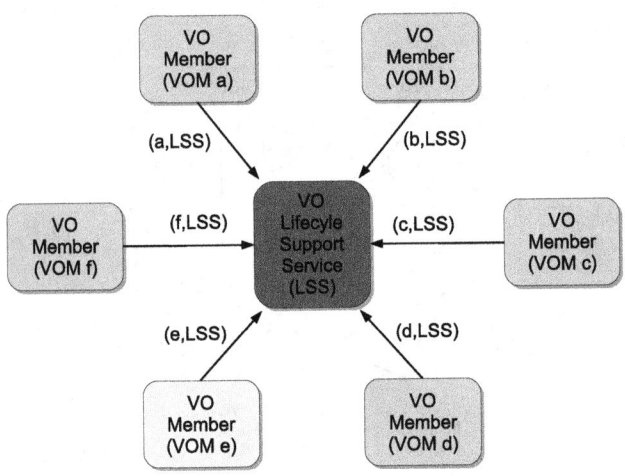

Figure 7.   An exemplary centralized "Big VO"

In the NextGRID project, this central component is called VO Lifecycle Support Service (LSS). It is a regular NextGRID service provider but not a regular core component of the NextGRID architecture.

4.2   Virtual Organization Lifecycle Phases

A Virtual Organization lives through different phases, which we call Lifecycle Phases. We propose the following four Lifecycle Phases:

Identification During this phase potential services, that means VO members, are discovered. Service discovery may be a process which occurs in multiple steps, starting with a potentially large list of candidate services which is gradually reduced to a small subset of services which will be selected as service providers for the VO. During this phase, SLA templates which a service provider offers may be taken into account.

Formation After the candidate services have been selected, a series of steps has to be accomplished before a VO may enter its productive phase. Bipartite SLAs have to be negotiated, supporting VO services have to be created and VO level policies and rules need to be distributed.

Operation & Evolution In this phase VO operations are taking place. This does not mean that the VO is immutable and stays in the state in which it was after the completion of the formation phase. On the contrary, the list of VO members might be extended or reduced, depending on the concrete operations which occur. Roles and responsibilities in the VO might change as well, so it can be said that the VO is subject to a certain kind of evolution.

Termination & Dissolution This phase effectively destroys the VO. All processes needed to produce logs and traces for provisioning or accounting procedures are executed before the VO is finally dissolved. Furthermore, all actions taken during the formation phase, for example enabling access to resources for VO participants, are revoked.

5. Implementing Virtual Organization Lifecycle Management

Figure 8 gives an overview of the components forming a VO realization, along with the relations between these components. The relations between the components building the VO (including the VO Admin Client Service) are determined through bipartite SLAs negotiated between the LSS and VO members.

These SLAs are displayed as lines with arrows between LSS and VO members. The lines without arrows between VO Admin Client Service and the administrator (connected through the VO Admin Client GUI) as well as between Customer Client Service and customer (connected through the Customer Client GUI) express a one-to-one relation between GUIs and services. This relation can be seen as proprietary in the sense that it is not subject to an SLA or something comparable. The connection of a service to a GUI client just serves to provide an interface to human users allowing interactive interference with the VO. In fact, this connection can be implemented in different ways and any VO member service implementation can freely decide on how to provide it.

In the realized "Big VO" system, all VO members, including the LSS, are embodied as Globus Toolkit 4 (GT4) services [14]. All services provide a common set of service methods related to SLA negotiation following the ne-

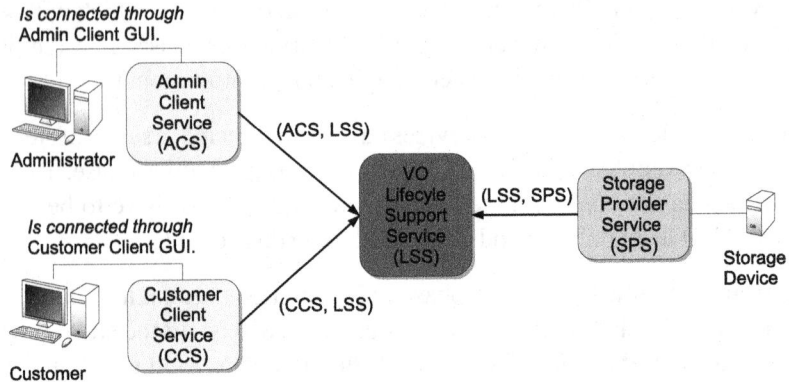

Figure 8.   Realization of a Big VO

gotiation logics as described in section 2.2 as well as SLA federation specific service methods. VO management resides on top of SLA management, which forms the basic building block of VO management. All involved components along with their specific features are listed in the following:

Lifecycle Support Service (LSS): This service is the heart of a VO and represents a VO's central management instance. The LSS invites VO members and, therefore, negotiates SLAs with potential VO members. To allow resource sharing within the VO, the LSS federates SLAs based on the negotiated SLAs and implements them between VO members to allow them to directly collaborate according to the terms of such a federated SLA. From a functional point of view the LSS exposes two different sets of service methods. The first set is accessible only to the VO Admin Client Service and all methods contained in this set are specific to the management of a VO whereas the second set can be invoked by all VO members. The first set comprises methods e.g. to invite new VO members, federate SLAs etc. The second set provides methods e.g. to retrieve information about available resources within the VO, request access to resources etc.

VO Admin Client Service & VO Admin Client GUI: The   VO   Admin Client Service represents the owner and administrative authority of the VO. This service is used to steer the LSS and, therefore, to carry out VO management. It is the only VO member authorized to access the LSS's VO management service methods. A VO Admin Client GUI is provided for this service, which is a GT4 client code allowing interactive usage of the VO Admin Client Service through a graphical user interface. Similar to the LSS from a functional point of view, this service provides two different sets of service methods as well. The first set connects to the VO management related service methods the LSS exposes while the second set comprises all service methods required to connect the GUI to the VO Admin Client Service. In principle, there can be more than one administraive authority acting coordinated with the LSS.

VO Storage Provider Service: This service represents an actual service provider. Besides the common service methods for SLA negotiation and federation, the storage provider service offers methods through which the actual storage provision service is made accessible to other VO members. This includes methods for uploading data, querying the stored data, downloading data and removing data from the service providers storage.

Customer Client Service & Customer Client GUI: This service differs from standard VO Member Services only in that it does not provide a service to the VO but only acts as service consumer. It is used to allow interactive access to VO resources by providing a Customer Client GUI to end users.

6. Stepping Through the Lifecycle Phases

Before entering the actual VO lifecycle, a user wishing to run a VO needs a VO Admin Client Service (ACS) to which he can connect through the VO Admin Client GUI. Once connected to the Admin Client Service, the lifecycle of the VO is entered by discovering potential LSS providers. The user selects one LSS provider and initiates SLA negotiation between the ACS and the LSS resulting in an SLA established between the two services as shown in Figure 9.

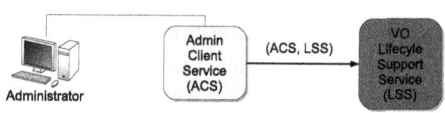

Figure 9. Formation of a Virtual Organization

The relevant SLA details of the SLA negotiated between the ACS and the LSS are shown in Figure 10. In order to populate the VO, the user adopting the role of the VO administrator discovers and selects a Storage Provider Service and a Customer Client Service. He requests the LSS (through the ACS) to negotiate SLAs with both services. This results in a VO as shown in Figure 8. The SLA negotiated with the Storage Provider Service contains two parts of special interest, one covering the amount of storage provided and the other allowing the acceptance of federated SLAs.

```
<Metric name="NumberSupportedMembers" defn="cc:NumberSupportedMembersType">
 <Target unit="MemberNumber" dialect="http://www.w3.org/TR/xquery/">
  <SuccessMeasure>
  $number = 1000
  </SuccessMeasure>
 </Target>
</Metric>
```

Figure 10.   Metric for number of VO members

The acceptance of federation has already been shown in Figure 2; the amount of storage provided can, in accordance with the NextGRID SLA schema, be specified as shown in Figure 11.

```
<Metric name="ProvidedStorage" defn="cc:ProvidedStorageType">
 <Target unit="GB" dialect="http://www.w3.org/TR/xquery/">
  <SuccessMeasure>
  $storage = 50
  </SuccessMeasure>
 </Target>
</Metric>
```

Figure 11.   Metric for storage provision

As the Customer Client Service (CCS) has been introduced for the sole purpose to consume resources within the VO without providing any, its SLA only contains one relevant term which covers the acceptance of federated SLAs, as already seen in the Storage Provider SLA. At this point the setup is done, the identification and formation phases are completed and the operation phase can begin. To demonstrate how collaboration between VO members can be realized through SLA federation, we assume that the Customer Client Service is searching for a certain amount of storage space. Therefore, the CCS queries the LSS for resources available within the VO. After having selected a specific resource, the CCS issues a collaboration request to the LSS for that resource and the respective resource amount. This causes the LSS to create a federated SLA covering the requested resource amount and establish it between the CCS and the Storage Provider.

In order for the LSS to be able to create a federated SLA, a set of rules for SLA federation must be specified. A simplistic approach could consist in using the Storage Provider's SLA template covering the full amount of storage (e.g. 50GB) that can be provided and establish it as a federated SLA. This, however, would imply that, even in the case that only a small part of the available storage space is requested (e.g. 5GB), the overall resource amount would always have to be allocated to the CCS. The approach adopted in the implementation presented in this paper is slightly more sophisticated. We have recognized that the process of federating an SLA could be driven to an arbitrary level of complexity, but this is not a key research topic to be presented here. The approach for SLA federation applied within this implementation relies on the basic rule to assign the consumer role to the party requesting collaboration and using the SLA template of the party assigned the provider role as root for the SLA to be created. Thereby, the resource amount in the SLA template is adjusted to the requested amount and the service consuming party is inserted in the SLA template. It is important to note that this closely links the LSS's tasks to resource brokerage as the LSS has to keep track of the resource amount covered by federated SLAs. A simple problem case can be constructed if the CCS has requested 25GB of storage space granted by a respective federated SLA and another VO member subsequently requests 30GB of storage space. The LSS hereby has to keep track of the actual resource usage for a specific VO member in order to make sure not to grant more resources than available through federated SLAs.

It is important to note that this approach entails a few implications as VO members engage to accept federated SLAs from the LSS, which implies a trust relationship between VO members and the LSS. However, there are as well a few possible approaches to circumvent these implications. One possible way to handle trust issues consists in the usage of a trusted third party federation service responsible for the creation of federated SLAs. Another way would be to allow VO members to reject federated SLAs received by the LSS in case the resource amount allocated through federated SLAs exceeds the overall resource amount granted to the VO through the SLA negotiated between a member and the LSS. In the latter case, it has to be ensured, e.g. through a trusted third party, that a reason for federation rejection is at hand.

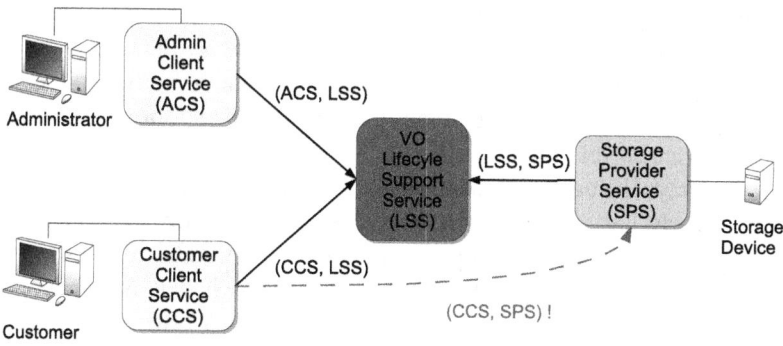

Figure 12. Established federated SLA

Assuming the CCS has requested 5GB storage space, a federated SLA is created by the LSS and established between the CCS and the Storage Provider by the LSS. The CCS is now able to collaborate with the Storage Provider based on this SLA as shown in Figure 12.

Once the CCS does not wish to collaborate with the Storage Provider any longer, the dissolution of the federated SLA is initiated. Similar to the federation logics, the dissolution is subject to some basic rules to be defined as well. The approach adopted in this implementation is to delegate the initial dissolution initiative to the service consumer, as in this scenario only the service consumer can decide when the collaboration can securely be terminated.

The last phase in the lifecycle of a VO is reached when the administrator decides to dissolve the whole VO. Then the ACS triggers the dissolution of all previously negotiated SLAs including the one negotiated between ACS and LSS.

7.   Conclusions

In this paper we presented an approach to the formation and operation of Virtual Organizations on the basis of bipartite Service Level Agreements combined with federation principles. The described model has been implemented as outlined and its ability to operate has been demonstrated to the European Commission. The demonstration shows that the proposed model for Virtual Organizations ameliorates classical Virtual Organization's deficiencies which consist mainly in the lack of dynamics. It also reduces the complexity of Virtual Organizations by dramatically decreasing the amount of negotiation which is necessary to reach a Virtual Organization where every member is, in principle, allowed to access services of each other member.

We have shown that different principles, like the negotiation protocol or service federation, developed in the NextGRID project, can be successfully applied to the area of Virtual Organizations. The resulting model combines these principles to form a powerful concept. It is mainly built around an additional component in Virtual Organizations, a Lifecycle Support Service, which acts as a central management instance. It provides two functionalities to the whole Virtual Organization: the management of membership and the management of bipartite Service Level Agreements.

As it is always the case with centralism, when building large-scale VOs, this approach clearly has its limits, since the LSS will certainly become a bottleneck. Bottleneck effects may appear when a certain number of VO members is reached or, even with less VO members, when there is extensive negotiation and federation happening. Precise figures for bottleneck effects have not been investigated.

Acknowledgments

This work has been supported by the NextGRID project and has been funded by the European Commission's IST activity of the 6th Framework Programme [15]. This paper expresses the opinions of the authors and not necessarily those of the European Commission. The European Commission is not liable for any use that may be made of the information contained in this paper.

References

[1] I. Foster, C. Kesselman and S. Tuecke. *The Anatomy of the Grid: Enabling scalabe Virtual Organizations.* Lecture Notes in Computer Science, 2001.

[2] D. Snelling and K. Jefferey. *Next Generation Grids 2.* European Commission, 2004.

[3] M. Surridge, S.J. Taylor, D. De Roure and E. Zaluska, *Experiences with GRIA – Industrial Applications on a Web Services Grid.* In Proceedings of the First International Conference on e-Science and Grid Computing, Melbourne, Dec 2005, pp 98-105. IEEE Press.

[4] M. Surridge, *VO Models in Next Generation Grids.* Private meeting of collaborating EU FP6 Grid projects, St Augustin, Jan 2007.
http://bscw.scai.fraunhofer.de/bscw/bscw.cgi/d105456/20070117_VO_Models.ppt.

[5] D. Snelling, A. Anjomshoaa, F. Wray, A. Basermann, M. Fisher, M. Surridge and P. Wieder, *NextGRID Architectural Concepts.*
http://www.nextgrid.org/download/publications/NextGRID_Architectural_Concepts.pdf.

[6] P. Hasselmeyer, C. Qu, L. Schubert, B. Koller and P. Wieder, *Towards Auotnomous Brokered SLA Negotiation.* In Exploiting the Knowledge Economy - Issues, Applications, Case Studies, October 2006. IOS.

[7] P. Hasselmeyer, B. Koller, L. Schubert and P. Wieder, *Towards SLA-Supported Resource Management.* Lecture Notes in Computer Science, HPCC-06, September 2006, pp 743-752. Springer.

[8] Hubert Hérenger and Stefan Wesner. *VO Lifecycle Models.* NextGRID Project Deliverable P5.4.4, August 2005.

[9] B. Mitchell and P. McKee, *SLAs: A Key Commercial Tool.* In P. Cunningham and M. Cunningham (eds), *Innovation and the Knowledge Economy: Issues, Applications, Case Studies,* 2005, IOS Press, Amsterdam, ISBN: 1-58603-563-0.

[10] Web Services Agreement Specification (WS-Agreement).
http://www.gridforum.org/Meetings/GGF11/Documents/draft-ggf-graap-agreement.

[11] Web Service Level Agreements (WSLA) Project. http://www.research.ibm.com/wsla.

[12] S. van den Berghe, M. Surridge and T.A. Leonard, *Dynamic Resource Allocation and Accounting in VOs.* NextGRID Project Deliverable P5.4.3, September 2005.

[13] René Heek, Hubert Hérenger and Roland Kübert. *VO Lifecycle Support Service Implementation.* NextGRID Project Deliverable P5.4.7, February 2007.

[14] The Globus Toolkit Homepage. http://www.globus.org/toolkit/.

[15] NextGRID - Architecture for Next Generation Grid Projects. http://www.nextgrid.org/.

MANAGING USER EXPECTATIONS WITH COMPONENT PERFORMANCE CONTRACTS*

Massimo Coppola, Domenico Laforenza, and Nicola Tonellotto
Information Science and Technologies Institute, National Research Council
Via G. Moruzzi 1, 56100, Pisa, Italy
{massimo.coppola, domenico.laforenza, nicola.tonellotto}@isti.cnr.it

Marco Danelutto and Marco Vanneschi
Computer Science Department, University of Pisa
Largo B. Pontecorvo 3, 56100, Pisa, Italy
{marcod,vannesch}@di.unipi.it

Corrado Zoccolo
IAC Search & Media Italia S.r.l., Corso Italia 58, Pisa, Italy
corrado.zoccolo@ask.com

Abstract   In this paper we introduce a definition of performance contract for hierarchical component applications communicating through one-way asynchronous communications. Component annotations allow to express a generic performance model, performance requirements and resource constraints. We propose an $O(n^{3.5})$ algorithm to obtain from user expectations the minimum resource requirements which ensure the desired QoS, to be exploited successively in a SLA negotiation phase. The technique is suitable for automatic execution, exploiting developer-provided annotations, and is validated with experiments on heterogeneous grid platforms.

Keywords: Software components, Service Level Agreements, Service Level Objective, QoS, automatic Grid deployment, performance modeling, performance prediction high level parallel programming, hierarchical composition

---

*This work has been supported by the European CoreGRID NoE (European Research Network on Foundations, Software Infrastructures and Applications for Large Scale, Distributed, GRID and Peer-to-Peer Technologies, contract no. IST-2002-004265).

1.   Introduction

It is becoming increasingly clear that the approach of existing Grid middleware, such as the Globus Toolkit, often does not efficiently enable application development and execution in a Grid environment [7], due to the complexity of the involved tasks.

Component-based programming [4] is currently the most promising approach to the programming of complex parallel Grid systems, easing problem decomposition and separation of aspects. One of the most promising component models in the Grid community is Fractal [5]. It offers a hierarchical abstract component model, featuring component introspection/intercession capabilities.

A hierarchical component model allows to build large scale Grid-aware applications where highly specialized components built by software specialists are easily composed to develop higher-level functionalities. The separation of developing roles is crucial to ease matching user-defined Service Level Objectives (SLOs) and resource-specific Service Level Agreements (SLAs).

To comply with the "invisible Grid" [1] approach, hierarchical application deployment should be completely in charge of the run-time, once the user-level SLOs have been specified. To tackle this problem, we push forward the similarity between parallel component models and Structured Parallel Programming (SPP) [2], by devising performance models for component compositions and exploiting them at deployment time. In Sect. 2 we define a form of *performance contract* [10] tailored to hierarchical component applications communicating streams of data through one-way asynchronous communications. Refer to our article [6] for a discussion of related works.

A contract for a given application couples the performance model with user-requested QoS. Our specification of a performance contract is as independent as possible from the runtime characteristics of resources, and allows contract composition in the very same way as new components are built wiring together existing components.

With this definition of contract, in Sect. 3 we propose an $O(n^{3.5})$ algorithm finding the minimum resource requirements in terms of performance which ensure the desired QoS, to be exploited successively in a SLA negotiation phase.

The algorithm allows to specify SLAs between simple components and Grid resources, and to quickly recompute these SLAs in case of dynamic rescheduling [3]. Moreover, due to its modular structure, we envision its full exploitation in components frameworks where a hierarchy of component controllers will be in charge of autonomic behavior of applications [2]. Sect. 4 reports on the experimental validation of the approach.

2.   Application Modeling

We model a component application as a directed graph, whose nodes represent computational components and edges represent one-way communications (links between interfaces). The graph can be non-simple, i.e. an edge can connect two or more nodes, and several distinct edges may link the same set of nodes.

Nodes can represent sequential and parallel computations. A sequential node has at most one active control flow (thread) at any time, while in a parallel node two scenarios are possible: **data-parallelism**, where only one computation, made up of several control flows, is active in the node, and **task-parallelism**, where several computations are active, each one being an independent control flow.

A computation can either start spontaneously, or be activated by one or more data receptions from incoming edges. To simplify the model, we assume that each incoming edge activates at most one computation in any node [9]. Computations can produce output data that activate further nodes through the outgoing edges.

Nodes can be connected according to three different patterns: **unicast** (i.e. one-to-one connection between two nodes), **merge** (i.e. many-to-one connection) and **broadcast** (i.e. one-to-many connection).

Performance Model.   The *execution rate* for each computation, and the *data transfer rate* for each input/output interface completely specify the application state from the point of view of its performance, therefore we will call them the **performance features** of our application.

In [6] a model for the dynamic behavior of such applications has been proposed. The main result states that, if the dynamic system is ergodic, the steady state behavior of the whole application can be described through a set of linear *balance equations*. The proof is given in [9], while empirical evidence is shown in [6].

These equations define the **performance model** of an application, describing the relations that hold among its performance features. With this approach, a compiler exploiting simple annotations (provided by the component developers) can build automatically analytical performance models for complex graph structures, obtaining the same predictive power provided by the performance models for skeletons, but not limited to few, well-known skeletons. Note that this model is completely independent from the application execution environment.

Performance Constraints and Requirements.   Given the definitions of performance features and performance model previously given, a **performance**

constraint is defined as an inequality in the form

$$x_i \geq c_i \tag{1}$$

where x_i is a performance feature (input, output or execution rate) and c_i is a strictly positive real number representing the desired operational value of the feature x_i. A constraint is *satisfied (at runtime)* if the measured value of the associated performance feature (x_i) is greater than or equal to the specified value (c_i).

Let a set of k performance constraints be given by the user. Such user-provided constraints are called **performance requirements**. They represent the user expected QoS of some components of the application at runtime. The following question arises: "What values the other performance features should assume at runtime to satisfy the performance requirements?". Clearly, given the interactions between the components, it should be possible, given few performance requirements, to derive performance constraints on each features of the performance model.

Deployment annotations.   From the performance constraints, we can determine the set of candidate resources that can satisfy them and a suitable mapping of components on the resources, by evaluating the match between component computations and computing resources, and between communications and network resources.

Computations can be characterized in terms of the *work* they perform per activation (e.g. number of operations, *MFlop/act*, amount of data exchanged, *MB/act*). We assume (*ergodicity*) that activation parameters are independent from the actual values of the received data. Analogously, we can characterize stream communications by their item size, or by the number of packets flowing on a stream.

Several metrics are possible [8], and multiple metrics can be considered simultaneously. The metrics outlined above are associated as meta-data to each component. We will refer to them as **deployment annotations**.

We will generally call *bandwidth* the work that a resource can perform in the time unit. Clearly, each computation metric has associated a resource bandwidth (e.g computational bandwidth measured in MFlop/s, memory bandwidth and I/O bandwidth in MB/s).

Part of the deployment annotations are actually provided by component developers, and part are automatically gathered and inferred from the application structure by the compiling tools. We underline that developer knowledge is needed only once, when shipping a new component, to provide a full set of component annotations.

By analyzing deployment annotations, the deployment tools can instantiate the abstract performance model for concrete resources, and thus evaluate any given mapping solution. Deployment annotations can include practical requirements (minimum hardware/software) to run a component. These constraints ensure that the execution model described by the component annotations is valid under a specific mapping onto the execution platform. Deployment annotations avoid, for instance, that due to insufficient memory on the resource, memory swapping effects invalidate the performance model of a memory-hungry computation.

Performance Contract. We can now define the performance contract for a hierarchical component model, as the way to convey users' SLOs, programmers knowledge of the components behavior, and the application hierarchical structure as a composition of components, that is as independent as possible from the runtime resource characteristics.

The **performance contract** for a component, primitive or composite, is a list of metadata containing the following items

- the component performance model, provided by the component and/or application developers;
- the component performance requirements, provided by the end-user;
- for each primitive component, deployment annotations for its computations, provided by the component developer (through profiling) or automatic tools (through execution traces analysis);
- for each composite component:
  - a performance contract for the composite component;
  - a mapping of its external performance features to the ones of the inner subcomponents.

Clearly the performance contract for a component-based application is the performance contract of its topmost component. A performance contract is said to be **assessed** if the performance requirements have been propagated to each component and the constraints for every performance feature has been calculated. This can be achieved with the algorithm we discuss in the following Section.

3. Constraints Resolution Algorithm

In the following we describe the algorithm computing an assessed performance contract. It is a three-step recursive procedure whose purpose is to deduce an assignement of values to all the features of the application model, which (1) satisfies all contract and resource constraints (2) chooses a feasible solution that optimizes application performance, (3) exploits the hierarchical structure of the application model. This goal is accomplished managing multiple low-level SLA features to match one or more high-level SLOs. The input of the algorithm is a performance contract with a performance model of size n, the number of performance features (either input, output or execution rates).

The balance equations (performance model) can be written in matrix notation, resulting in an homogeneous system. For more details on this model, please refer to [6].

Let $c \in \mathbb{R}^k$ denote the vector of the performance requirement values, and $x \in \mathbb{R}^n$ indicate the performance features. The vector $x_c \in \mathbb{R}^k$ represents the features constrained by the user requirements, and $x_{uc} \in \mathbb{R}^{n-k}$ indicates the unconstrained ones. For simplicity, the elements of x (and correspondingly, the rows of the performance model matrix) are ordered in such a way to have $x = [x_{uc}|x_c]^T$, in order to express every performance feature as a function of the constrained ones. Exploiting the Gauss-Jordan elimination algorithm (*first step*), the performance matrix is row reduced into block-echelon form. This representation allows to recognize if the set of constraints is well specified, over- or under-specified. In general a performance model with n performance features and m equations is fully specified by a set of k constraints if the resulting matrix and system have the form

$$\left[\begin{array}{c|c} I_{(n-k)\times(n-k)} & D_{(n-k)\times k} \\ \hline 0_{(m-n+k)\times(n-k)} & E_{(m-n+k)\times k} \end{array} \right] \left[\begin{array}{c} x_{uc} \\ x_c \end{array} \right] = 0 \qquad (2)$$

Note that $m - n + k$ can be zero, and in that case the form of the coefficient matrix is $\left[\begin{array}{c|c} I_{m\times m} & D_{m\times(n-m)} \end{array} \right]$.

The set of solutions of the system is a vector subspace of $\mathbb{R}^n$. We call the dimension of the solution space the number of **degrees of freedom** of the application. This value determines how many constraints have to be provided in order to derive expected values for every performance feature. The degenerate case of a solution space with dimension 0 (the only solution is the null vector) predicts a deadlocking steady-state, in which no computation or communication can proceed. Clearly, only positive values of the rates are meaningful, so we regard any assignment of positive values for the vector $\left[\begin{array}{cc} x_{uc}^T & x_c^T \end{array} \right]^T \in \mathbb{R}^n$ that is a solution of the system, as a possible "operation point" for the modeled application.

Since the set of possible operation points is infinite (excluding the deadlock case), we can add a further optimization constraint to the problem: find the cheapest solution among the admissible ones. Our problem is transformed in the following linear optimization problem (*second step*):

$$\min \sum h_i \quad \text{s.t.} \quad \begin{cases} x_{uc} + Dx_c = 0 \\ Ex_c = 0 \\ x_c = c + h \\ x_{uc} \geq 0 \\ h \geq 0 \end{cases} \qquad (3)$$

where the first two matrix equations are simply derived by unrolling the matrix-vector multiplication in (2), the user constraints must be satisfied (the vector inequality $x_c \geq c$ was rewritten as an equality using the positive slack variables h_i), and the distance $(\sum h_i)$ between user specified constraints and actual values for the constrained variables should be minimized.

Application to Hierarchical Compositions. When applied to a hierarchical composition, the contract assessment algorithm is recursive: given an application (i.e. its topmost component) and its performance contract, the algorithm computes the expected values of the performance features using the performance model (first and second step), and maps them to the interfaces of each sub-component. Then it can be applied to the performance contract of each sub-component (*recursive step*), using as input requirements the computed values of rates at component interfaces, to determine the performance values associated to each module of the sub-component. Applied recursively, the algorithm can compute the performance requirements for every simple component of the application.

Complexity of the algorithm. The computational complexity of the provided algorithm is polynomial in time, w.r.t. the input size n of the contract description. For a basic component we have $T(n) = T_{GJ}(n) + T_{LP}(n)$, where $T_{GJ}(n)$ is the time complexity of the Gauss Jordan algorithm (first step) $O(n^3)$, and $T_{LP}(n)$ is the complexity of the Linear Solver (second step) $O(n^{3.5})$ for the well-known Karmarkar algorithm). For a complex component we have that the contract size n is the sum of the complex part n_0 and of the contract size of the sub-components n_i, and the time complexity results ($T(n_i)$ is the complexity of the recursive step on the ith sub-component):

$$T\left(\sum_{i=0}^{k} n_i\right) = T_{GJ}(n_0) + T_{LP}(n_0) + \sum_{i=1}^{k} T(n_i)$$

Since $\sum n_i = n \Rightarrow \sum n_i^k = O(n^k) \qquad \forall k \geq 1$, we conclude

$$T(n) = O(n^{3.5})$$

The requirements of an application could vary at run-time, hence the performance contract is not fixed during the execution. When changes affect the performance required from a component, the contract assessment algorithm has to be applied at run-time, to derive the new assignments for all components. Our algorithm meets the requirements for on-line use, as it has a low computational cost, and it can be distributed over the management hierarchy, (computing in parallel the subproblems generated by the recursive step) among the components constituting the application.

Typical values for n (that roughly correspond to the total number of component interfaces in the application) are in the range between few tens up to several hundreds, for reasonably sized Grid applications. The algorithm running time is usually a small fraction of the total time needed to determine the application mapping, and start the application (the longest parts consisting in retrieving all candidate resources and staging the applications binaries onto remote machines).

Deriving SLA parameters.   The user specifies the overall performance requirements, describing the QoS goal for the whole application. Components, in the general case, will have **component annotations** attached, describing the steady-state relationships between activation of computations and of output interfaces (see Sect. 2). The component annotations should be given just once, by the component developer, and belong to the component's metadata.

The work performed by a computation can be expressed as an array of metric values, $l = [l_1, \ldots, l_n]$, either obtained by the developer (code profiling) or by the user from historical records (by execution on reference resources).

With a simple metrics of work l (e.g. MFlop/act), it is straightforward to translate a performance constraint c (e.g. act/s) into a resource bandwidth requirement w (MFlop/s) and vice-versa: $w = l \cdot c$.

With multidimensional metrics of computation and communication, given a work vector $l = [l_1, \ldots, l_n]$ describing an activation, and a bandwidth vector $w = [w_1, \ldots, w_n]$ describing a resource, the equation is easily extended if we write it with respect to the service time, $t_s(l, w) = 1/c$,

$$t_s(l, w) = \bigoplus_{i=1}^{n} \frac{l_i}{w_i} \qquad (4)$$

Here the combining operator $\bigoplus$ acts on metric components according to the kind of work they measure. It is a sum operator when the metrics deal with sequentialized work, and a maximum when work can be carried out in parallel.

4.   Experimental Validation

In the following, a demonstration of the applicability of the proposed approach to select resource for a test application is shown. The application is the one depicted in Fig. 1. W.r.t. a group of 12 pictures (GOP), the performance model for the application fixes the following relationships among execution (C_{Xe}), input (C_{Xi}) and output rates (C_{Xo}) of the various computations. The model has exactly one degree of freedom.

$$C_{1e} = C_{1o} = C_{2i} = C_{2o} = C_{3i} = 12 \cdot C_{3o}, \quad C_{3o} = C_{4i} = C_{4o} = C_{5i}$$

Suppose that the user wants 1 frame/s at the last stage (the constraint is expressed by $C_{5i} \geq 1/12$, because each input for C_5 is composed by 12 frames). Applying the performance model, we can derive the computation and transfer

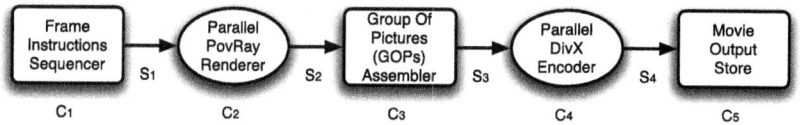

Figure 1.   Graph of the render-encode application

rates for each computation and communication that are required to satisfy the contract.

We measured the weight of computations in MFlop per task and MB transferred to/from memory, and the weight of communications by their size only (see Tab. 1). We then expressed the service time applying equation (4), with work description $l = [l_{MFlop}, l_{MB}]^T$, resource bandwidths $w = [w_{MFlop/s}, w_{MB/s}]^T$ and *sum* as combining operator.

Imposing the constraint and solving back w.r.t. w, we can derive for each computation node a set of matching resource requirements.

As an example, the requirement for stream $S_2 = C_{2o}$ is to carry 1.19 MB messages with minimum rate 1 message/s, thus a link providing 9.52 Mb/s is sufficient. Likewise, the test application will never scale above 10 frames/s with a 100 Mb/s network, and needs to be redesigned, if higher performances are required.

In Fig. 2, two execution runs are displayed with mapping onto homogeneous (left) and heterogeneous (right) resources, and the same performance contract. The mappings computed using the performance model fulfill the constraints, for most of the application runtime. We notice that the application workload (the smoothed curve) deviates from that measured on the first movie frames, being heavier in the middle of the computation. This occurs because, in order to build the model, we sampled the performance on the first frames of the movie, but the application workload slightly changes with the evolution of the movie. This is unavoidable in complex applications, and may require dynamic rescheduling [3]. Although the heterogeneous run shows greater variance in the achieved bandwidth, the average bandwidth is comparable with the homo-

Table 1.   Deployment annotations for the application.

Component	C_1	C_2	C_3	C_4	C_5	Stream	S_1	S_2	S_3	S_4
Processor	i686	i686	i686	i686	i686	data type	param	pic	GOP	zip
Memory (MB)	-	64	256	64	-	data size	54	1.19	14.24	2
CPU Work	-	3307	-	52	-		(B)	(MB)	(MB)	(MB)
Mem. Work	-	302	-	104	-					

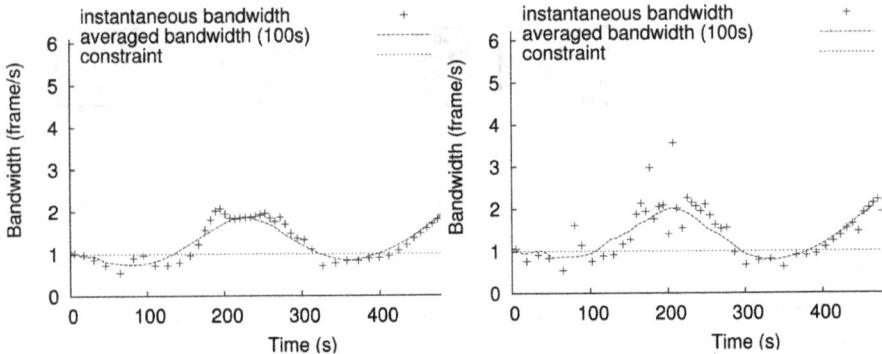

Figure 2.   Execution results: left) homogeneous cluster, Athlon XP 2600+,   right) heterogeneous resources (9 P4@2GHz, 1 Athlon XP 2800+, 1 P4@2.8GHz).

geneous case. This provides evidence that the performance model properly handles heterogeneous resources.

5.   Conclusions

We have described a way to specify performance models and contracts for hierarchical component-based applications, and we presented an algorithm exploiting component annotations to translate a user-specified performance contract into elementary resource requirements. Our approach is suitable to complete automatization, and can easily be adopted in component runtime environments, to determinate the resource SLAs needed to provide a stated QoS. The obtained results match our expectations, as the algorithm handles homogeneous and heterogeneous sets of resources, and it runs fast enough to be adopted for runtime reconfigurations.

References

[1] M. Aldinucci, M. Coppola, S. Campa, M. Danelutto, M. Vanneschi, and C. Zoccolo. Structured Implementation of Component-based Grid Programming Environments. In V. Getov, D. Laforenza, and A. Reinefeld, editors, *Future Generation Grids*, CoreGRID series, pages 217–239. Springer Verlag, November 2005.

[2] M. Aldinucci, M. Coppola, S. Campa, M. Danelutto, M. Vanneschi, and C. Zoccolo. Structured implementation of component based grid programming environments. In V. Getov, D. Laforenza, and A. Reinefeld, editors, *Future Generation Grids*, CoreGRID series. Springer, 2006.

[3] M. Aldinucci, A. Petrocelli, E. Pistoletti, M. Torquati, M. Vanneschi, L. Veraldi, and C. Zoccolo. Dynamic reconfiguration of Grid-aware applications in ASSIST. In J. C. Cunha and P. D. Medeiros, editors, *Euro-Par 2005 Parallel Processing*, volume 3648 of *Lecture Notes in Computer Science*, pages 771–781. Springer, August 2005.

[4] Francoise Baude, Denis Caromel, and Matthieu Morel. From Distributed Objects to Hierarchical Grid Components. In *Proc. of the International Symposium on Distributed Objects and Applications (DOA)*, volume 2888 of *LNCS*, pages 1226–1242, Dresden, Germany, November 2003. Springer Verlag.

[5] E. Bruneton, T. Coupaye, M. Leclercq, V. Quèma, and J.-B. Stefani. The FRACTAL component model and its support in Java: Experiences with Auto-adaptive and Reconfigurable Systems. *Software Practice & Experience*, 36(11/12):1257–1284, 2006.

[6] M. Danelutto, N. Tonellotto, M. Vanneschi, and C. Zoccolo. A Performance Model for Stream-based Computations. In *Proc. of 15th Euromicro Conf. on Parallel, Distributed, and Network-Based Processing*. IEEE C.S., Feb 2007.

[7] Expert Group Report. Next Generation Grids 2: Requirements and Options for European Grids Research 2005-2010 and Beyond. `ftp://ftp.cordis.europa.eu/pub/ist/docs/ngg2_eg_final.pdf`, July 2004.

[8] Antonios Litke, Athanasios Panagakis, Anastasios Doulamis, Nikolaos Doulamis, Theodora Varvarigou, and Emmanuel Varvarigos. An Advanced Architecture for a Commercial Grid Infrastructure. In *Grid Computing*, volume 3165 of *LNCS*, pages 32–41, Berlin, Germany, 2004. Springer Verlag.

[9] N. Tonellotto and C. Zoccolo. Characterization of the performance of assist programs. Technical Report TR-0007, CoreGRID - Network of Excellence, June 2005.

[10] F. Vraalsen, R.A. Aydt, C.L. Mendes, and D.A. Reed. Performance Contracts: Predicting and Monitoring Grid Application Behavior. In *Proc. of 2nd International Workshop on Grid Computing*, Nov 2001.

SERVICE LEVEL AGREEMENTS IN CATALLAXY-BASED GRID MARKETS

Liviu Joita and Omer F. Rana
Cardiff University, School of Computer Science and Welsh e-Science Centre Queen's Buildings, 5 The Parade, Roath, Cardiff, CF24 3AA, UK
(L.Joita, O.F.Rana)@cs.cardiff.ac.uk

Isaac Chao, Pablo Chacin, Felix Freitag, and Leandro Navarro
Computer Architecture Department, Technical University of Catalonia Jordi Girona 1-3, Campus Nord D6 Barcelona 08035, Spain
(ichao, pchacin, felix, leandro)@ac.upc.edu

Oscar Ardaiz
Department of Mathematics and Informatics, Public University of Navarra Campus de Arrosadia, Pamplona 31006, Spain
oscar.ardaiz@unavarra.es

Abstract   Grid computing is an important paradigm for managing computationally demanding applications composed of a collection of services. Experience of using Service Level Agreements (SLAs) within the context of a Catallaxy-enabled "proof-of-concept" prototype is described. The approach uses the Catallaxy concept to enable the dynamic discovery of services and resources. The concept of "social utility" is then used to evaluate the benefits of using the Catallaxy-based approach.

Keywords: Service Level Agreements, Web services, Grid markets, social utility economic index, Catallaxy

1.   Introduction

There has been significant interest in utilizing an economic paradigm for exchanging Grid resources and services [3]. This approach provides the capability to schedule access to services based on a market mechanism (such as auctions), leading to a fair and efficient approach to sharing high demand resources. Most existing approaches in this context rely on a centralized broker, and are implemented alongside an existing Grid middleware. An alternative approach, which does not necessitate centralised brokers, is the Catallaxy mechanism of von Hayek [5]. Catallaxy is a coordination mechanism for systems consisting of autonomous decentralized agents that make use of a "free-market" for goods exchange. It enables prices within the market to be adjusted based on negotiation and price signalling between agents [4]. Catallaxy provides a way to inform the individual (agent) about the knowledge that may be contained within other agents. Exchange of information between agents leads to the generation of prices which reflect the value each individual (agent) assigns to the respective good [1]. Catallaxy therefore leads to the development of self-organizing individuals (agents) that are highly dynamic – thereby leading to systems which behave in a Peer-2-Peer fashion. Such an approach is particularly suited to "Open Systems", where detailed knowledge about other agents may not be known *apriori*. Service Level Agreements (SLAs) provide a contract between an application user requiring services/resources, and application providers determining what should be made available for external use. To enable service/resource sharing/usage in application environments, SLAs may be used to define: (a) requirements that such an application would place on services (and resources) owned by a third party; (b) check whether these requirements have been met during use. An SLA also specifies the penalty that a service provider may incur if terms in the SLA are violated.

Our approach utilizes a policy from which the configuration of individual components within the system is derived. Hence, self-managing services make use of Service Level Agreements (SLA) as a way to discover resources that guarantee an adequate Quality of Service (QoS), and provide a management interface to monitor and control service life-cycle. Social utility is used as a basis to evaluate the effectiveness of the approach – and provides a measure of SLA compliance in service allocation and use.

This paper demonstrates the use of SLAs in Catallaxy-based markets and the experience of using and integrating SLAs within a decentralized economic self-organisation mechanism for service/resource allocation. Section 2 introduces the social utility economic index and the composition process used to derive this index. Section 3 describes the application scenario and the SLAs used. Section 4 gives an overview of SLAs at the application layer, while Section

5 contains a discussion of the evaluation framework and experimental results. Conclusions are presented in Section 6.

2. Social utility - a composite index

Figure 1 describes the layers within a performance metrics framework for on-demand service allocation, and shows the single composite index – "social utility" – on top of these layers. Social utility is a factor considered in macroe-conomic models, and is used to measure the "welfare" within a system as a whole. This term originates in social systems, where the benefit to a group or society is considered to be more significant than benefit to an individual. In a social system, it is possible to make a distinction between the maximum utility *of* and the maximum utility *for* a group of users/providers. The latter is the point where each individual has attained the maximum possible private satisfaction. The former refers to the maximum utility of the group or society as a whole, not of individuals. Only the second type can be treated by the economist; he can consider only the wants of individuals who are dissimilar and whose satisfactions therefore cannot be added up to yield a measure of the maximum utility for the entire group or society. Social utility therefore provides a useful way to measure the "utility" of a group, rather than an individual. Figure 1 also shows a view of the data analysis at different layers and how a single composite index is derived. Our intention is to be start from performance metrics that can be easily measured, and combine these to determine social utility. In this way, it is possible to use raw data that can be easily measured for individual components within a system, and process it to generate a metric that could be used to effectively measure the benefit to a group/system as a whole.

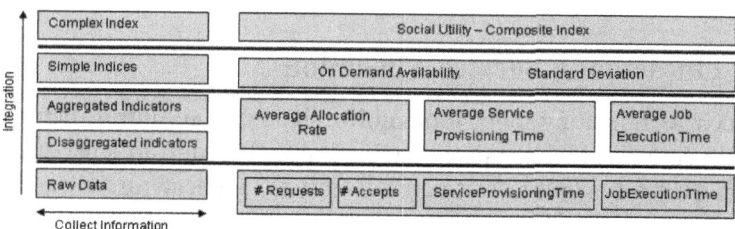

Figure 1. Layer metrics - Logical view of composite index

Performance/technical metrics include easy to measure parameters which can subsequently be aggregated. Technical metrics include: (a) efficiency measures – number of requests, number of acceptances; and (b) time metrics – service provisioning time and job execution time. Some examples include: (i) Number of Requests: these include metrics that measure demand, and are counted as the number of requests for service execution; (ii) Number of Acceptance:

the number of successfully acknowledged requests for services; (iii) Service Provisioning Time: the time of service usage in one transaction, including the on-demand request time, discovery, negotiation, and execution times; (iv) Job Execution Time: time to execute the on-demand service. From figure 1, the next layer from the bottom provides a first integration stage based on individually measured values. On DeMand availability (ODM) is a composite of indicators obtained at the application layer within one experiment run, and can be obtained as in equation (1). ODM lies between [0, 1], where an optimal on-demand service allocation mechanism would have an ODM=1. The Standard deviation (std_u) is obtained as in equation (2).

$$ODM = \frac{1}{2}(mean(service.prov.time) + mean(job.exec.time)) \quad (1)$$

$$std\_u = \frac{1}{2}(std(service.prov.time) + std(job.exec.time)) \quad (2)$$

The top layer in figure 1 presents the economic utility value used for comparing different alternatives. The social utility is based on a loss function – a full description of this function is presented in [8]. The loss function is calculated using two indicators: the composite indicator ODM and the standard deviation (std_u) – both considered as stochastic variables that aggregate the raw metrics.

$$L = \alpha((1 - ODM)^2 + std\_u^2) \quad (3)$$

where "L" is the social utility, and α is a weight between [0, 1]. In our experiments α is set to 0.5. "L" lies between [0, 1], where an optimal social utility would be close to zero.

3.   On-demand Service Allocation

Current Grid Computing applications utilize static resource infrastructure which is usually connected by physically stable links. The shift to a pervasive Grid demands a more dynamic infrastructure, leading to applications built as complex services accessed on demand. Figure 2 shows our application that makes use of a Catallaxy-based market.

We use on an economic Service Oriented Architecture implemented using the Grid Market Middleware (GMM) – a resource allocation middleware which incorporates decentralized economic models [2]. The GMM is accessed by an application as a Web Service, and provides an access point to a market, enabling the application to negotiate (and subsequently enforce) SLAs. The application does not have to know details about the operation of the market, only the location of the access point, and the message format to access it. The GMM exposes the interface to the access point and describes these message formats.

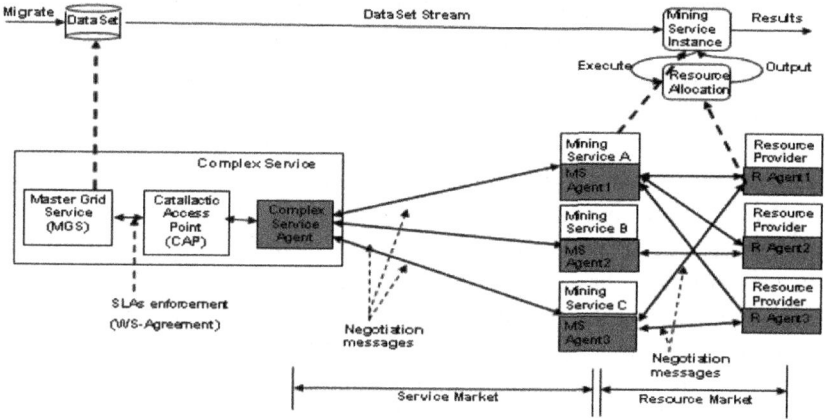

Figure 2. Cat-DataMining prototype - agents and Grid Markets Middleware

The GMM also provides mechanisms to register, manage, locate and negotiate for services and resources. It allows trading agents to interact with each other and engage in negotiations. Furthermore, the middleware offers a set of generic negotiation mechanisms, and provides a plug-in architecture enabling additional negotiation strategies to be included. The GMM has a layered architecture, which allows a clear separation between platform specific concerns from the economic mechanisms, to cope with highly heterogeneous environments. A detailed description of both the design and implementation of the GMM architecture can be found in [2].

3.1 Data Mining Services

In the Cat-DataMining prototype, the basic problem addressed is the dynamic allocation of CPU resources for the processing of low-level data, to support transformation models that compress/summarize the data (for example, produce a short report), make it more abstract (for example, a descriptive approximation or model of the process that generated the data), or make it more useful (for example, a predictive model for estimating the value of future cases). The prototype makes use of specific data-mining methods for pattern discovery and extraction. This process is often structured into a discovery pipeline/workflow, involving access, integration and analysis of data from disparate sources, and uses data patterns and models generated through intermediate stages. The data mining algorithms have been derived from the WEKA toolkit [10].

Figure 2 shows also the prototype components and related GMM agents as buyers and sellers in the Grid service and resource markets, and consists of only one service invocation. The prototype is composed of four main components: the Master Grid Service (MGS) – a Complex Service requestor, the Catallactic

Access Point (CAP), the Data Mining Services – as types of complex and basic services respectively, and job execution resources - as computational resources. The complex service agent acting on the request of MGS is the buyer entity in the service market, and the basic service is the seller entity in the service market.

A complex service could be represented by a proxy, which needs basic service capabilities for execution – with support for a service selector instance. Complex services do not need to have details of the resource layer. A basic service is split into a basic service logic and a resource allocator. The logic is able to negotiate with the complex service and to translate the requirements for service execution on a resource instance (e.g. CPU and storage, etc.) A resource allocator gets the resource specification and broadcasts the respective demand to the local resource managers. This leads to the formation of resource bundles and requires resource co-allocation. In thie context, a bundles is an *n-tuple* of resource types (e.g. a 3-tuple would be: CPU, storage, and bandwidth); co-allocation describes resources for one single service transaction from various local resource managers simultaneously.

The Data Mining basic service is the buyer entity in the resource market, and the Local Resource Managers are the seller entity on the resource market. The main functionalities of basic service agent at the resource market are: (i) co-allocation of resources (resource bundles) by parallel negotiation with different resource providers (local resource manager entities); (ii) informing the complex service about the outcome of resource negotiation.

4.   SLAs at application layer

Currently, SLAs are defined in a static manner, i.e. the terms within an SLA must adhere to strict constraints, and are monitored during application execution – such as in WS-Agreement. However, within many applications, it is often difficult to define such constraints very precisely, thereby leading to a large number of violations. There is a need to modify an agreement that had already been established, especially if the agreement is used at a time much later than when the agreement had been defined. These requirements relate to comparing the cost of re-establishing a new agreement vs. being able to adapt an agreement that is already in place. Secondly, there is a need to support flexibility in the agreement if an agreement initiator is not fully aware of the operating environment when the agreement is defined. In this case, the agreement initiator may not have enough information to determine what to ask for from a provider. This is likely to be the case when an agreement initiator or provider operates with imprecise knowledge about the other party involved in the agreement.

4.1 SLAs in Cat-DataMining

The data mining scenario of the Cat-DataMining prototype involves an MGS which needs to run a data mining job. The MGS sends an AgreementOffer (AO), see Listing 2, based on the AgreementTemplate (AT), see Listing 1, downloaded from the CatallacticAccessPoint (CAP), to the CAP to find a Data Mining service. The CAP provides an entry point into the market and allows existing Grid applications to make requests directly to it. The Complex Service Agent, acting on behalf of the MGS (as a complex service) chosen by the CAP, negotiates with the Basic Service Agents, in the GMM environment, for Data Mining services. WS-Agreement is used in the Cat-DataMining prototype, and forms the basis for choosing between multiple service and resource providers. When using WS-Agreement in our prototype, several parts need to be specified [1]: agreement name, the agreement context (parties to the agreement), reference to the service(s) provided in support of the agreement, and the lifetime of the agreement. Agreement terms, which describe the agreement itself, can contain the service description terms, which provide information needed to instantiate or otherwise identify a service to which this agreement belongs. Finally, guarantee terms which specify the service levels the parties agree to. An example of an Agreement Template and Offer used by Cat-DataMining is provided in Figure 3 and in Figure 4.

```
<AgreementLite>
    <Name>DataMiningService</Name>
    <Context>
        <AgreementInitiator>cardiff</AgreementInitiator>
        <AgreementOfferSubmitter></AgreementOfferSubmitter>
        <ExpirationTime>2007-12-31</ExpirationTime>
    </Context>
    <Terms>
        <BasicServiceType>J48</BasicServiceType>
        <NumberOfBasicServiceNodes>1</NumberOfBasicServiceNodes>
        <BasicServiceConstraints/>
        <PayForService></PayForService>
        <Equity><!-- it evaluates catallaxy integrity --></Equity>
        <ExperimentID><!-- needed for tests --></ExperimentID>
    </Terms>
</AgreementLite>
```

Figure 3. Agreement Template

```
<AgreementLite>
    <Name>DataMiningService</Name>
    <Context>
        <AgreementInitiator>cardiff</AgreementInitiator>
        <AgreementOfferSubmitter>barcelona</AgreementOfferSubmitter>
        <ExpirationTime>2007-12-31</ExpirationTime>
    </Context>
    <Terms>
        <BasicServiceType>J48</BasicServiceType>
        <NumberOfBasicServiceNodes>1</NumberOfBasicServiceNodes>
        <BasicServiceConstraints/>
        <PayForService>50</PayForService>
        <Equity><!-- it evaluates catallaxy integrity --></Equity>
        <ExperimentID><!-- needed for tests --></ExperimentID>
    </Terms>
</AgreementLite>
```

Figure 4. Agreement Offer

5.   Evaluation and results

This section presents an evaluation of the Cat-DataMining prototype, by using "social utility" described in Section 2. This parameter is obtained by combining the raw data collected during the experiments. The purpose of the evaluation process presented here is to see how the variation of the budget influences the distribution of welfare through the community of buyers and sellers involved in the Cat-DataMining application – and as measured using the social utility index. This welfare distribution is valid for both users' application, which provides the budget, and the agents deployed at the middleware, which make use of the budget. The hypothesis is that the proposed Cat-Data Mining prototype achieves a fair distribution of social utility between the participant agents.

To be able to use economic concepts, it is necessary to specify a virtual policy maker – essentially a logic entity whose functionality is implemented via the Catallactic Access Point (CAP) module within the prototype. The role of the policy maker is to minimizing inequality and maximise the fair distribution of gain. In our metric framework, the equity metric (equity) is introduced within the SLA contract as a term to measure the behaviour the Catallaxy mechanism from the perspective of the application user. A CAP makes use of the client's application budget in a fair way (i.e. without any predefined preferences for any services) within the market through the complex service agent. The equity metric can be obtained as in equation (4) – where *agent satisfaction* is a metric measured at the GMM level and presented in [8]:

$$equity = 1 - agent\ satisfaction \qquad (4)$$

Agent satisfaction measures the utility gained by an agent in a single transaction, which is the difference between the lowest price he is willing to pay in this transaction, and the final price of the agreement. It is defined as a ratio between the subjective transaction value and the budget. If this difference is greater, the gain is better. The agent's gain has to be fair, and the agent must not speculate by using all his budget for buying services – as by doing this, the agent's satisfaction is high (towards 1), while the equity metric, the fairness view from the user's application perspective, is low (towards 0). The (client) user's satisfaction is higher by paying less than the budget (which is the maximum price the user's application can buy a service for), if agent satisfaction is lower, but still the agent has a gain.

A description of parameters measured within the Cat-DataMining prototype is presented in [6]. The results presented in this section consider only metrics measured at the application layer, while economic parameters (such as overall cost of computation or data access) and other metrics, measured at the middleware layer, are not taken into consideration - so their values will be zero. Therefore, the parameters considered are: total time within one transaction of an experiment – service.prov.time and the job execution time – job.exec.time. Experiments make use of ZIP (Zero Intelligence Plus) agents [7]– as economic agents within the GMM; these agents use a gradient algorithm to set the price for resources. In order to run the tests, we setup controlled experiments deploying several instances of the GMM in a Linux server farm. Each node has 2 CPUs (Intel PIII, 1 GHz and 512 MB of memory). The nodes in the farm are connected by an internal Ethernet network of 100 Mb/s. We consider three initial parameters to start the prototype with: (i) the number of prototype instances to run, (ii) the delay between each instance run, and (iii) the budget the client has for the specific data mining service needed. We also consider the data set needed to be executed as 1 KB and the data mining service needed to run the application job as J48 (from WEKA). This is deployed as a Web Service in an Apache Tomcat container. The scenarios for the tests are presented in Figure 5, in which a group of two tests running in two different conditions are specified.

Test scenario	OnDeMand availability (ODM)	Standard Deviation (std_u)	Social Utility (L)
1.a – 50 clients, budget=50, delay=1s	0.099254	0.470013	0.516128
1.b – 50 clients, budget 100, delay=10s	0.090467	0.242400	0.443004
2.a – 100 clients, budget=50, delay=1s	0.147664	0.504291	0.490393
2.b – 100 clients, budget=100, delay=10s	0.134398	0.409765	0.458587

Figure 5. Experiment results - final index (social utility)

L must lie between 0 and 1 – a system behaves better if L is closer to zero (0). The main observation following the results presented in Figure 5 is that system behaves better when the budget is bigger under similar conditions: i.e. number of instances running in one experiment, and the delay between each user's application transactions. The factor L also shows the fairness of the system through the distribution of welfare among the population (the "agents"). By varying the price, one can see a fairness of the negotiations and the stability of the market – as the number of agents trying to speculate on price is reduced to minimum. A reduced standard deviation is lower it shows again that there is low speculative behaviour of agents on the market, and negotiations converge in a short space of time.

6. Conclusions

Details of using Service Level Agreements (SLAs) within the context of a Catallaxy-enabled "proof-of-concept" prototype have been presented, where the dynamic discovery of services and resources, and the selection of a particular service instance, are based on Catallaxy-based markets. The design and implementation of an applications that could operate within such a market – referred to as the Cat-DataMining application – has been presented.

An evaluation framework using economic concept based on social utility is used, and the results obtained are based on a decentralized economic self-organisation mechanism for on-demand service allocation in application layer networks.

Acknowledgement: This work has partially been funded by the EU in the IST programme "Future and Emerging Technologies" under grant FP6-003769 "CATNETS".

References

[1] O. Ardaiz, P. Artigas, T. Eymann, F. Freitag, L. Navarro, M. Reinicke, The Catallaxy Approach for Decentralized Economic-based Allocation in Grid Resource and Service

Markets. In *International Journal of Applied Intelligence*. Special Issue on Agent based Grid Computing. Volume 25 , Issue 2, pages: 131 - 145, October 2006.

[2] O. Ardaiz, P. Chacin, I. Chao, F. Freitag, L. Navarro - "An Architecture for Incorporating Decentralized Economic Models in Application Layer Networks", in *International Workshop in Smart Grid Technologies*, Utrecht, Holanda, July 25 - 29, 2005.

[3] R. Buyya, D. Abramson, J. Giddy, H. Stockinger - "Economic Models for Resource Management and Scheduling in Grid Computing. In *Journal of Concurrency and Computation: Practice and Experience (CCPE)*, Wiley, May 2002.

[4] T. Eymann, O. Ardaiz, M. Catalano, P. Chacin, I. Chao, F. Freitag, M. Gallegati, G. Giulioni, L. Joita, L. Navarro, D. Neumann, O. Rana, M. Reinicke, R. C. Schiaffino, B. Schnizler,W. Streitberger, D. Veit, and F. Zini - "Catallaxy based Grid markets", in *Proceedings of the First International Workshop on Smart Grid Technologies (SGT05)*, 2005.

[5] F. A. Hayek, W. Bartley, P. Klein, B. Caldwell, The collected works of F. A. Hayek. In *University of Chicago Press*, 1989

[6] L. Joita, O.F. Rana, P. Chacin, I. Chao, F. Freitag, L. Navarro, O. Ardaiz - "A Catallactic Market for Data Mining Services", in *International Journal of Future Generation Computer Systems (FGCS), Grid Computing: Theory, Methods and Applications, Volume 23, Issue 1, January 2007, ISSN 0167-739x, pages: 146-153*, 2006.

[7] C. Preist, M. van Tol - "Adaptive agents in a persistent shout double auction", in *Proceedings of the First international Conference on Information and Computation Economies (Charleston, South Carolina, United States, October 25 - 28, 1998)*. ICE '98. ACM Press, New York, NY, 11-18, 1998.

[8] W. Streitberger, T. Eymann, D. Veit, M. Catalano, G. Giulioni, L. Joita, O.F. Rana - "Evaluation of Economic Resource Allocation in Application Layer Networks - A Metric Framework", in *8. Internationale Tagung Wirtschaftsinformatik – eOrganisation: Service-, Prozess-, Market-Engineering*, 28 February - 2 March 2007, Karlsruhe, Germany.

[9] Web Services Agreement Specification (WS-Agreement), 14 June 2006, Grid Resource Allocation Agreement Protocol WG (GRAAP-WG). Available at (Last accessed on 30 May 2006):`https://forge.gridforum.org/projects/graap-wg`

[10] Waikato Environment for Knowledge Analysis. Available at: `www.cs.waikato.ac.nz/ml/weka/`. Last accessed: August 2007.

IMPROVING BUSINESS OPPORTUNITIES OF FINANCIAL SERVICE PROVIDERS THROUGH SERVICE LEVEL AGREEMENTS

Henning Mersch and Philipp Wieder
Central Institute for Applied Mathematics, Research Centre Jülich,
52425 Jülich, Germany
{h.mersch | ph.wieder}@fz-juelich.de

Bastian Koller
Höchstleistungsrechenzentrum Stuttgart,
70550 Stuttgart, Germany
koller@hlrs.de

Gerard Murphy, Ron Perrot, and Paul Donachy
Belfast e-Science Centre, School of Computer Science, The Queen's University of Belfast,
Belfast, BT7 1NN, United Kingdom
{g.m.murphy | r.perrot | p.donachy}@qub.ac.uk

Ali Anjomshoaa
EPCC, University of Edinburgh, Edinburgh, EH9 3JZ, United Kingdom
ali@epcc.ed.ac.uk

Abstract   The calculation of the Implied Volatility of stock options is a computationally expensive process which in general exceeds the resources available at a customer's site. Financial service providers therefore offer the required Implied Volatility services, adapting dynamically their own resource consumption to the customer's demands. The success of such a business model relies on carefully negotiated and observed Service Level Agreements between the different parties involved. The NextGRID project, driven by the adaption of several business scenarios to next generation Grid technologies, has designed and implemented an Implied Volatility framework which applies dynamic negotiation of Service Level Agreements to improve the existing solution. In this paper we describe the business scenario and the different core components which we integrated to realise the Implied Volatility framework.

Keywords: Implied Volatility, negotiation protocol, NextGRID, Service Level Agreements, UDAP

1.   Introduction

The development of next generation Grid concepts and methods and the application of business scenarios to evaluate those are two major research and development areas of the NextGRID project [9]. One of the business scenarios is the calculation of Implied Volatility parameters for stock options (cf. Section 2). Since previous experiments revealed the potential business benefits of the application of NextGRID's Service Level Agreement Driven Dynamics concept [10] to this scenario, we integrated and extended NextGRID components (cf. Section 3) to realise the NextGRID Implied Volatility Framework described in Section 3. This framework shows some differences compared to other solutions, but offers convincing arguments for other projects to already make use of it (cf. Section 5). The development so far is promising and encourages future investment into maturing the existing solution (cf. Section 6).

2.   Business Scenario

2.1   An Introduction to Implied Volatility

Within the stock market, stock and stock options can be purchased. Stock signifies an ownership position within a corporation. Options represent an option to buy (in the case of a call option) or sell (in the case of a put option) a set amount of stock from/to a third party at a set price (the strike price) in the future (the maturity date of the option). An option is purchased from the third party and if it is profitable on the maturity date (for example, the strike price of a call option is less than the current value of the stock, allowing the holder of the option to buy the stock more cheaply than would otherwise be possible) it will be exercised - otherwise it will be left to expire.

When the stock market is open, stocks and option prices are constantly being updated. Stock options are normally priced using the Black Scholes model. This equation contains a volatility parameter which can not be observed in practice. There is a one-to-one relationship between the theoretical price of a stock option and its volatility. Unfortunately there is no closed form solution for implying the volatility from the stock option price. If the volatility is known, trades can be executed to take advantage of volatility spikes. The Implied Volatility must be calculated using a numerical method; a Newton-Raphson iterative process is normally used, which is computationally expensive. The peak rate of the option market is 120,000 prices per second.

2.2   Current Implementation

The current implementation of this service relies on software being deployed on a local machine which is then hooked into a constant market feed. The limitations of this service are on the number of options which can be monitored at any time. As the number of options monitored increases the processing power required to calculate volatility increases exponentially, rapidly exceeding available resources.

2.3 NextGRID's Financial Service Scenario

In the NextGRID Implied Volatility scenario there are four actors: the *Financial Customer*, the *Financial Provider*, the *Compute Provider*, and the *Data Provider*.

Instead of the Financial Customers having the software running on a local machine or on one supplied by the Financial Provider they will have access to a Grid Portal where they can search for financial services (Implied Volatility being only one such service). They may also browse what Data Feeds are available to supply these services. When a Financial Customer selects a service he will be offered a choice of available Service Level Agreements (SLAs) [6] with the corresponding Financial Provider and will then choose the most suitable. The completion of the SLA negotiation will stimulate the Financial Provider to discover from the Grid the necessary Compute and Data resources and set up the corresponding SLAs with Compute and Data providers (see Fig. 1 for the SLAs being negotiated between the different actors). Once all the agreements are in place the necessary software will be deployed onto the chosen compute resource, the chosen data resource will be connected and the subsequent output data stream will be supplied to the Financial Customer.

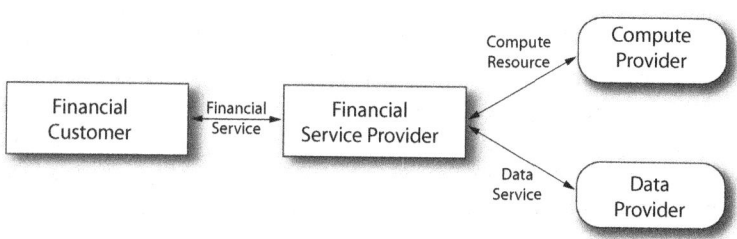

Figure 1. SLA relationships between parties

One essential customer requirement in the given scenario is high reliability, which implies the fast and correct response of the system to failure. As an example, one could imagine the partial or complete failure of the resource provided by the Compute Provider. In the current implementation this usually would mean either significant down time or the switch over to a shadow resource which has been mirroring the primary service. In this scenario the failure of the compute resource will be detected and the SLA between the Financial Provider and the Compute Provider will be breached. The Financial Provider will initially halt the supply of the data feed, discover a new suitable compute resource, agree a new SLA with the new Compute Provider and deploy the software. The data feed may then be re-started pointing at the new compute resource which will then begin supplying the Financial Customer with the output data stream. From the point of view of the customers the SLA breach will only affect them in terms of a short delay while the Financial Provider switches Compute Providers.

The main driver for designing and implementing a framework (cf. Section 3) to fulfil the requirements of the scenario are the business benefits for the different actors: Financial Customers can now operate through a single access point (the Grid Portal) with a large range of services and smaller customers have access to a market not previously available. In case of the Financial Provider new revenue streams are created, specialisation in providing financial services not hardware or data expertise is now easier, and potential penalties due to breaching an SLA are reduced or prevented. And also the Compute and Data Providers can create new revenue streams because of the possibility to dynamically provide services to new Financial Providers.

3.   The NextGRID Solution to dynamic SLAs

The two core components of NextGRID's Implied Volatility Framework are the *NextGRID SLA Framework* and the *Universal Dynamic Activity Package* (UDAP), which are both central entities of the NextGRID architecture [10]. The following two sections describe these components and their contributions to the architecture outlined in Section 3.

3.1   NextGRID SLA Framework

During the runtime of the NextGRID project a negotiation framework for Service Level Agreements has been developed [3]. The design of this framework is based on requirements from industrial applications which have been collected and analysed within the project. Based on this design, a proof-of-concept SLA Negotiation Framework implementation has been realised which is used to validate NextGRID's concepts and principles. This framework together with UDAP is the backbone of the Implied Volatility Framework.

Fig. 2 shows the design of the SLA Negotiation Framework. The two core components are Negotiators located at each of the business parties, the Financial Customer and the Financial Service Provider. These Negotiators are directly communicating and are responsible for Service Level Agreement negotiation in the NextGRID SLA Framework. NextGRID has chosen the so-called *Discrete-Offer-Protocol* for negotiation [10], which does not intend any refinements of negotiation parameters. In the beginning, the Customer Negotiator sends a request for an offer (a bid) to the Service Provider Negotiator. A bid has the same structure as an SLA template, but with empty information tags (service provider details, price, etc.). The Service Provider Negotiator has to check

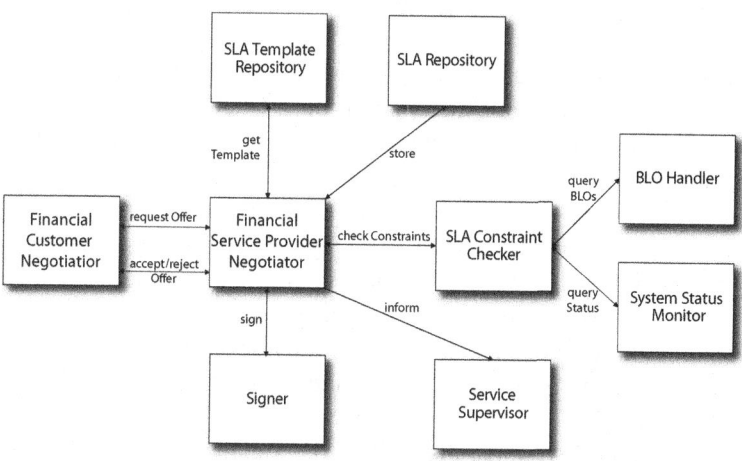

Figure 2. The NextGRID SLA Framework

whether or not it is able to provide the requested service. For that purpose it checks the SLA Template Repository (where Service Providers store their own service descriptions) for matching templates. If such a template exists, it has to be checked whether the current system status allows to offer this service to the Customer. The respective component – the SLA Constraint Checker – retrieves this information based on the selected service template from the System Status Monitor and from the Business Level Objective (BLO) Handler [4]. The BLO Handler is the component that has knowledge about the business preferences of the Service Provider (e.g. "prefer customer A to customer B", "maximise profit", "maximise resource usage", et cetera). Based on this knowledge, the SLA Constraint Checker validates the possible offer, and, if possible, advises the Service Provider Negotiator to fill the Customer's bid with the required information and send it back as an offer. Now the Customer has to decide whether to accept or reject an offer. In case of an acceptance, the Service Provider is informed and retrieves the SLA offer signed by the Customer. To become a valid SLA, the SLA offer has also to be signed by the Service Provider and a copy has to be sent to the Customer. Now each party has an SLA document signed by both parties. This SLA is stored in the SLA Repository component. After the negotiation process, the Service Supervisor component on the Service Provider's side is informed that a new SLA has been agreed upon and it starts to configure the system and the service(s) accordingly.

Please note that not all components of the framework have been implemented yet, since it was important to check the validity of the negotiation protocol first, a step that was possible with just a subset of the components.

3.2   UDAP

The Universal Dynamic Activity Package brings a new uniformity and coherency to managing activity information on a Grid. In the current state of Grid architectures, information about activities is fragmented and dispersed. Activity information, such as resource usage, security data, activity state, data requirements, et cetera, is currently captured using a variety of schemata and it is stored in different ways and by different logical components. This dispersion of activity information leads to management, security, and logistical overheads in discovering, accessing, and using that information. UDAP aims to bring all of the information fragments that are associated with an activity, regardless of the various schemata that are used to describe and capture these fragments, into one logical package.

The core of the UDAP model is the UDAP Document defined by the UDAP package, which is not discussed in detail here. The UDAP Manager is the entity that manages information in the UDAP Document. The UDAP Manager should have a standardised public interface that allows any Grid component to invoke its management functions for read, update and append operations of activity information. A UDAP Client is any Grid component that uses and/or produces activity information. UDAP Clients invoke the public management interface of the UDAP Manager for read, update and append operations of activity information. A UDAP Client can subscribe to the interface of a UDAP Manager, in order to receive notification of activity information based events. The subscription of a UDAP Client may be conditional, where the condition dictates the type of activity information based event that the client is interested in, e.g. "notify me if the state of the activity changes to running" or "notify me if the resource usage of the activity has exceeded the budget of the activity owner". An overview of the component's interactions is provided in Fig. 3.

3.2.1   UDAP applied to Implied Volatility.   In this paper we will apply UDAP to the presented scenario for two purposes. On the one hand, Compute-, Data, and Financial Service Providers will be *discovered*. On the other hand, we will track a negotiated SLA to *evaluate* Providers (their QoS) as well as Customers. This means that UDAP is independent of the provider and the customer and lives in a separate third domain (see Fig. 3; different colours illustrate different domains). Nevertheless for other scenarios, the UDAP package could be used in other ways, which allows UDAP to participate either on the customer or provider side.

3.2.2   UDAP SLA Evaluation.   In a case where a UDAP user discovers a list of providers suitable for its purposes, it might be not enough to simply select the fastest or cheapest one. The UDAP user might want to order the providers additionally based on experience, either its own experience or experience other

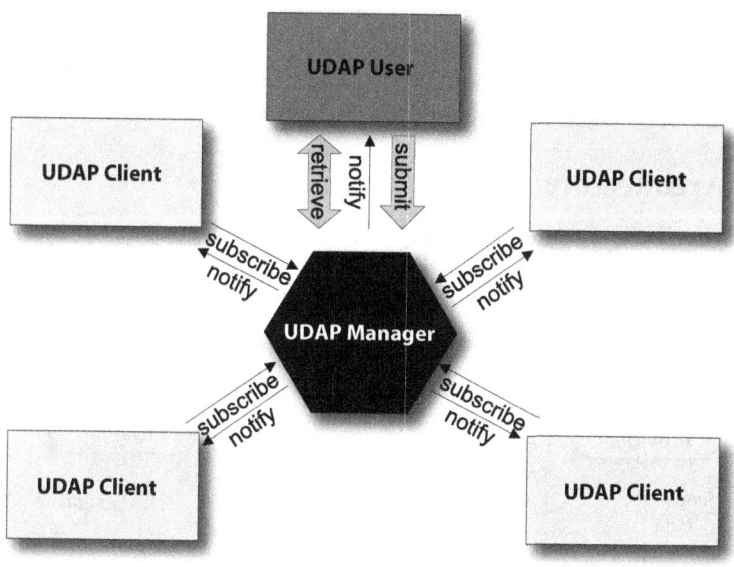

Figure 3.   UDAP components and their interaction

users have made. The same yields for the provider, which might want to make different offers (SLA Templates associated with the discovery result) depending on experience with this particular user. We call this the Quality-of-Service (QoS) of a provider respectively customer. For determining the QoS of a party, an evaluation system should be capable of tracking various SLAs, which belong to one party. This means this component could appraise a party depending on the history of its negotiated SLAs and associated QoS information.

Within the UDAP discovery step, it might be required to negotiate a SLA before consuming this service. UDAP could be used to track these negotiated SLAs for later evaluation. An SLA Activity Tracking instance could be instantiated by either the customer or the provider of the service via the UDAP Manager providing the negotiated SLA. Afterwards, the other party has to be informed about the location of this instance. Now both parties are in the position to append new information to this SLA Activity Tracking called "Rankings". These items contain an overall integer representation of the satisfaction of the other party's QoS; additional statements of the other party like "violated an SLA" or "has not paid the bill" could be appended, too. The evaluation component could later on query UDAP to return all SLAs where a particular party is involved. This brings the evaluator in the position to appraise a party by building the average over the provided satisfaction values. So, if a customer would like to order a list of providers, it could simply go to the evaluation component and retrieve the required information.

In case that some providers or customers do not want to publish their contracts, the presented evaluation system is still fully functional. If parties reject to support the system, no Rankings about their SLAs will be tracked and the SLAs will not be taken into account for evaluation.

4.   Architecture

The NextGRID Implied Volatility Framework design aims to harness the Grid to allow fluctuating demand to be met by available resources on the Grid. In this section we describe and picture (cf. Fig. 4) the architecture of this framework.

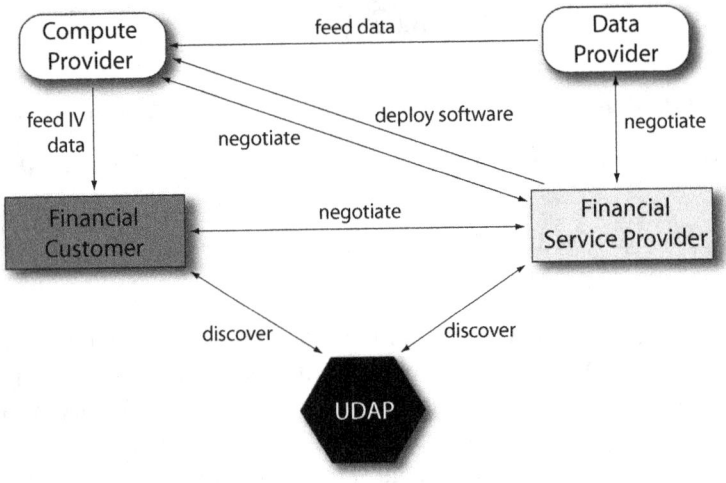

Figure 4.   The Implied Volatility Framework

A Financial Customer is interested in retrieving a continuous data feed containing their interested information. To achieve this, it starts with discovering a service, providing this capability. This is done using the above described UDAP discovery facility. Afterwards, the customer retrieved a list of Financial service providers, which could be ranked by contacting the Evaluation system (not shown in the diagram). This uses prior agreed and tracked SLAs to rank the provided list. After choosing one Financial Service Provider, the customer needs to establish a SLA with this provider by contacting its negotiator part. This will - if a SLA is established - check, if additional compute and/or data resources are required for fulfilling the requirements of the Financial Customer and will negotiate new Compute and Data Providers by discovering via UDAP and negotiate with the Negotiator Components of the providers. New compute resources need to have the software, which will be used afterwards, which means the software must be deployed in a way that it could be used. Afterwards, the Data Provider could support the Compute Provider with required data for computing the Financial Customer required data feed.

4.1   Architectural Components

The **Financial Customer** is interested in an Implied Volatility data feed, which is provided by a Financial Service Provider. Therefore the customer first needs to discover a suitable Financial Service Provider using UDAP and then negotiate an SLA with the provider to agree upon the service level.

UDAP, as described in Section 3.2, provides two functions for our system: (i) discovery of different service types and (ii) the tracking of an SLA.

The **Financial Service Provider** requires compute and data resources to provide the Implied Volatility service (or other financial services). Both of them have to be discovered from UDAP and afterwards an SLA has to be negotiated with the Compute and the Data provider respectively.

A **Data Provider** provides a data feed which is the foundation for the Implied Volatility calculation.

A **Compute Provider** provides resources for computing the Implied Volatility data feed out of the data feed provided by a Data Provider.

4.2   Dynamic (Re-)Allocation

Normally the failure of a compute resource implies that the SLA between the Financial Service Provider and the Financial Customer is breached. In our architecture, the Financial Service Provider could - after detecting the failure - simply discover new compute resources with the help of UDAP, negotiate with the respective Compute Provider, and set up the machine by deploying the necessary software. Afterwards this compute resource replaces the old one, the Implied Volatility data feed is re-connected and the negotiated SLA with the Financial Customer has not been breached (in case the re-allocation was fast enough to provide the agrees QoS level).

5.   Related Work

Apart from NextGRID a number of other projects is doing research in the area of Service Level Agreements in business-oriented Grid environments. AssessGrid, for example, introduces risk assessment and management to SLA negotiation [5], implementing, contrary to NextGRID, the WS-Agreement specification [1]. The same specification has been used by the Japanese Business Grid which provided solutions to share IT resources based on SLAs among distributed centres in an enterprise and trusted partners' data centres, thus making it possible for an Application Service Provider to dispatch a complex job through a single portal [7]. The reason for NextGRID not to use WS-Agreement, which combines a vocabulary for SLAs and a protocol to offer and negotiate them, are the project's requirements regarding the SLA vocabulary. NextGRID supports the concept of self-similar SLAs [8], but WS-Agreement does not, although the protocols of both approaches are the same. The BREIN [2] project, on the other hand, develops solution based on the NextGRID SLA Framework and is therefore examined closer in the following section.

5.1   BREIN

BREIN [2] aims at realising flexible Virtual Organisation support to reduce the complexity of business-to-business collaborations. As already mentioned in Chapter 3.1, NextGRID concentrates on the conceptualisation of the framework, delivering reference implementations of selected parts of the framework. In the BREIN project, conceptual ideas of a set of projects (including NextGRID) have been taken up to develop an initial design of a prototype implementation of an "intelligent" negotiation framework.

In contrast to the NextGRID approach, BREIN wants to support a multiphase negotiation protocol. The customer sends an offer to the Service Provider Negotiator, which extracts the offer parameters and hands them over to an optimisation component. This optimisation component retrieves the business goals/business criteria of the Service Provider and the capability information for the resources as well as their availabilities. Based on this information, the optimisation component refines the parameters, hands them back to the Service Provider Negotiator, which then sends a counter-offer to the Service Customer. To automate these functionalities, BREIN will make usage of technologies and concepts from the Semantic Web and multi-agent area. At the point in time of writing this paper, the prototyping activity was not finished yet, which means that the presented approach is only a snapshot of the current status.

6.   Status and Future Perspectives

In the course of this paper we described a business scenario, the provision of Implied Volatility services, which is used in the NextGRID project to drive the architectural development and to evaluate prototype developments. This scenario has been implemented integrating and enhancing NextGRID components, notably the NextGRID SLA Framework and UDAP (plus some auxiliary services that are of minor importance to this work). The resulting Implied Volatility Framework underpins the benefit of dynamic SLA negotiation to the actors involved in the business scenario. It is planned to demonstrate the function of the framework at different occasions. Moreover, the uptake of the concepts and prototype implementations by other projects like BREIN is ongoing work which will lead to more complete and advanced implementations of what has been presented here.

Acknowledgments

This work has been supported by the NextGRID project and has been partly funded by the European Commission's IST activity of the 6th Framework Programme under contract number 511563. In addition, this work has been supported by the BREIN project (http://www.gridsforbusiness.eu) and has been partly funded by the European Commission's IST activity of the 6th Framework Programme under contract number 034556. This paper expresses the opinions of the authors and not necessarily those of the European Commission. The European Commission is not liable for any use that may be made of the information contained in this paper.

References

[1] A. Andrieux, K. Czajkowski, A. Dan, K. Keahey, H. Ludwig, T. Nakata, J. Pruyne, J. Rofrano, S. Tuecke, and M. Xu. WS-Agreement - Web Services Agreement Specification. Technical report, Open Grid Forum, May 2007. Grid Forum Document GFD.107.

[2] BREIN – Business objective driven reliable and intelligent grids for real business, 2007. Web site, 16 Jun 2007 <http://www.eu-brein.com/>.

[3] P. Hasselmeyer, H. Mersch, H.-N. Quyen, L. Schubert, B. Koller, and Ph. Wieder. Implementing an SLA Negotiation Framework. In *Proc. of the eChallenges Conference (e-2007)*, The Hague, The Netherlands, October 24–26, 2007. To appear.

[4] P. Hasselmeyer, L. Schubert, B. Koller, and Ph. Wieder. Towards SLA-supported Resource Management. In *Proc. of the 2006 International Conference on High Performance Computing and Communications (HPCC-06)*, 4208, pages 743–752. Springer, 2006.

[5] M. Hovestadt, O. Kao, and K. Voss. The First Step of Introducing Risk Management for Preprocessing SLA. In *Proc. of the IEEE International Conference on Services and Computing 2006 (SCC'06)*, pages 36–43. IEEE Computer Society, 2006.

[6] J. Lee and R. Ben-Natan. *Integrating Service Level Agreements: Optimizing Your OSS for SLA Delivery*. Wiley, 2002.

[7] H. Ludwig, T. Nakata, O. Wäldrich, Ph. Wieder, and W. Ziegler. Reliable Orchestration of Resources using WS-Agreement. In *Proc. of the 2006 International Conference on High Performance Computing and Communications (HPCC-06)*, volume 4208 of *LNCS*, pages 753–762. Springer, 2006.

[8] P. Masche, P. Mckee, and B. Mitchell. The Increasing Role of Service Level Agreements in B2B Systems. In *Proc. of the 2nd International Conference on Web Information Systems and Technologies*, Setubal, Portugal, April 2006.

[9] NextGRID – Architecture for Next Generation Grids, 2007. Web site, 16 Jun 2007 <http://www.nextgrid.org/>.

[10] D. Snelling, A. Anjomshoaa, F. Wray, A. Basermann, M. Fisher, M. Surridge, and Ph. Wieder. NextGRID Architetural Concepts. In T. Priol and M. Vanneschi, editors, *Towards Next Generation Grids (Proc. of the CoreGRID Symposium in conjunction with the Euro-Par 2007)*, pages 3–13. Springer, 2007.

IMPLEMENTING WS-AGREEMENT IN A GLOBUS TOOLKIT 4.0 ENVIRONMENT*

Dominic Battré and Odej Kao
Berlin University of Technology
Secr. E-N 50, Einsteinufer 17, 10587 Berlin
Germany
dominic.battre@tu-berlin.de
odej.kao@tu-berlin.de

Kerstin Voss
University of Paderborn
Fuerstenallee 11, 33102 Paderborn
Germany
kerstinv@upb.de

Abstract   Service Level Agreements are an integral part on the path towards the commercial uptake of Grids in industry. A paying user of the Grid needs assurances that jobs are processed according to negotiated procedures and requires financial compensation in case these are violated. The WS-Agreement specification serves this purpose and went into recommendation status recently. Now, independent implementations are necessary to prove interoperability in order to allow the standardization effort proceed. At the same time, several research projects would like to build on a framework instead of developing a WS-Agreement implementation from scratch. This paper presents first experiences with implementing a negotiation service with WS-Agreement using the Globus Toolkit 4.0. It presents the architecture and discusses advantages and disadvantages of using the Globus Toolkit as well as difficulties implementing WS-Agreement and how these were addressed. Thereby, it shall support other projects which want to employ WS-Agreement and need to select a Grid middleware.

Keywords: WS-Agreement, Globus Toolkit, AssessGrid, architecture, Service Level Agreements

*The authors would like to thank the EU for partially supporting this work within the 6th Framework Programme under contract IST-031772 "Advanced Risk Assessment and Management for Trustable Grids" (AssessGrid).

1. Introduction

Service Level Agreements (SLAs) are an integral part towards the commercial uptake of Grids in industry. A paying user of the Grid needs assurances that jobs are processed according to negotiated procedures and requires financial compensation in case these are violated. Otherwise business users will not be willing to give critical jobs to external resource providers, knowing that the fate of their business is given to the arbitrariness of a possibly unknown resource provider. The WS-Agreement specification [1] serves this purpose and went into recommendation status recently. This paper presents early experiences with implementing a negotiation service with WS-Agreement using the Globus Toolkit 4.0. It shows the advantages of building upon the Globus Toolkit but also the disadvantages of this choice. Our implementation was and is being developed within the AssessGrid project. A detailed description of the architecture shall give the reader some insight whether our implementation might serve as a basis for their work. The implementation is available at the AssessGrid website [2]. This paper addresses only the negotiation component. For the broader picture or more details of AssessGrid, please refer to [2].

As mentioned before, the purpose of WS-Agreement is to facilitate the negotiation of SLAs. The specification follows the WS-Resource Factory Pattern. A WS-AgreementFactory is responsible for creating new SLAs that are represented by WS-Agreement resources. Once created, a WS-Agreement resource provides access to the state information of the agreement. An agreement consists of context information and agreement terms. While the context defines information such as participating parties, agreement terms describe the negotiated terms of the agreement. Since these are domain specific, they are not subject of this paper. The agreement template data structure is an extension of agreements. It comprises additional creation constraints that help the user by pointing to locations in the template that may be modified and inform him or her about possible values that may be defined in the SLA (e.g. maximum CPU speed that can be requested from a certain provider).

The open source community provides several solutions for implementing a specification such as the WS-Agreement. Among these is Apache Axis2/Java, a recent development within the Apache Software Foundation to implement SOAP. Add-ons such as Apache Sandesha2, Kandula2, and Rampart provide implementations for WS-ReliableMessaging, WS-Coordination, and WS-Security. Apache Muse represents a framework based on Axis2/Java that provides WS-ResourceFramework 1.2, WS-Notification 1.3, WS-DistributedManagement 1.1, and WS-MetadataExchange. The WSAG4J [3] implementation of WS-Agreement is based on this software stack.

A different approach that is presented in this paper uses the infrastructure provided by the Globus Toolkit 4.0. This has several advantages but certain disadvantages as well. A major benefit of relying on the Globus Toolkit is the software ecosystem that grew around it and therefore the scale of the community reached. The Globus Toolkit itself provides a plentitude of useful services; among these are authentication, authorization, credential delegation, GridFTP, the Monitoring and Discovery System (MDS), WS-Notification, and others. At the same time, external projects like the GridSphere portal framework support the development of a front-end.

A decision in favor of the Globus Toolkit brings, however, several disadvantages that should not be concealed. The Globus Toolkit 4.0 is based on Apache Axis 1.2RC2, which does not support XML Schema Substitution Groups nor choice-elements whose maxOccurs attribute is set to "unbounded". Tiny modifications to the WS-Agreement WSDL files allow Axis 1.2RC2 to handle these parts without losing compatibility to other implementations. On the other hand, the Globus Toolkit 4.0 uses different versions of WS-Addressing and WS-ResourceFramework than required by WS-Agreement. This prevents full compliance to the WS-Agreement specification and makes interoperability with WS-Agreement compliant implementations difficult. Efforts exist in the GT community to update to the new versions and by the OGF GRAAP group to write a translation proxy between our implementation and WSAG4J.

Therefore, at the moment, one has to decide between using the Globus Toolkit with all services provided by the toolkit and the community on the one hand and full WS-Agreement compliance on the other hand. Grid Sphere and GridFTP were some of the reasons for the AssessGrid project to pick the Globus Toolkit approach. Once the Globus Toolkit picks up the required versions of WS-Addressing and WS-ResourceFramework, interoperability issues should be solved—at least on the protocol layer.

After this short summary of advantages and disadvantages of using the Globus Toolkit, section 2 addresses the negotiation protocol assumed in our implementation. Section 3 then describes the architecture arisen from this. Section 4 addresses related work and section 5 concludes the paper.

2. Negotiation Protocol

The WS-Agreement protocol is very limited for negotiation, basically resembling a one-phase commit protocol. This is unfortunately insufficient for AssessGrid. The project considers three different parties, an end-user, who is interested in the consumption of compute resources, a resource broker, and a resource provider. We will not consider the AssessGrid specific tasks of the broker but regard it as a common broker here whose tasks are finding suitable resources and handling workflows.

Three different usage scenarios are subject of the AssessGrid project. Generalized these are:

Scenario 1 – Direct SLA negotiation with provider: In the simplest scenario, an end-user negotiates an SLA directly with a known suitable resource provider. A broker is not involved in this negotiation.

Scenario 2 – Broker as intermediary: In this case, the end-user submits an SLA request to the broker, which then looks for suitable resources and forwards the request to suitable providers. The broker returns the SLA offers to the end-user, ranked by price, penalty, or some other domain specific criteria. The end-user is then free to select and commit to an SLA offer by interacting directly with the corresponding provider.

Scenario 3 – Broker as a higher-level provider: The broker can act as a virtual provider. In that case, the end-user agrees an SLA with the broker, which in turn agrees SLAs with all providers involved in executing the end-user's application. The broker can be used to map entire workflows to resources.

From these scenarios we can conclude that the current negotiation interface of WS-Agreement does not satisfy our needs. Currently a resource consumer issues an SLA request to a resource provider. By this act, the consumer is already committed to the request. The provider can only accept or reject the request. This has certain shortcomings presented in the following:

It is common real-world practice that a customer asks several companies for offers for a particular job. The companies state their price and the customer can pick the cheapest offer. This is not possible in the current WS-Agreement specification. By submitting an SLA request, the user is committed to that request. At the moment, we neglect this assumption. A user can submit a non-binding SLA request and the provider is allowed to modify the request by answering with an SLA offer that has a price tag. The provider is bound to this offer and the user can either commit to the offer or let it expire. Even though this is common among several implementations (see section 4) the GRAAP group has strong arguments against it (scalability and byzantine faults of the Internet environment, see e.g. [4]). Therefore, the approach will be changed in the future.

3.   Architecture

Figure 1 presents a high level view of the NegotiationManager (NegMgr), the service implementing WS-Agreement, on top of a resource management system. The consumer of this negotiation service can be either an end-user interface, such as a portal or command line tools, or even a broker service. The consumer accesses the NegMgr over the WS-Agreement interface for creating or negotiating new SLAs and checking the status of existing SLAs.

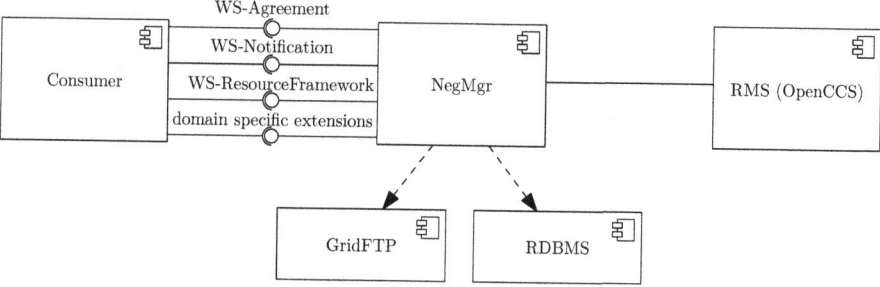

Figure 1.   High level component architecture

WS-Notification allows to monitor all kind of changes. A broker might be interested in keeping a cache of offered SLA templates from providers and might therefore subscribe to a provider's templates. An end user might monitor the status of its SLAs to get notified when a job finishes. Similarly a broker might monitor SLAs of the subtasks of a workflow to trigger the creation of new ones for following tasks or reacting upon failures. Furthermore, state information can be requested by WS-ResourceFramework means at any time.

Besides the mentioned implementations of WS-Agreement, WS-Notification, and WS-ResourceFramework, we have extended the interface by logging mechanisms that allow a user to see time-stamped human readable log messages and by a commit method because of the altered commit protocol.

The architecture is depicted in more detail in figure 2. The figure shows components with gray and white background. Gray components are generic while white components carry the domain specific logic. The components are described in the following paragraphs.

Similarly to WSAG4J, we have implemented two services, AgreementFactory and Agreement, that delegate the business logic to concrete implementation classes. In terms of design patterns, these are strategy implementations. The concrete AgreementFactory makes use of two components, one being the TemplateStore, the other one being the DecisionProcess, a component to decide whether an agreement request is valid.

The TemplateStore is responsible for the persistence of templates. Our WS-Agreement implementation assumes that templates are static and do not depend on runtime information. The WS-ResourceFramework offers means to add new templates to the database while using the authentication and authorization services offered by the Globus Toolkit. This was realized by implementing a new org.globus.wsrf.impl.BaseResourceProperty extension. The Agreement-Factory can delegate most work in this regard to the TemplateStore.

Task of the DecisionProcess component is to validate agreement requests. An SLA request is valid if it fulfills the requirements of the WS-Agreement

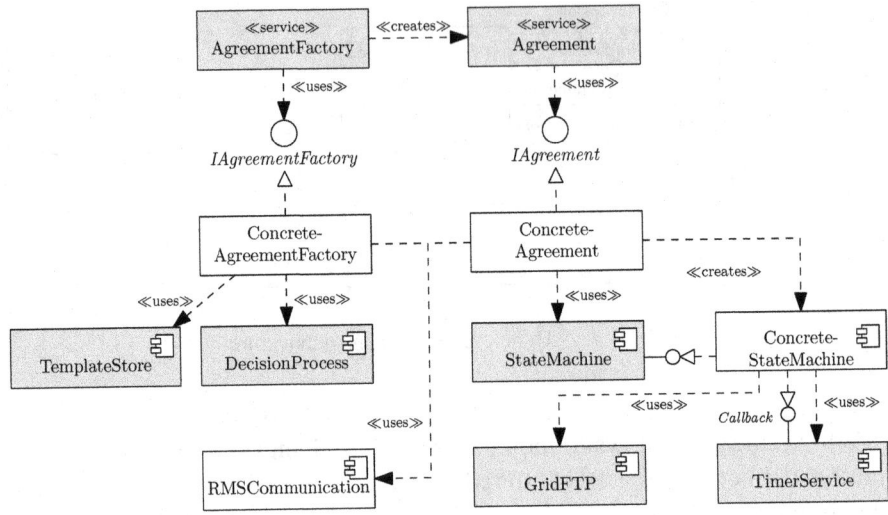

Figure 2.   Detailed component architecture

specification and conforms to the template it originated from. While WS-Agreement compliance tests are rather easy to implement, the test for compliance to creation constraints is rather difficult. Each creation constraint of an agreement template consists of an XPath expression filtering some nodes and the actual constraint description (wsag:ItemConstraint). Free-form constraints are not supported at the moment. Two challenges arise from the definition of the creation constraints. First the XPath evaluation is difficult because Globus/Axis generates Java Beans that are derived from the SOAP messages. In the process of generating these Java Beans, the entire XML context is lost, and therewith also the binding of namespace prefixes that are used in the XPath expressions. For that reason, our implementation assumes fixed bindings of namespace prefixes. The second challenge originates from the problem of XML Schema validation. The wsag:ItemConstraints use a subset of XML Schema to restrict possible values. As these are quite difficult to handle thoroughly, currently only a small subset is supported: Minimum and maximum bounds of numbers, enumerations and correct date/time formats are checked.

If an SLA request has been found to be template compliant, it is passed to the resource management system for finding a decision whether to make an SLA offer and determining the price tag. Our project uses OpenCCS, a planning based scheduler, for this process. The job is integrated into a tentative schedule which forms the decision base. In case the job fits into the schedule and no previously agreed SLAs need to be violated, an offer is generated.

So far we have implicitly assumed that an SLA consists merely of a conjunction of requirements that need to be fulfilled. WS-Agreement provides, however, means to specify alternative ways to fulfill an agreement (e.g. many CPUs for a short time or few CPUs for a long time). Such alternatives can be described by statements of logical and-, or-, and xor-expressions. This is not supported at the moment, but can be handled in the future by converting the expressions into disjunctive normal form and evaluating each one individually.

We have seen that the creation of an agreement and the decision whether to create it are handled completely by the AgreementFactory and the resource management system. The right hand side of figure 2 describes the life-time handling of an agreement which is subject of the following paragraphs.

In principle it would be great to use the WS-GRAM implementation of Globus to process jobs. It is widely tested and there are plenty of backends for WS-GRAM. However, WS-GRAM does not appear suitable for a scenario with SLAs for two reasons. First, it is implemented for queueing based schedulers for which it is difficult to provide guarantees. In particular, users will be interested in deadlines for the job completion, which are difficult to support in queueing based systems. The second shortcoming of WS-GRAM relates to the fact that an SLA needs to terminate in one of three states: Completed, violated by provider, or violated by consumer. Finding the cause of a violation is not supported sufficiently by WS-GRAM.

We substitute WS-GRAM by a new state machine that models a Moore automata. The state machine is composed of states, transitions, and actions. Associated to each state is a (possibly empty) set of actions that are executed when entering the state. A state can handle several events that cause the transition to a new (possible identical) state. Each exception that can be thrown by an event handler or an action has a destination state attached. In case such an exception is raised, the state machine moves into this state. That way, each error is either compensated or leads to a final state that indicates the party responsible for an SLA violation.

As we use planning based schedulers, events need to be triggered at certain times. For example file staging needs to begin at the time specified in the SLA. This is another shortcoming of WS-GRAM. A TimerService is responsible in our implementation for generating such timer events.

A job consists—as in WS-GRAM—of stage in, execution, stage out, and cleanup. The difference is that the stage-in, the beginning of the execution, and the cleanup phase are triggered at certain times. Stage-out begins immediately after the execution has finished.

The points in time when certain phases begin are defined in the SLA. The SLAs used in our project define time boundaries as depicted in figure 3. First, the SLA defines at what time the resource consumer guarantees to provide stage-in files. At this time, the resource provider starts the stage-in procedure. Furthermore, the consumer specifies when the job can start earliest, when it has to finish latest, and how much CPU (wall clock) time it requires. When

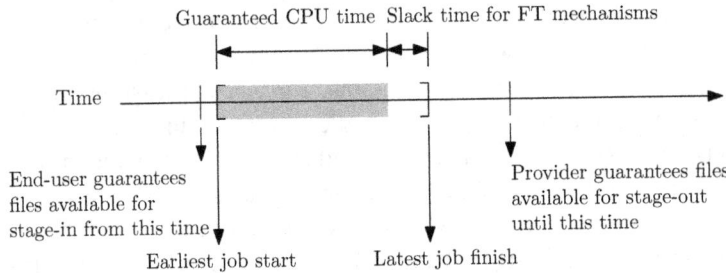

Figure 3.   Life Cycle of an SLA

specifying the earliest start time, the consumer needs to provide sufficient time for the stage-in. Determining an adequate timeslot for this from the provider is non-trivial and out of our project's scope. The interval between earliest start and latest finish time may provide some slack time that can be used by the provider for fault-tolerance mechanisms such as checkpointing. Finally, the stage out is triggered directly after the job finishes. Files are kept until a negotiated cleanup time.

3.1   Security and Roles

So far we have been oblivious to any security aspects. Most security aspects are handled in the generic AgreementFactory and Agreement web services. We have identified four different roles with different privileges. These roles are described in the following and summarized in table 1. Each row is dedicated to one role. The first three columns identify the user who takes these roles in each of the three scenarios discussed before. The final four columns describe the rights that are associated to the roles.

An *administrator* has read and write access to everything. A person belongs to the group of administrators if his or her distinguished name is listed in a specific gridmap file. The *SLA creator* is the identity who creates the SLA by calling createAgreement at the AgreementFactory. This can be the service consumer (in scenario 1), a broker who requests SLA offers on behalf of a prospective service consumer (scenario 2), or a broker who requests SLA offers in order to act as a virtual provider (scenario 3). The SLA creator role is not sufficient to actually establish the agreement by committing to it. The only person who is allowed to commit to the SLA is the *SLA owner*, whose identity is explicitly listed in the SLA. As committing to an SLA brings several legal responsibilities, this differentiation is very important. Finally, in case a resource broker acts as a virtual service provider, we need the role of a *service user*. This role grants access to the services or resources covered by the SLA.

Table 1. Roles and privileges.

Scen. 1	Scen. 2	Scen. 3	Role	Read status	Commit	Terminate	Access to resources
			Admin.	X	X	X	X
End User	Broker	Broker	Creator	X			
End User	End User	Broker	Owner	X	X	X	X
End User	End User	Broker	User	X			X
			Other				

3.2 SLA Fulfillment

A final topic to be discussed here is the question who is responsible for an SLA violation. Our concept may be not optimal but quite pragmatic. The first rule is that the first detected violation of a guarantee is considered as the cause for a failed SLA and determines who has to pay a penalty. In case the SLA fails, only one penalty is paid but no reward. As it is difficult to find the cause of an SLA violation—it can be a hardware or software failure—the following rule is used: If the provider did not allocate the resources on time or any part of the resources failed and it could not be resolved through fault-tolerance mechanisms, the provider is liable for the failure. It may be that no resource failure is detected, e.g. when a violation is caused by a software problem. In this case the simplifying assumption is that this is the end-user's fault.

This approach follows common practice in insurance industry. If the cause of an accident appears obvious, this is considered the true cause (ostensible evidence). If any party disagrees, an independent expert in the field is asked to investigate the situation and the dispute is solved in court. In order to realize this in a Grid context, providers need to be certified that they keep auditable (unmodifiable) logs and allow external investigators to check the equipment at any time without prior notice. This is, however, not part of our current research. A perfect and automated decision process cannot be found because it requires provable correct hardware and software.

4. Related Work

Our WS-Agreement implementation has been developed within the Assess-Grid project [2]. Currently the only other public and actively developed WS-Agreement implementation known to the authors is WSAG4J [3] by Wäldrich. As mentioned above, it is based on Axis2/Java and is therefore capable of sticking closer to the WS-Agreement specification while being not native to the Globus Toolkit ecosystem. The Cremona implementation [5] was developed within the IBM Emerging Technologies Toolkit and builds on an earlier version of WS-Agreement. However, the source codes are closed and no updates have been published for more than one year. Mobach et al. describe in [6] the use of WS-Agreement for mobile agents. [3] and [6] use or support a request-offer-commit protocol as our implementation. Interoperability tests are planed for the near future between our implementation, WSAG4J, and an implementation by the SORMA project [7].

5.   Conclusion

Within this paper we have argued why service level agreements are important for the commercial update of the Grid. We have presented the advantages and disadvantages of implementing a WS-Agreement negotiation service with the Globus Toolkit. We have shown the current shortcoming of the negotiation protocol assumed by WS-Agreement and how this is addressed. Based on this we have presented our implementation and how it makes use of the services provided by the Globus Toolkit. We have described our process to decide whether to accept SLA requests and how computational jobs described by these SLAs are processed during their lifetime. Finally, security aspects were described.

We invite everybody to take a look at our implementation, which is available on the AssessGrid website [2].

References

[1] Andrieux, A., Czajkowski, K., Dan, A., Keahey, K., Ludwig, H., Kakata, T., Pruyne, J., Rofrano, J., Tuecke, S., Xu, M.: Web Services Agreement Specification (WS-Agreement). In: OGF Document Series. (2007)

[2] AssessGrid - Advanced Risk Assessment and Management for Trustable Grids. http://www.assessgrid.eu/ (2007)

[3] Wäldrich, O.: WS-Agreement Framework (WSAG4J). http://packcs-e0.scai.fhg.de/mss-project/wsag4j/ (2007)

[4] Parkin, M., Kuo, D., Brooke, J., Macculloch, A.: Challenges in EU Grid Contracts. In Exploiting the Knowledge Economy: Issues, Applications, Case Studies. (2006)

[5] Ludwig, H., Dan, A., Kearney, R.: Cremona: An Architecture and Library for Creation and Monitoring of WS-Agreements. In: ICSOC '04: Proc. of the 2nd international conference on Service oriented computing, New York, NY, USA, ACM Press (2004) 65–74

[6] Mobach, D., Overeinder, B., Brazier, F.: A WS-Agreement Based Resource Negotiation Framework for Mobile Agents. Scalable Computing: Practice and Experience **7**(1) (2006) 23–36

[7] SORMA - Self-Organizing ICT Resource Management. http://www.iw.uni-karlsruhe.de/sormang/ (2007)

Index